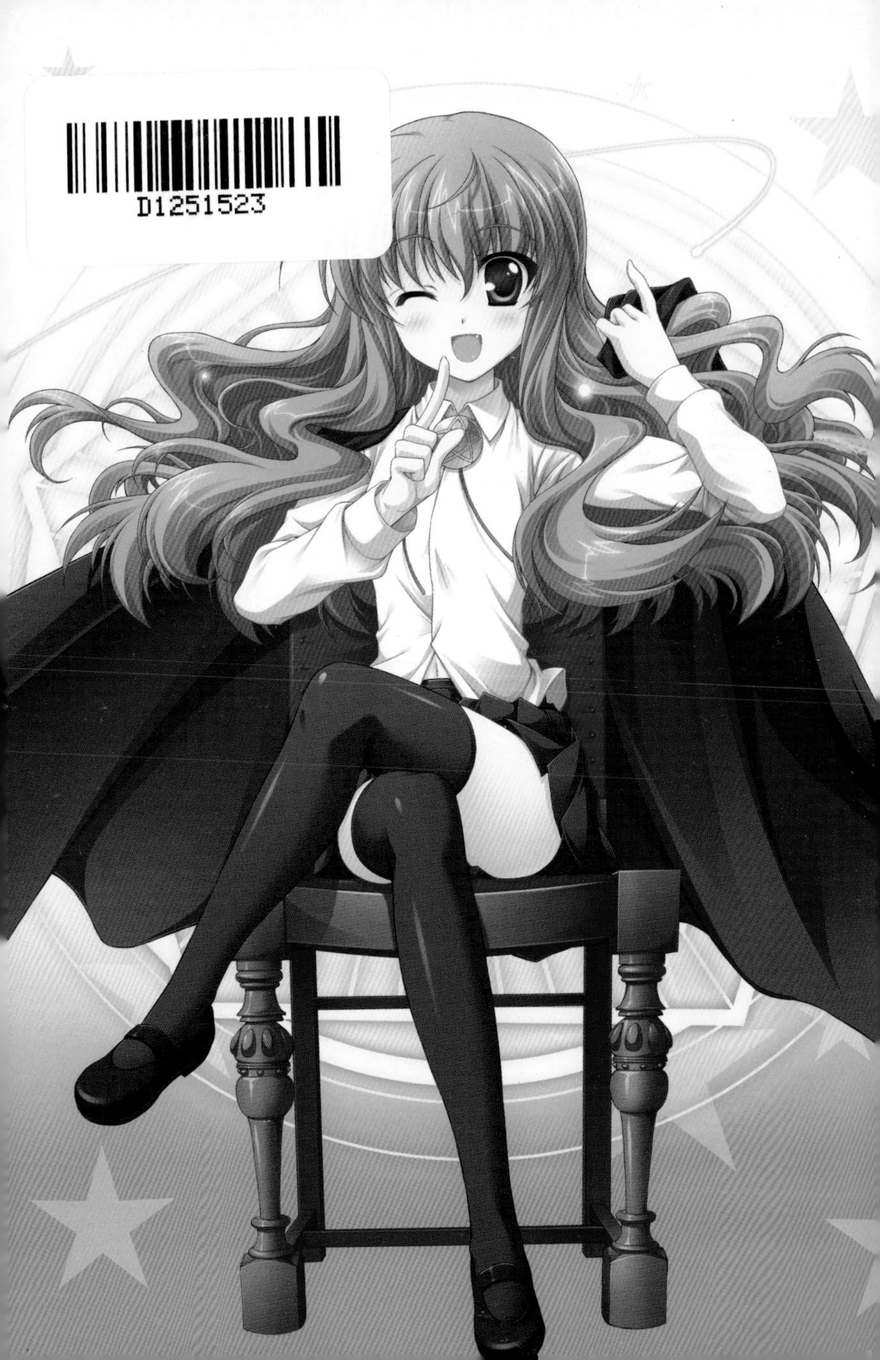

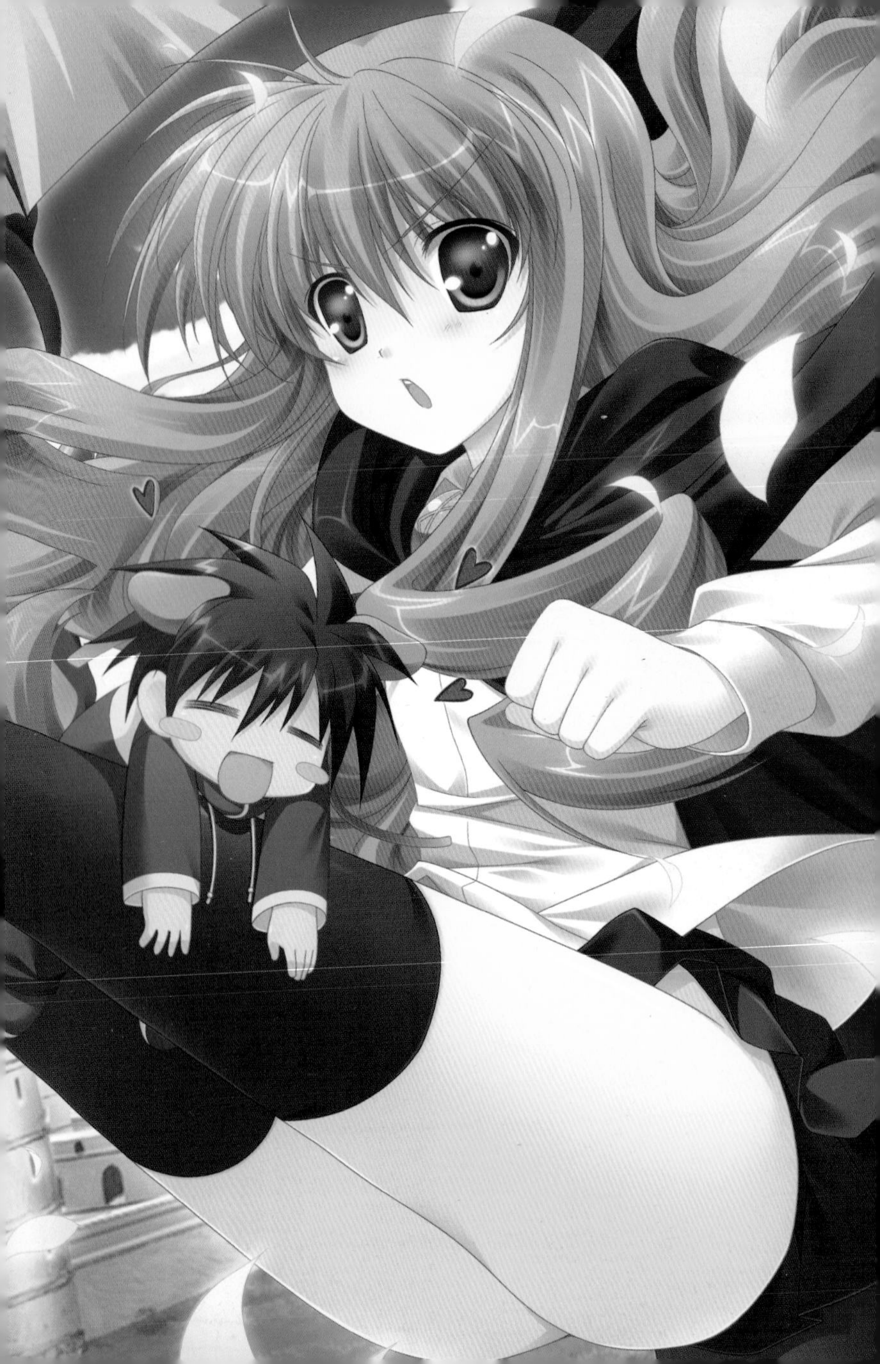

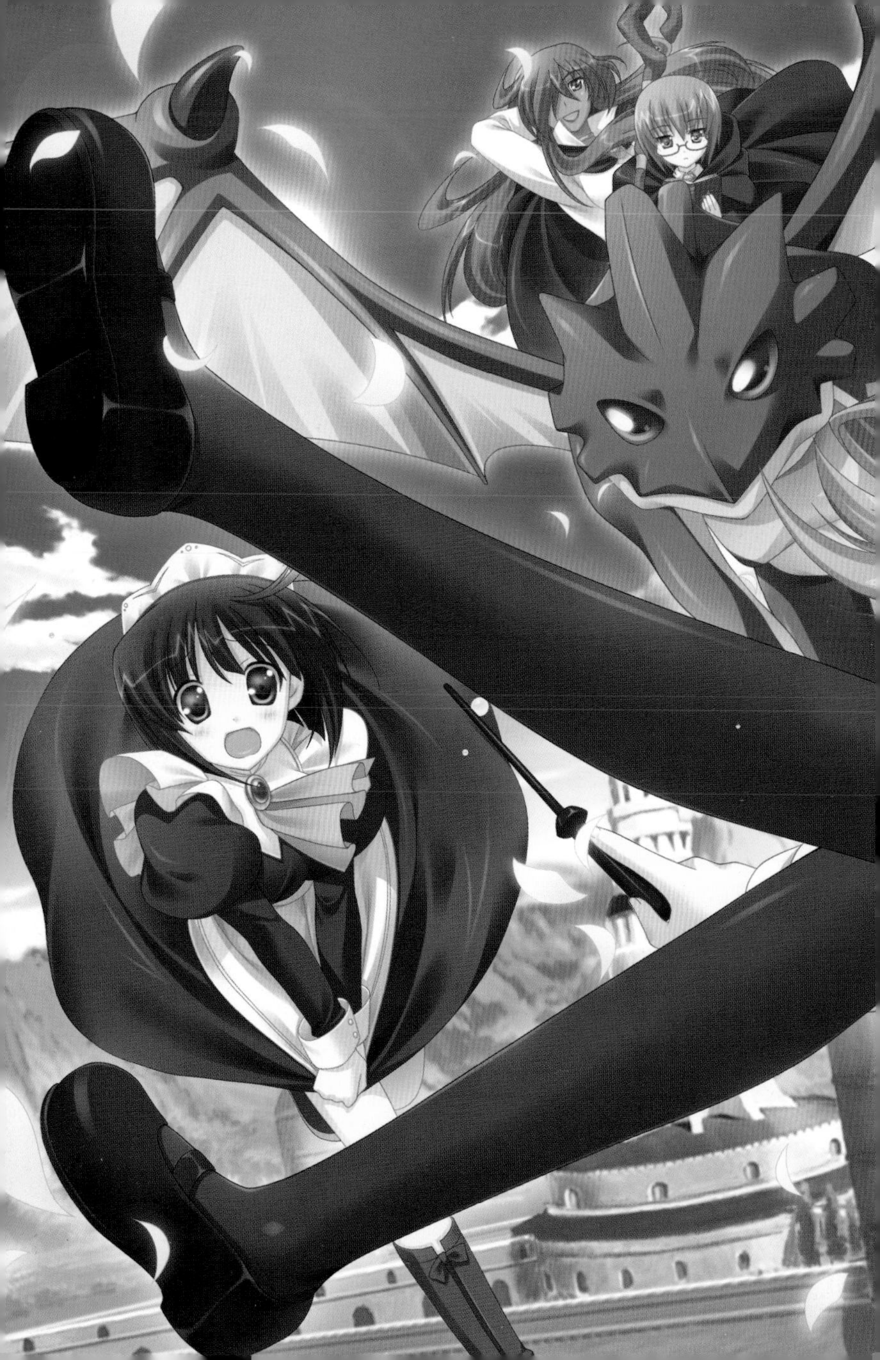

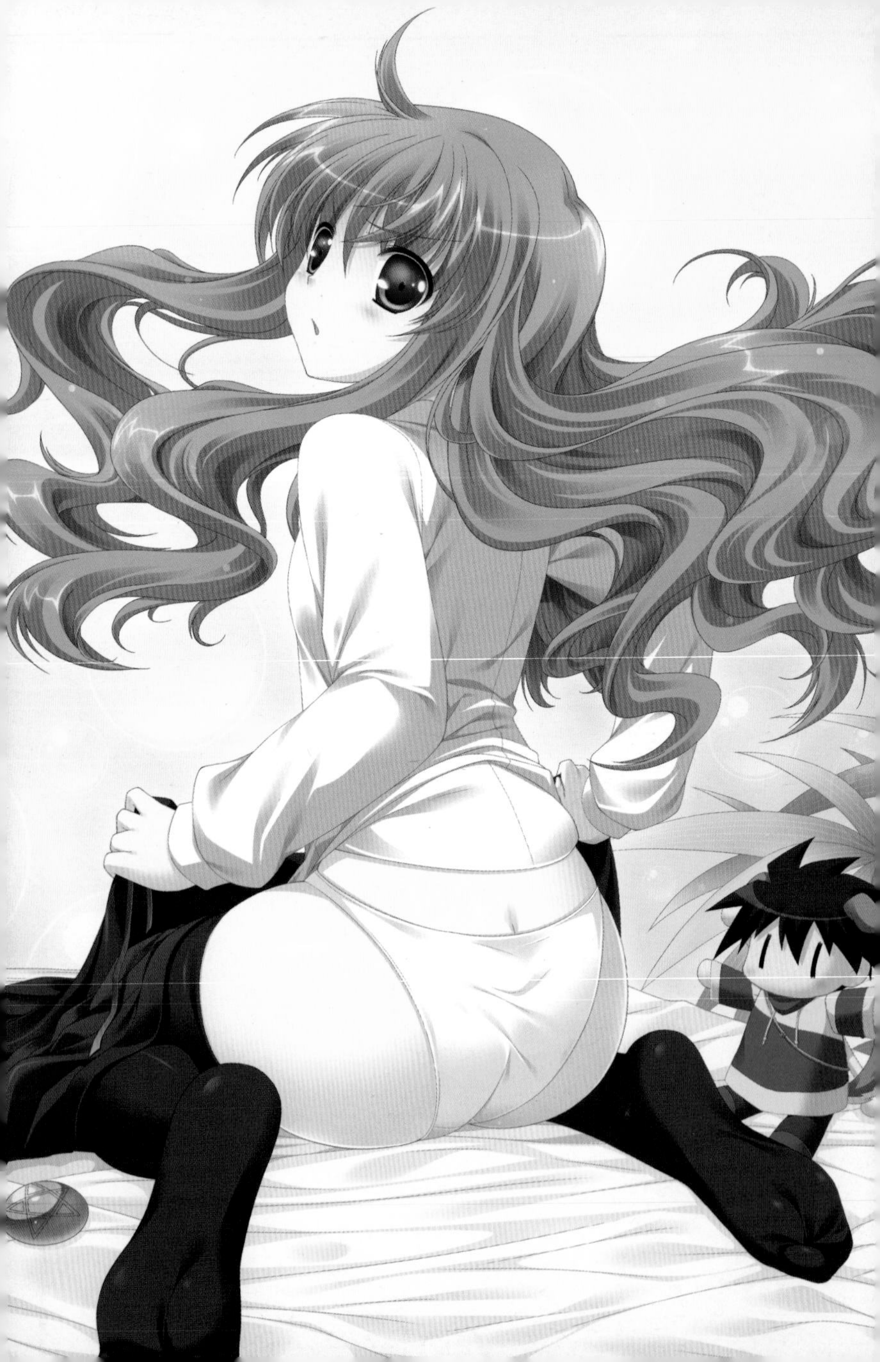

Le Familier de

ZERO'S FAMILIAR Chevalier 2

Art: Yukari Higa
Story: Noboru Yamaguchi
Character Design: Eiji Usatsuka

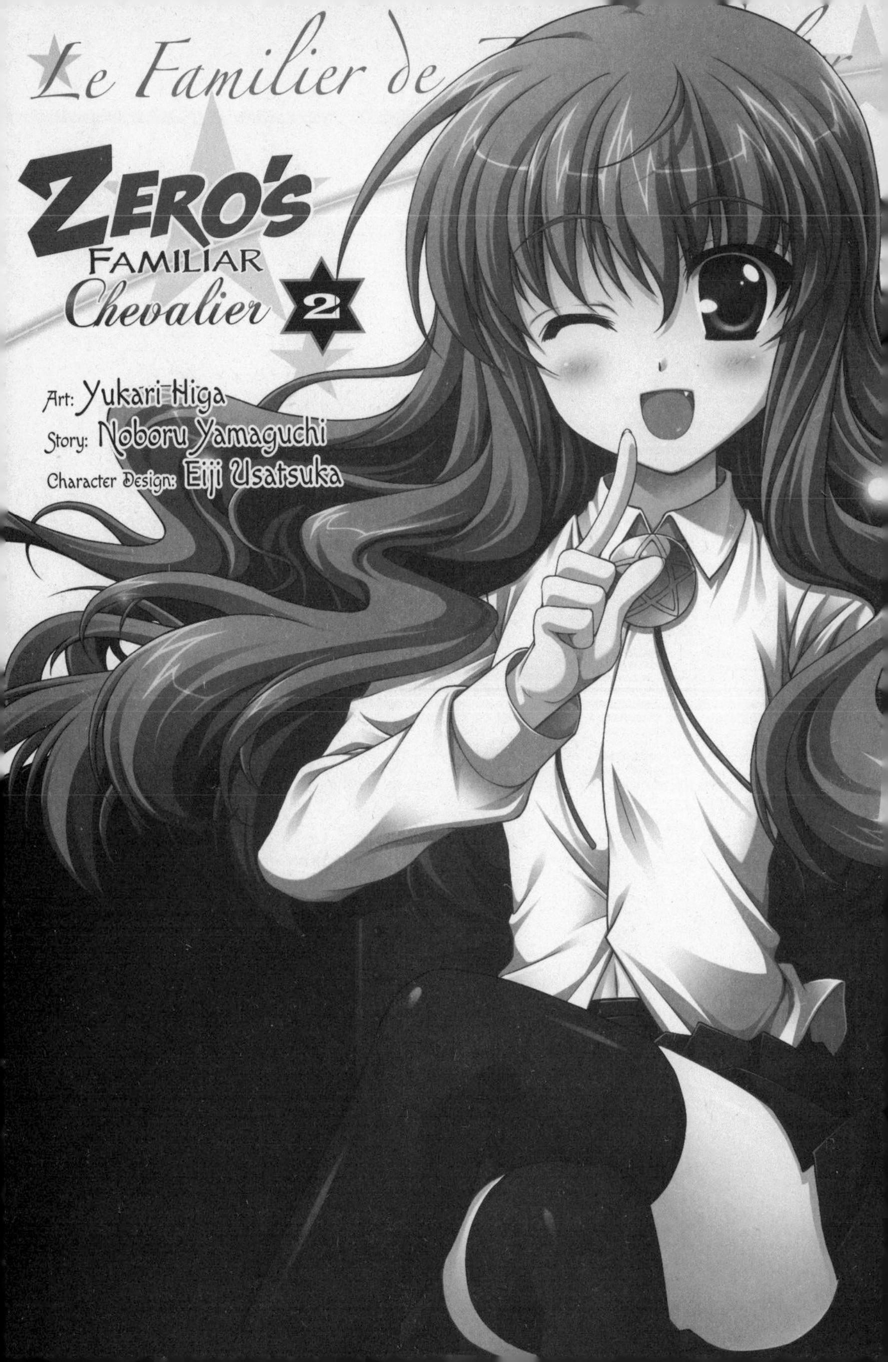

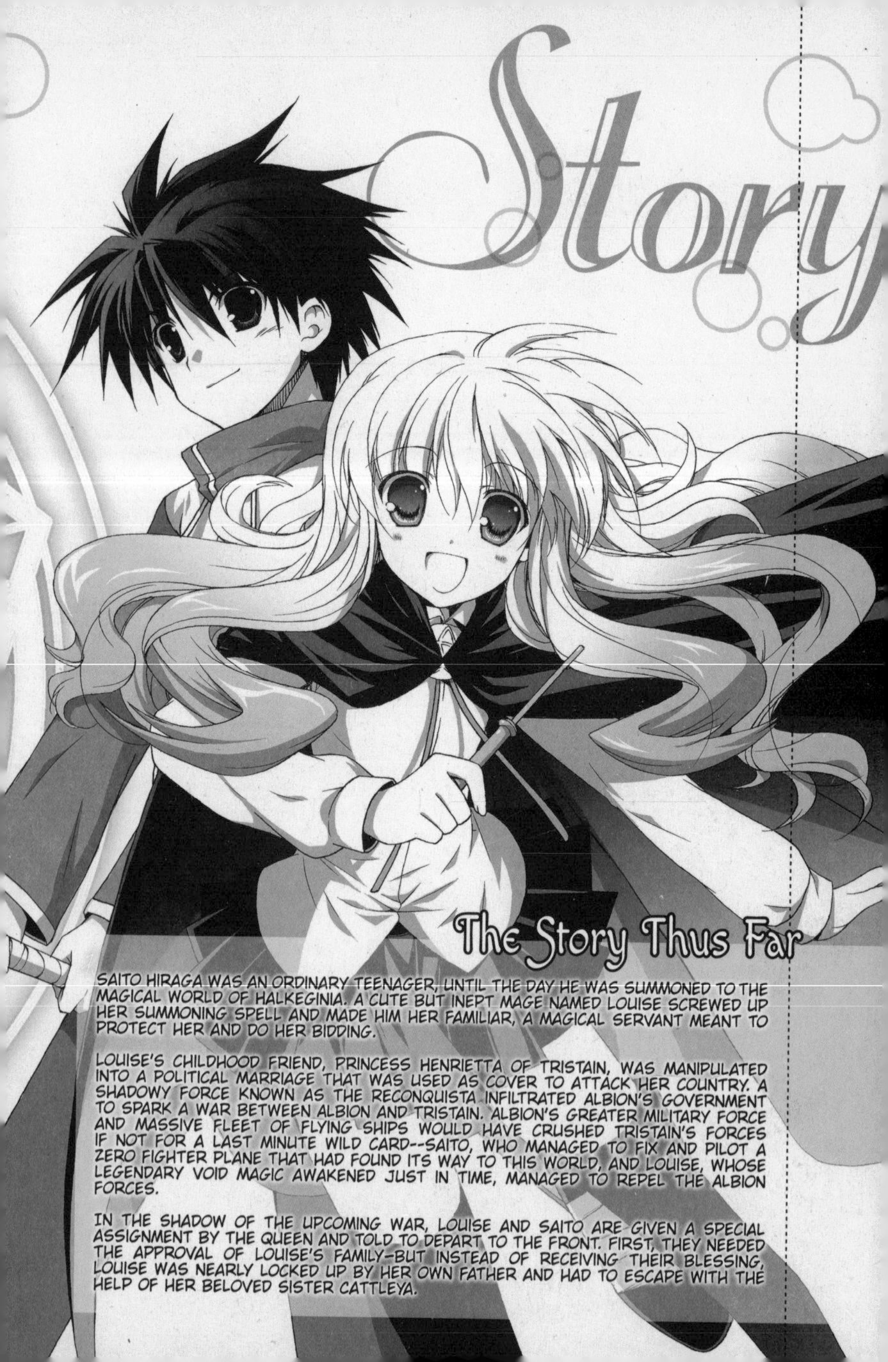
Story

The Story Thus Far

SAITO HIRAGA WAS AN ORDINARY TEENAGER, UNTIL THE DAY HE WAS SUMMONED TO THE MAGICAL WORLD OF HALKEGINIA. A CUTE BUT INEPT MAGE NAMED LOUISE SCREWED UP HER SUMMONING SPELL AND MADE HIM HER FAMILIAR, A MAGICAL SERVANT MEANT TO PROTECT HER AND DO HER BIDDING.

LOUISE'S CHILDHOOD FRIEND, PRINCESS HENRIETTA OF TRISTAIN, WAS MANIPULATED INTO A POLITICAL MARRIAGE THAT WAS USED AS COVER TO ATTACK HER COUNTRY. A SHADOWY FORCE KNOWN AS THE RECONQUISTA INFILTRATED ALBION'S GOVERNMENT TO SPARK A WAR BETWEEN ALBION AND TRISTAIN. ALBION'S GREATER MILITARY FORCE AND MASSIVE FLEET OF FLYING SHIPS WOULD HAVE CRUSHED TRISTAIN'S FORCES IF NOT FOR A LAST MINUTE WILD CARD--SAITO, WHO MANAGED TO FIX AND PILOT A ZERO FIGHTER PLANE THAT HAD FOUND ITS WAY TO THIS WORLD, AND LOUISE, WHOSE LEGENDARY VOID MAGIC AWAKENED JUST IN TIME, MANAGED TO REPEL THE ALBION FORCES.

IN THE SHADOW OF THE UPCOMING WAR, LOUISE AND SAITO ARE GIVEN A SPECIAL ASSIGNMENT BY THE QUEEN AND TOLD TO DEPART TO THE FRONT. FIRST, THEY NEEDED THE APPROVAL OF LOUISE'S FAMILY–BUT INSTEAD OF RECEIVING THEIR BLESSING, LOUISE WAS NEARLY LOCKED UP BY HER OWN FATHER AND HAD TO ESCAPE WITH THE HELP OF HER BELOVED SISTER CATTLEYA.

Halkeginia Map

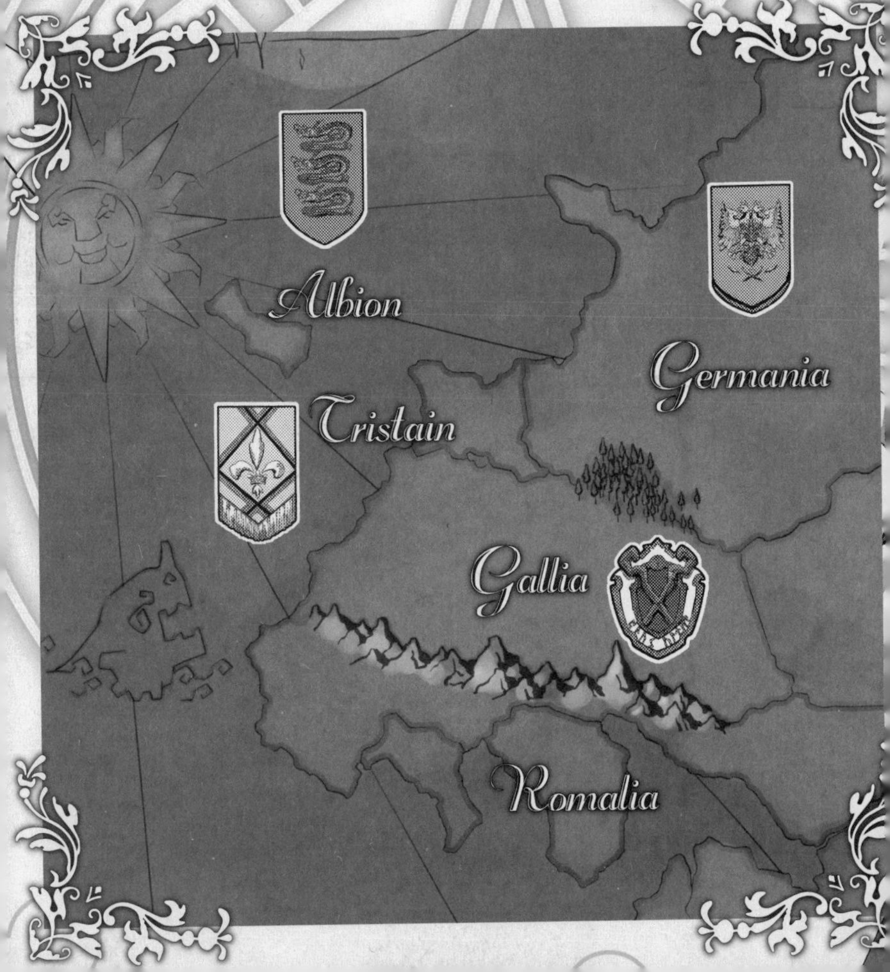
Albion
Germania
Tristain
Gallia
Romalia

Characters

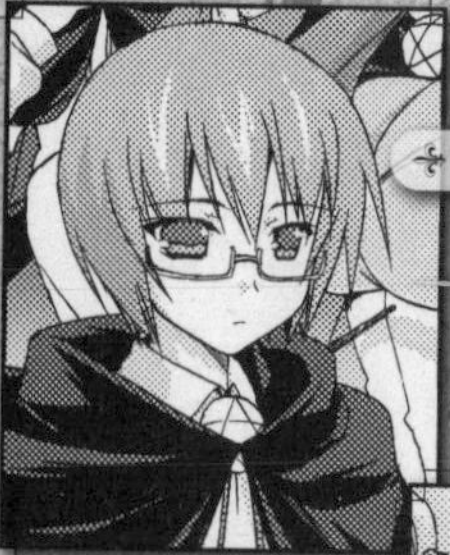

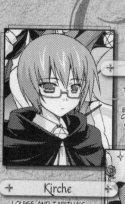

Tabitha

A TOP STUDENT AT TRISTAIN'S MAGIC ACADEMY. DESPITE BEING A GIRL OF FEW WORDS AND FEWER EXPRESSIONS, SHE IS VERY CLOSE WITH LOUISE AND CO. ALSO KNOWN AS "TABITHA THE SNOWSTORM."

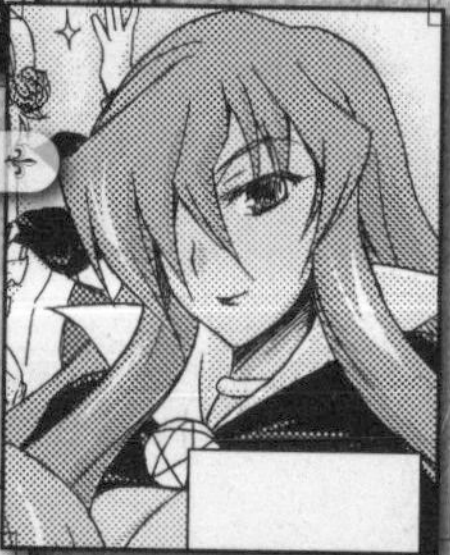

Kirche

LOUISE AND TABITHA'S FRIEND AND ANOTHER STUDENT AT THE MAGIC ACADEMY. SHE HAS A BRIGHT, WILD PERSONALITY AND SPECIALIZES IN FIRE MAGIC. ALSO KNOWN AS "KIRCHE THE ARDENT."

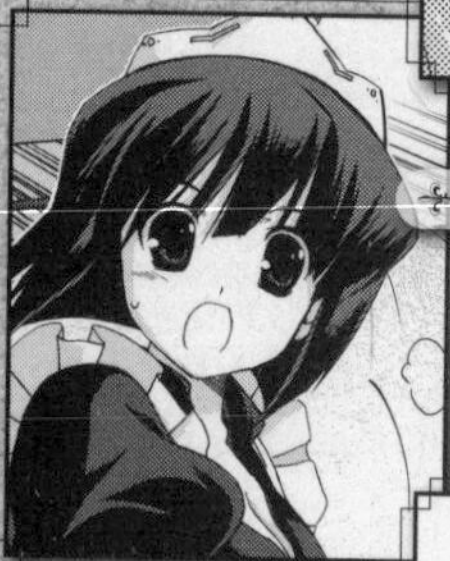

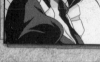

Siesta

A COMMONER. SIESTA IS 17 YEARS OLD AND WORKS AS A MAID AT THE TRISTAIN MAGIC ACADEMY. SHE HAS FEELINGS FOR SAITO AND MAKES THEM KNOWN OFTEN. HAS AN IMPRESSIVE RACK.

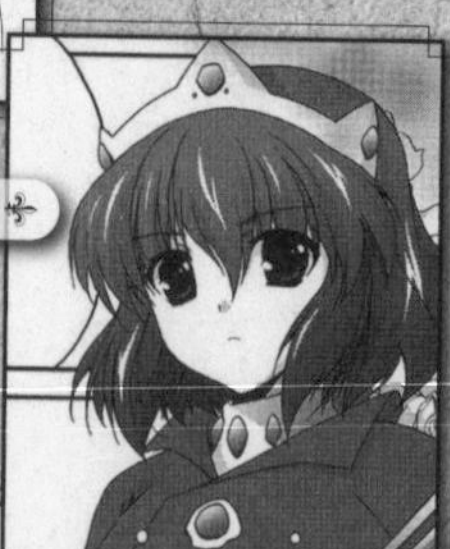

Henrietta

PRINCESS, AND LATER QUEEN, OF THE KINGDOM OF TRISTAIN. SHE TOOK THE THRONE AT THE START OF THE WAR WITH ALBION. LOUISE'S CHILDHOOD FRIEND.

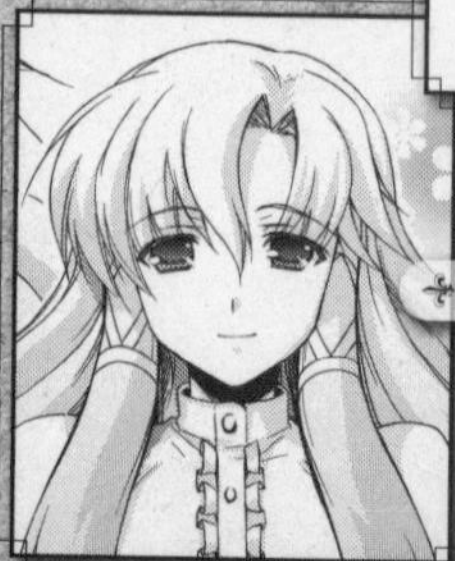

Cattleya

LOUISE'S SECOND-OLDEST SISTER. LOUISE ABSOLUTELY ADORES HER.

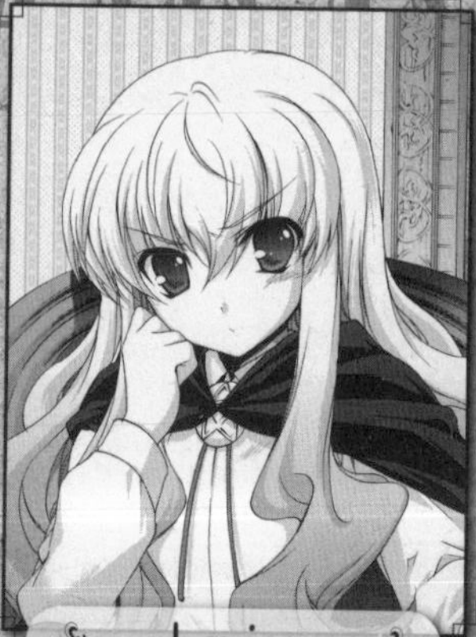

Louise

A SECOND-YEAR STUDENT AT TRISTAIN'S MAGIC ACADEMY. SAITO'S MASTER, SHE HAS PINK-BLOND HAIR AND REDDISH-BROWN EYES. SHE WIELDS THE LEGENDARY ELEMENT KNOWN AS "VOID." DAUGHTER OF A POWERFUL NOBLE FAMILY, SHE IS EXTREMELY PRIDEFUL AND STUBBORN. ALSO KNOWN AS "LOUISE THE ZERO."

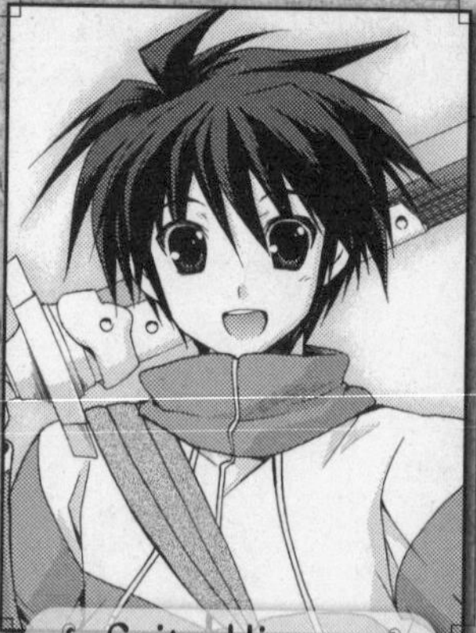

Saito Hiraga

AN ORDINARY JAPANESE HIGH SCHOOL STUDENT, SAITO WAS SUMMONED BY LOUISE AS HER FAMILIAR. HE LATER DISCOVERED THAT HE'S THE LEGENDARY FAMILIAR KNOWN AS "GANDALFR," WITH THE ABILITY TO WIELD ANY WEAPON. HE USUALLY FIGHTS WITH DERFLINGER, A MAGICAL BLADE THAT'S CAPABLE OF SPEECH.

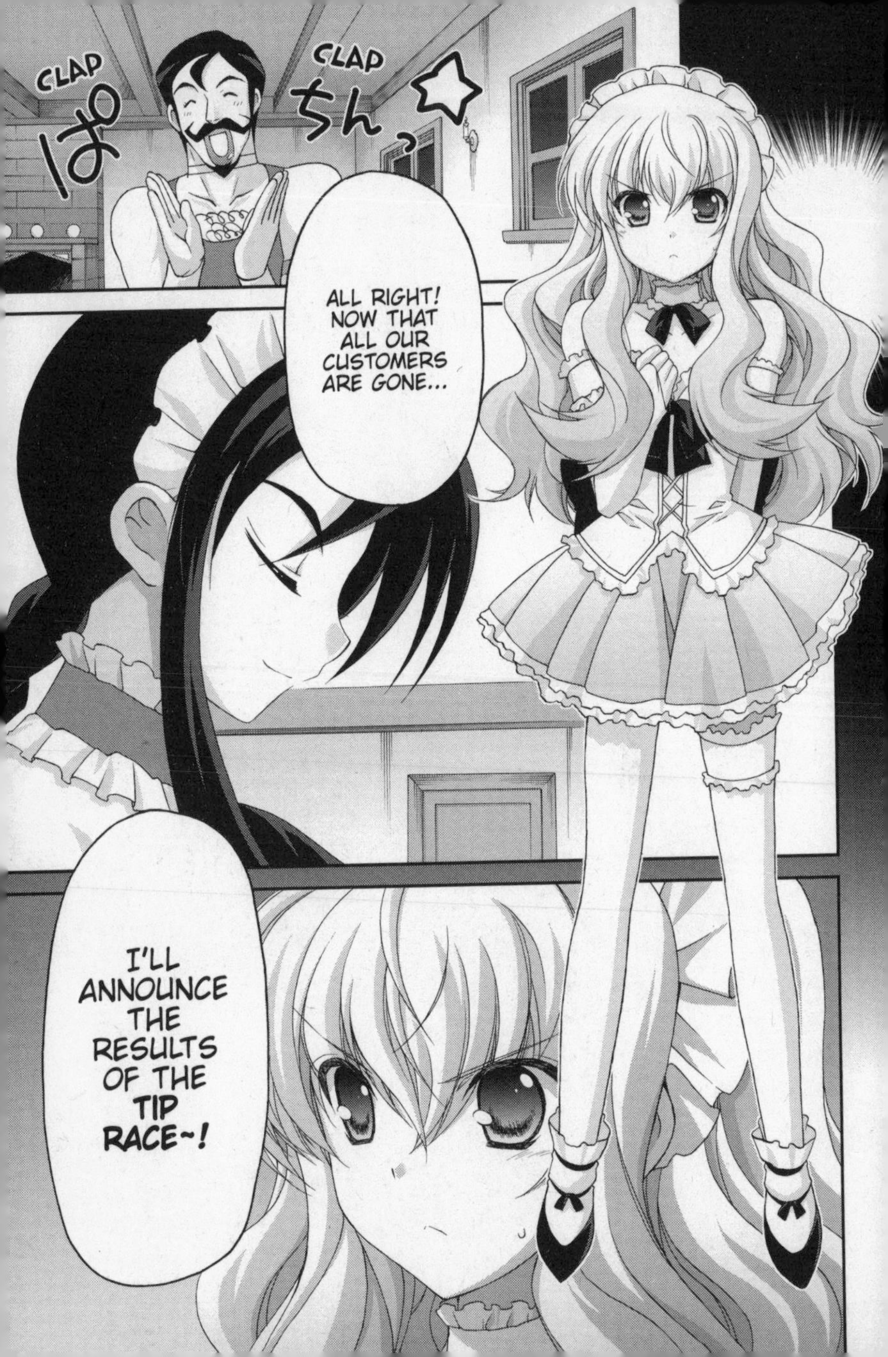
CLAP
ちん
CLAP
ぱ
ALL RIGHT! NOW THAT ALL OUR CUSTOMERS ARE GONE...
I'LL ANNOUNCE THE RESULTS OF THE TIP RACE~!

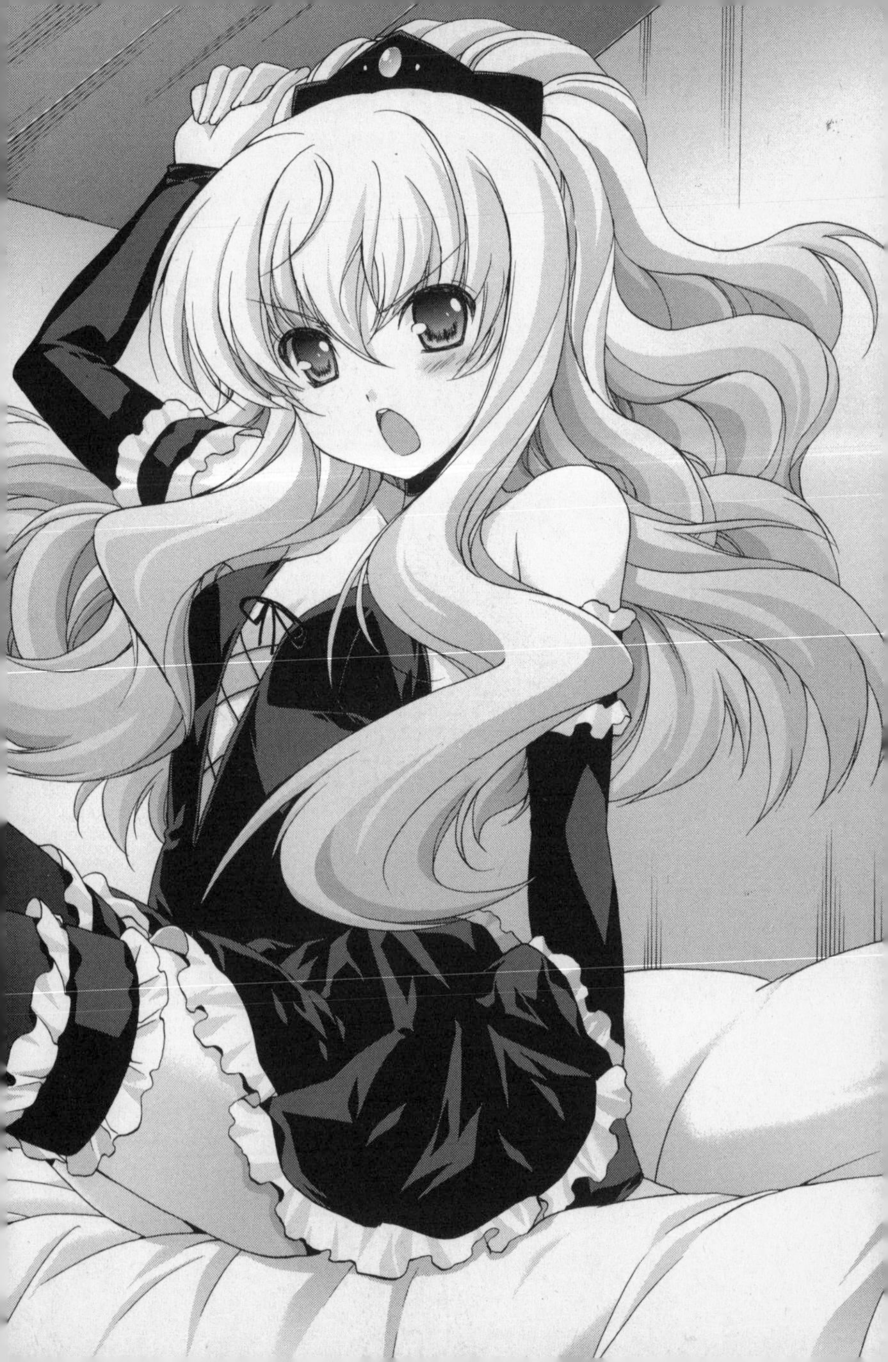

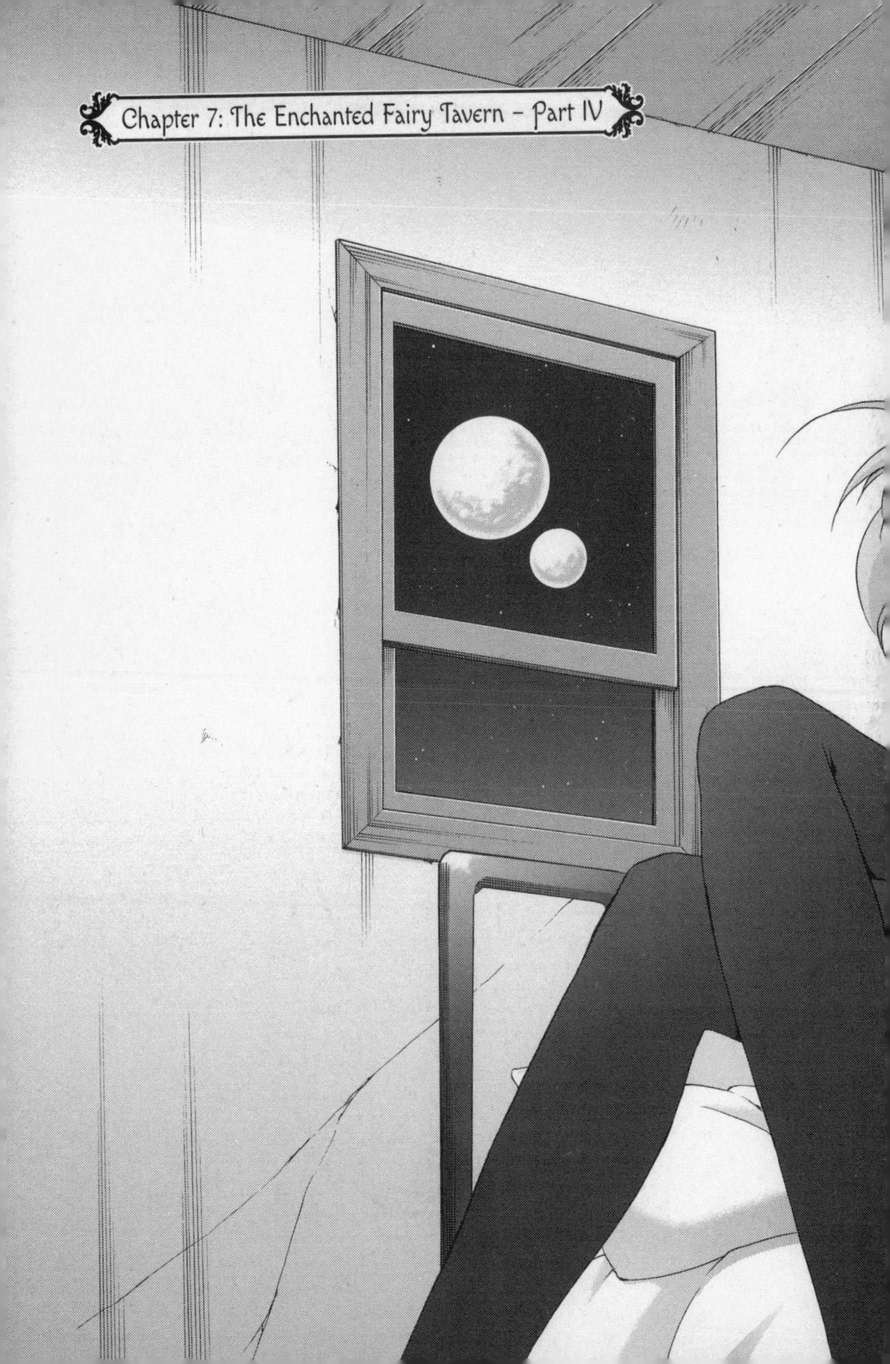
Chapter 7: The Enchanted Fairy Tavern – Part IV

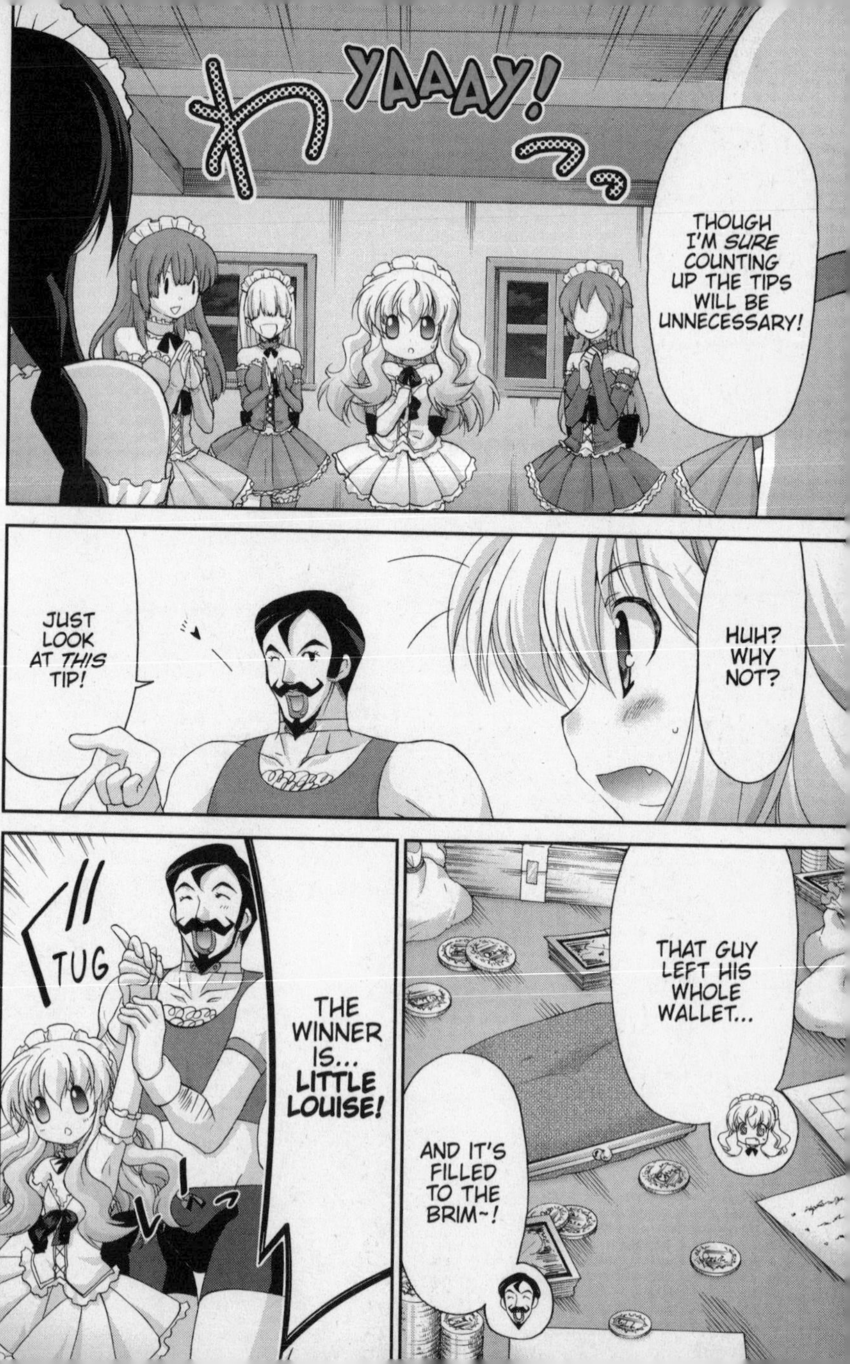
YAAAY!
THOUGH I'M *SURE* COUNTING UP THE TIPS WILL BE UNNECESSARY!
HUH? WHY NOT?
JUST LOOK AT *THIS* TIP!
THAT GUY LEFT HIS WHOLE WALLET...
AND IT'S FILLED TO THE BRIM~!
TUG
THE WINNER IS... **LITTLE LOUISE!**

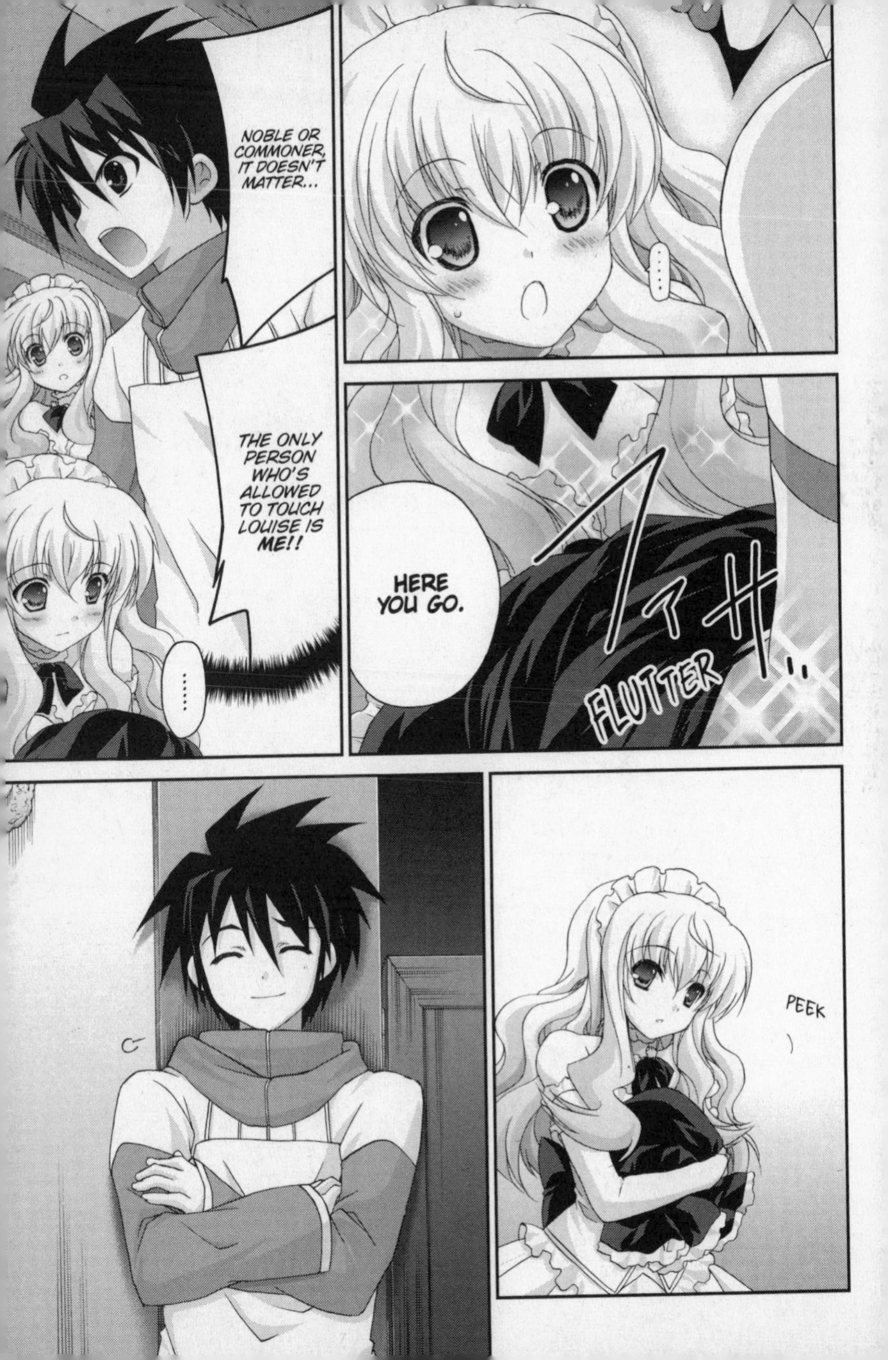
......
HERE YOU GO.
FLUTTER
NOBLE OR COMMONER, IT DOESN'T MATTER...
THE ONLY PERSON WHO'S ALLOWED TO TOUCH LOUISE IS ME!!
......
PEEK

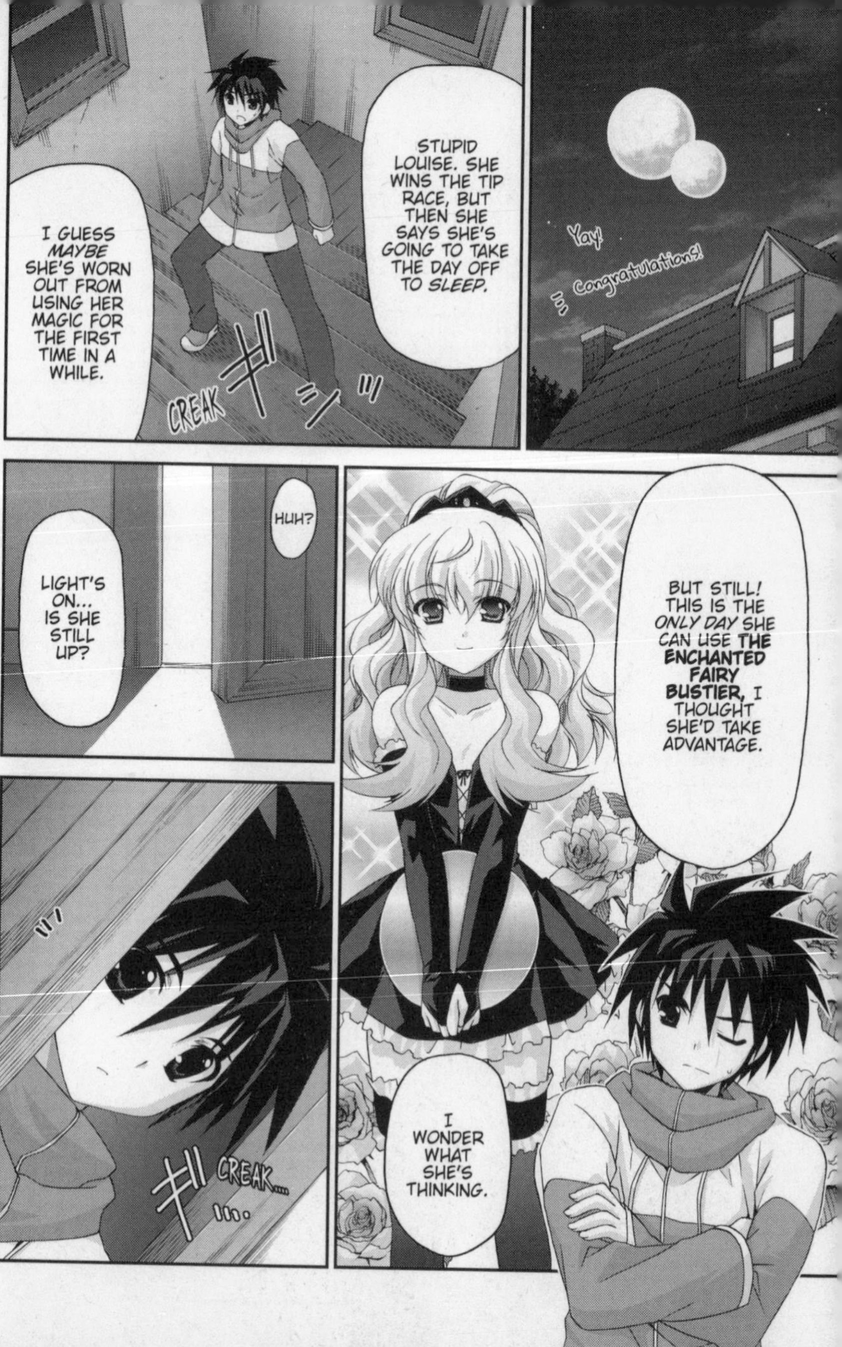
Yay!
Congratulations!
STUPID LOUISE. SHE WINS THE TIP RACE, BUT THEN SHE SAYS SHE'S GOING TO TAKE THE DAY OFF TO *SLEEP*.
I GUESS *MAYBE* SHE'S WORN OUT FROM USING HER MAGIC FOR THE FIRST TIME IN A WHILE.
CREAK
BUT STILL! THIS IS THE *ONLY DAY* SHE CAN USE **THE ENCHANTED FAIRY BUSTIER,** I THOUGHT SHE'D TAKE ADVANTAGE.
I WONDER WHAT SHE'S THINKING.
HUH?
LIGHT'S ON... IS SHE STILL UP?
CREAK...

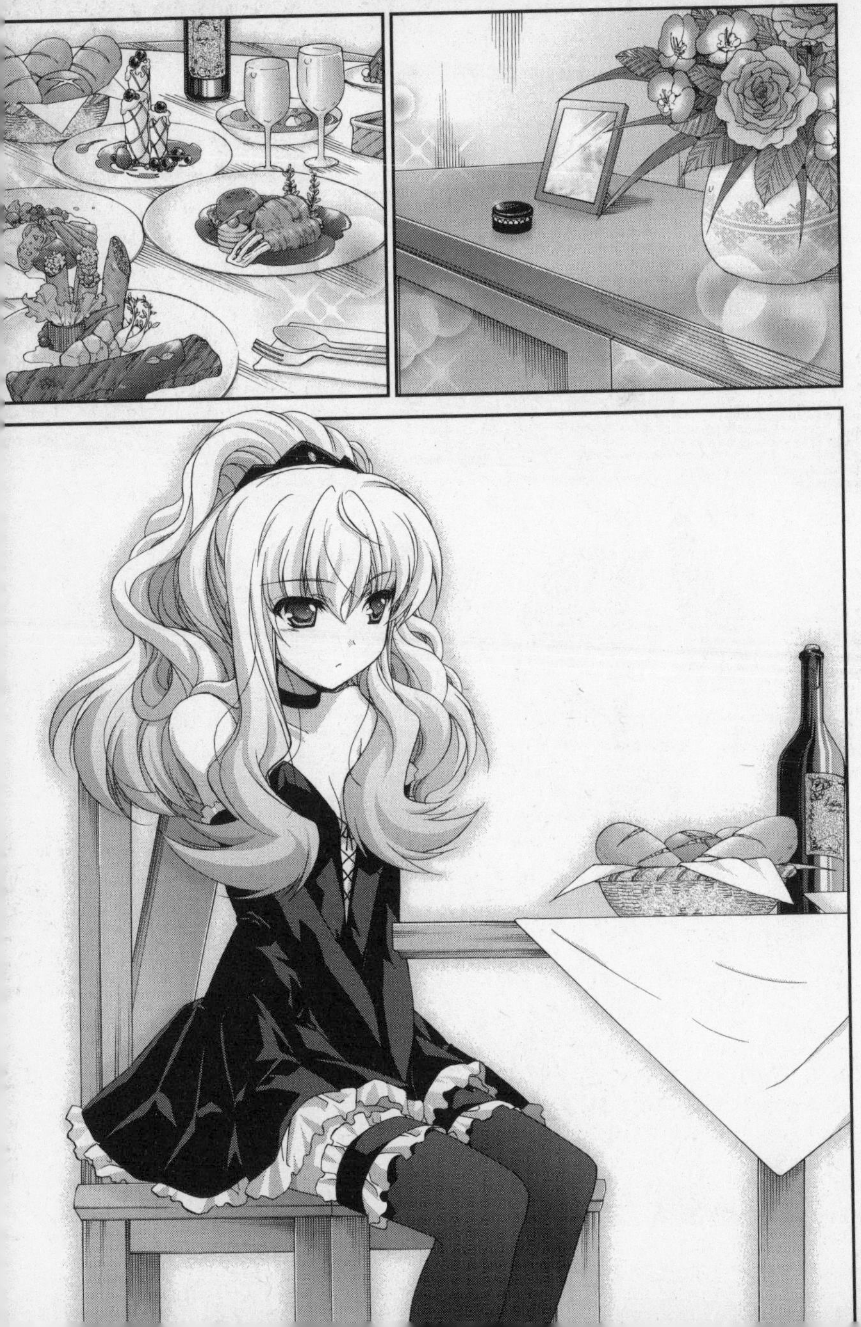

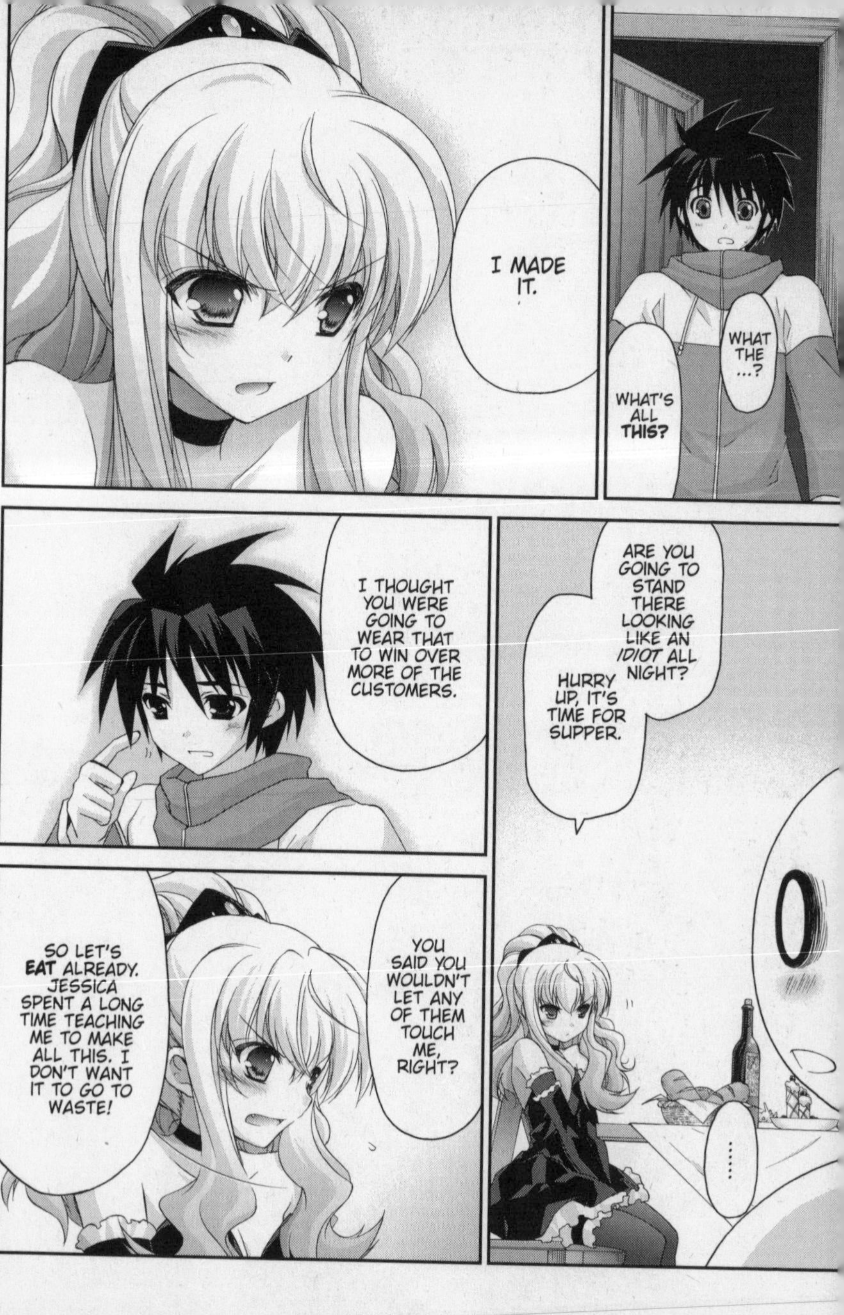
WHAT THE ...?
WHAT'S ALL THIS?
I MADE IT.
ARE YOU GOING TO STAND THERE LOOKING LIKE AN IDIOT ALL NIGHT?
HURRY UP, IT'S TIME FOR SUPPER.
......
I THOUGHT YOU WERE GOING TO WEAR THAT TO WIN OVER MORE OF THE CUSTOMERS.
YOU SAID YOU WOULDN'T LET ANY OF THEM TOUCH ME, RIGHT?
SO LET'S EAT ALREADY. JESSICA SPENT A LONG TIME TEACHING ME TO MAKE ALL THIS. I DON'T WANT IT TO GO TO WASTE!

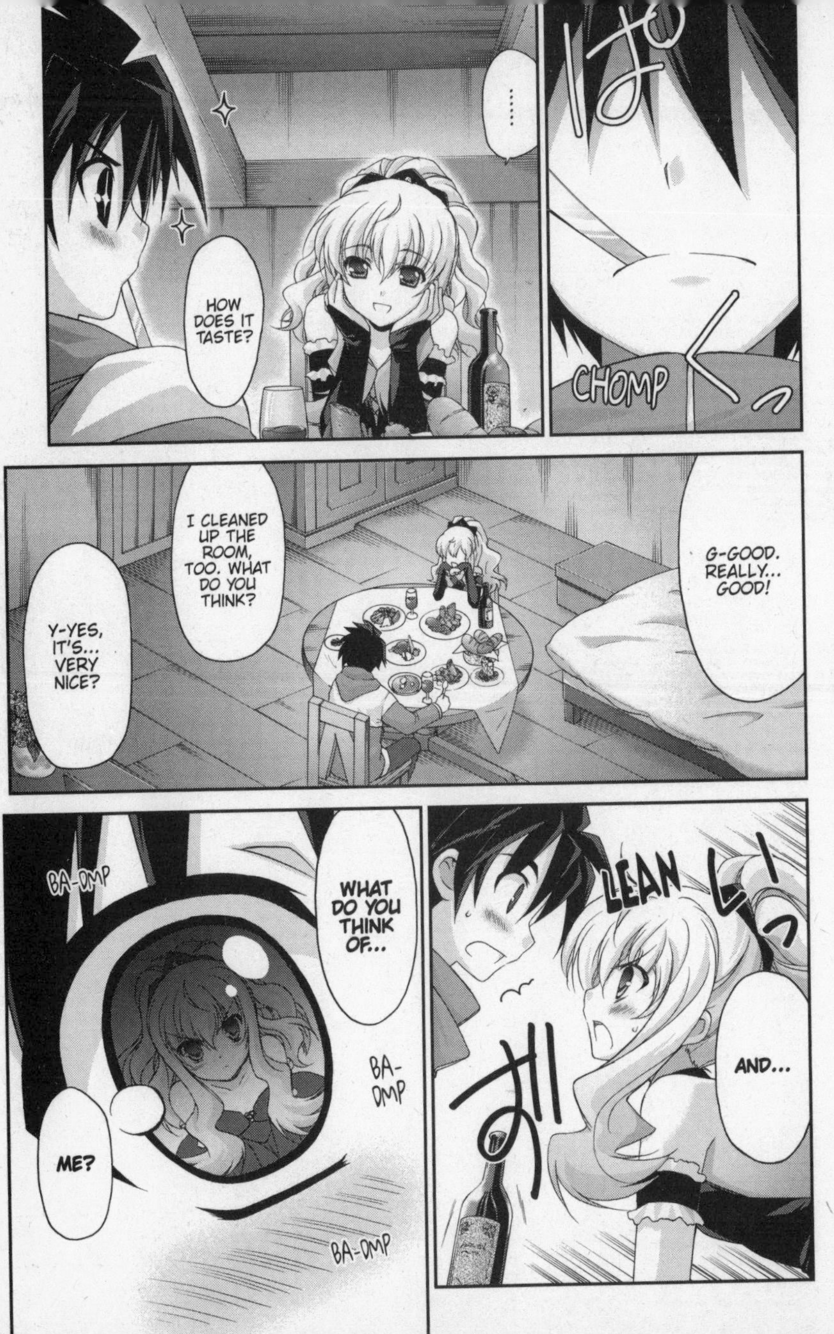
......
CHOMP
HOW DOES IT TASTE?
G-GOOD. REALLY... GOOD!
I CLEANED UP THE ROOM, TOO. WHAT DO YOU THINK?
Y-YES, IT'S... VERY NICE?
LEAN
AND...
WHAT DO YOU THINK OF...
BA-DMP
BA-DMP
ME?
BA-DMP

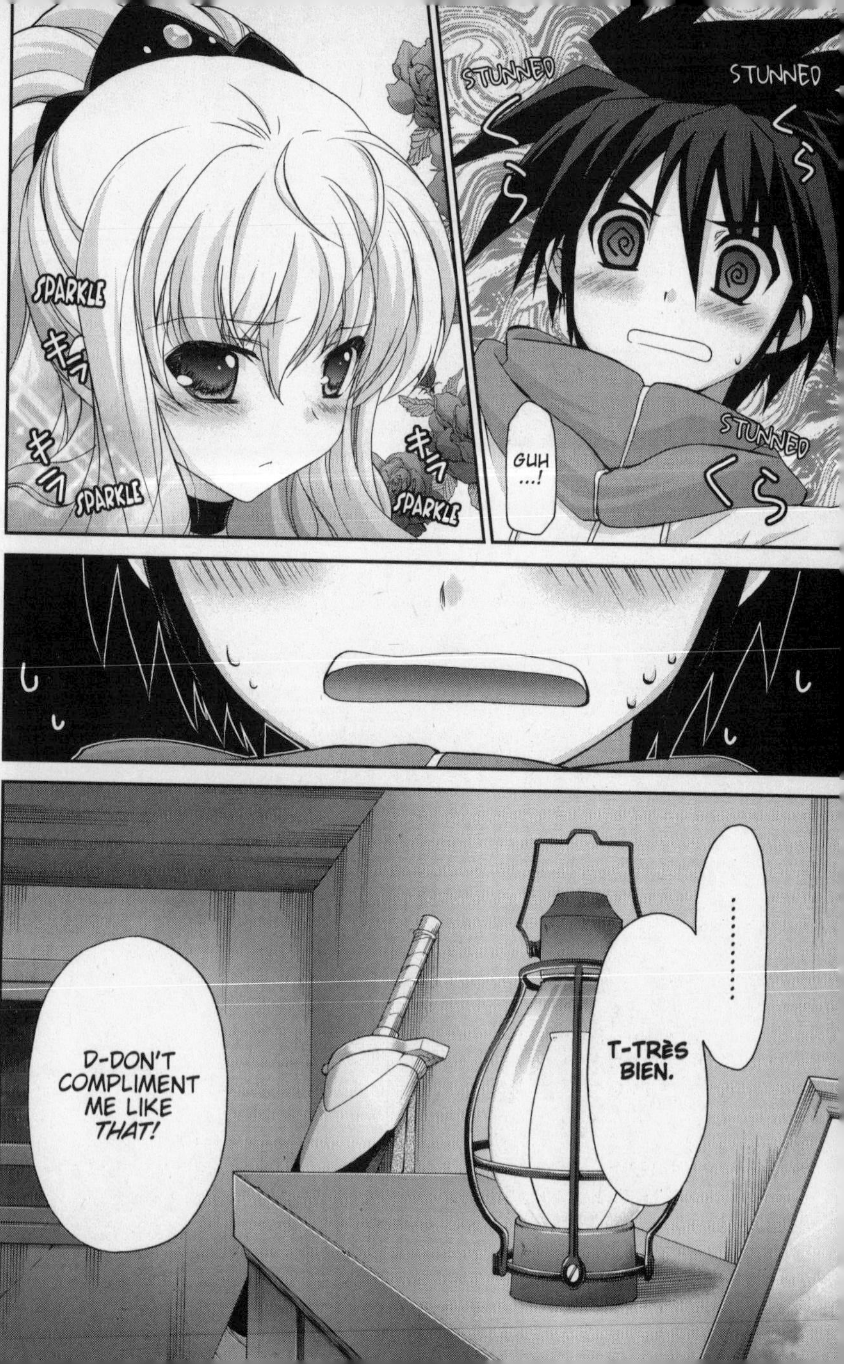
STUNNED
くら
STUNNED
くら
GUH ...!
STUNNED
くら
SPARKLE
キラ
SPARKLE
キラ
SPARKLE
キラ
SPARKLE
......
T-TRÈS BIEN.
D-DON'T COMPLIMENT ME LIKE *THAT!*

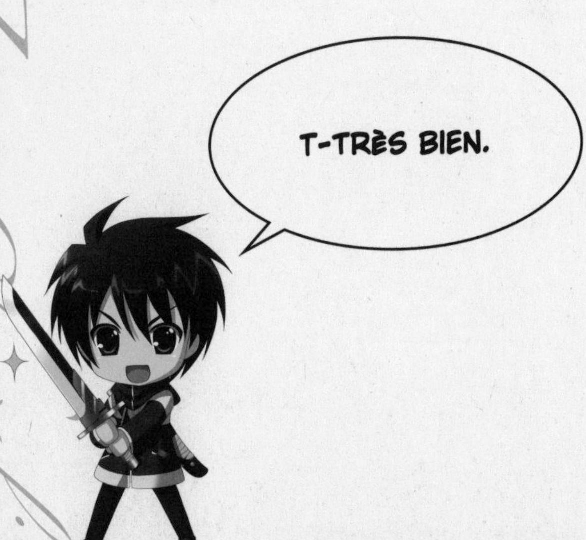
T-TRÈS BIEN.

Le Familier de Zero Chevalier

ZERO'S
FAMILIAR
Chevalier

Chapter 8: A Tristanian Holiday – Part I

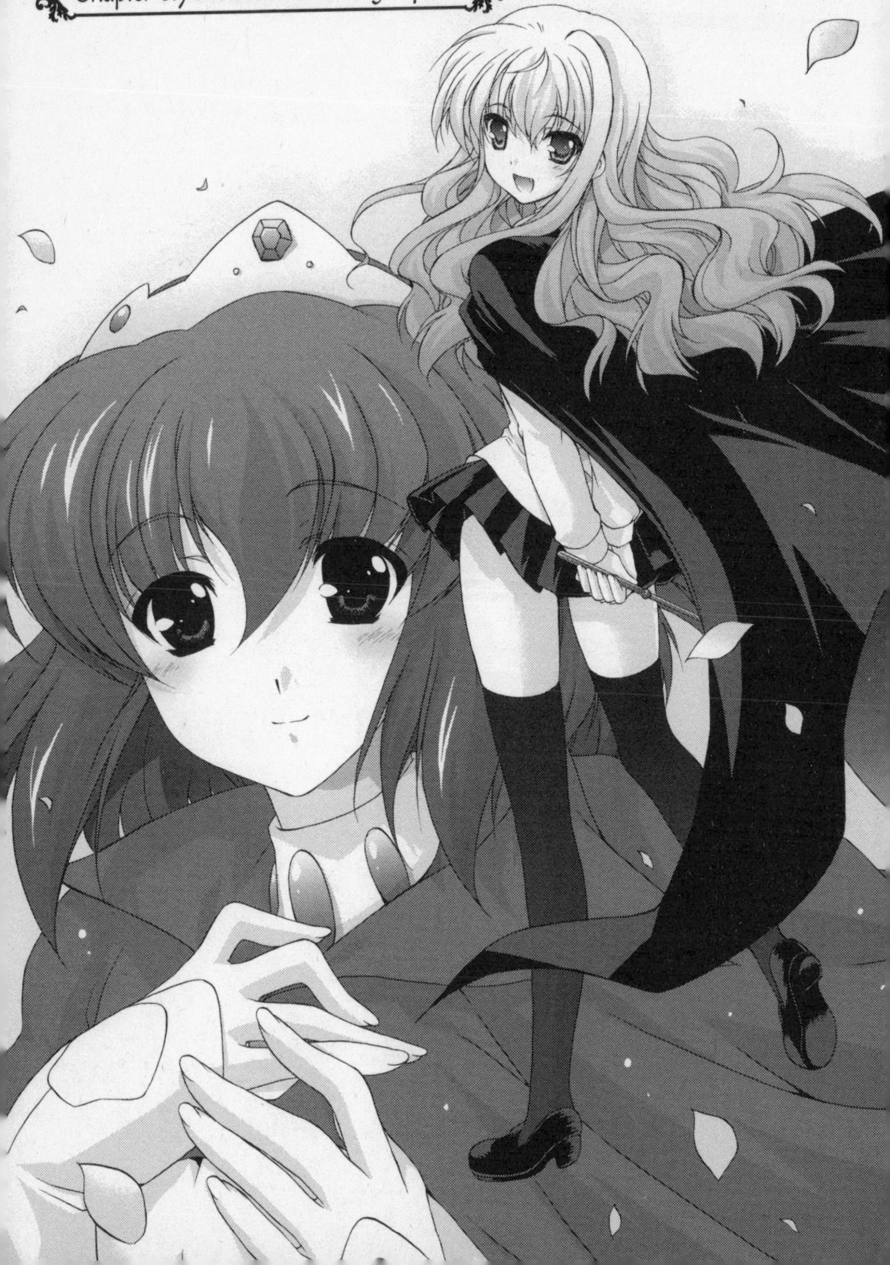

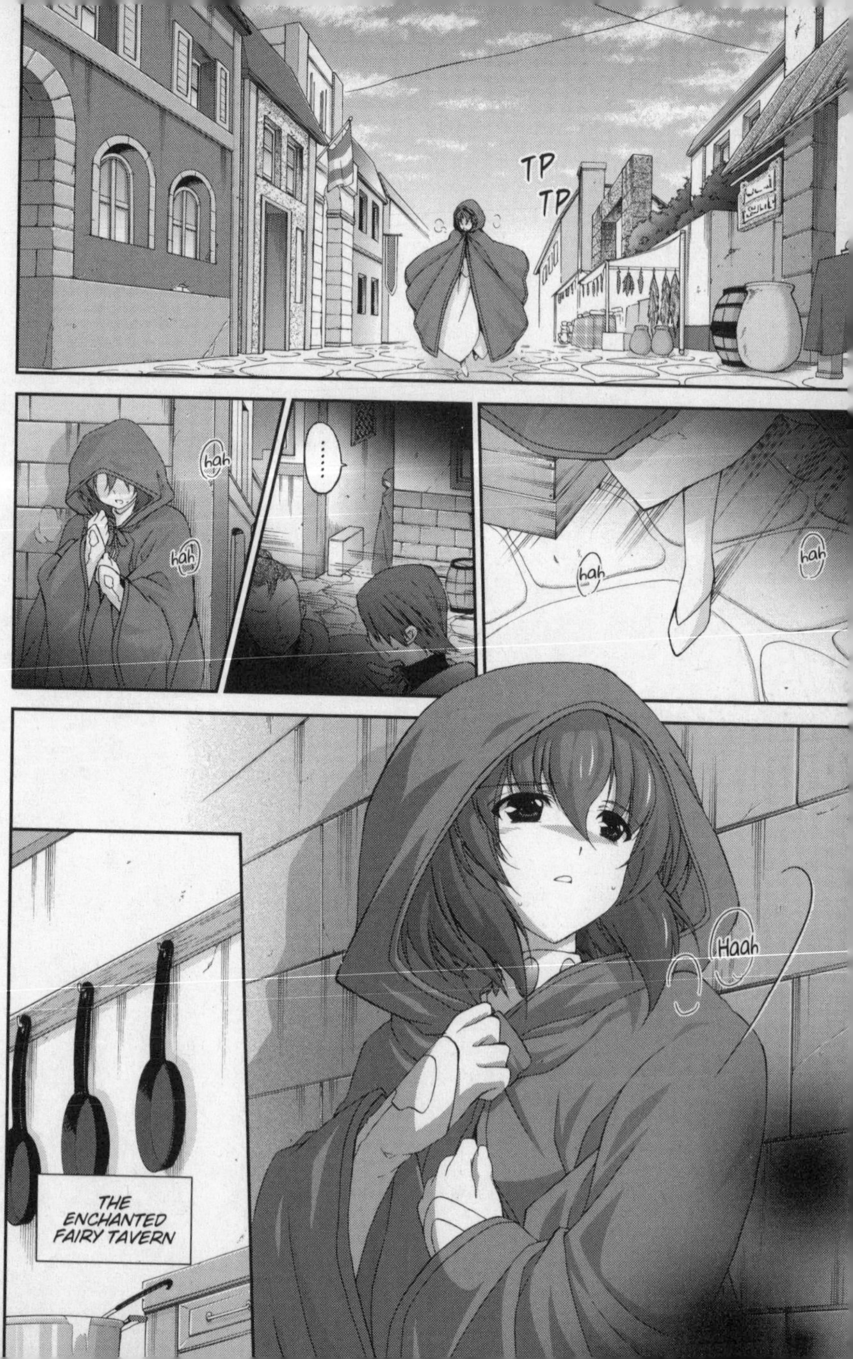
TP
TP
hah
hah
......
hah
hah
Haah
THE ENCHANTED FAIRY TAVERN

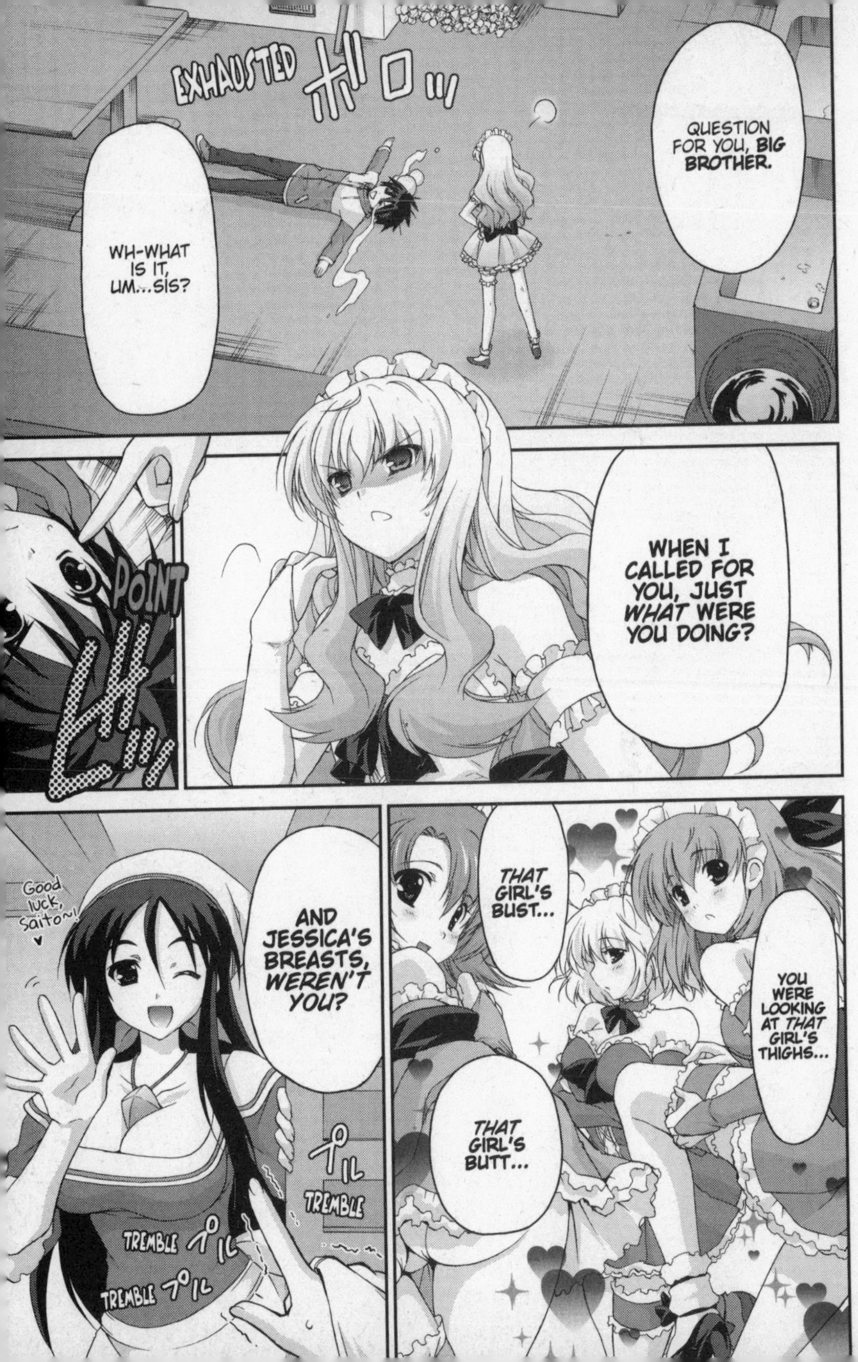

QUESTION FOR YOU, BIG BROTHER.
EXHAUSTED
WH-WHAT IS IT, UM...SIS?
WHEN I CALLED FOR YOU, JUST *WHAT* WERE YOU DOING?
POINT
YOU WERE LOOKING AT *THAT* GIRL'S THIGHS...
THAT GIRL'S BUST...
THAT GIRL'S BUTT...
AND JESSICA'S BREASTS, *WEREN'T* YOU?
Good luck, Saito~!
TREMBLE
TREMBLE
TREMBLE

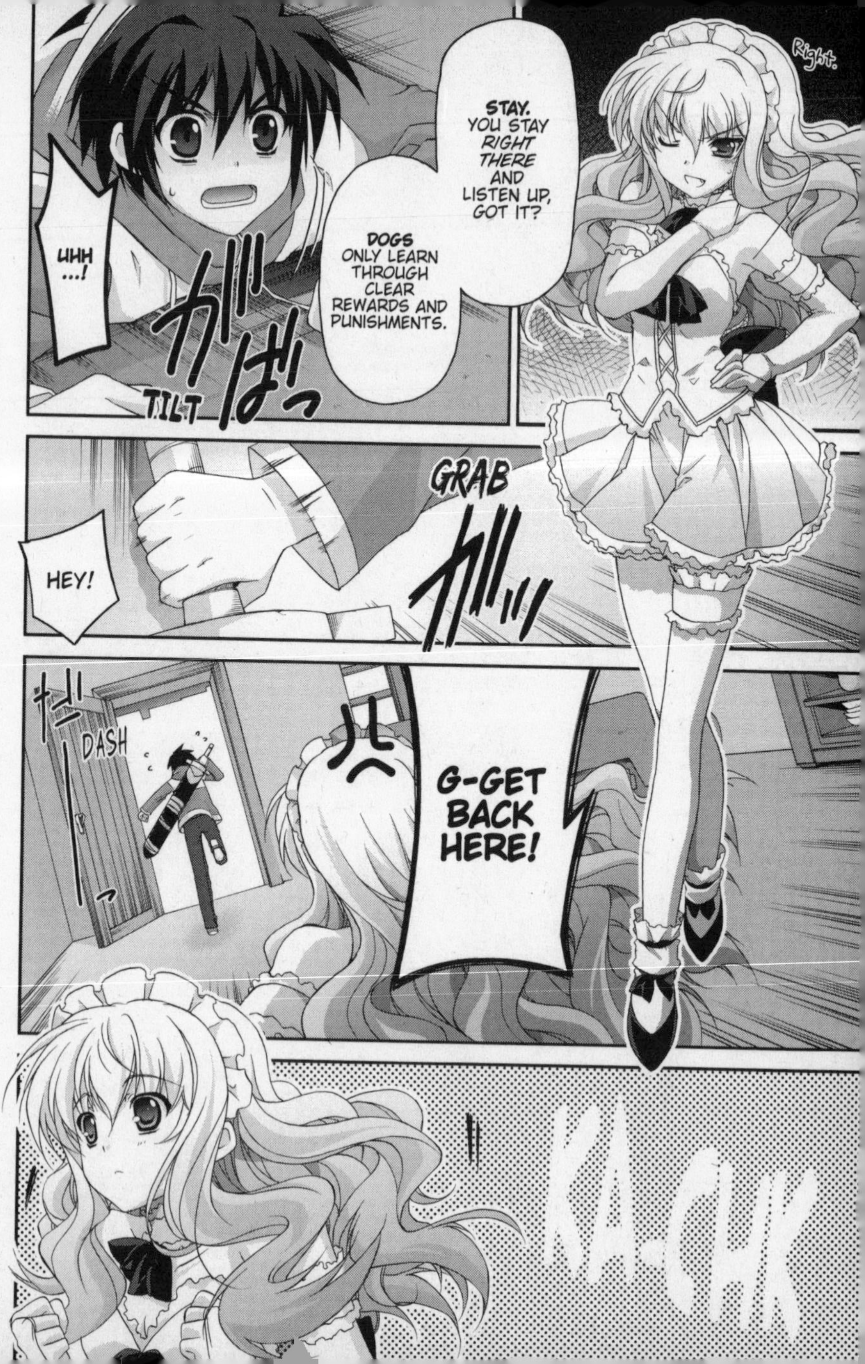
Right.
STAY. YOU STAY RIGHT THERE AND LISTEN UP, GOT IT?
DOGS ONLY LEARN THROUGH CLEAR REWARDS AND PUNISHMENTS.
UHH ...!
がばっ
TILT
GRAB
HEY!
G-GET BACK HERE!
DASH
KA-CHK

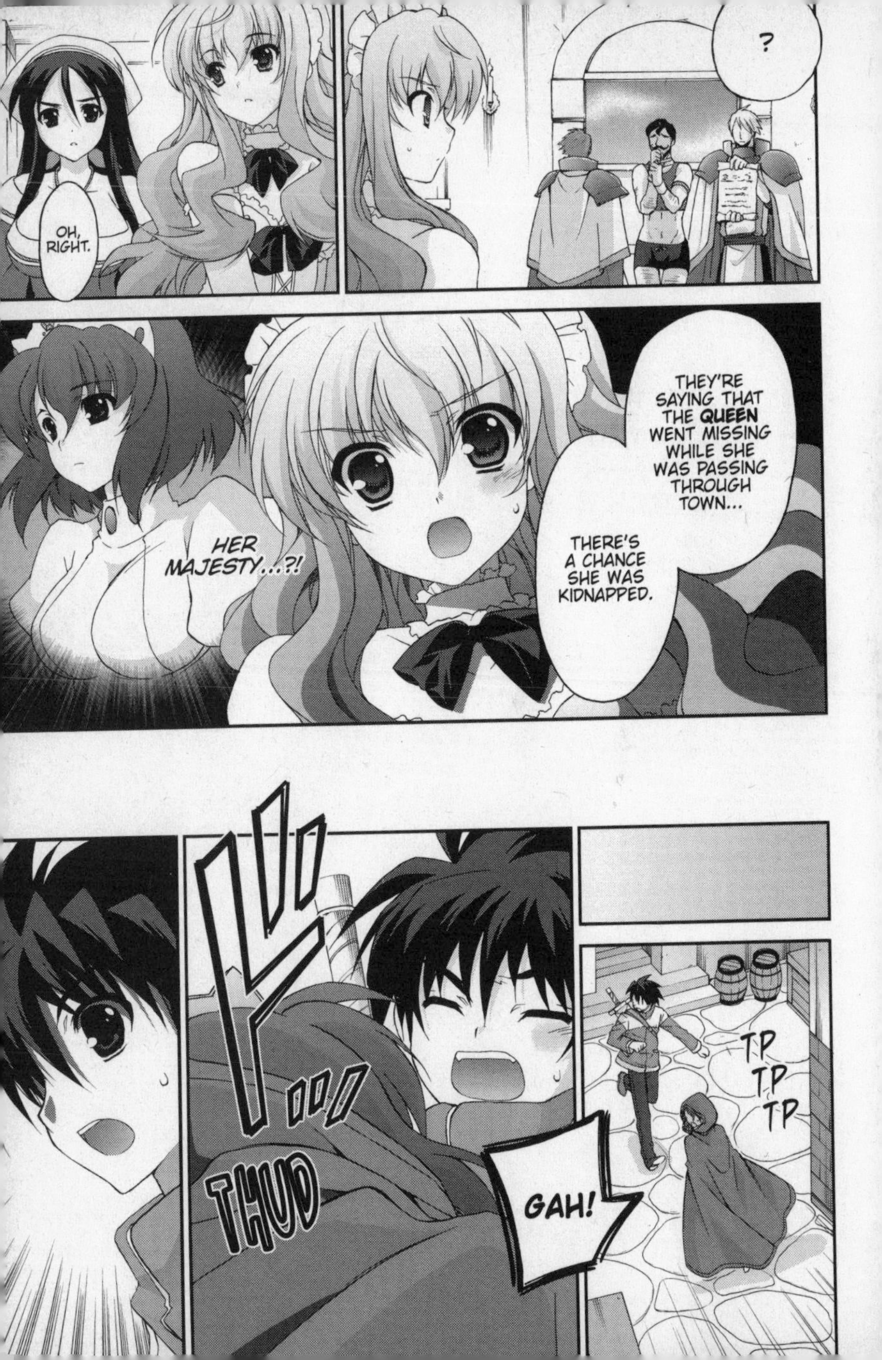
?
OH, RIGHT.
THEY'RE SAYING THAT THE QUEEN WENT MISSING WHILE SHE WAS PASSING THROUGH TOWN...
THERE'S A CHANCE SHE WAS KIDNAPPED.
HER MAJESTY...?!
TP TP TP
GAH!
THUD

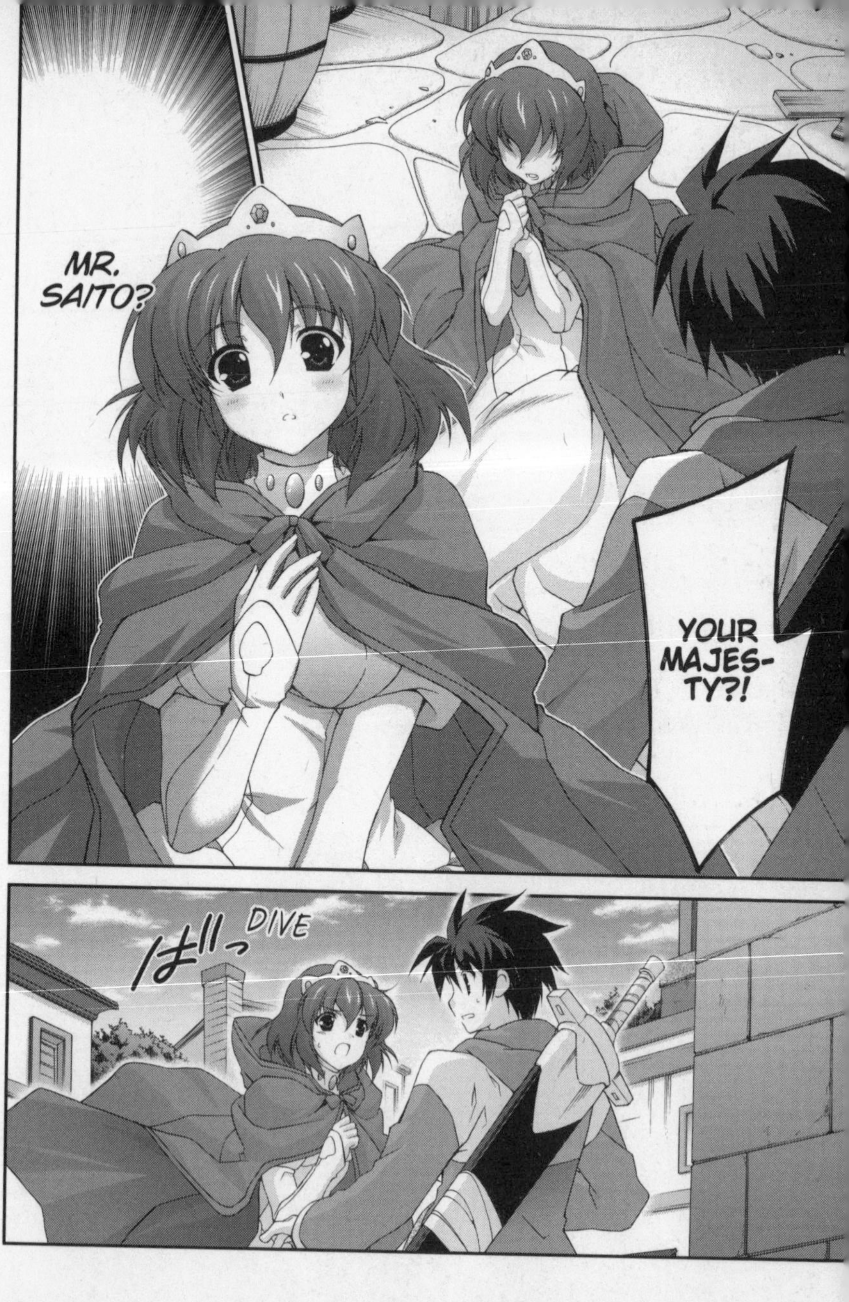
YOUR MAJES-TY?!
MR. SAITO?
ぱっ DIVE

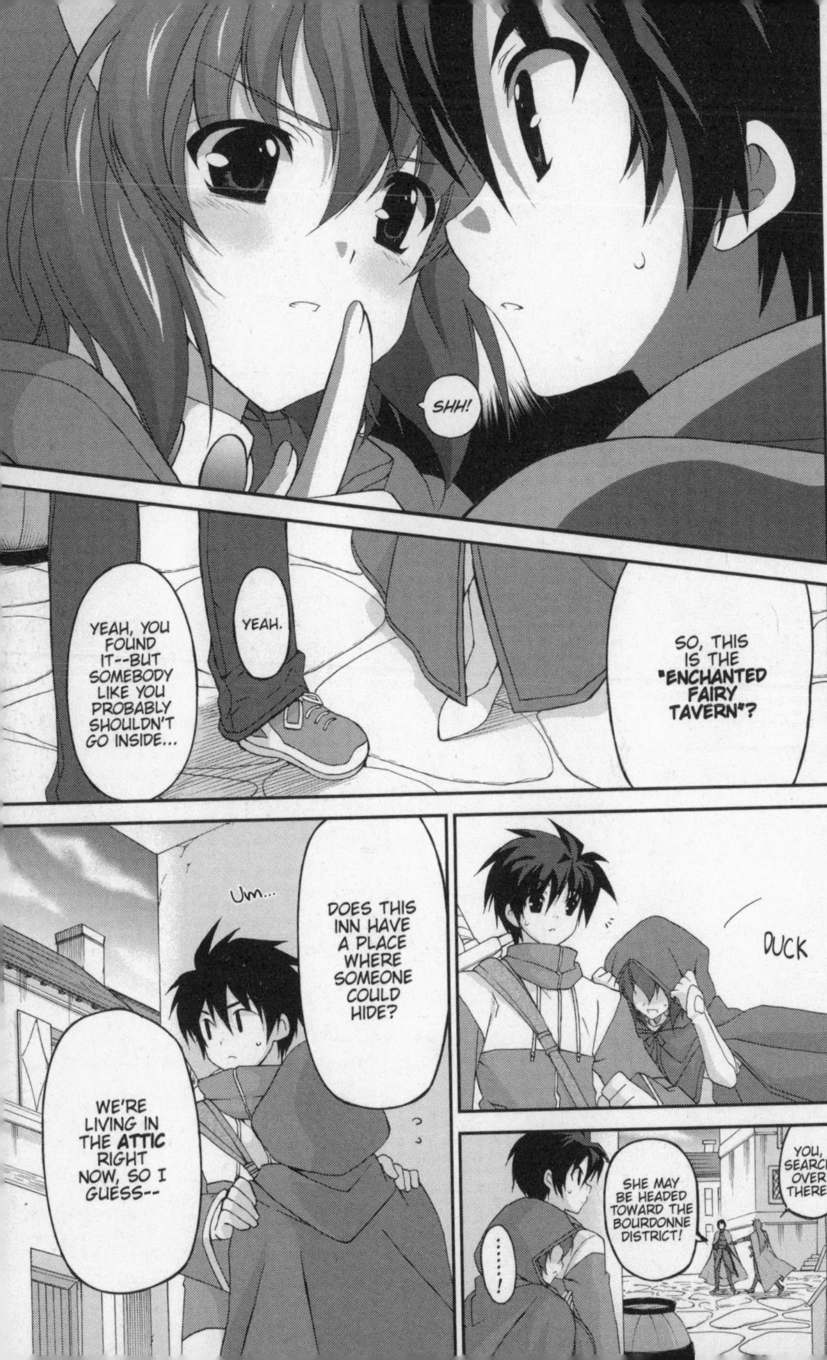
SHH!
SO, THIS IS THE "ENCHANTED FAIRY TAVERN"?
YEAH.
YEAH, YOU FOUND IT--BUT SOMEBODY LIKE YOU PROBABLY SHOULDN'T GO INSIDE...
DUCK
YOU, SEARCH OVER THERE!
SHE MAY BE HEADED TOWARD THE BOURDONNE DISTRICT!
......!
Um...
DOES THIS INN HAVE A PLACE WHERE SOMEONE COULD HIDE?
WE'RE LIVING IN THE ATTIC RIGHT NOW, SO I GUESS--

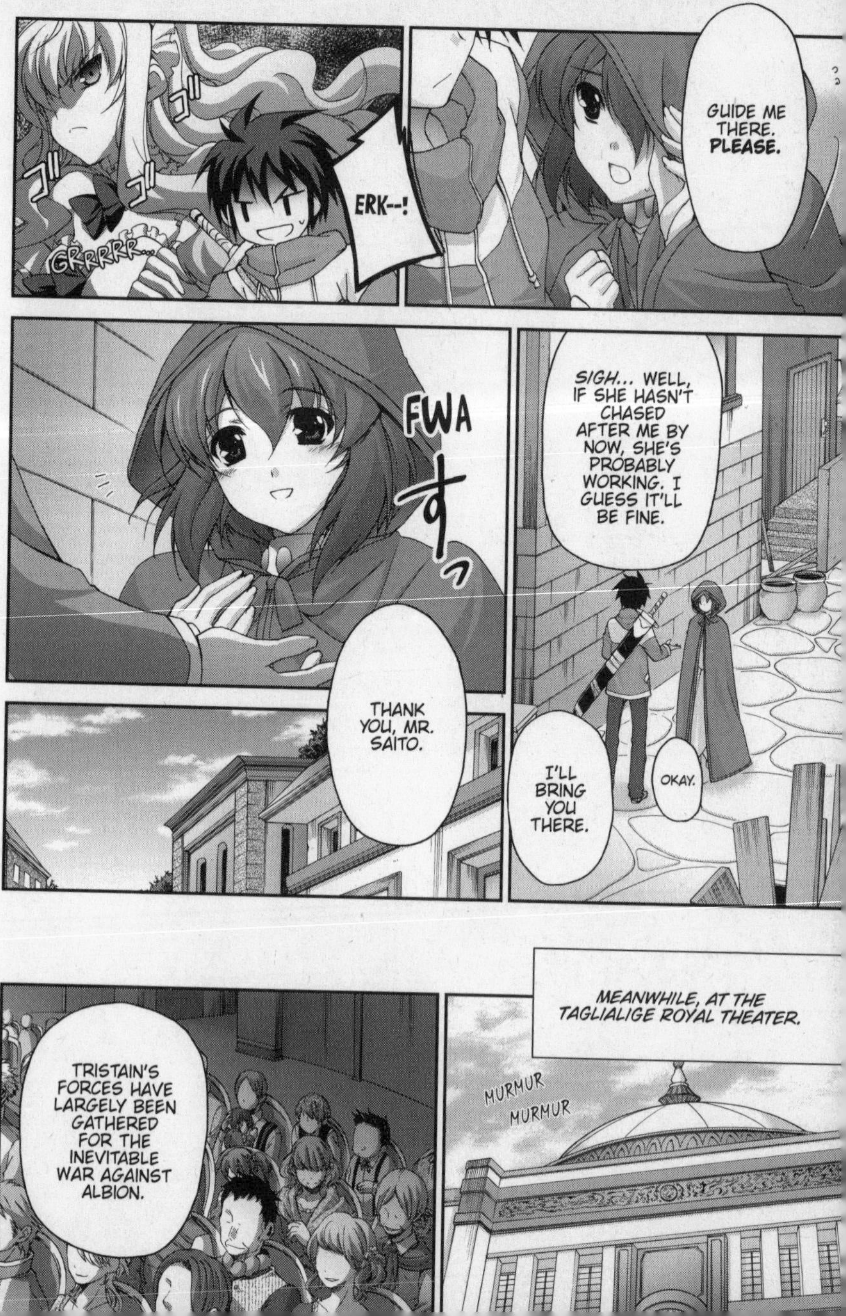
GUIDE ME THERE. **PLEASE.**
ERK--!
ゴ ゴ ゴ
GRRRRR...
SIGH... WELL, IF SHE HASN'T CHASED AFTER ME BY NOW, SHE'S PROBABLY WORKING. I GUESS IT'LL BE FINE.
I'LL BRING YOU THERE.
OKAY.
FWA
すっ
THANK YOU, MR. SAITO.
MEANWHILE, AT THE TAGLIALIGE ROYAL THEATER.
MURMUR
MURMUR
TRISTAIN'S FORCES HAVE LARGELY BEEN GATHERED FOR THE INEVITABLE WAR AGAINST ALBION.

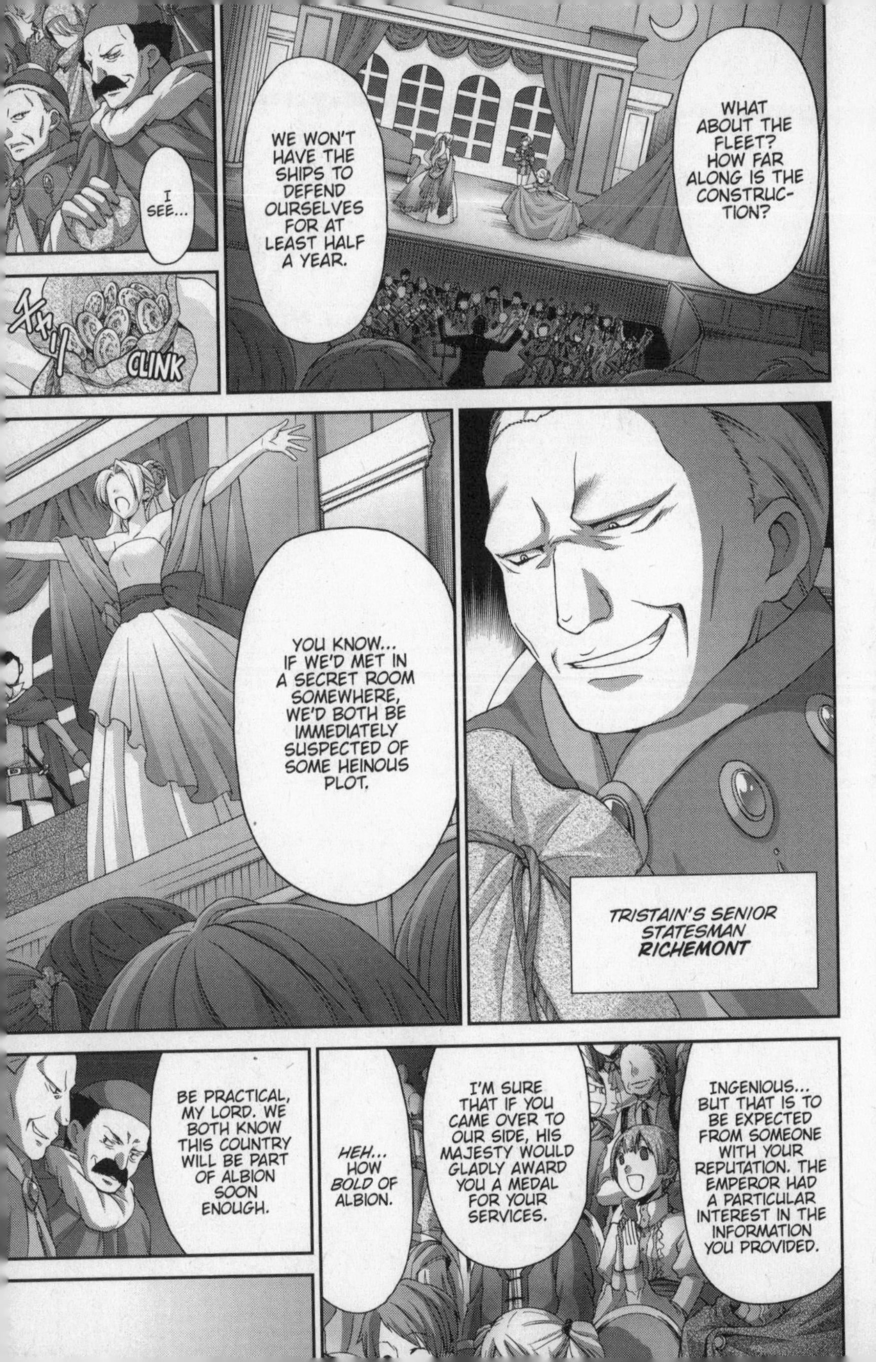
WHAT ABOUT THE FLEET? HOW FAR ALONG IS THE CONSTRUCTION?
WE WON'T HAVE THE SHIPS TO DEFEND OURSELVES FOR AT LEAST HALF A YEAR.
I SEE...
CLINK
YOU KNOW... IF WE'D MET IN A SECRET ROOM SOMEWHERE, WE'D BOTH BE IMMEDIATELY SUSPECTED OF SOME HEINOUS PLOT.
TRISTAIN'S SENIOR STATESMAN RICHEMONT
INGENIOUS... BUT THAT IS TO BE EXPECTED FROM SOMEONE WITH YOUR REPUTATION. THE EMPEROR HAD A PARTICULAR INTEREST IN THE INFORMATION YOU PROVIDED.
I'M SURE THAT IF YOU CAME OVER TO OUR SIDE, HIS MAJESTY WOULD GLADLY AWARD YOU A MEDAL FOR YOUR SERVICES.
HEH... HOW BOLD OF ALBION.
BE PRACTICAL, MY LORD. WE BOTH KNOW THIS COUNTRY WILL BE PART OF ALBION SOON ENOUGH.

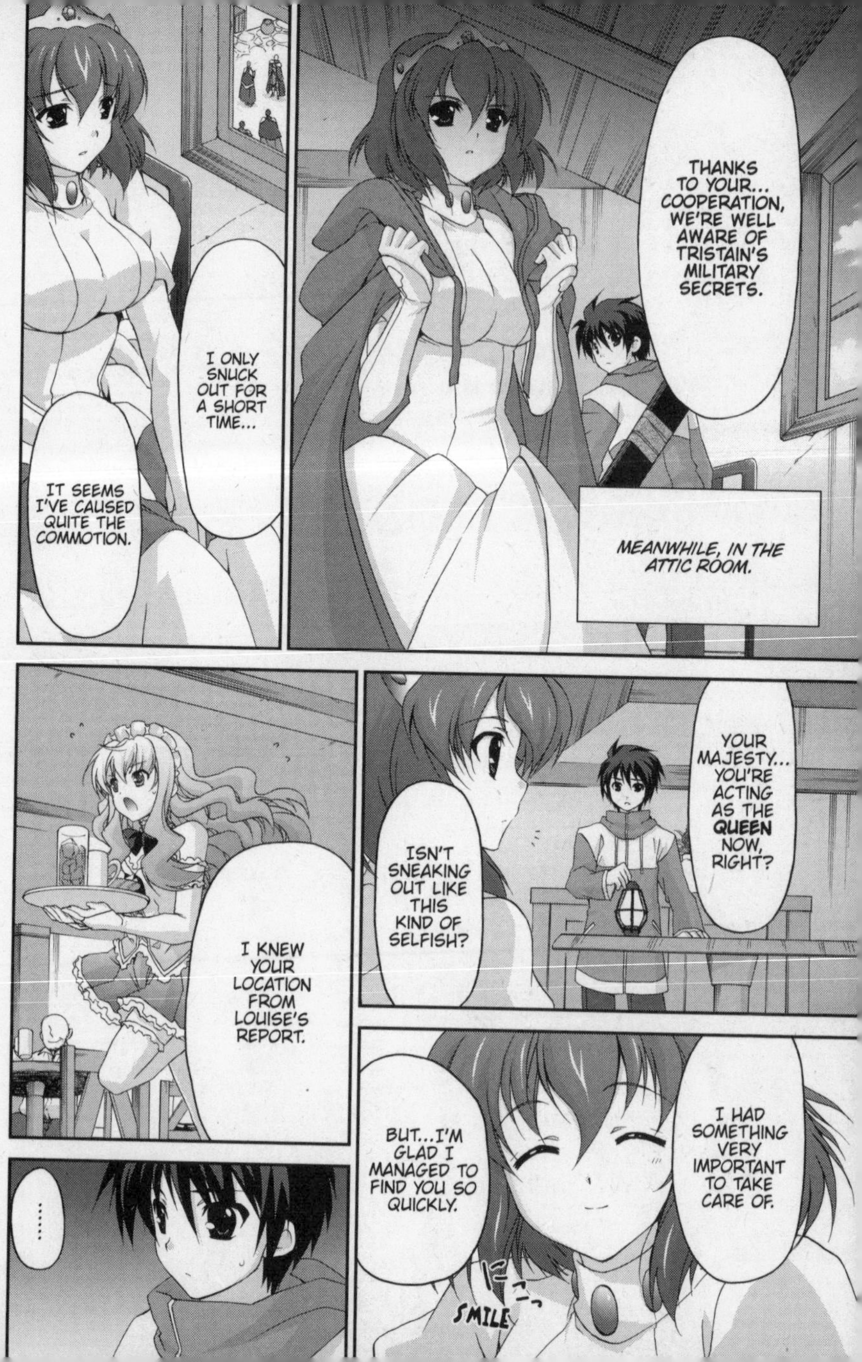
THANKS TO YOUR... COOPERATION, WE'RE WELL AWARE OF TRISTAIN'S MILITARY SECRETS.
MEANWHILE, IN THE ATTIC ROOM.
I ONLY SNUCK OUT FOR A SHORT TIME...
IT SEEMS I'VE CAUSED QUITE THE COMMOTION.
YOUR MAJESTY... YOU'RE ACTING AS THE **QUEEN** NOW, RIGHT?
ISN'T SNEAKING OUT LIKE THIS KIND OF SELFISH?
I HAD SOMETHING VERY IMPORTANT TO TAKE CARE OF.
BUT...I'M GLAD I MANAGED TO FIND YOU SO QUICKLY.
にこっ
SMILE
I KNEW YOUR LOCATION FROM LOUISE'S REPORT.
......

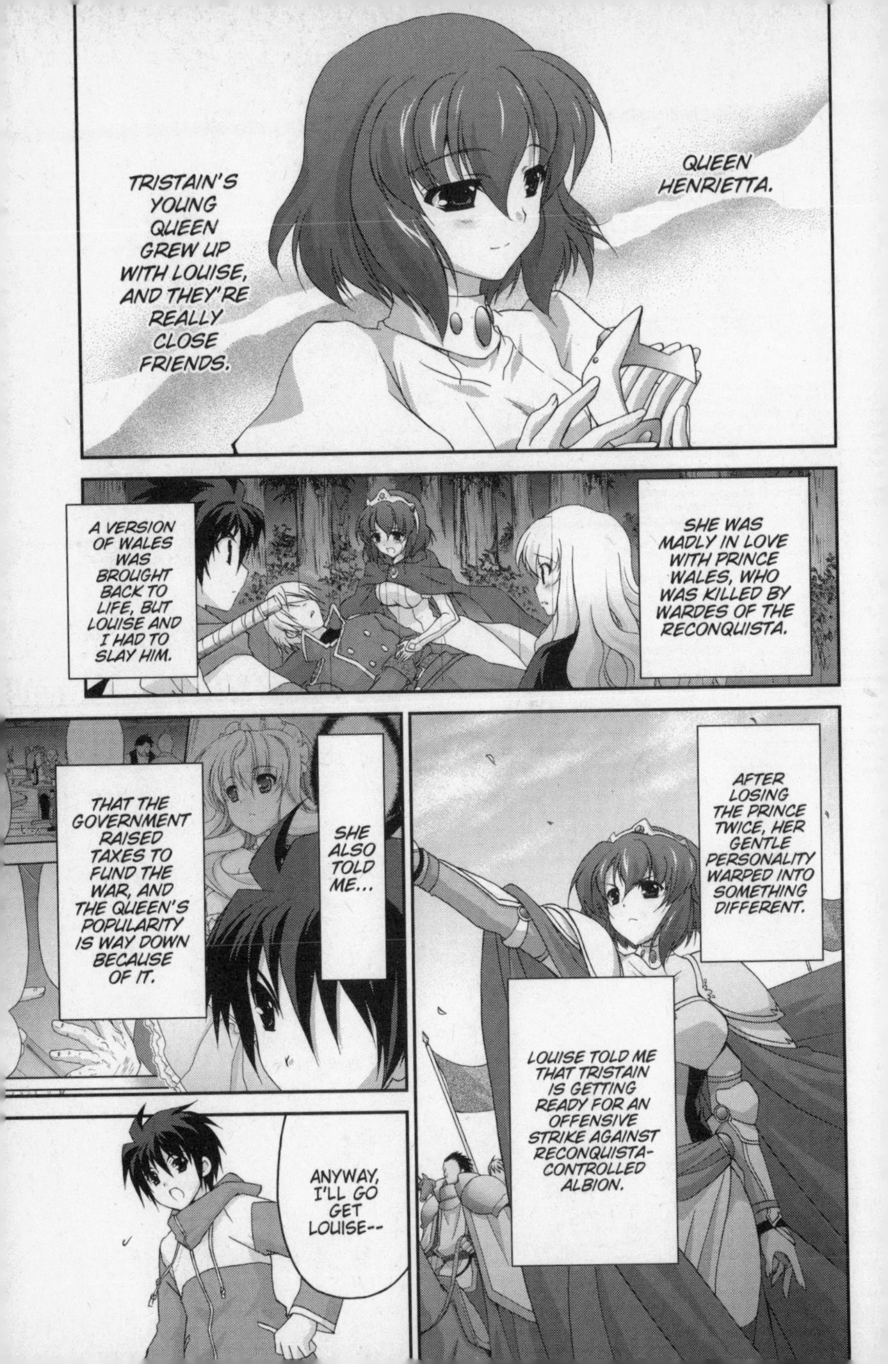
QUEEN HENRIETTA.
TRISTAIN'S YOUNG QUEEN GREW UP WITH LOUISE, AND THEY'RE REALLY CLOSE FRIENDS.
SHE WAS MADLY IN LOVE WITH PRINCE WALES, WHO WAS KILLED BY WARDES OF THE RECONQUISTA.
A VERSION OF WALES WAS BROUGHT BACK TO LIFE, BUT LOUISE AND I HAD TO SLAY HIM.
AFTER LOSING THE PRINCE TWICE, HER GENTLE PERSONALITY WARPED INTO SOMETHING DIFFERENT.
LOUISE TOLD ME THAT TRISTAIN IS GETTING READY FOR AN OFFENSIVE STRIKE AGAINST RECONQUISTA-CONTROLLED ALBION.
SHE ALSO TOLD ME...
THAT THE GOVERNMENT RAISED TAXES TO FUND THE WAR, AND THE QUEEN'S POPULARITY IS WAY DOWN BECAUSE OF IT.
ANYWAY, I'LL GO GET LOUISE--

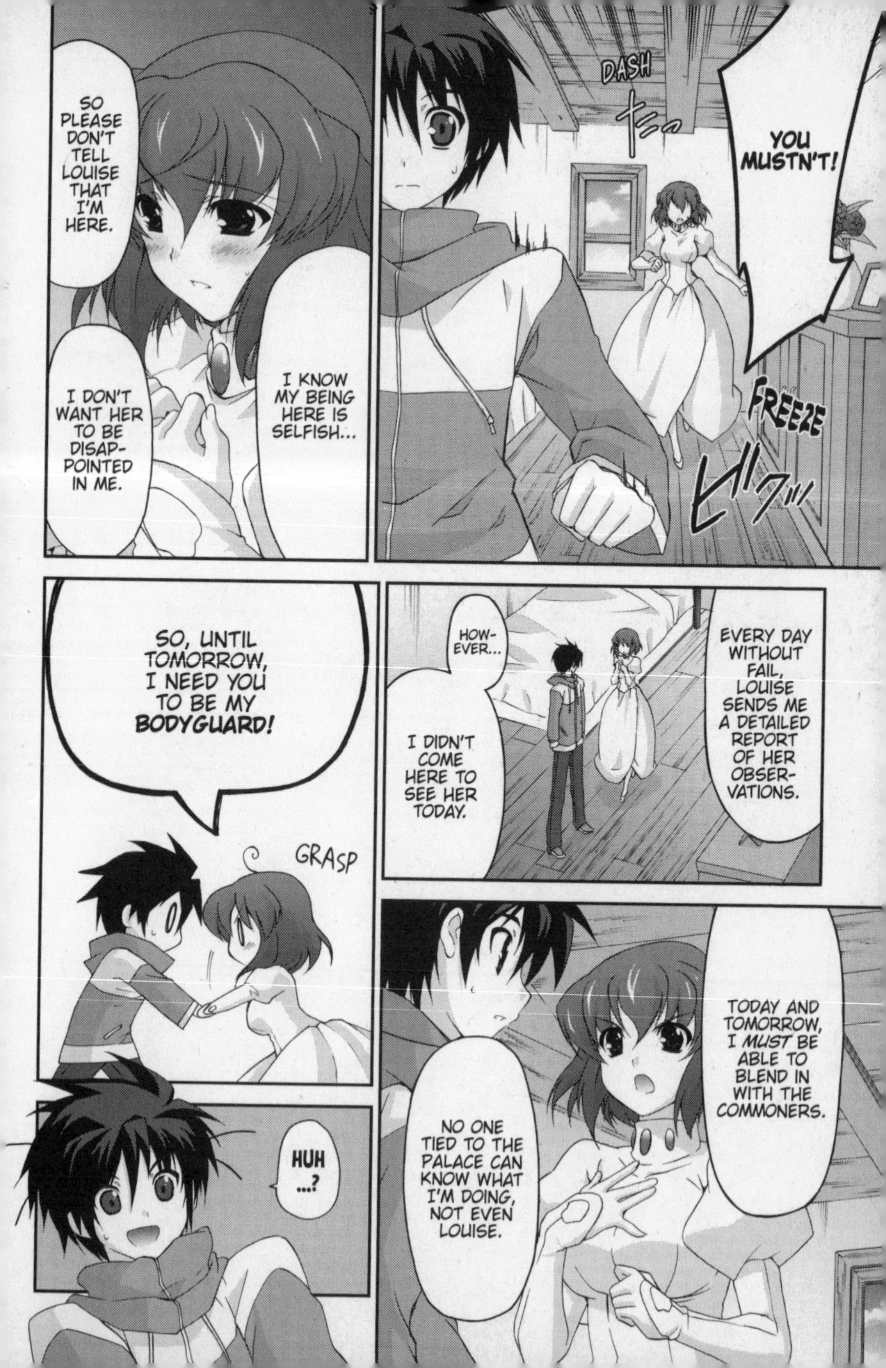
DASH
YOU MUSTN'T!
FREEZE
SO PLEASE DON'T TELL LOUISE THAT I'M HERE.
I KNOW MY BEING HERE IS SELFISH...
I DON'T WANT HER TO BE DISAP-POINTED IN ME.
EVERY DAY WITHOUT FAIL, LOUISE SENDS ME A DETAILED REPORT OF HER OBSERVATIONS.
HOW-EVER...
I DIDN'T COME HERE TO SEE HER TODAY.
TODAY AND TOMORROW, I *MUST* BE ABLE TO BLEND IN WITH THE COMMONERS.
NO ONE TIED TO THE PALACE CAN KNOW WHAT I'M DOING, NOT EVEN LOUISE.
SO, UNTIL TOMORROW, I NEED YOU TO BE MY **BODYGUARD!**
GRASP
HUH ...?

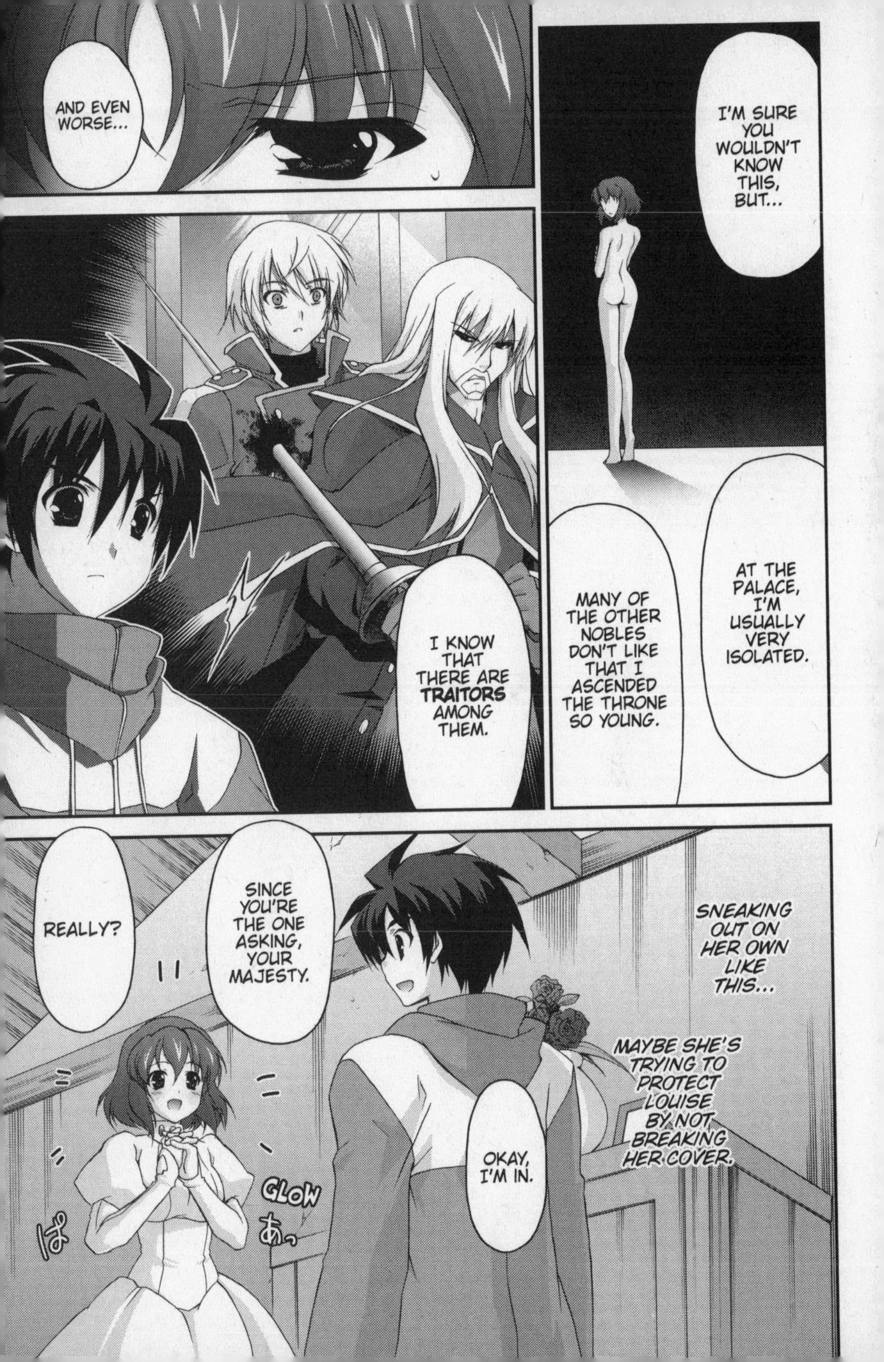
I'M SURE YOU WOULDN'T KNOW THIS, BUT...
AT THE PALACE, I'M USUALLY VERY ISOLATED.
MANY OF THE OTHER NOBLES DON'T LIKE THAT I ASCENDED THE THRONE SO YOUNG.
AND EVEN WORSE...
I KNOW THAT THERE ARE **TRAITORS** AMONG THEM.
SNEAKING OUT ON HER OWN LIKE THIS...
MAYBE SHE'S TRYING TO PROTECT LOUISE BY NOT BREAKING HER COVER.
OKAY, I'M IN.
SINCE YOU'RE THE ONE ASKING, YOUR MAJESTY.
REALLY?
GLOW
ぱあっ

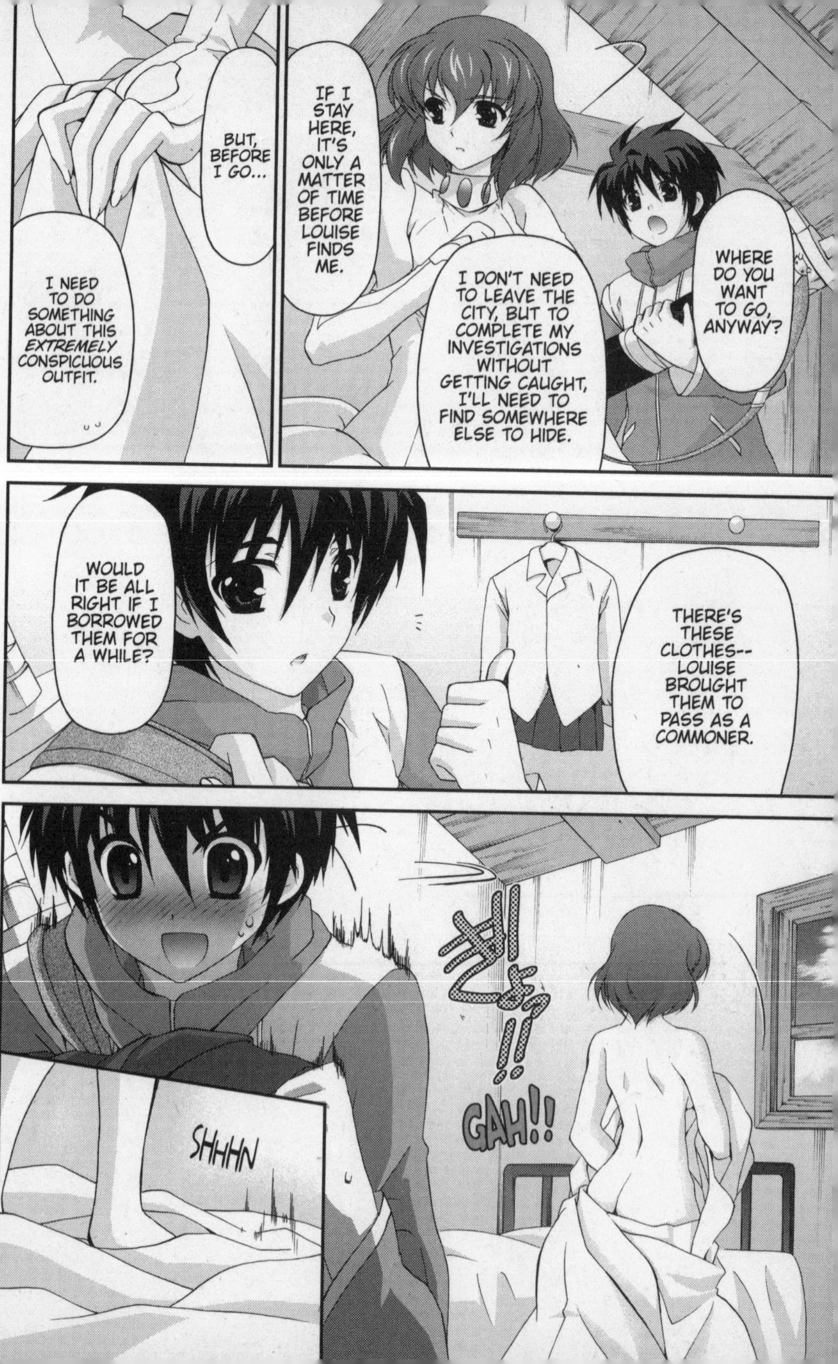

WHERE DO YOU WANT TO GO, ANYWAY?
I DON'T NEED TO LEAVE THE CITY, BUT TO COMPLETE MY INVESTIGATIONS WITHOUT GETTING CAUGHT, I'LL NEED TO FIND SOMEWHERE ELSE TO HIDE.
IF I STAY HERE, IT'S ONLY A MATTER OF TIME BEFORE LOUISE FINDS ME.
BUT, BEFORE I GO...
I NEED TO DO SOMETHING ABOUT THIS *EXTREMELY* CONSPICUOUS OUTFIT.
THERE'S THESE CLOTHES-- LOUISE BROUGHT THEM TO PASS AS A COMMONER.
WOULD IT BE ALL RIGHT IF I BORROWED THEM FOR A WHILE?
GAH!!
SHHHN

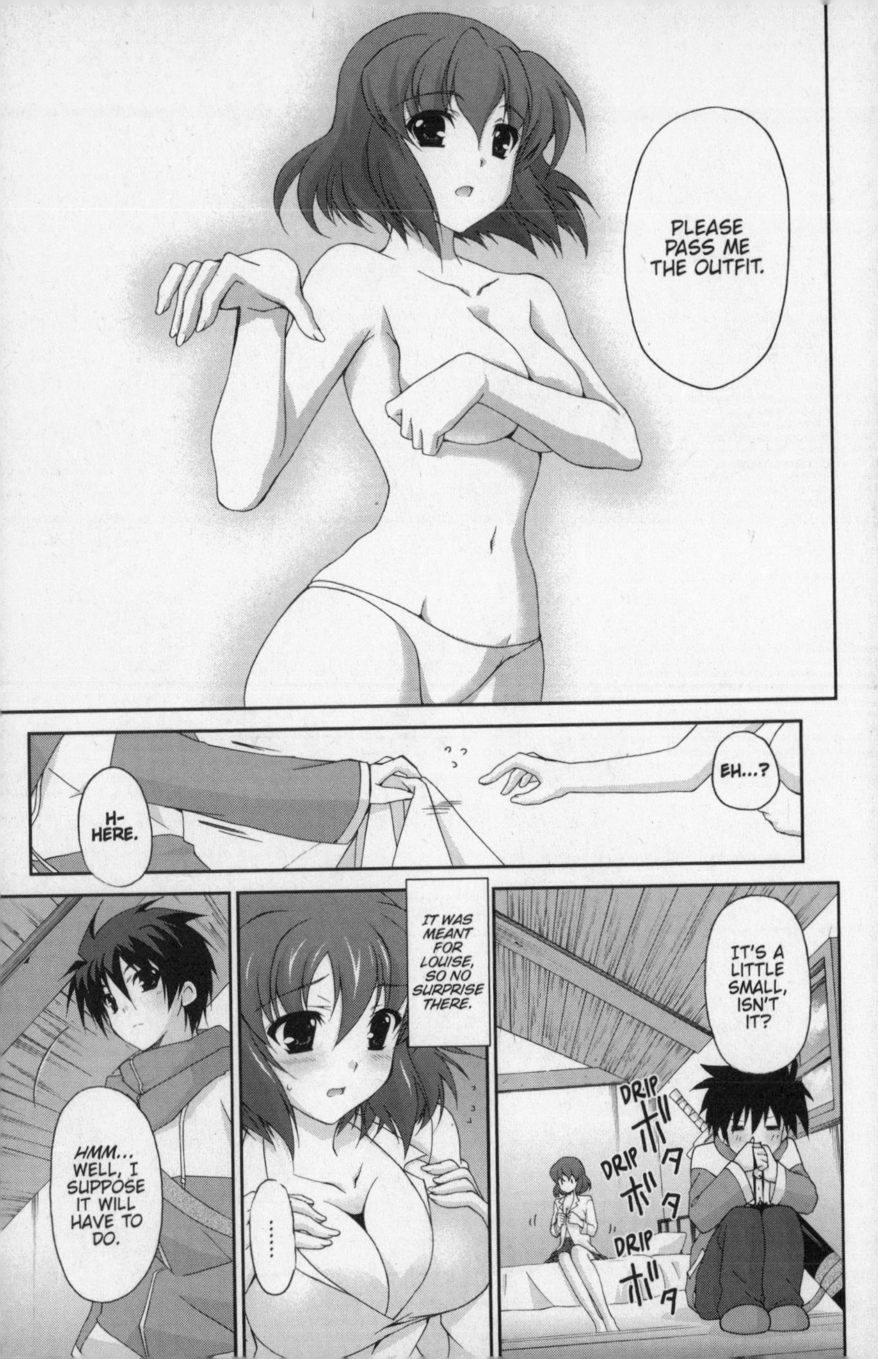
PLEASE PASS ME THE OUTFIT.
EH...?
H-HERE.
IT'S A LITTLE SMALL, ISN'T IT?
DRIP ボタ
DRIP ボタ
DRIP ボタ
IT WAS MEANT FOR LOUISE, SO NO SURPRISE THERE.
......
HMM... WELL, I SUPPOSE IT WILL HAVE TO DO.

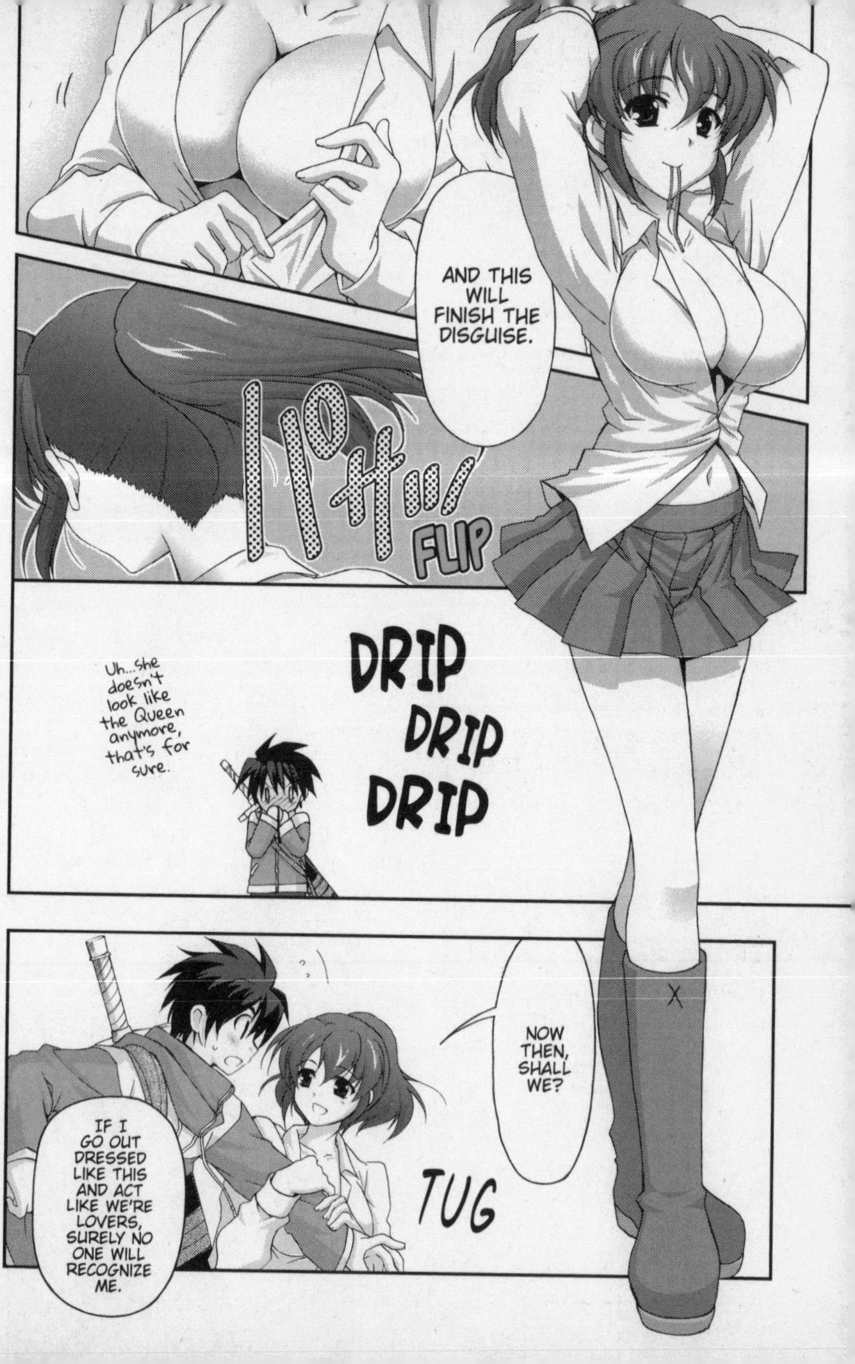
AND THIS WILL FINISH THE DISGUISE.
FLIP
DRIP DRIP DRIP
Uh...she doesn't look like the Queen anymore, that's for sure.
NOW THEN, SHALL WE?
TUG
IF I GO OUT DRESSED LIKE THIS AND ACT LIKE WE'RE LOVERS, SURELY NO ONE WILL RECOGNIZE ME.

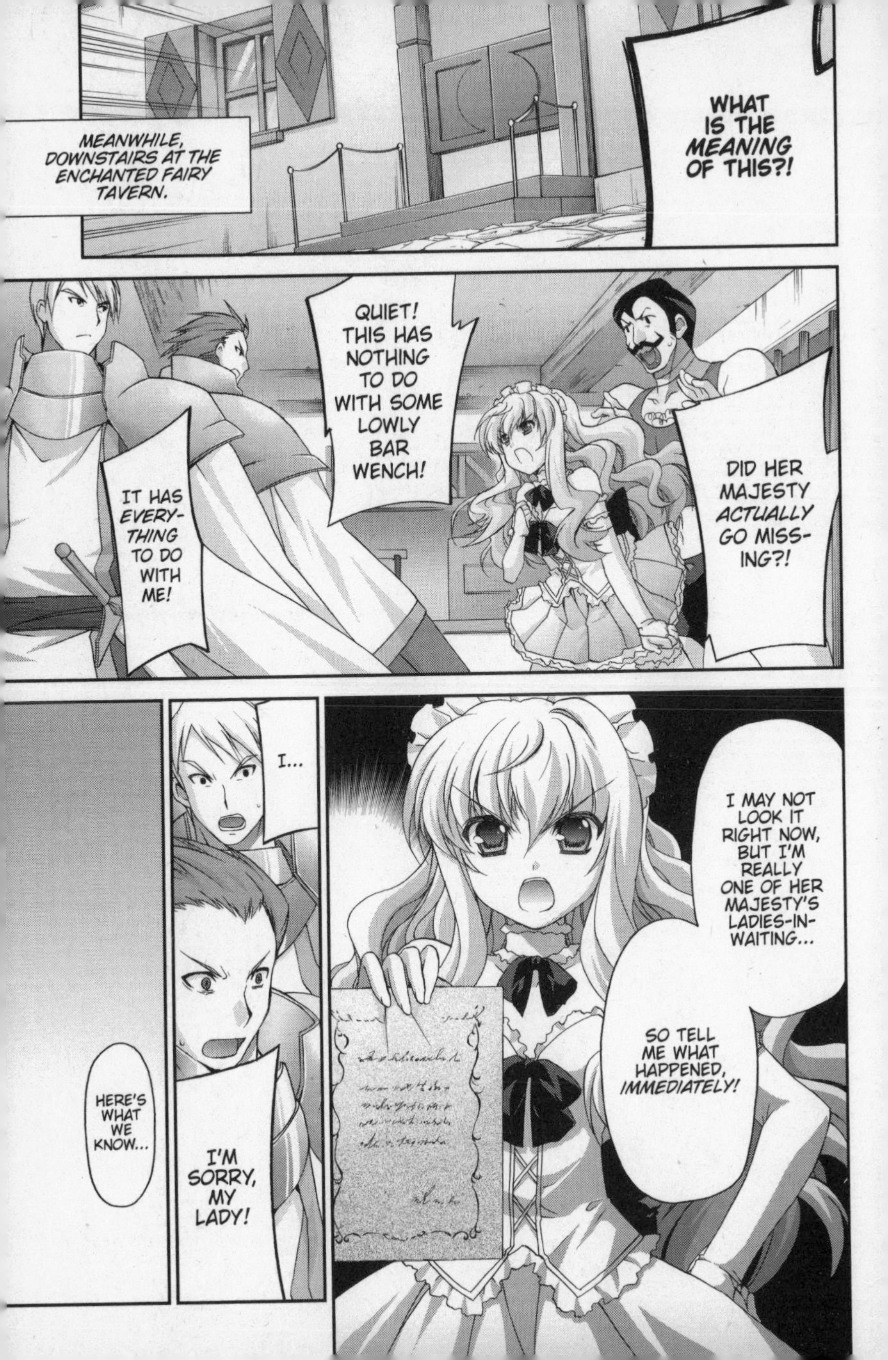
WHAT IS THE MEANING OF THIS?!
MEANWHILE, DOWNSTAIRS AT THE ENCHANTED FAIRY TAVERN.
DID HER MAJESTY ACTUALLY GO MISSING?!
QUIET! THIS HAS NOTHING TO DO WITH SOME LOWLY BAR WENCH!
IT HAS EVERYTHING TO DO WITH ME!
I MAY NOT LOOK IT RIGHT NOW, BUT I'M REALLY ONE OF HER MAJESTY'S LADIES-IN-WAITING...
SO TELL ME WHAT HAPPENED, IMMEDIATELY!
I...
I'M SORRY, MY LADY!
HERE'S WHAT WE KNOW...

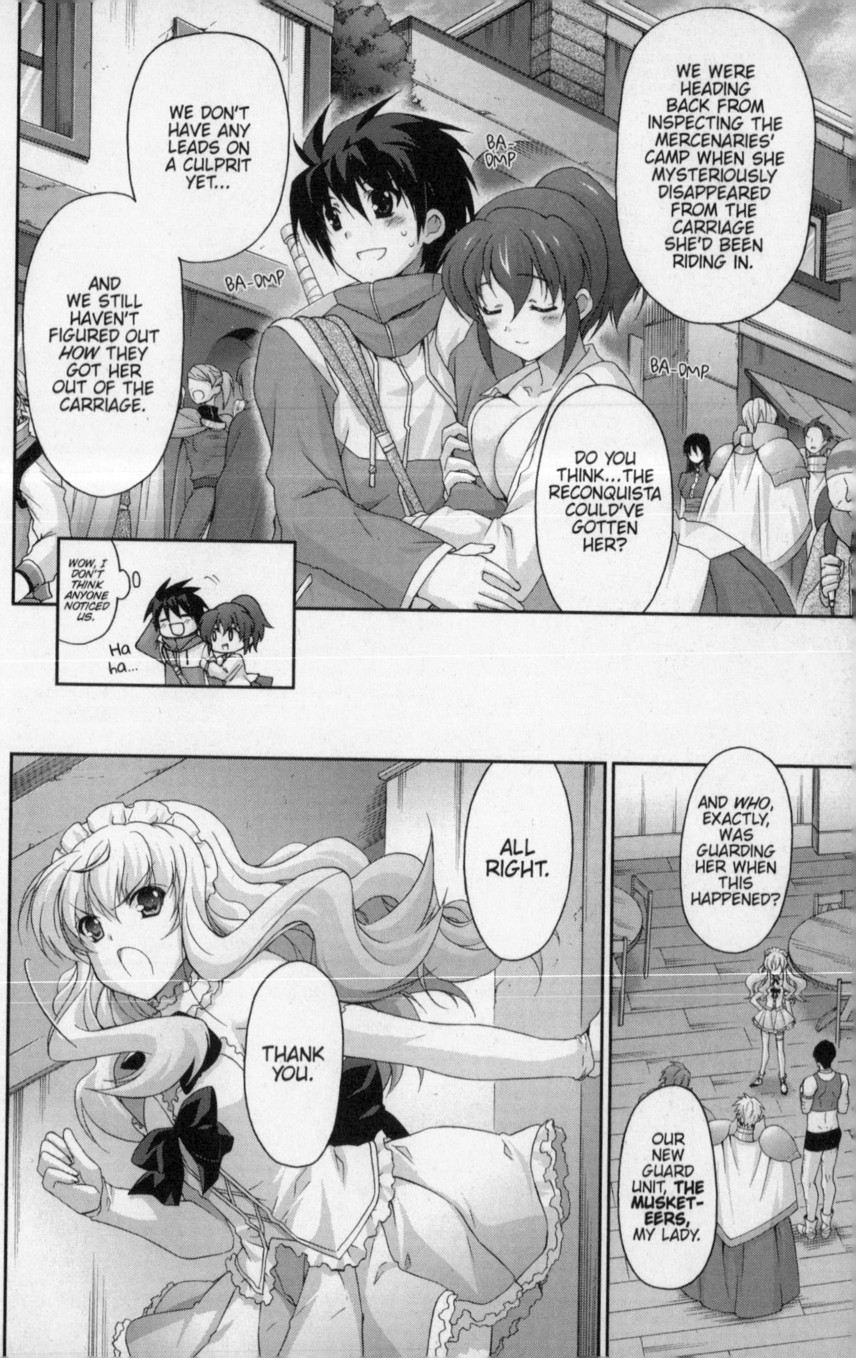
WE WERE HEADING BACK FROM INSPECTING THE MERCENARIES' CAMP WHEN SHE MYSTERIOUSLY DISAPPEARED FROM THE CARRIAGE SHE'D BEEN RIDING IN.
BA-DMP
BA-DMP
BA-DMP
DO YOU THINK...THE RECONQUISTA COULD'VE GOTTEN HER?
WE DON'T HAVE ANY LEADS ON A CULPRIT YET...
AND WE STILL HAVEN'T FIGURED OUT *HOW* THEY GOT HER OUT OF THE CARRIAGE.
WOW, I DON'T THINK ANYONE NOTICED US.
Ha ha...
AND *WHO*, EXACTLY, WAS GUARDING HER WHEN THIS HAPPENED?
OUR NEW GUARD UNIT, **THE MUSKETEERS,** MY LADY.
ALL RIGHT.
THANK YOU.

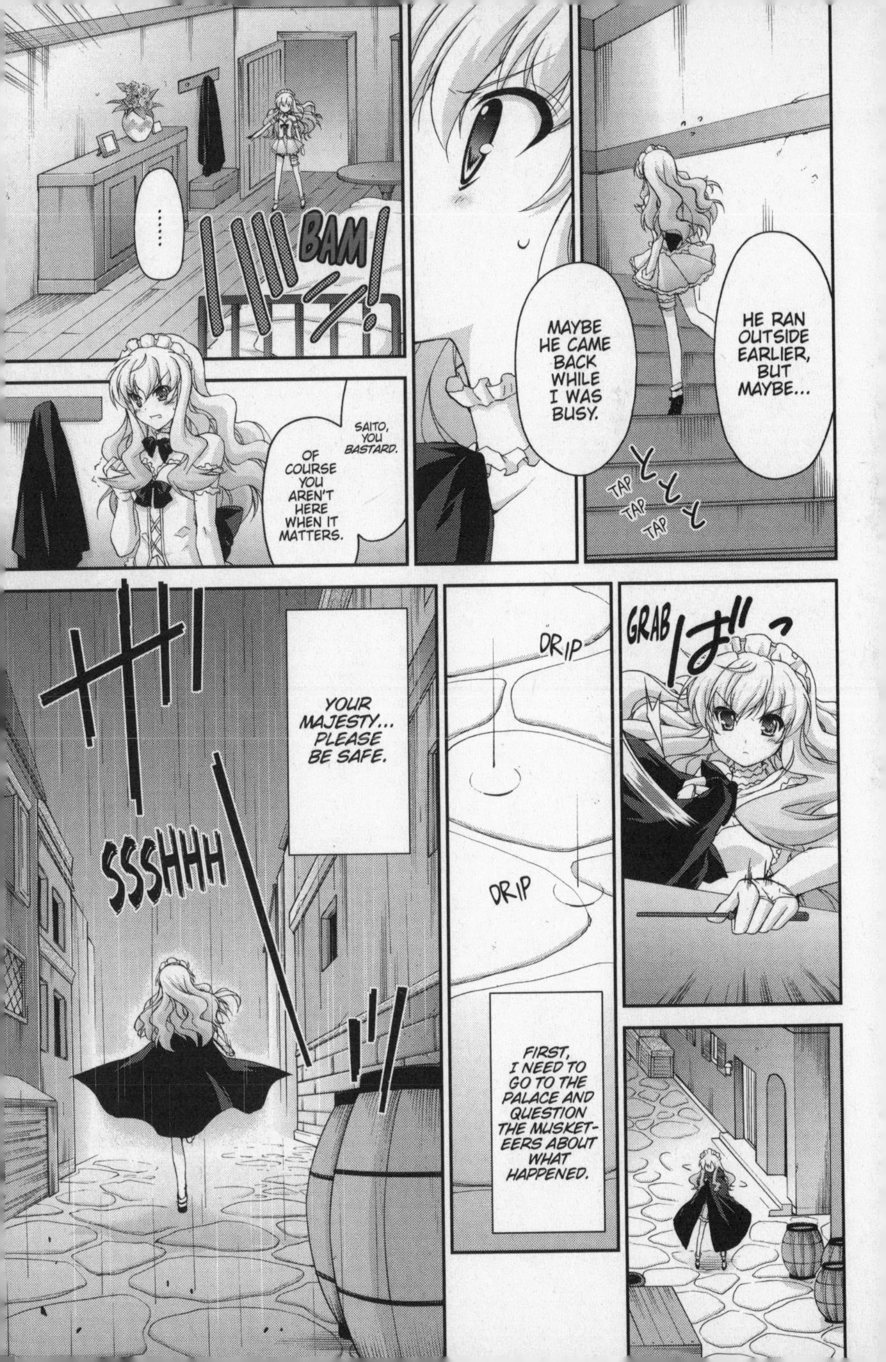
HE RAN OUTSIDE EARLIER, BUT MAYBE...
MAYBE HE CAME BACK WHILE I WAS BUSY.
TAP TAP TAP
BAM
......
SAITO, YOU BASTARD.
OF COURSE YOU AREN'T HERE WHEN IT MATTERS.
GRAB
DRIP
DRIP
FIRST, I NEED TO GO TO THE PALACE AND QUESTION THE MUSKET-EERS ABOUT WHAT HAPPENED.
YOUR MAJESTY... PLEASE BE SAFE.
SSSHHH

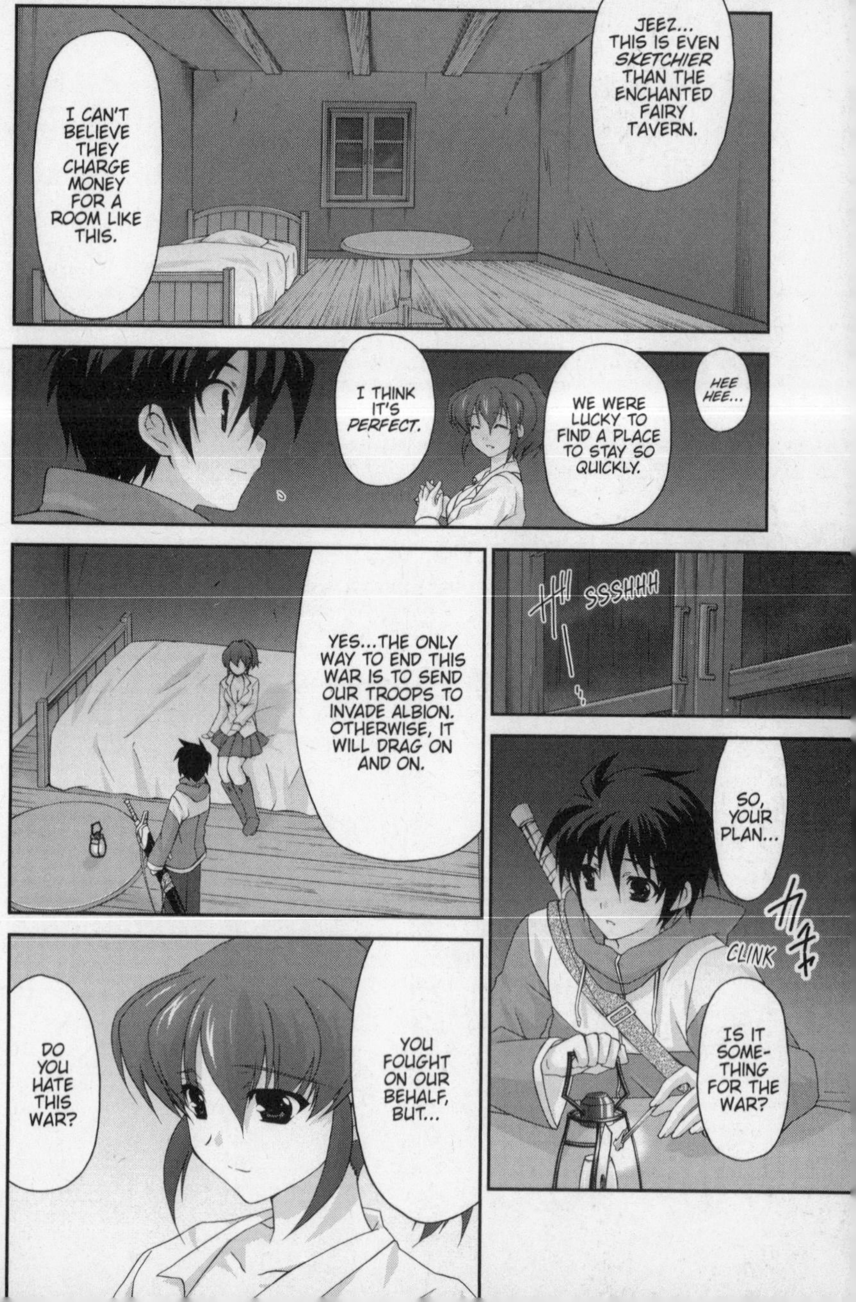
JEEZ... THIS IS EVEN *SKETCHIER* THAN THE ENCHANTED FAIRY TAVERN.
I CAN'T BELIEVE THEY CHARGE MONEY FOR A ROOM LIKE THIS.
HEE HEE...
WE WERE LUCKY TO FIND A PLACE TO STAY SO QUICKLY.
I THINK IT'S *PERFECT*.
SSSHHH
SO, YOUR PLAN...
CLINK
IS IT SOME-THING FOR THE WAR?
YES...THE ONLY WAY TO END THIS WAR IS TO SEND OUR TROOPS TO INVADE ALBION. OTHERWISE, IT WILL DRAG ON AND ON.
YOU FOUGHT ON OUR BEHALF, BUT...
DO YOU HATE THIS WAR?

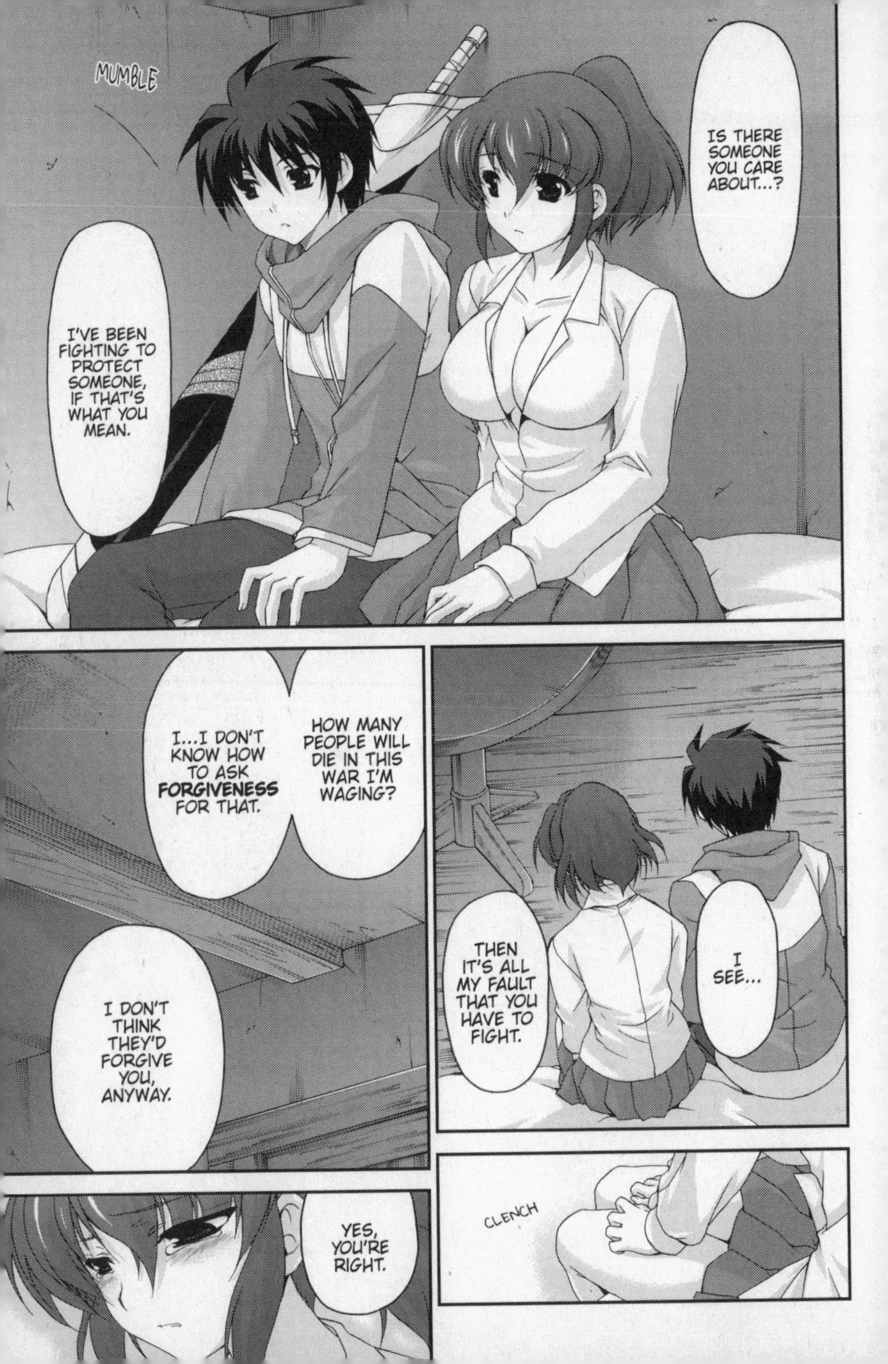
IS THERE SOMEONE YOU CARE ABOUT...?
MUMBLE
I'VE BEEN FIGHTING TO PROTECT SOMEONE, IF THAT'S WHAT YOU MEAN.
I SEE...
THEN IT'S ALL MY FAULT THAT YOU HAVE TO FIGHT.
HOW MANY PEOPLE WILL DIE IN THIS WAR I'M WAGING?
I...I DON'T KNOW HOW TO ASK **FORGIVENESS** FOR THAT.
I DON'T THINK THEY'D FORGIVE YOU, ANYWAY.
CLENCH
YES, YOU'RE RIGHT.

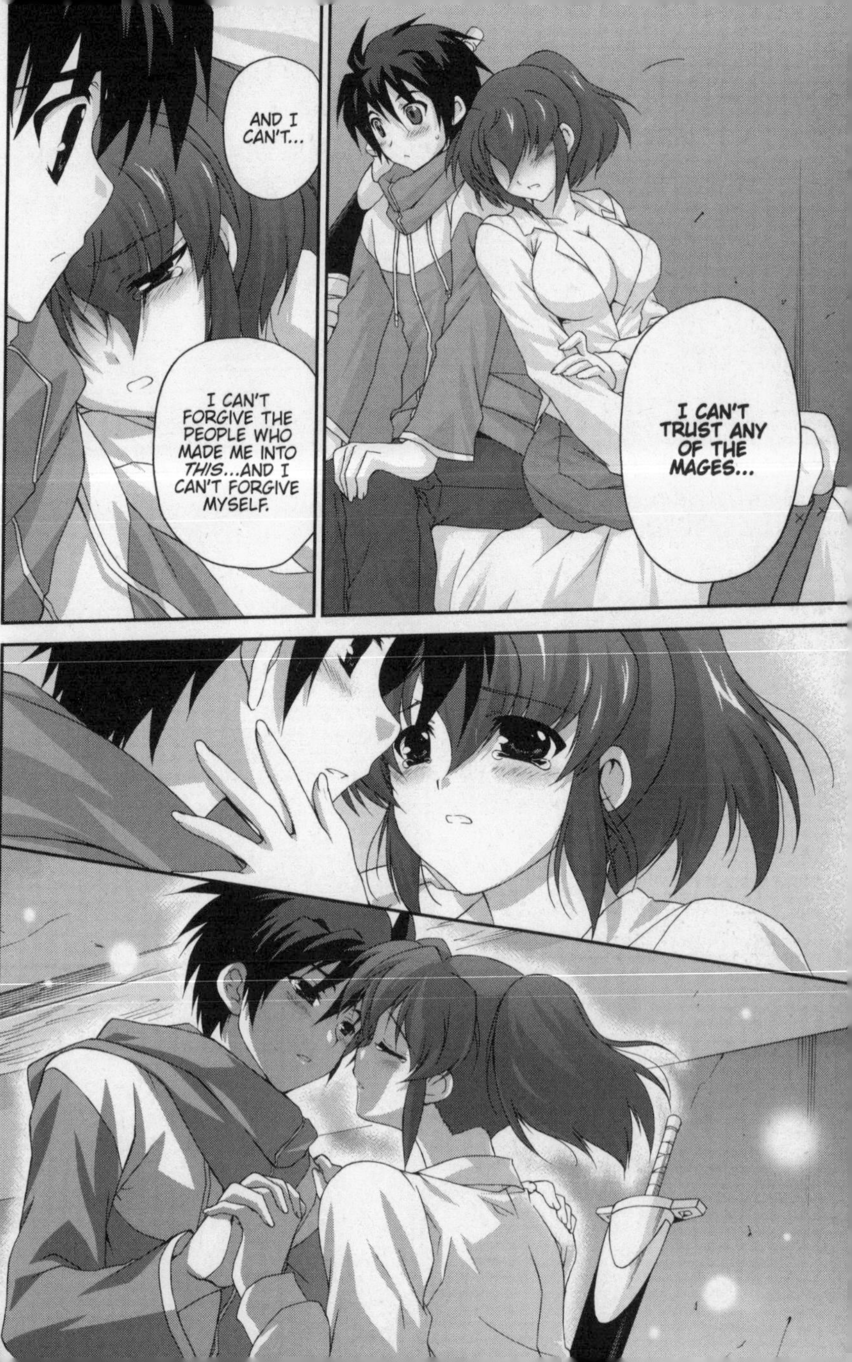
I CAN'T TRUST ANY OF THE MAGES...
AND I CAN'T...
I CAN'T FORGIVE THE PEOPLE WHO MADE ME INTO *THIS*...AND I CAN'T FORGIVE MYSELF.

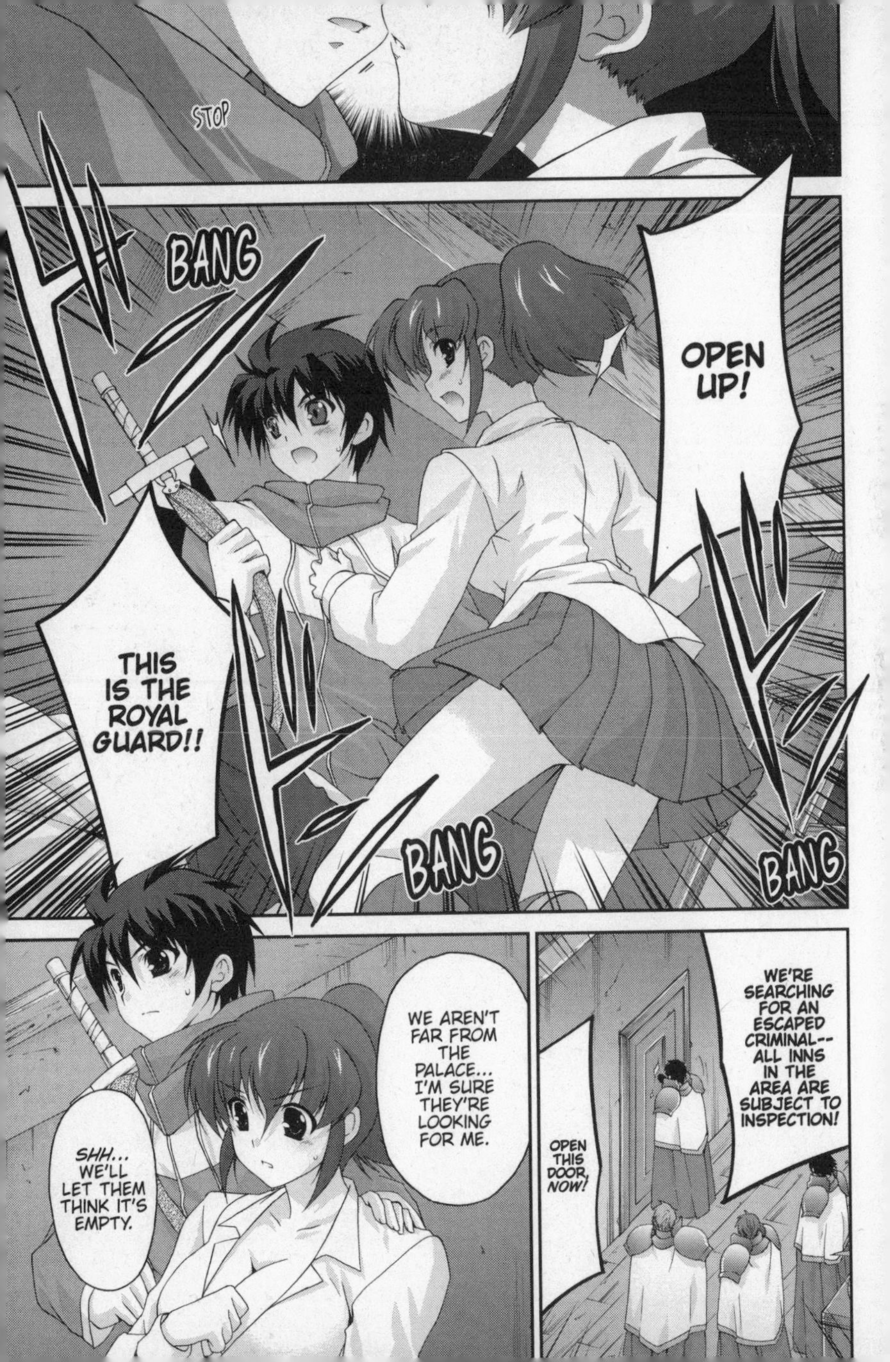
STOP
OPEN UP!
BANG
BANG
THIS IS THE ROYAL GUARD!!
BANG
WE'RE SEARCHING FOR AN ESCAPED CRIMINAL-- ALL INNS IN THE AREA ARE SUBJECT TO INSPECTION!
OPEN THIS DOOR, NOW!
WE AREN'T FAR FROM THE PALACE... I'M SURE THEY'RE LOOKING FOR ME.
SHH... WE'LL LET THEM THINK IT'S EMPTY.

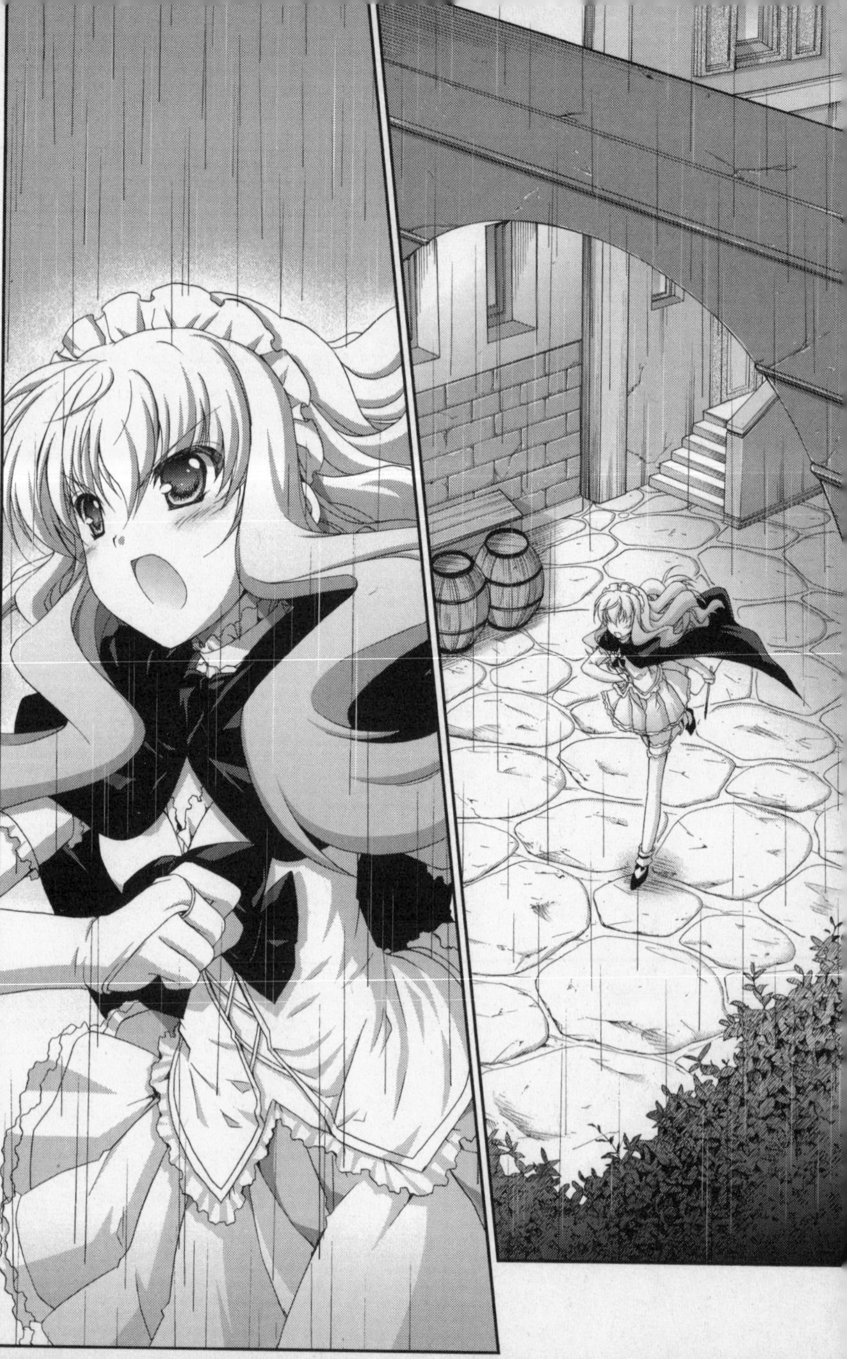

Le Familier de Zero Chevalier

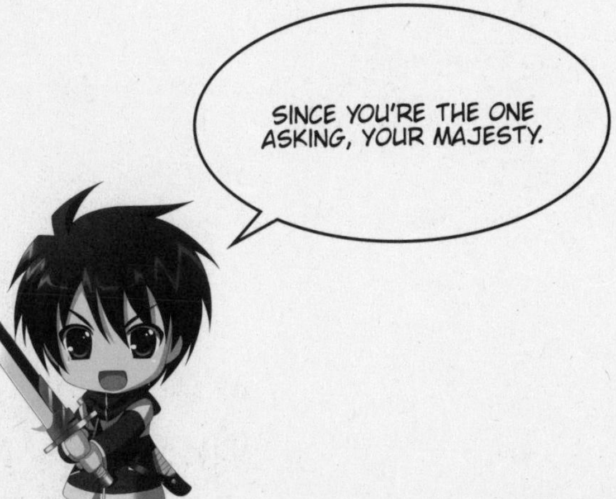

Le Familier de Zero Chevalier

ZERO's FAMILIAR Chevalier

Chapter 9: A Tristanian Holiday – Part II

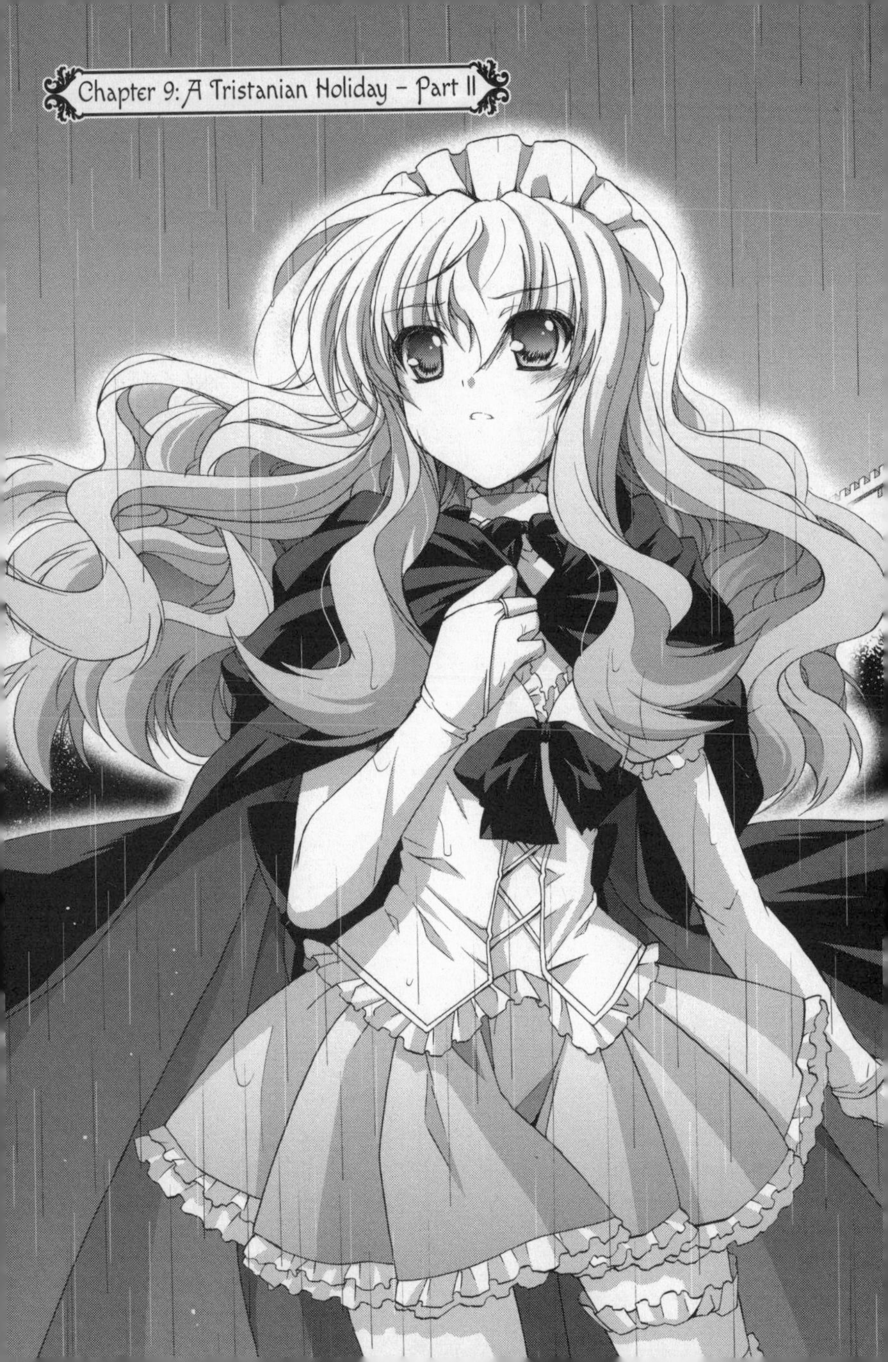

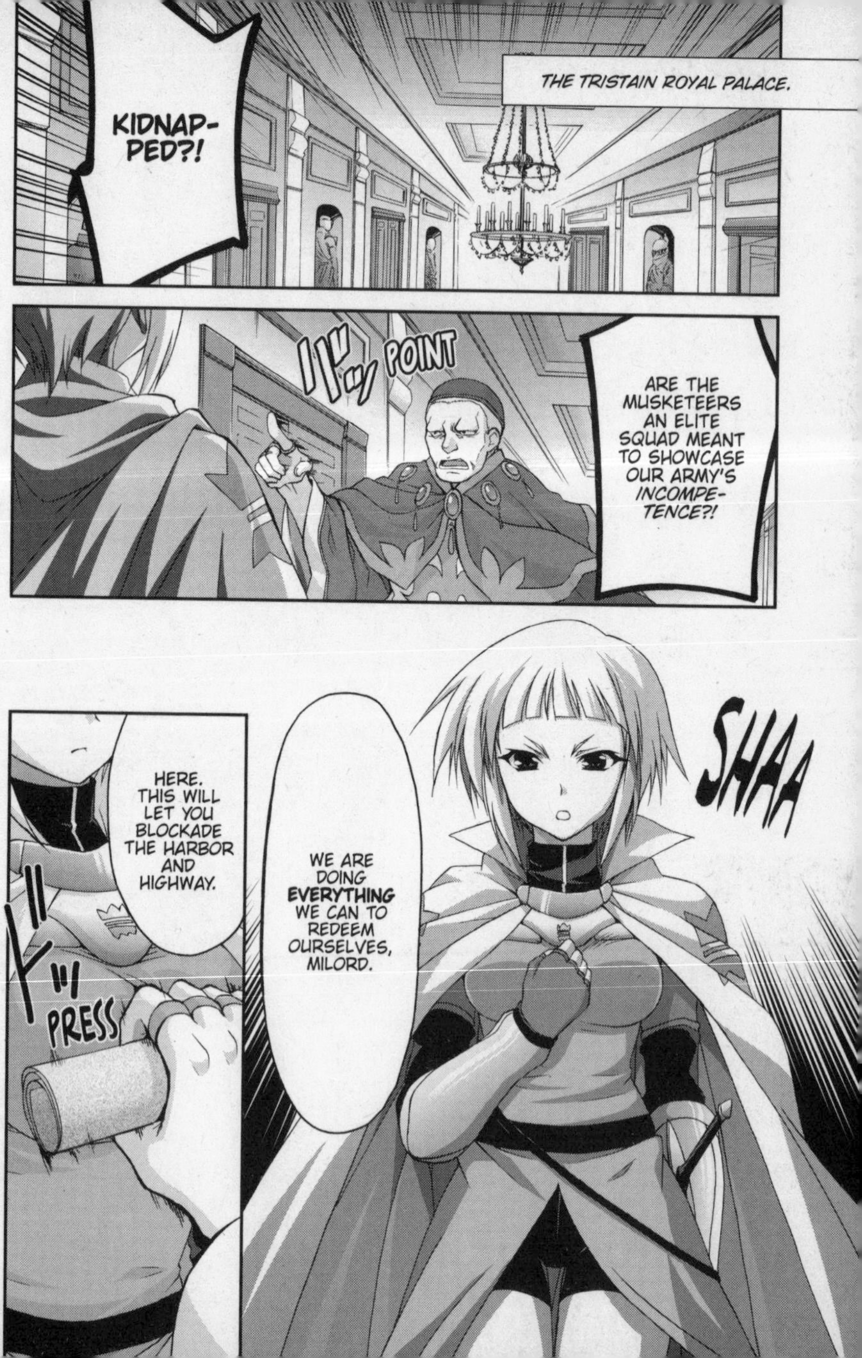
THE TRISTAIN ROYAL PALACE.
KIDNAP-PED?!
ARE THE MUSKETEERS AN ELITE SQUAD MEANT TO SHOWCASE OUR ARMY'S INCOMPE-TENCE?!
POINT
SHAA
WE ARE DOING EVERYTHING WE CAN TO REDEEM OURSELVES, MILORD.
HERE. THIS WILL LET YOU BLOCKADE THE HARBOR AND HIGHWAY.
PRESS

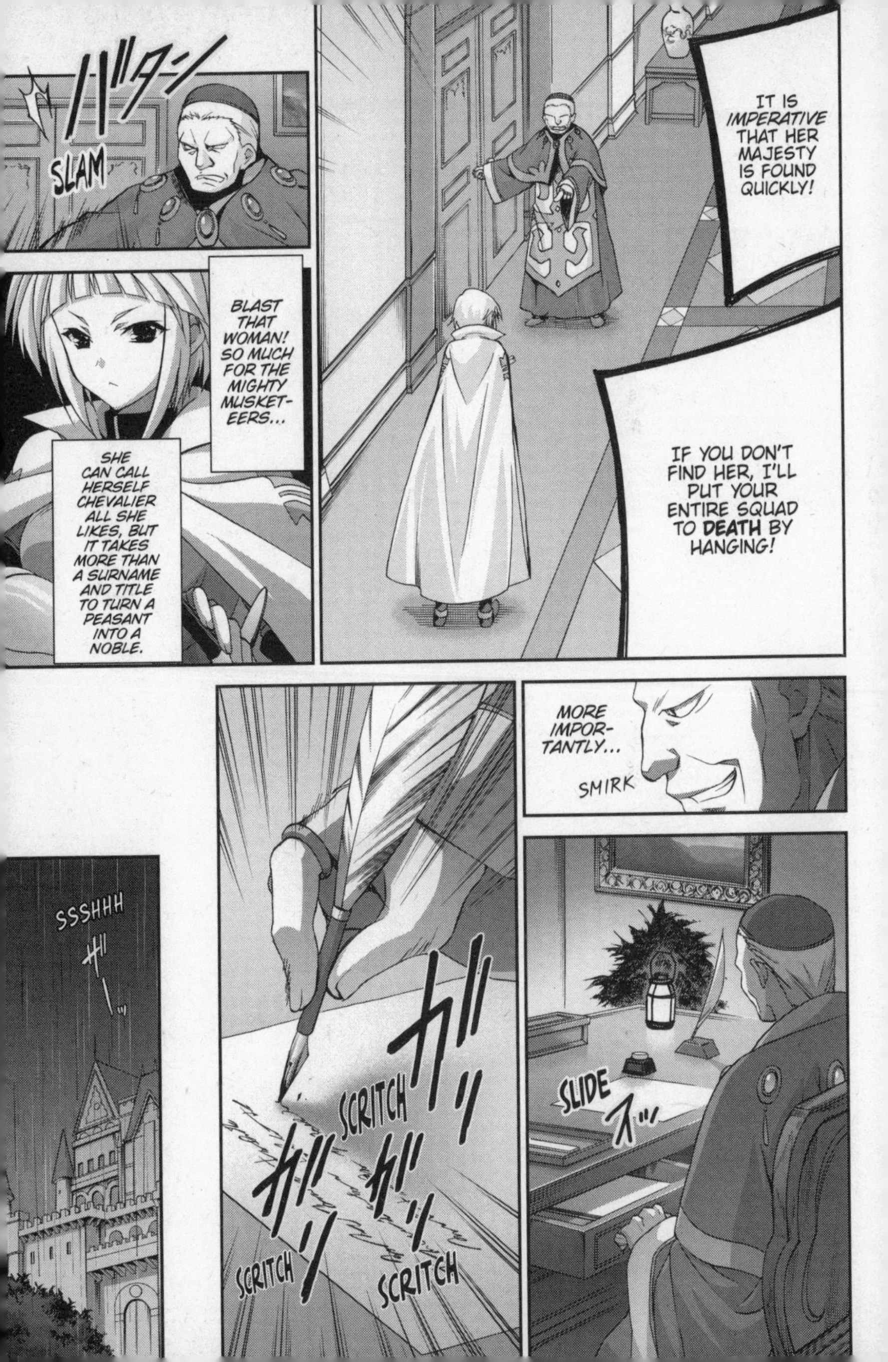
IT IS IMPERATIVE THAT HER MAJESTY IS FOUND QUICKLY!
IF YOU DON'T FIND HER, I'LL PUT YOUR ENTIRE SQUAD TO **DEATH** BY HANGING!
SLAM
BLAST THAT WOMAN! SO MUCH FOR THE MIGHTY MUSKET-EERS...
SHE CAN CALL HERSELF CHEVALIER ALL SHE LIKES, BUT IT TAKES MORE THAN A SURNAME AND TITLE TO TURN A PEASANT INTO A NOBLE.
MORE IMPOR-TANTLY...
SMIRK
SLIDE
SCRITCH
SCRITCH
SCRITCH
SSSHHH

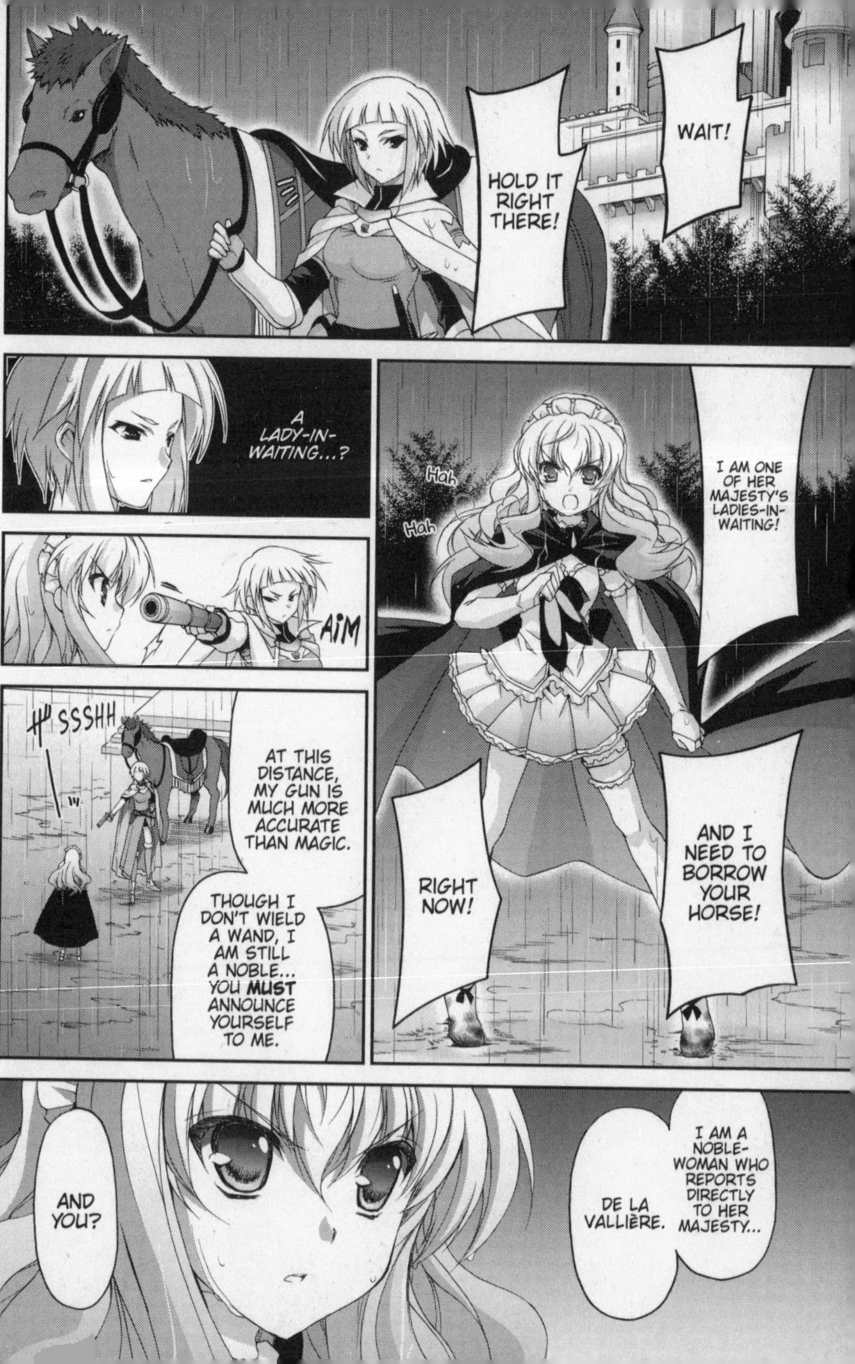
WAIT!
HOLD IT RIGHT THERE!
I AM ONE OF HER MAJESTY'S LADIES-IN-WAITING!
Hah
Hah
AND I NEED TO BORROW YOUR HORSE!
RIGHT NOW!
A LADY-IN-WAITING...?
AiM
SSSHH
AT THIS DISTANCE, MY GUN IS MUCH MORE ACCURATE THAN MAGIC.
THOUGH I DON'T WIELD A WAND, I AM STILL A NOBLE... YOU **MUST** ANNOUNCE YOURSELF TO ME.
I AM A NOBLE-WOMAN WHO REPORTS DIRECTLY TO HER MAJESTY...
DE LA VALLIÈRE.
AND YOU?

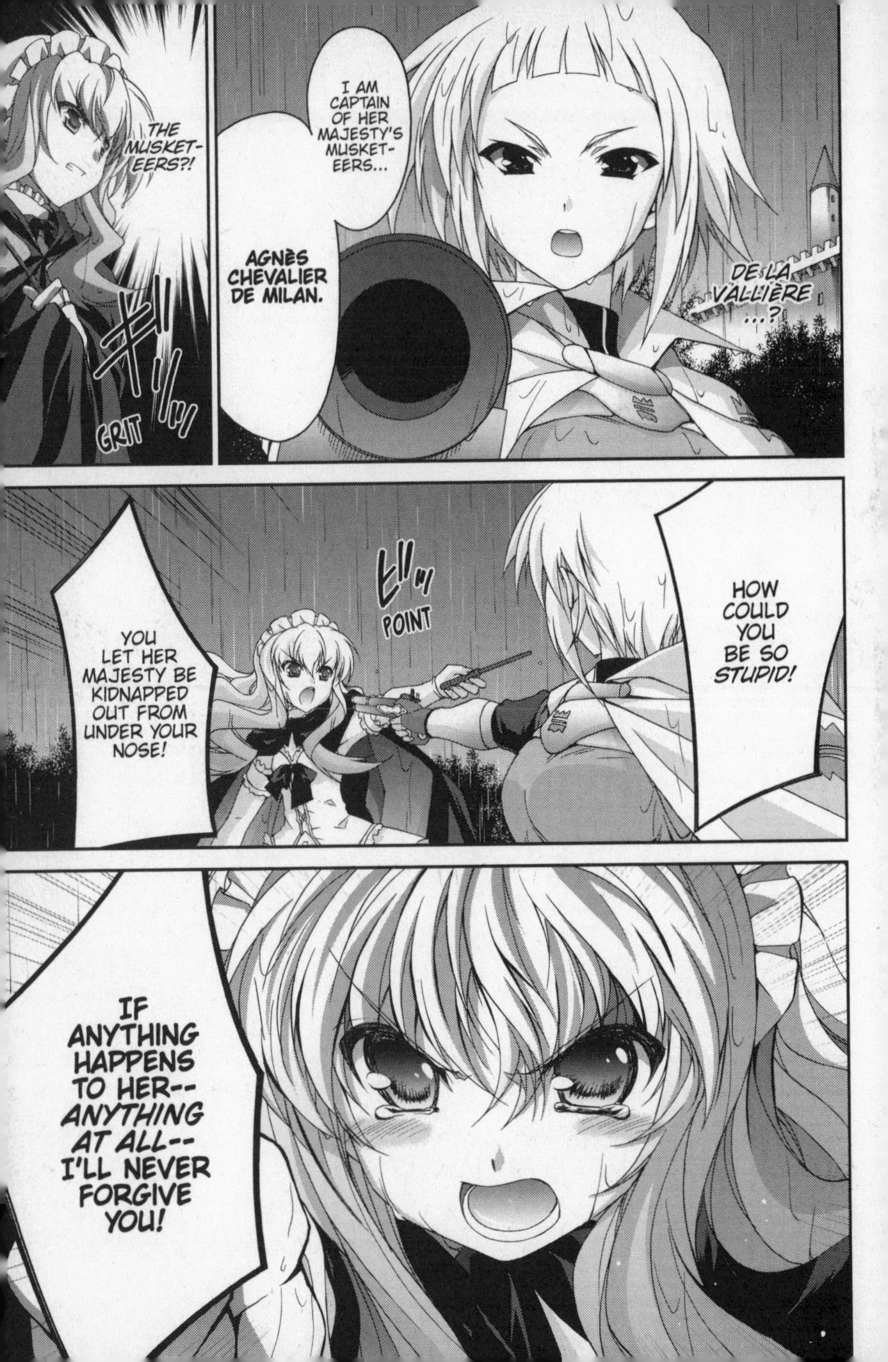
DE LA VALLIÈRE ...?
I AM CAPTAIN OF HER MAJESTY'S MUSKETEERS...
AGNÈS CHEVALIER DE MILAN.
THE MUSKETEERS?!
GRIT
HOW COULD YOU BE SO STUPID!
POINT
YOU LET HER MAJESTY BE KIDNAPPED OUT FROM UNDER YOUR NOSE!
IF ANYTHING HAPPENS TO HER-- ANYTHING AT ALL-- I'LL NEVER FORGIVE YOU!

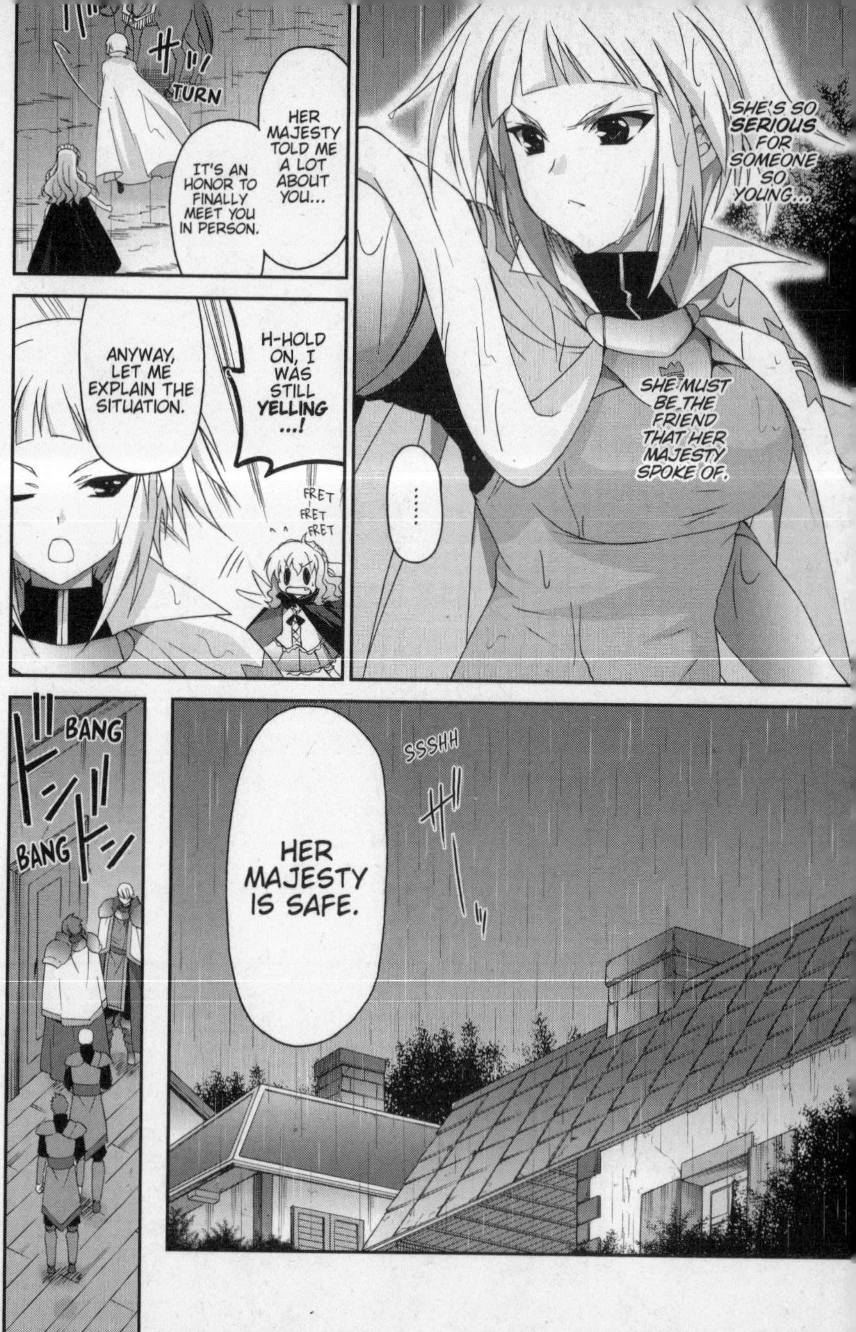
SHE'S SO SERIOUS FOR SOMEONE SO YOUNG...
SHE MUST BE THE FRIEND THAT HER MAJESTY SPOKE OF.
......
HER MAJESTY TOLD ME A LOT ABOUT YOU...
IT'S AN HONOR TO FINALLY MEET YOU IN PERSON.
TURN
ANYWAY, LET ME EXPLAIN THE SITUATION.
H-HOLD ON, I WAS STILL YELLING ...!
FRET FRET FRET
SSSHH
HER MAJESTY IS SAFE.
BANG
BANG

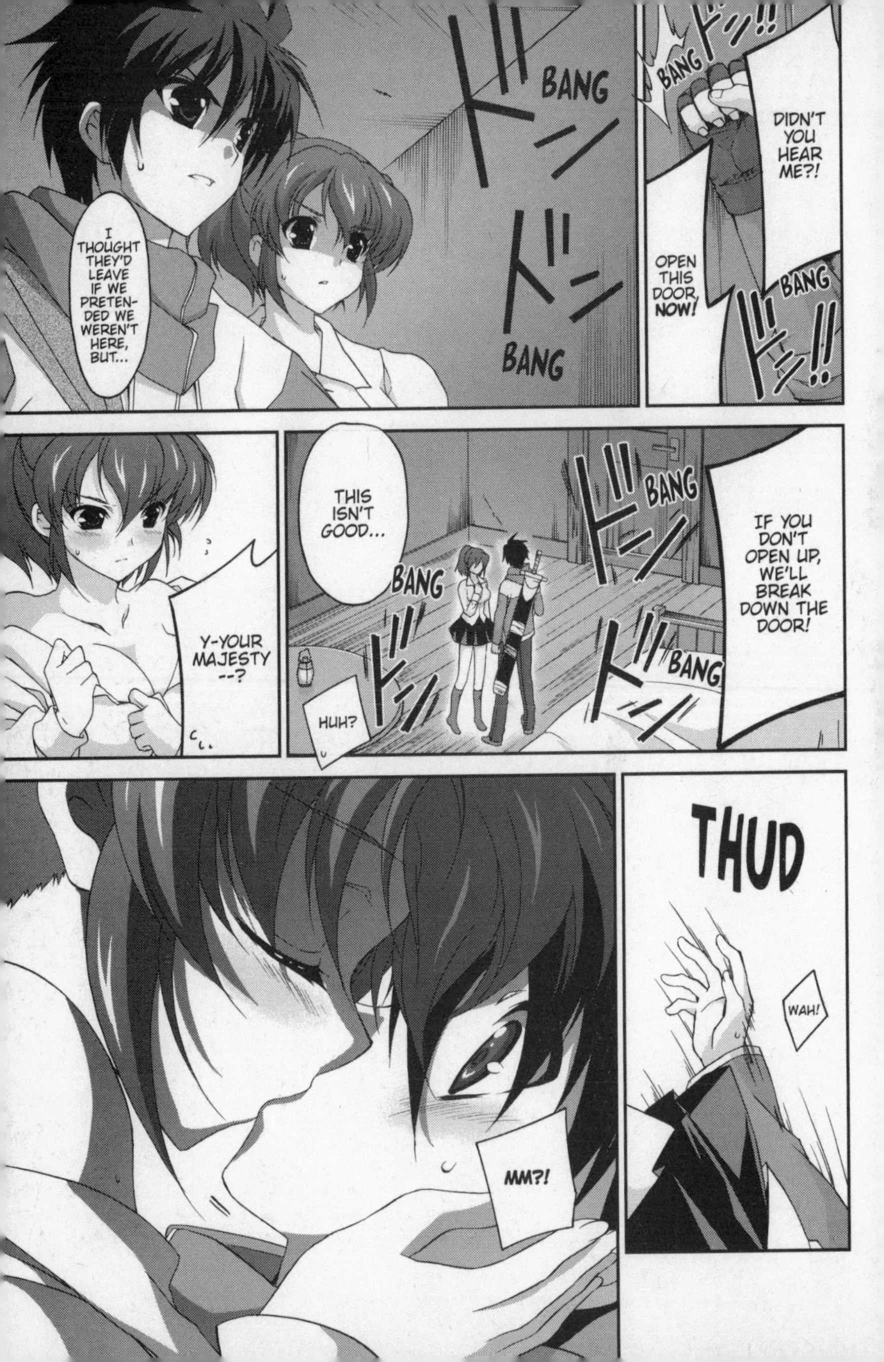
BANG
DIDN'T YOU HEAR ME?!
OPEN THIS DOOR, NOW!
BANG
BANG
BANG
I THOUGHT THEY'D LEAVE IF WE PRETEN-DED WE WEREN'T HERE, BUT...
IF YOU DON'T OPEN UP, WE'LL BREAK DOWN THE DOOR!
BANG
BANG
BANG
THIS ISN'T GOOD...
HUH?
Y-YOUR MAJESTY --?
THUD
WAH!
MM?!

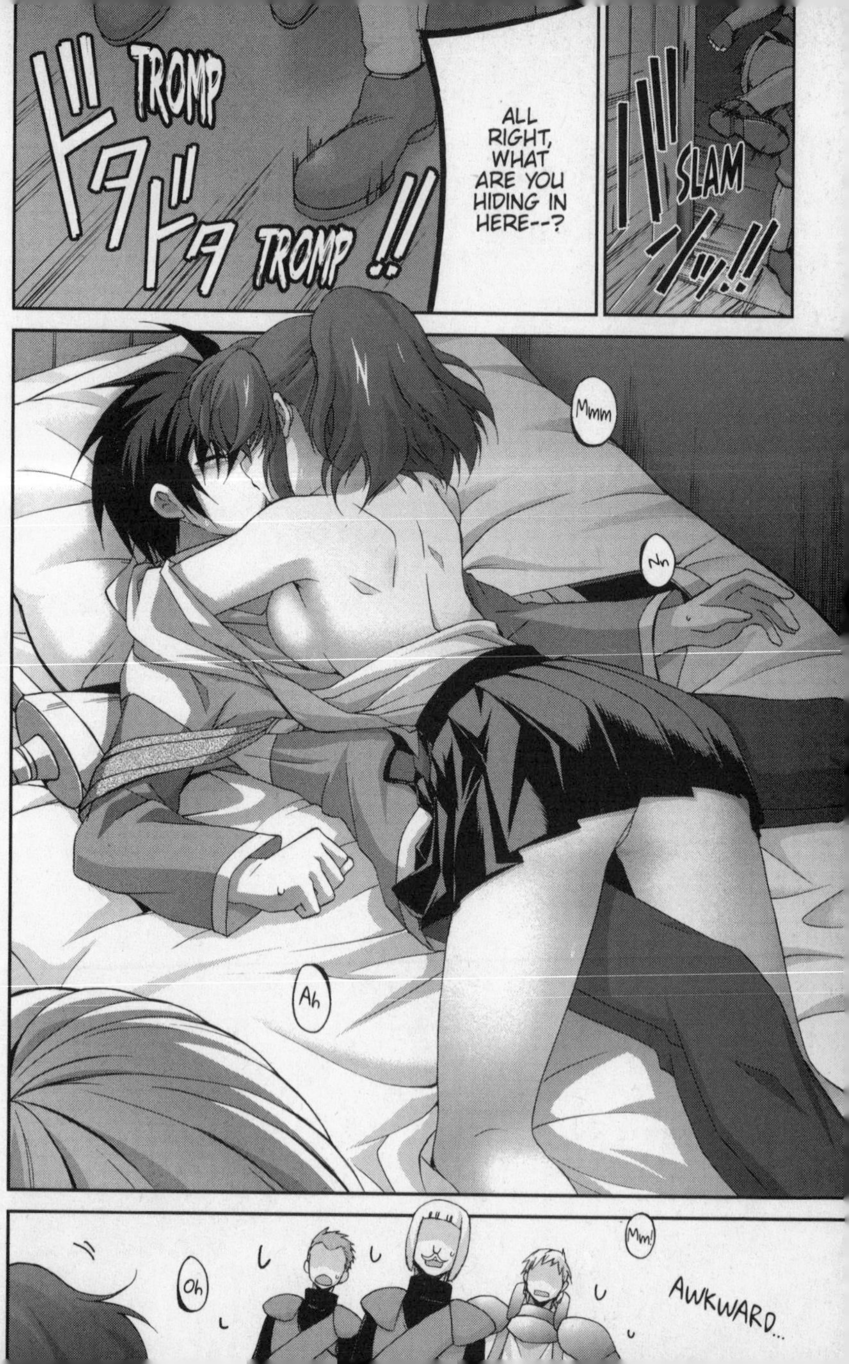
バンッ!!
SLAM
ALL RIGHT, WHAT ARE YOU HIDING IN HERE--?
ドタドタ
TROMP
TROMP!!
Mmm
Nn
Ah
Mm!
AWKWARD...
Oh

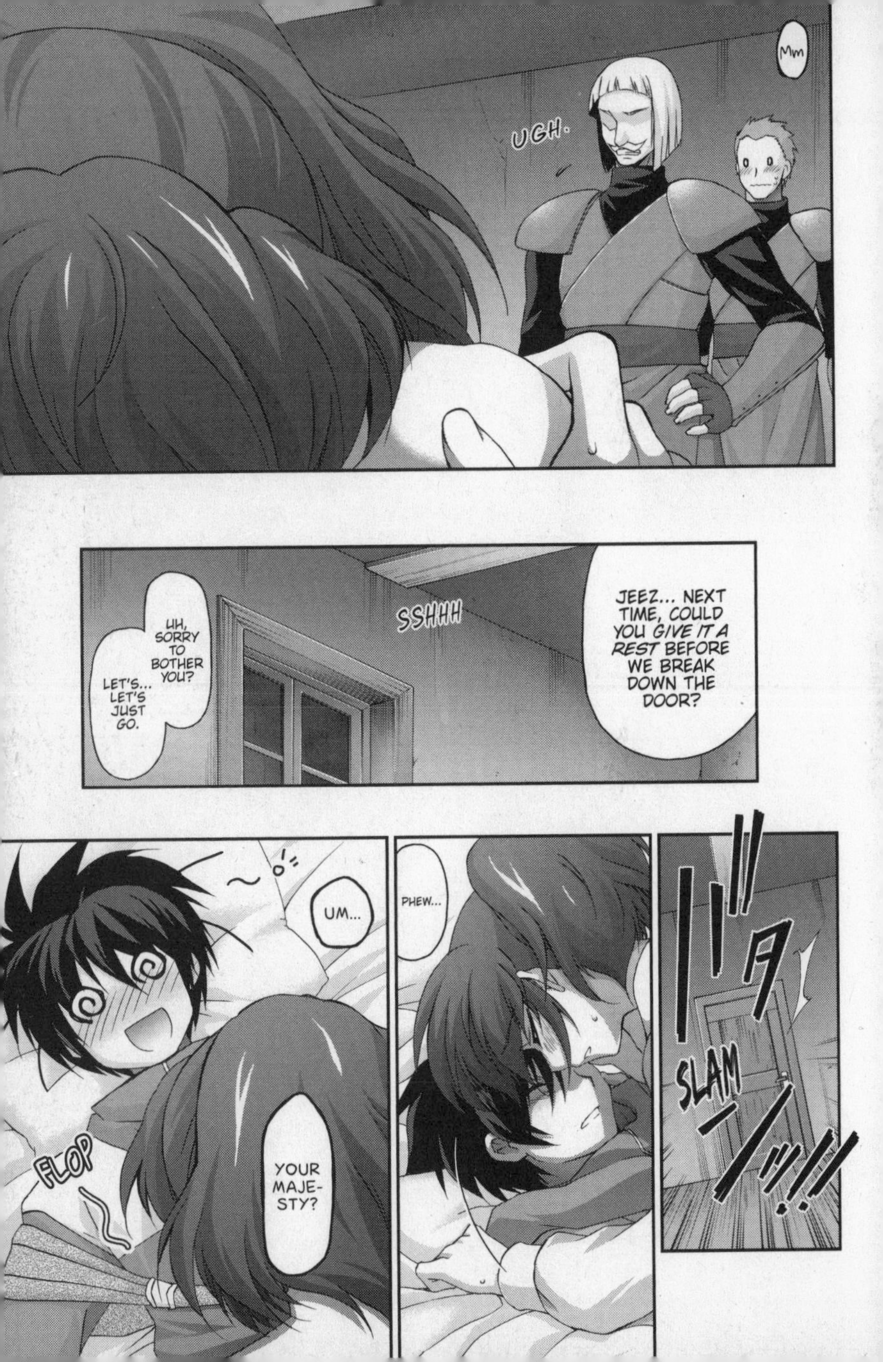
Mm
UGH.
JEEZ... NEXT TIME, COULD YOU *GIVE IT A REST* BEFORE WE BREAK DOWN THE DOOR?
SSHHH
UH, SORRY TO BOTHER YOU?
LET'S... LET'S JUST GO.
SLAM
PHEW...
YOUR MAJESTY?
UM...
FLOP

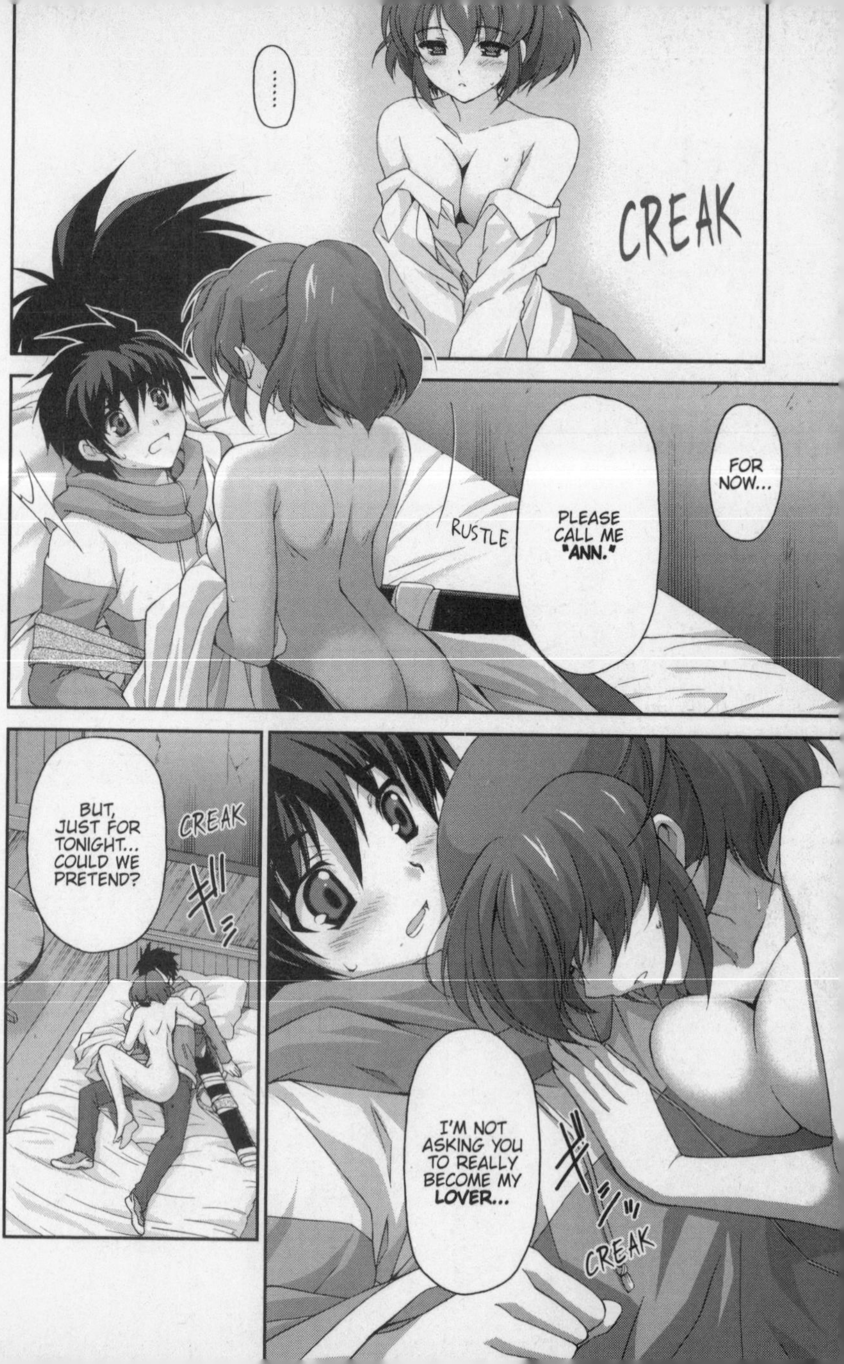
......
CREAK
FOR NOW...
PLEASE CALL ME "ANN."
RUSTLE
I'M NOT ASKING YOU TO REALLY BECOME MY LOVER...
CREAK
BUT, JUST FOR TONIGHT... COULD WE PRETEND?
CREAK

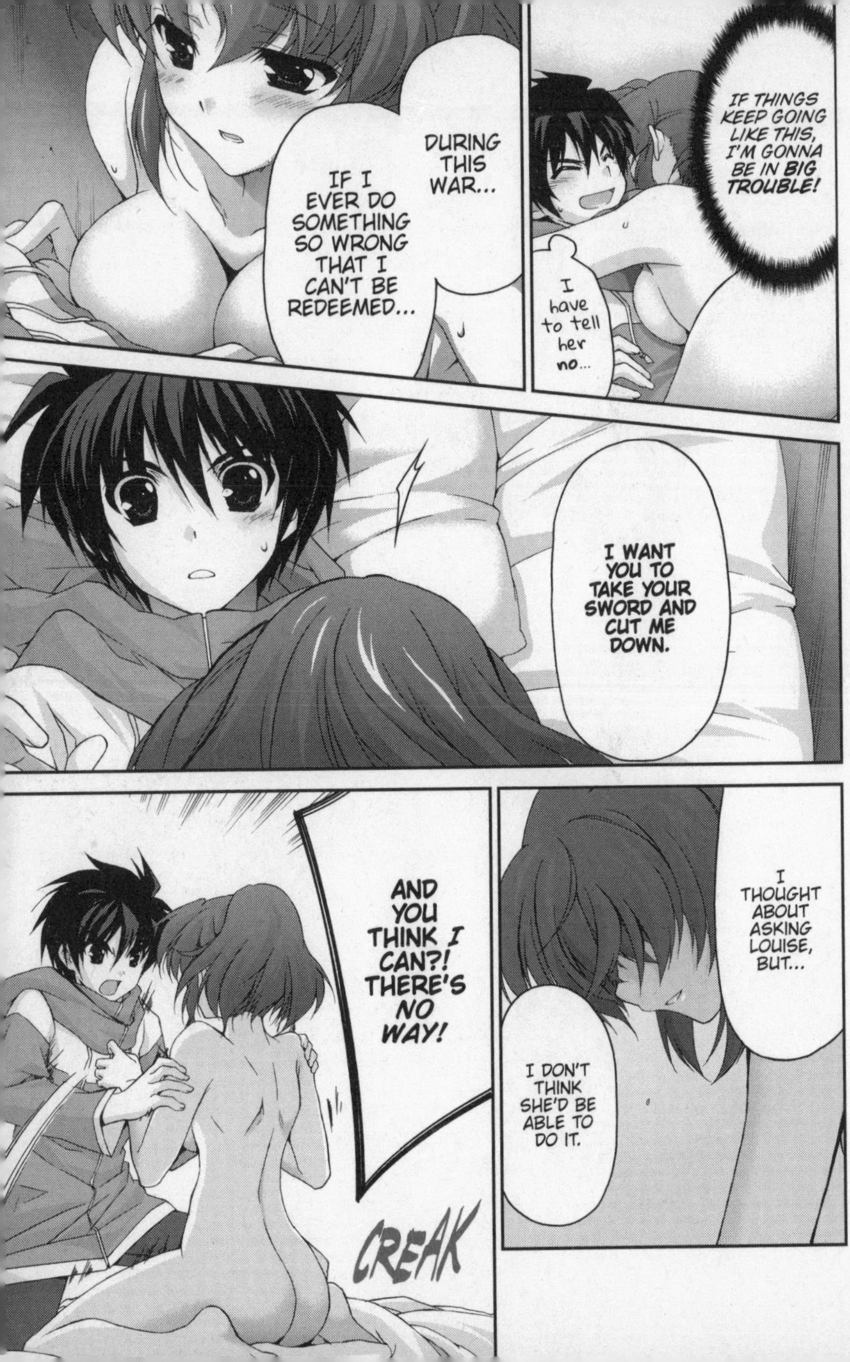
IF THINGS KEEP GOING LIKE THIS, I'M GONNA BE IN **BIG TROUBLE!**
I have to tell her no...
DURING THIS WAR...
IF I EVER DO SOMETHING SO WRONG THAT I CAN'T BE REDEEMED...
I WANT YOU TO TAKE YOUR SWORD AND CUT ME DOWN.
I THOUGHT ABOUT ASKING LOUISE, BUT...
I DON'T THINK SHE'D BE ABLE TO DO IT.
AND YOU THINK *I* CAN?! THERE'S *NO WAY!*
CREAK

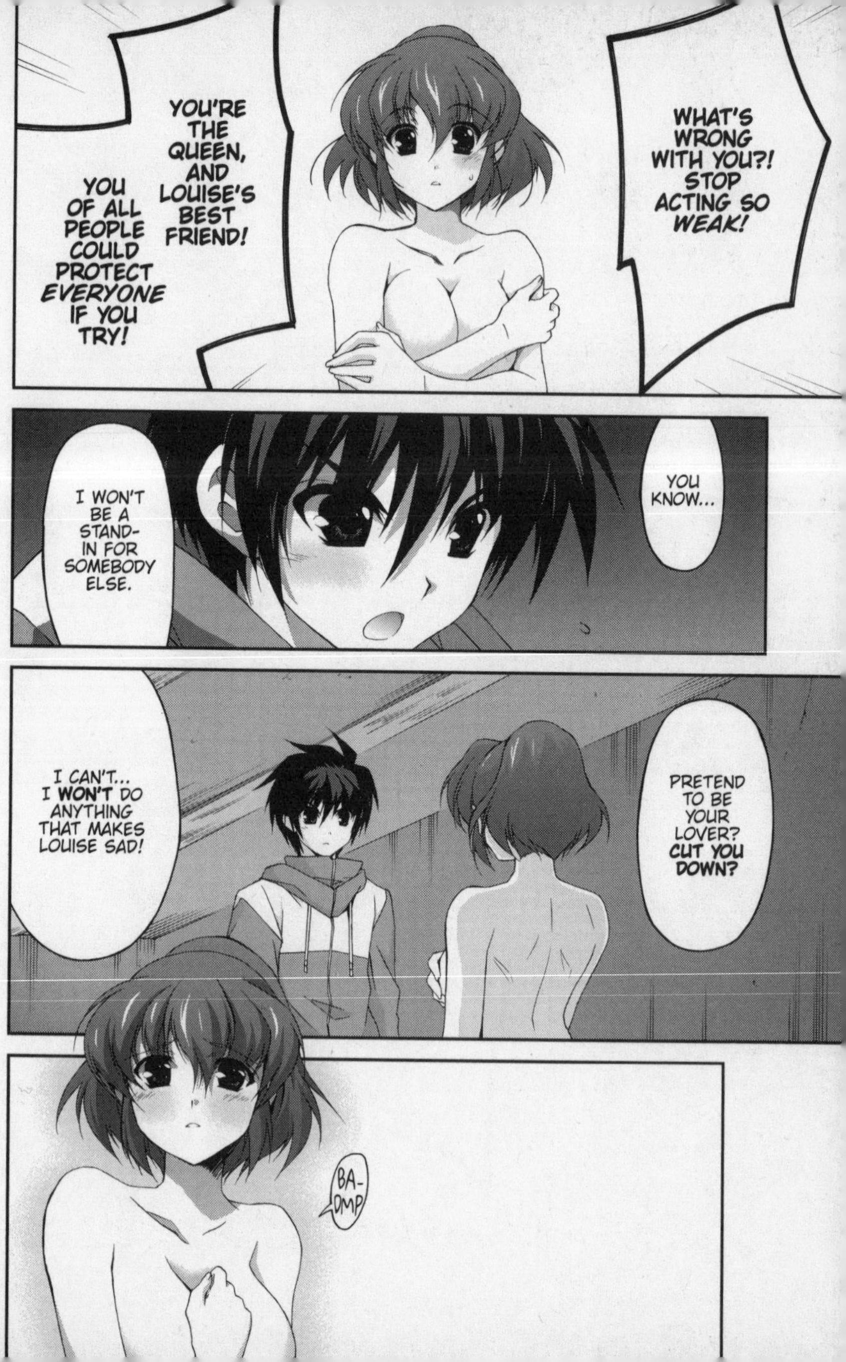
WHAT'S WRONG WITH YOU?! STOP ACTING SO *WEAK!*
YOU'RE THE QUEEN, AND LOUISE'S BEST FRIEND!
YOU OF ALL PEOPLE COULD PROTECT *EVERYONE* IF YOU TRY!
YOU KNOW...
I WON'T BE A STAND-IN FOR SOMEBODY ELSE.
PRETEND TO BE YOUR LOVER? **CUT YOU DOWN?**
I CAN'T... I **WON'T** DO ANYTHING THAT MAKES LOUISE SAD!
BA-DMP

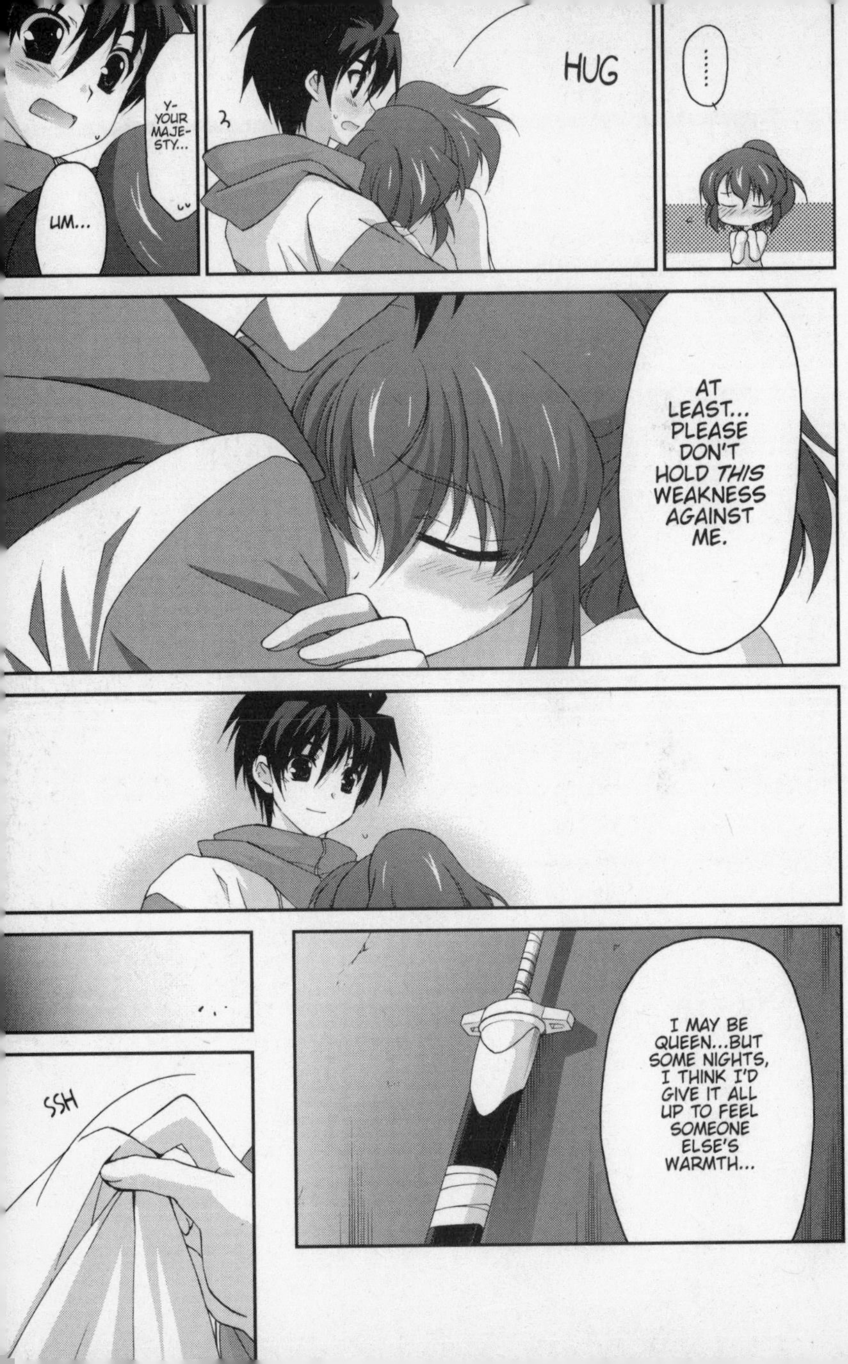
......
HUG
Y-YOUR MAJESTY...
UM...
AT LEAST... PLEASE DON'T HOLD *THIS* WEAKNESS AGAINST ME.
I MAY BE QUEEN...BUT SOME NIGHTS, I THINK I'D GIVE IT ALL UP TO FEEL SOMEONE ELSE'S WARMTH...
SSH

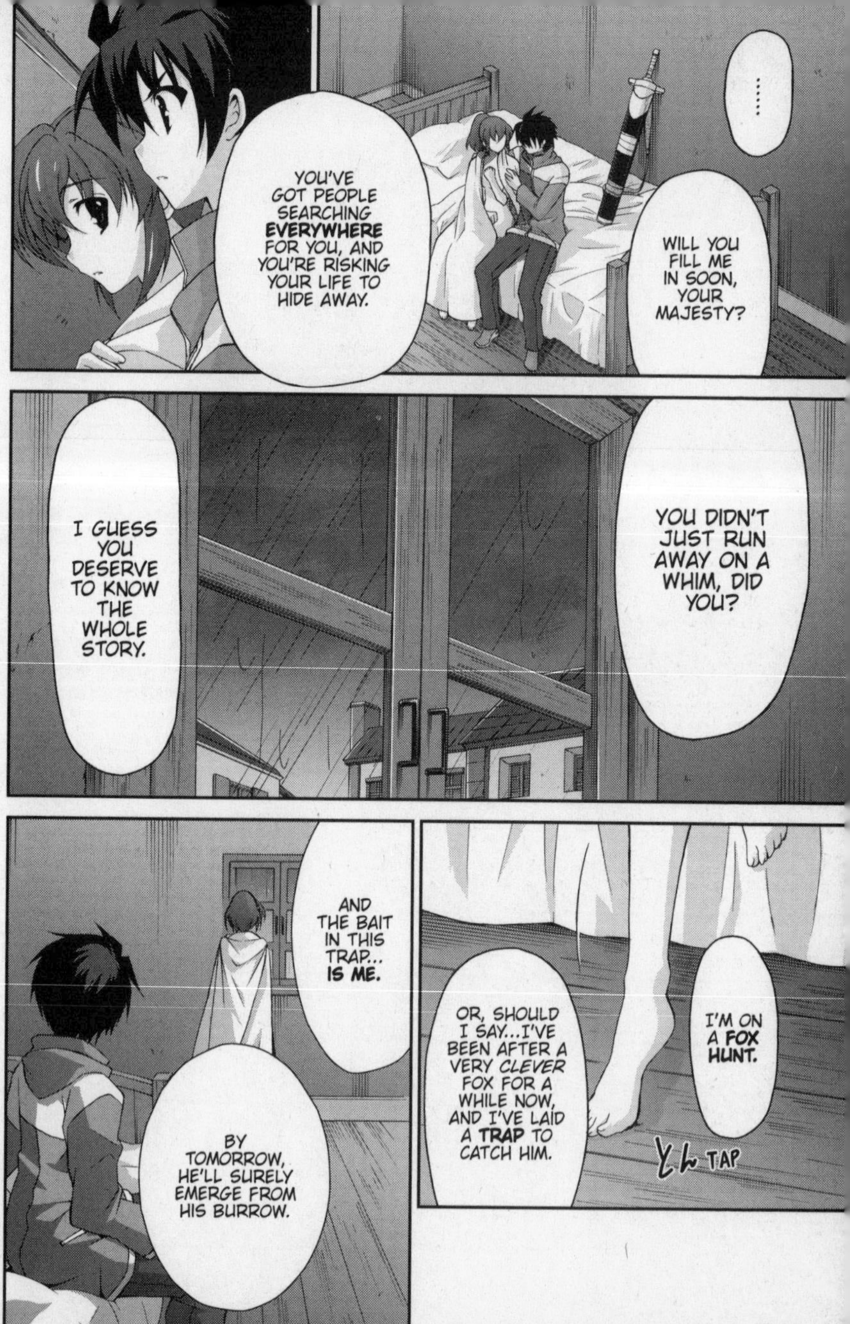
......
WILL YOU FILL ME IN SOON, YOUR MAJESTY?
YOU'VE GOT PEOPLE SEARCHING EVERYWHERE FOR YOU, AND YOU'RE RISKING YOUR LIFE TO HIDE AWAY.
YOU DIDN'T JUST RUN AWAY ON A WHIM, DID YOU?
I GUESS YOU DESERVE TO KNOW THE WHOLE STORY.
I'M ON A FOX HUNT.
OR, SHOULD I SAY...I'VE BEEN AFTER A VERY CLEVER FOX FOR A WHILE NOW, AND I'VE LAID A TRAP TO CATCH HIM.
TAP
AND THE BAIT IN THIS TRAP... IS ME.
BY TOMORROW, HE'LL SURELY EMERGE FROM HIS BURROW.

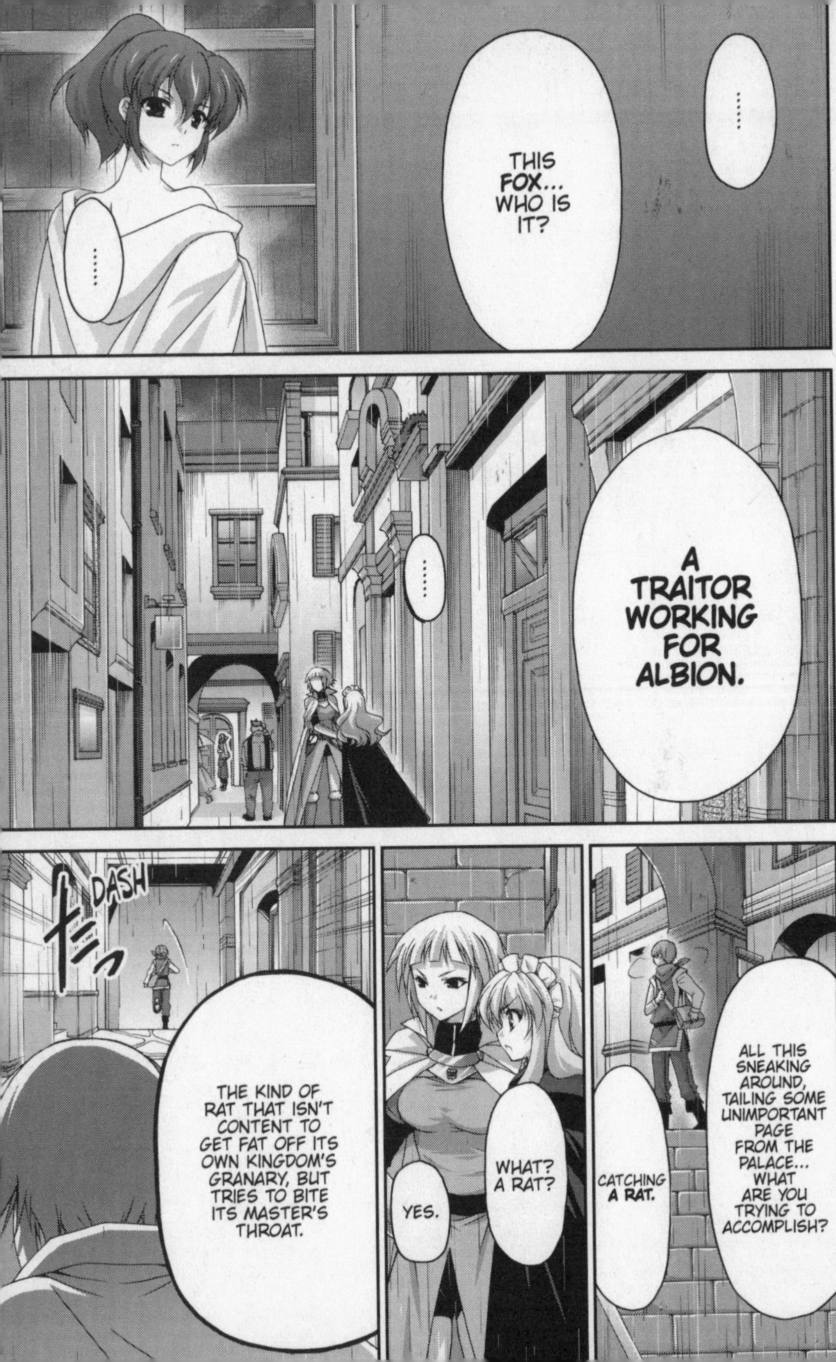
......
THIS FOX... WHO IS IT?
......
A TRAITOR WORKING FOR ALBION.
......
ALL THIS SNEAKING AROUND, TAILING SOME UNIMPORTANT PAGE FROM THE PALACE... WHAT ARE YOU TRYING TO ACCOMPLISH?
CATCHING A RAT.
WHAT? A RAT?
YES.
DASH
THE KIND OF RAT THAT ISN'T CONTENT TO GET FAT OFF ITS OWN KINGDOM'S GRANARY, BUT TRIES TO BITE ITS MASTER'S THROAT.

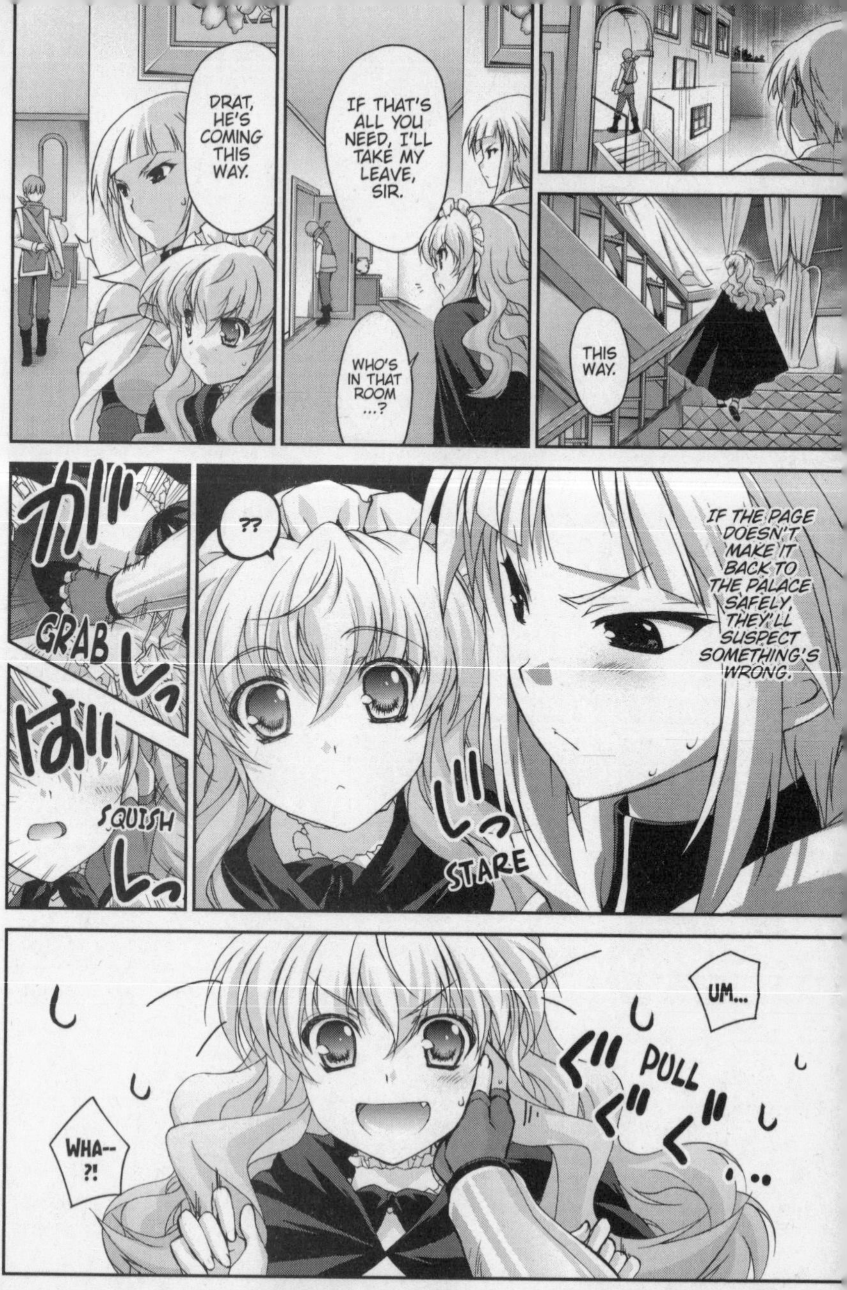
THIS WAY.
IF THAT'S ALL YOU NEED, I'LL TAKE MY LEAVE, SIR.
WHO'S IN THAT ROOM ...?
DRAT, HE'S COMING THIS WAY.
??
IF THE PAGE DOESN'T MAKE IT BACK TO THE PALACE SAFELY, THEY'LL SUSPECT SOMETHING'S WRONG.
STARE
GRAB
SQUISH
UM...
PULL
WHA-- ?!

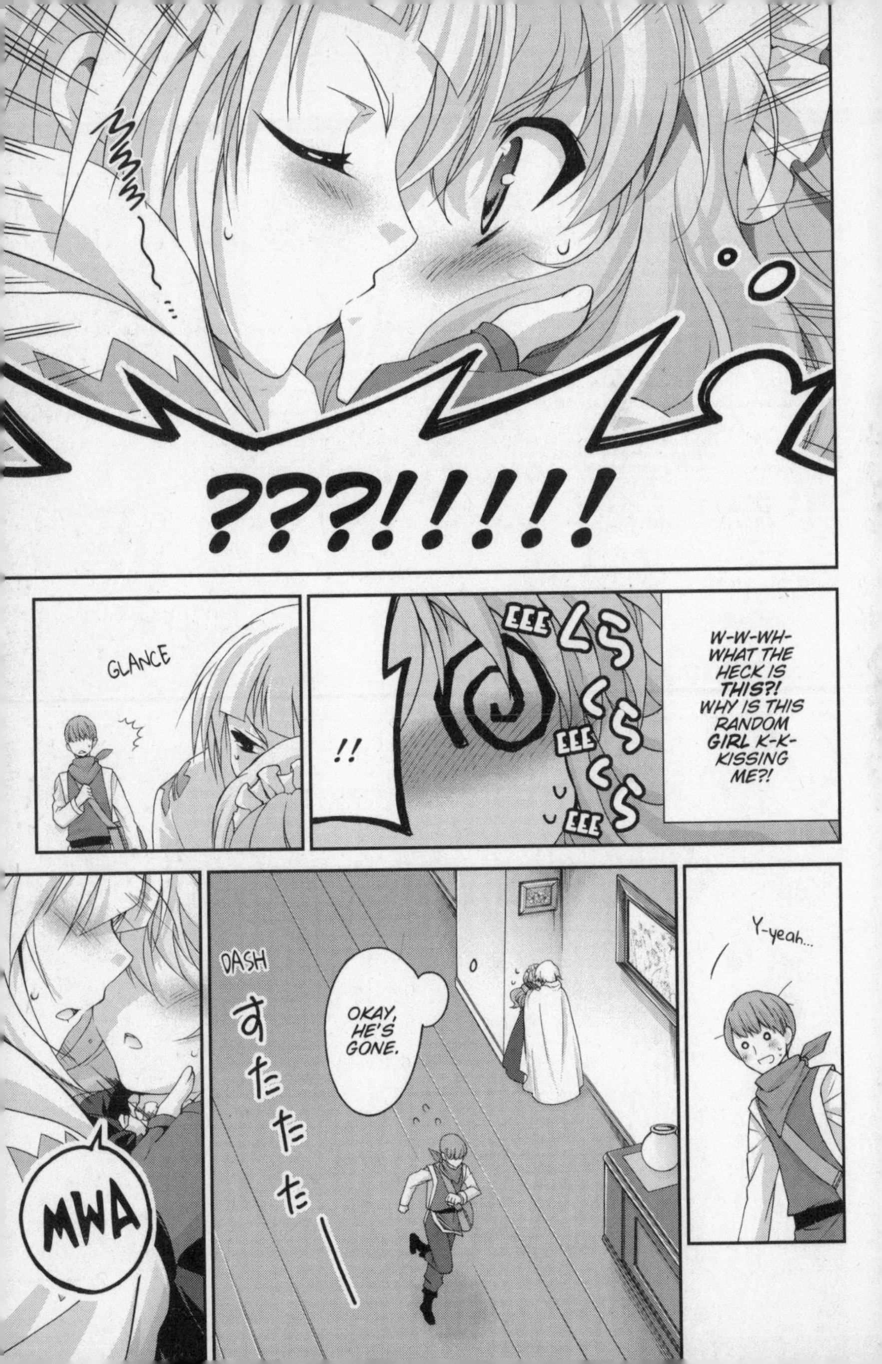
MMM~...
???!!!!!
W-W-WH-WHAT THE HECK IS THIS?! WHY IS THIS RANDOM GIRL K-K-KISSING ME?!
EEE くら EEE くら EEE くら
!!
GLANCE
Y-yeah...
OKAY, HE'S GONE.
DASH
すたたたー
MWA

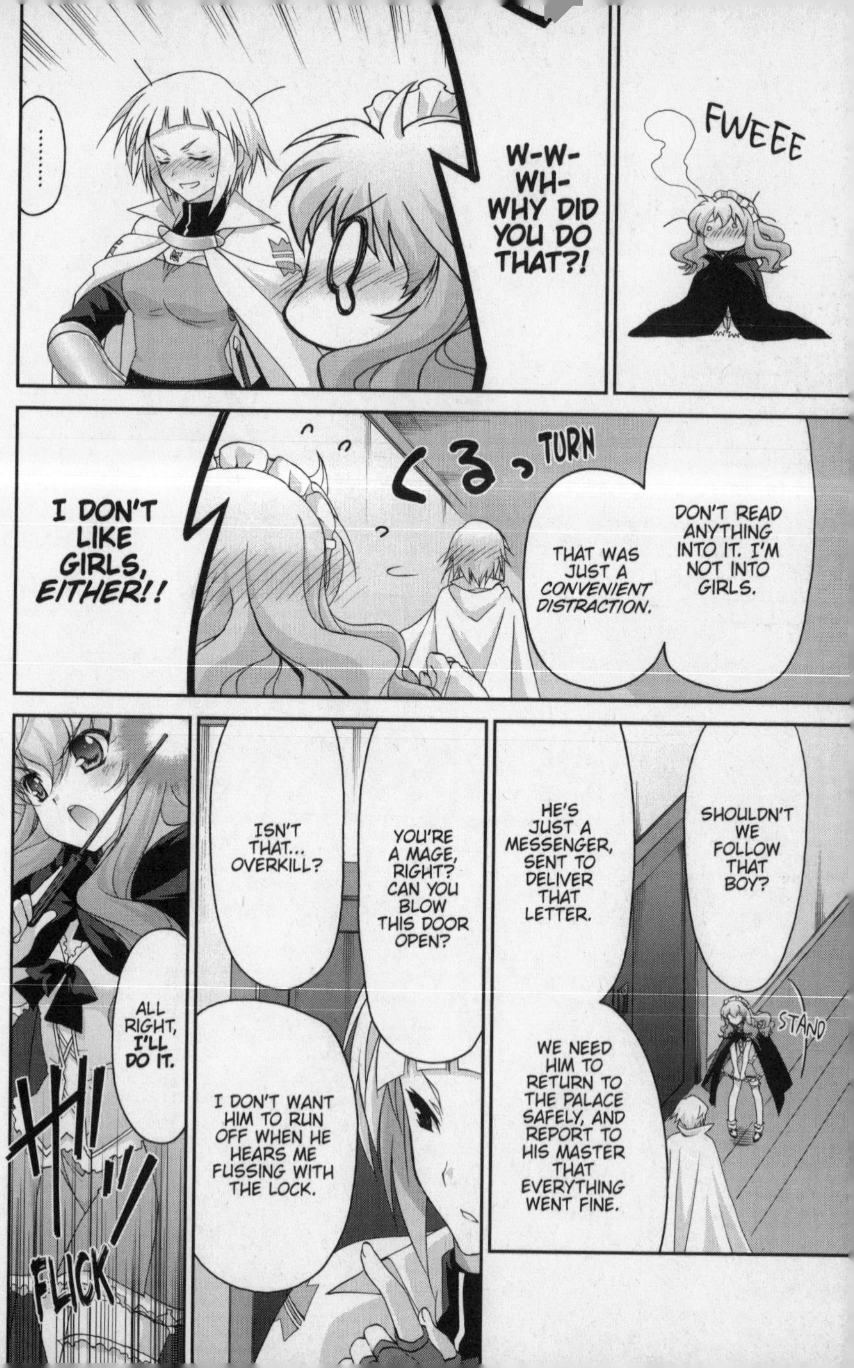
FWEEE
W-W-WH-WHY DID YOU DO THAT?!
......
DON'T READ ANYTHING INTO IT. I'M NOT INTO GIRLS.
THAT WAS JUST A CONVENIENT DISTRACTION.
TURN
I DON'T LIKE GIRLS, EITHER!!
SHOULDN'T WE FOLLOW THAT BOY?
HE'S JUST A MESSENGER, SENT TO DELIVER THAT LETTER.
WE NEED HIM TO RETURN TO THE PALACE SAFELY, AND REPORT TO HIS MASTER THAT EVERYTHING WENT FINE.
STAND
YOU'RE A MAGE, RIGHT? CAN YOU BLOW THIS DOOR OPEN?
ISN'T THAT... OVERKILL?
I DON'T WANT HIM TO RUN OFF WHEN HE HEARS ME FUSSING WITH THE LOCK.
ALL RIGHT, I'LL DO IT.
FLICK

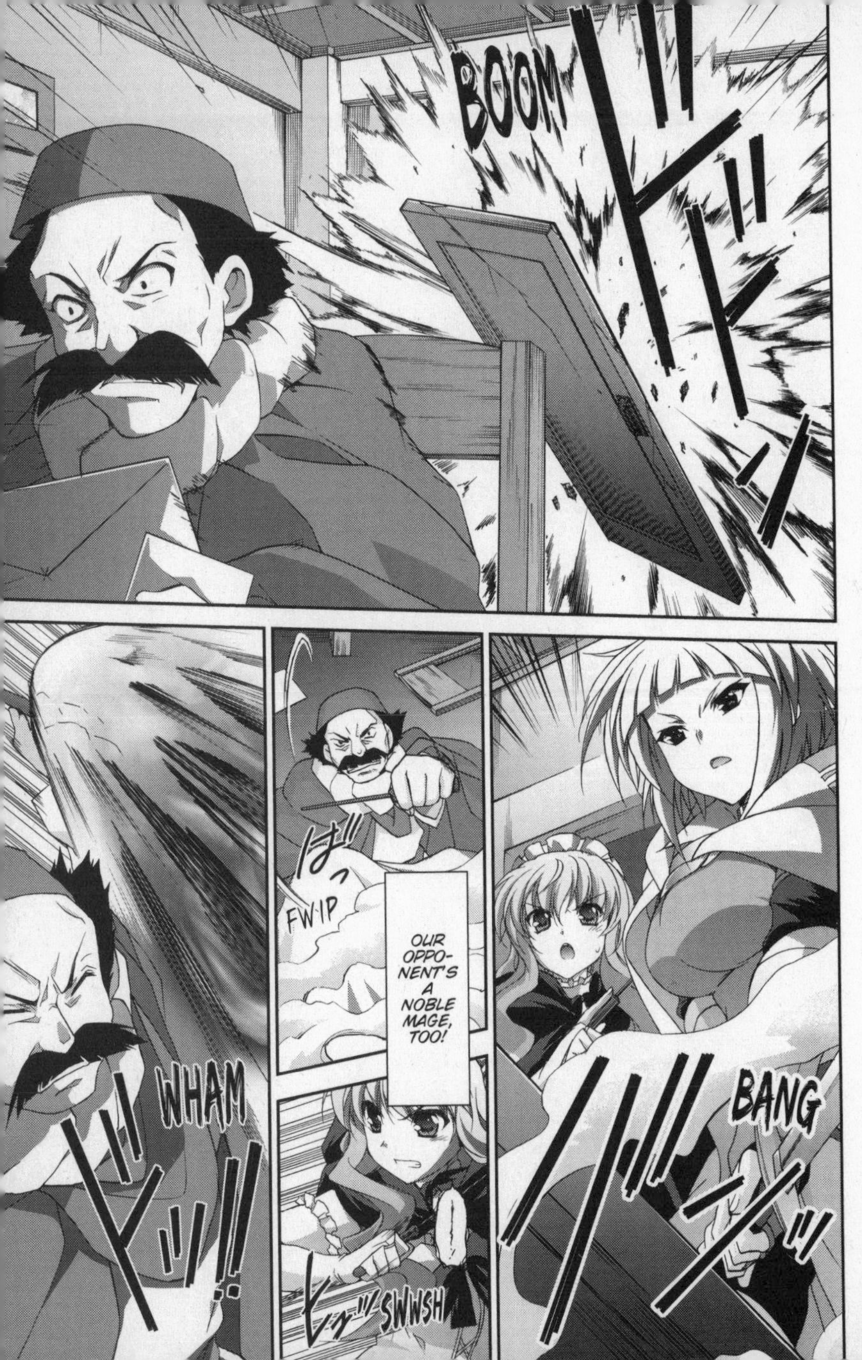
BOOM
BANG
ばっ
FWIP
OUR OPPONENT'S A NOBLE MAGE, TOO!
SWWSH
WHAM

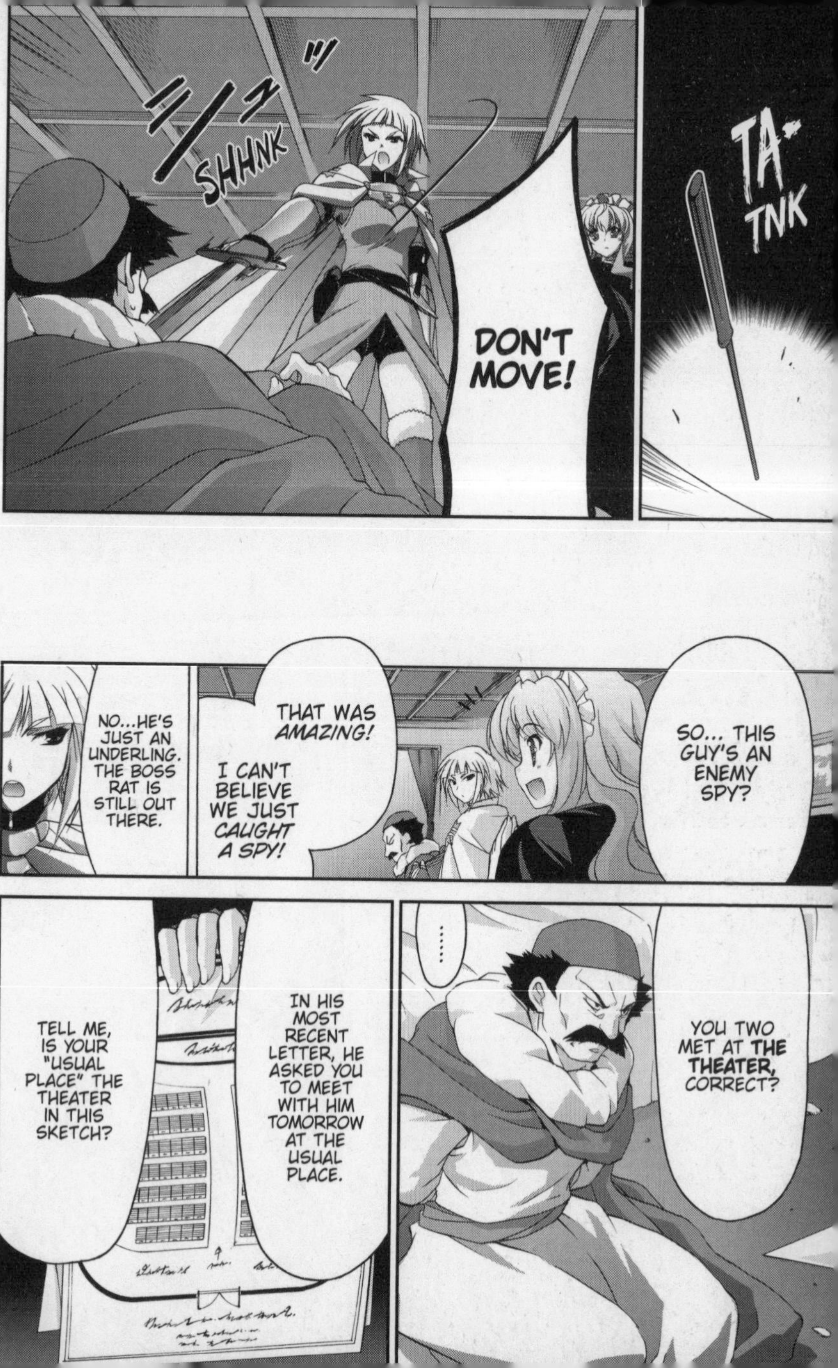
TA-TNK
DON'T MOVE!
SHHNK
SO... THIS GUY'S AN ENEMY SPY?
THAT WAS AMAZING!
I CAN'T BELIEVE WE JUST CAUGHT A SPY!
NO...HE'S JUST AN UNDERLING. THE BOSS RAT IS STILL OUT THERE.
YOU TWO MET AT THE THEATER, CORRECT?
......
IN HIS MOST RECENT LETTER, HE ASKED YOU TO MEET WITH HIM TOMORROW AT THE USUAL PLACE.
TELL ME, IS YOUR "USUAL PLACE" THE THEATER IN THIS SKETCH?

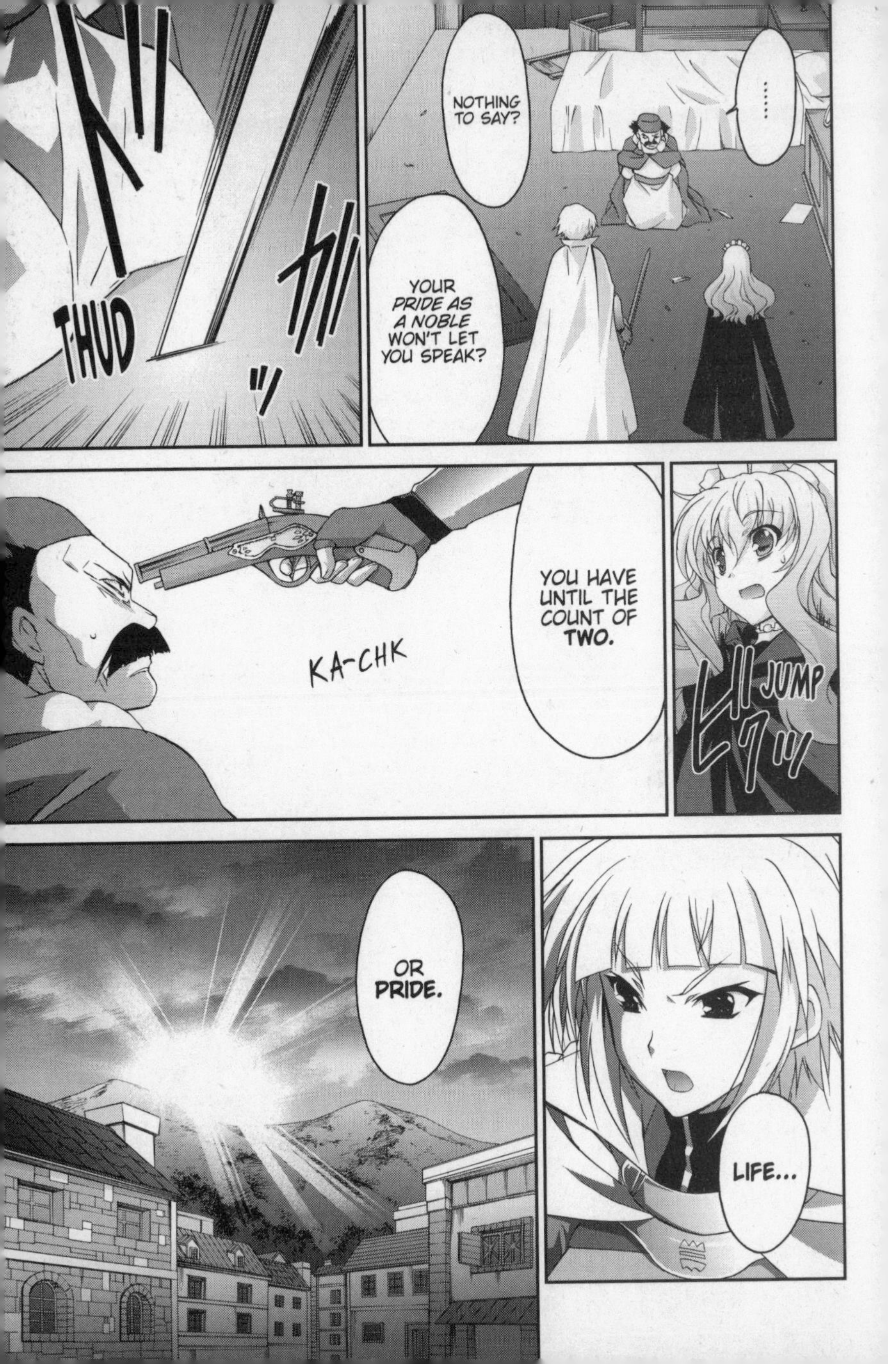
......
NOTHING TO SAY?
YOUR PRIDE AS A NOBLE WON'T LET YOU SPEAK?
THUD
JUMP
ビクッ
YOU HAVE UNTIL THE COUNT OF TWO.
KA-CHK
LIFE...
OR PRIDE.

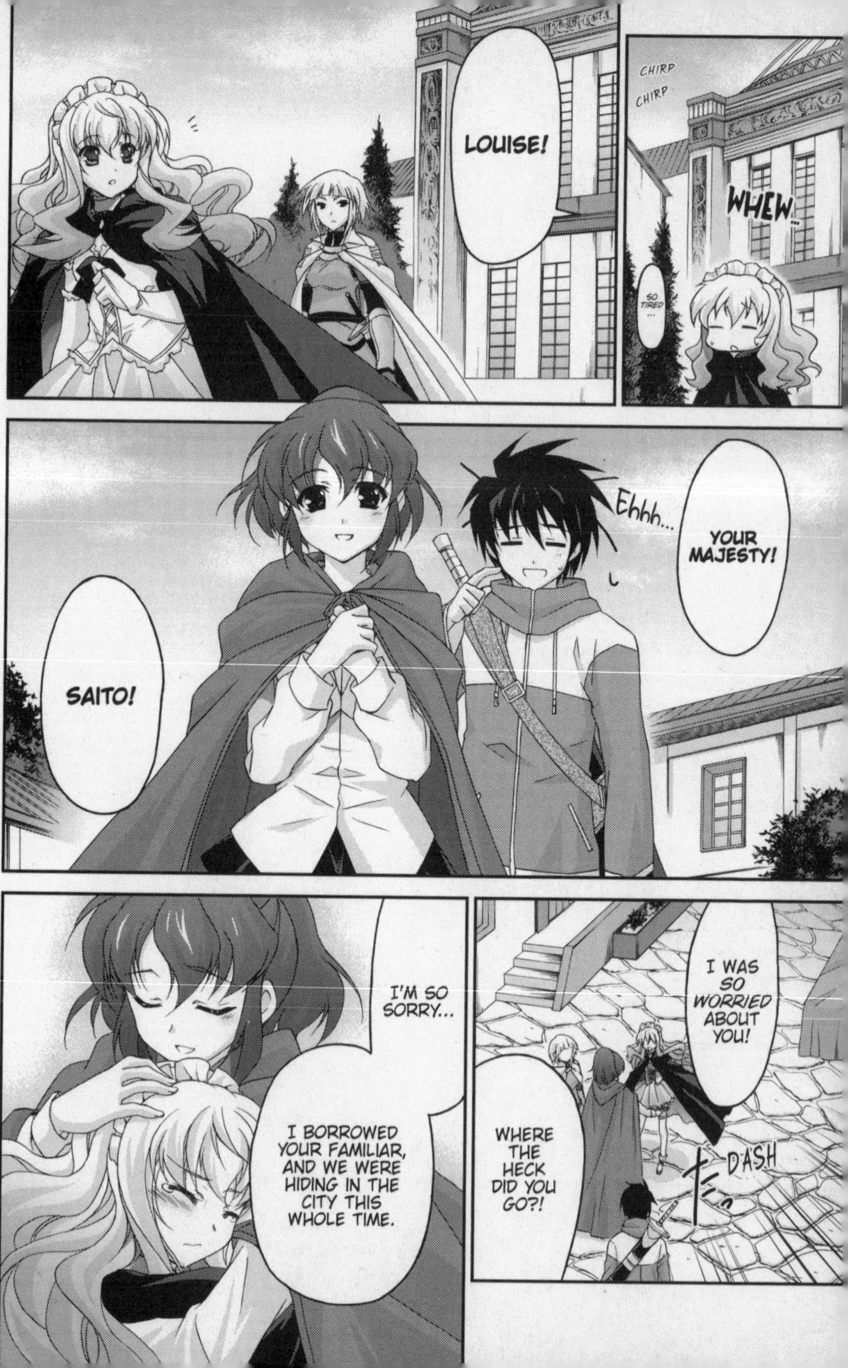
CHIRP
CHIRP
WHEW...
SO TIRED...
LOUISE!
YOUR MAJESTY!
Ehhh...
SAITO!
I WAS SO WORRIED ABOUT YOU!
WHERE THE HECK DID YOU GO?!
DASH
I'M SO SORRY...
I BORROWED YOUR FAMILIAR, AND WE WERE HIDING IN THE CITY THIS WHOLE TIME.

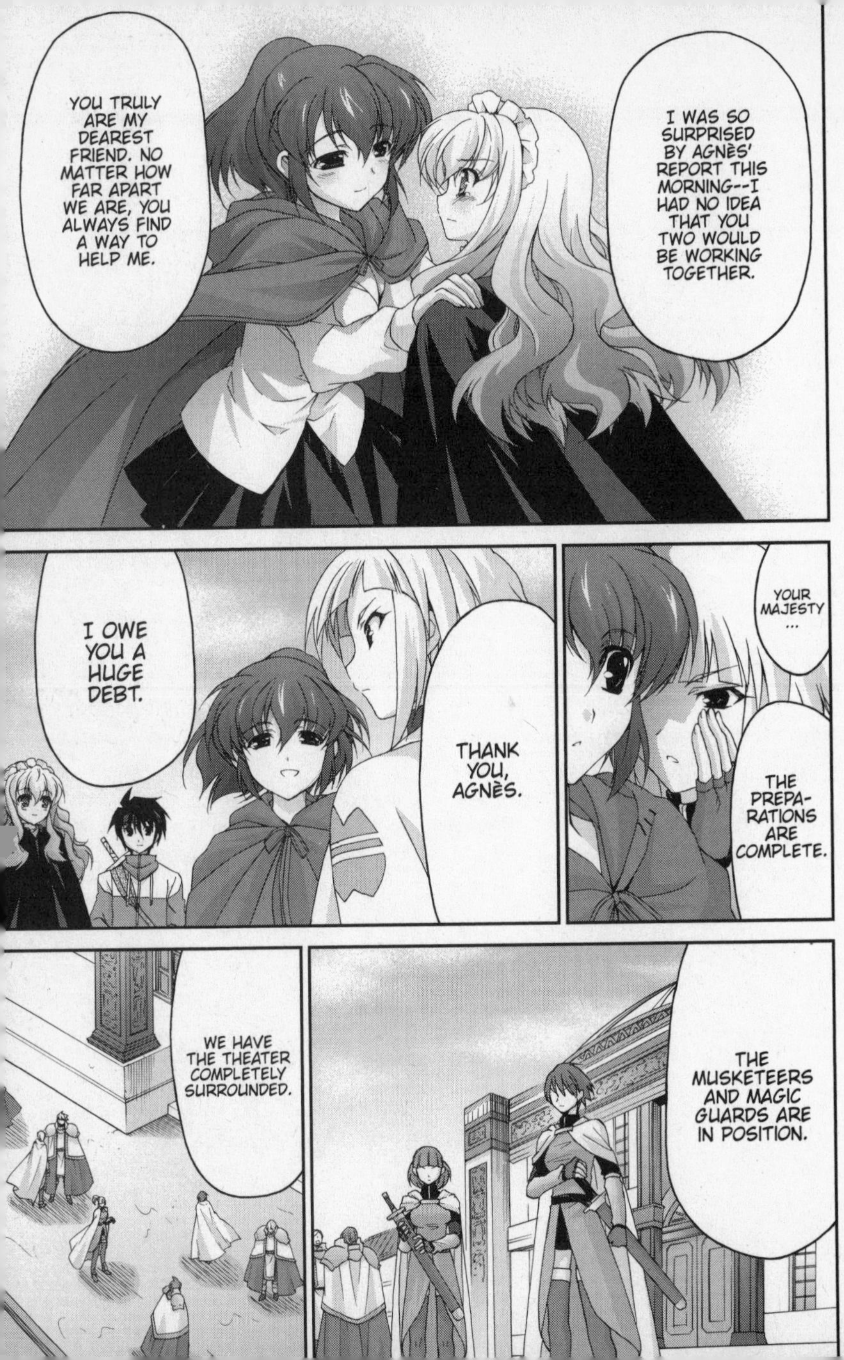
I WAS SO SURPRISED BY AGNÈS' REPORT THIS MORNING--I HAD NO IDEA THAT YOU TWO WOULD BE WORKING TOGETHER.
YOU TRULY ARE MY DEAREST FRIEND. NO MATTER HOW FAR APART WE ARE, YOU ALWAYS FIND A WAY TO HELP ME.
YOUR MAJESTY ...
THE PREPARATIONS ARE COMPLETE.
THANK YOU, AGNÈS.
I OWE YOU A HUGE DEBT.
THE MUSKETEERS AND MAGIC GUARDS ARE IN POSITION.
WE HAVE THE THEATER COMPLETELY SURROUNDED.

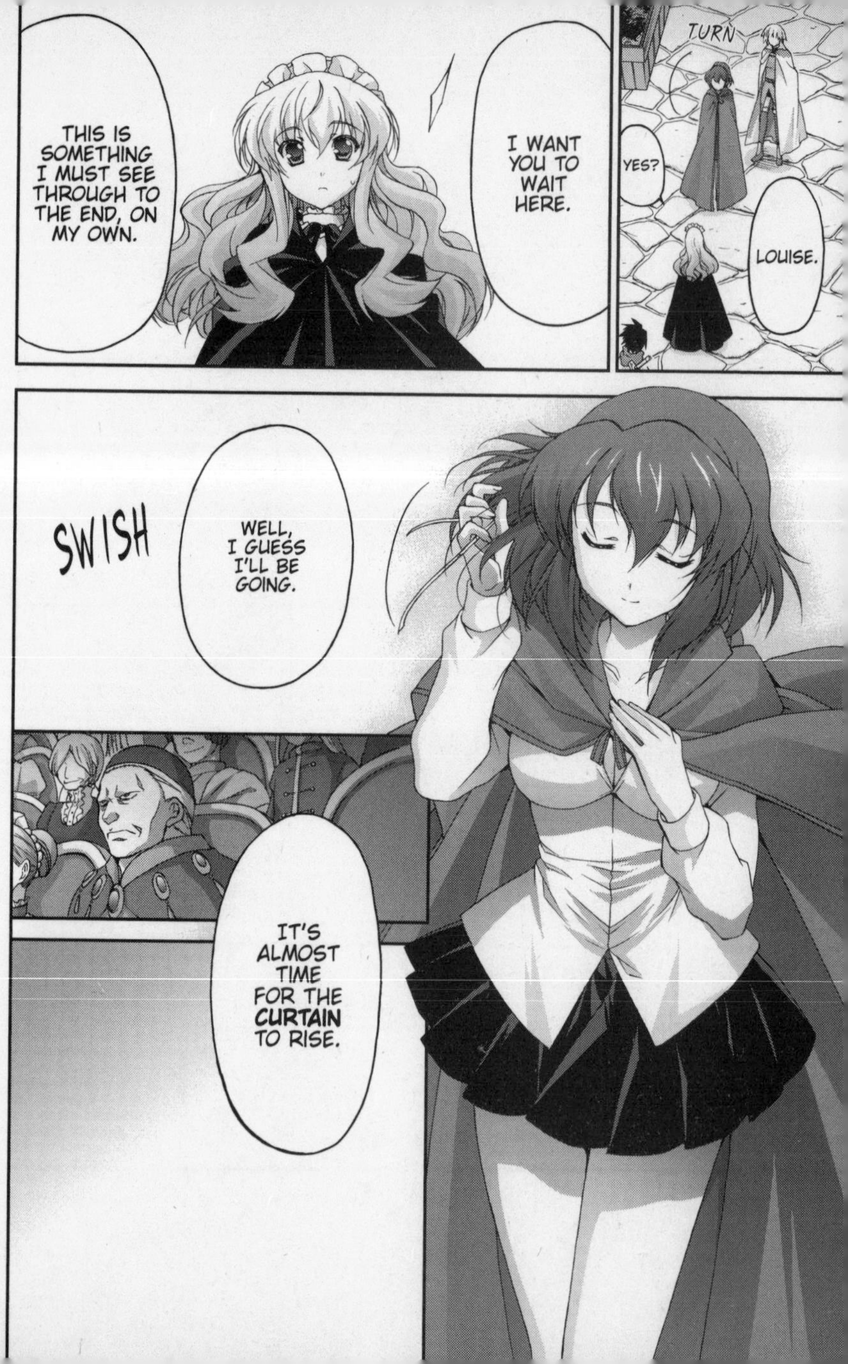
TURN
LOUISE.
YES?
I WANT YOU TO WAIT HERE.
THIS IS SOMETHING I MUST SEE THROUGH TO THE END, ON MY OWN.
WELL, I GUESS I'LL BE GOING.
SWISH
IT'S ALMOST TIME FOR THE **CURTAIN** TO RISE.

IF THINGS KEEP GOING LIKE THIS, I'M GONNA BE IN BIG TROUBLE!

Le Familier de Zero Chevalier

ZERO'S
FAMILIAR
Chevalier

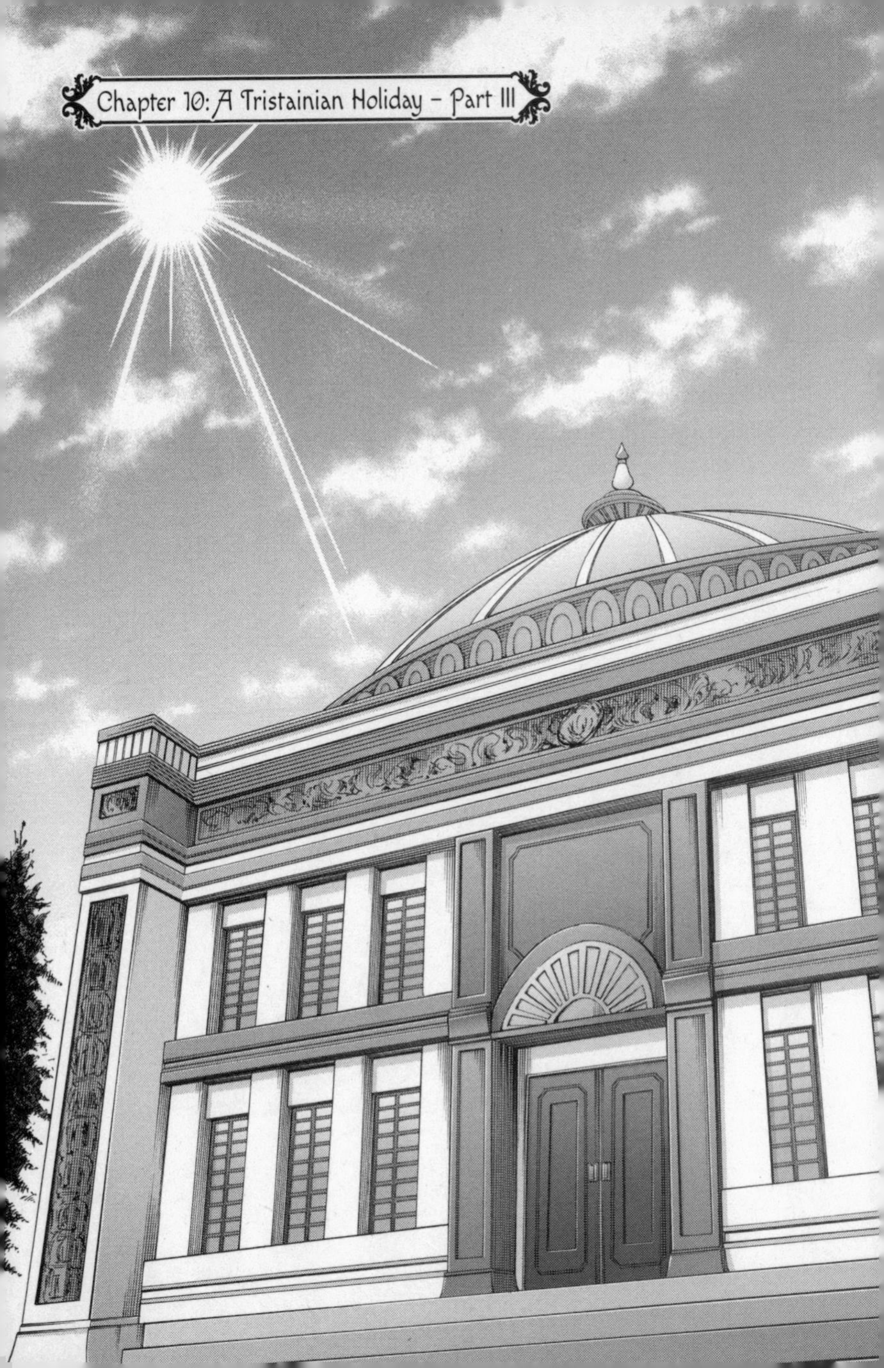
Chapter 10: A Tristainian Holiday - Part III

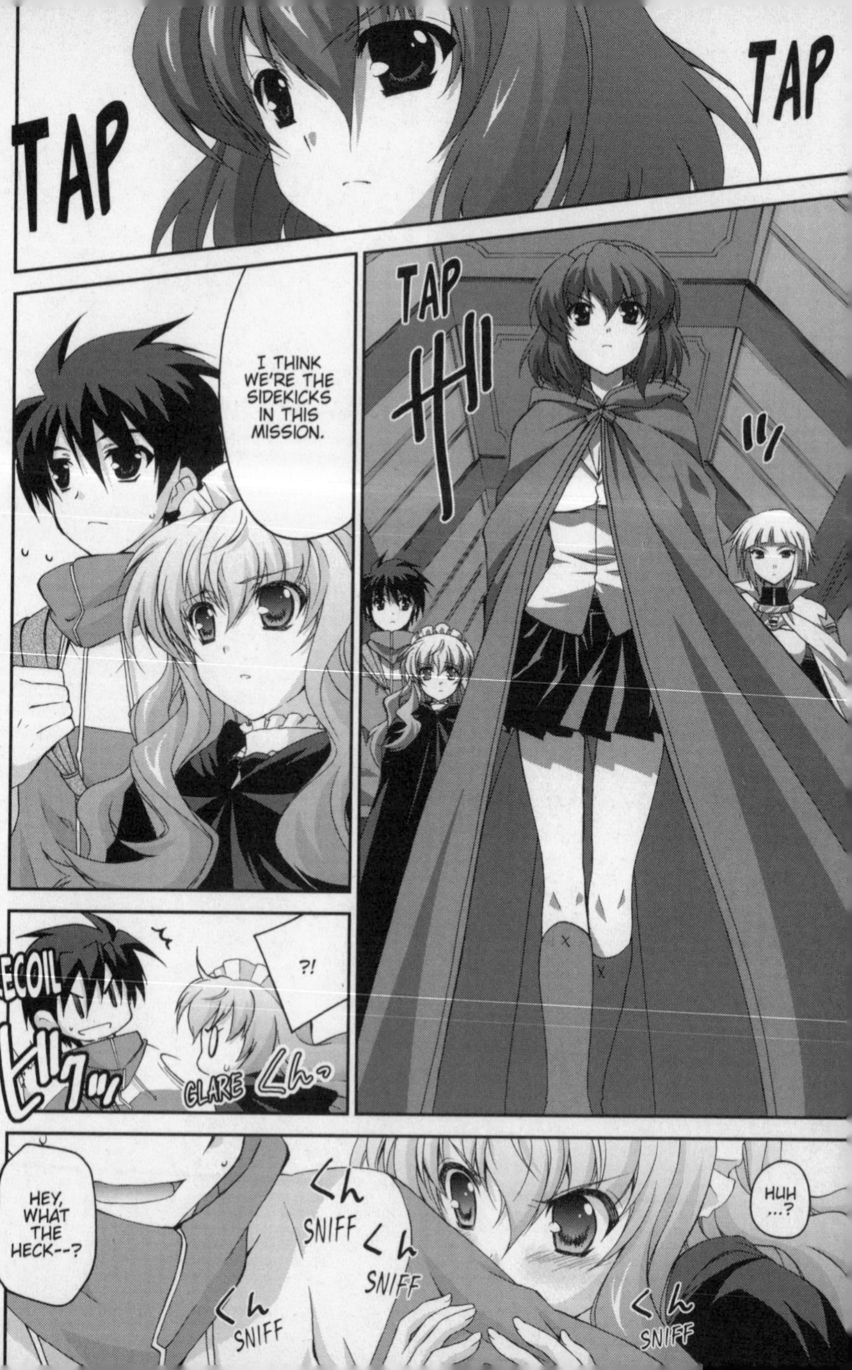
TAP
TAP
TAP
TAP
I THINK WE'RE THE SIDEKICKS IN THIS MISSION.
?!
RECOIL
GLARE
HUH ...?
くん SNIFF
くん SNIFF
くん SNIFF
くん SNIFF
HEY, WHAT THE HECK--?

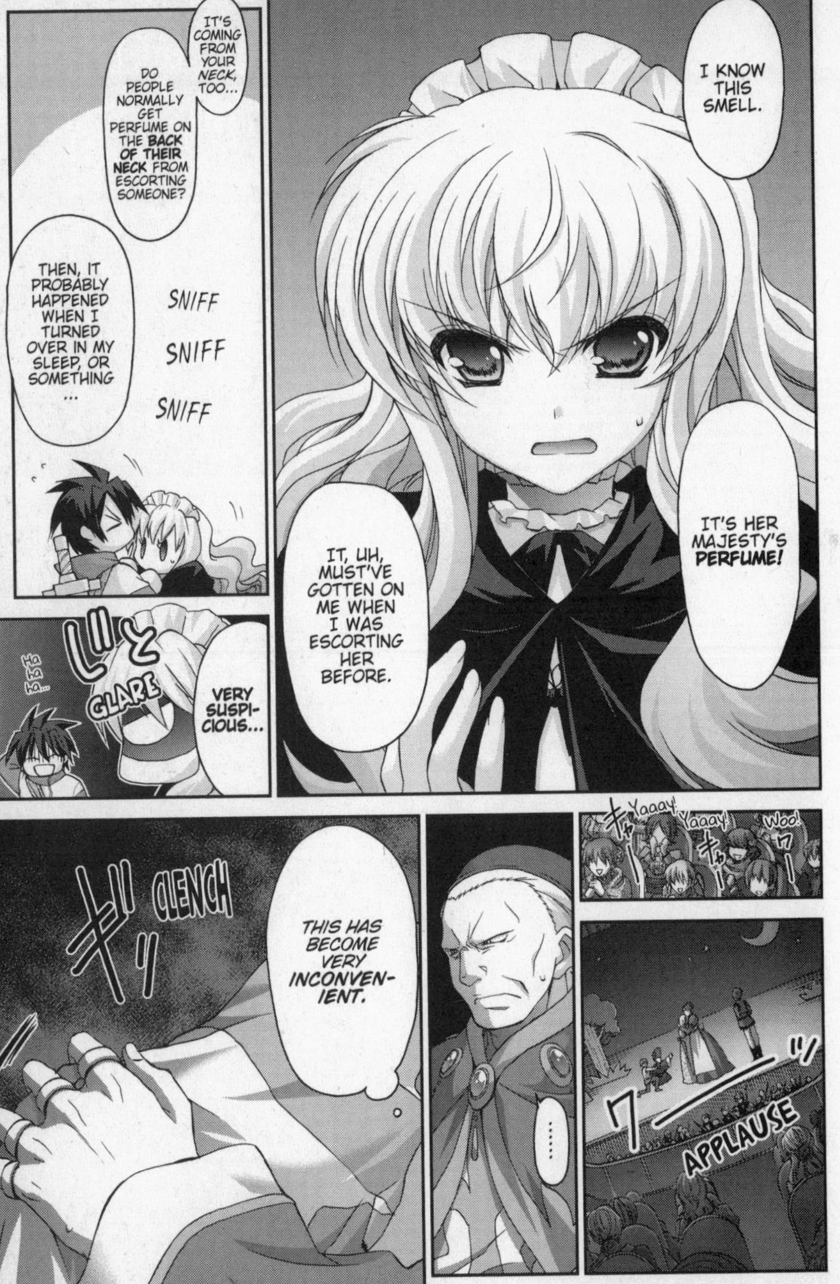
I KNOW THIS SMELL.
IT'S HER MAJESTY'S **PERFUME!**
IT, UH, MUST'VE GOTTEN ON ME WHEN I WAS ESCORTING HER BEFORE.
IT'S COMING FROM YOUR NECK, TOO...
DO PEOPLE NORMALLY GET PERFUME ON THE **BACK OF THEIR NECK** FROM ESCORTING SOMEONE?
SNIFF
SNIFF
SNIFF
THEN, IT PROBABLY HAPPENED WHEN I TURNED OVER IN MY SLEEP, OR SOMETHING ...
VERY SUSPICIOUS...
GLARE
Ha ha ha...
Yaaay!
Yaaay!
Woo!
APPLAUSE
......
THIS HAS BECOME VERY INCONVENIENT.
CLENCH

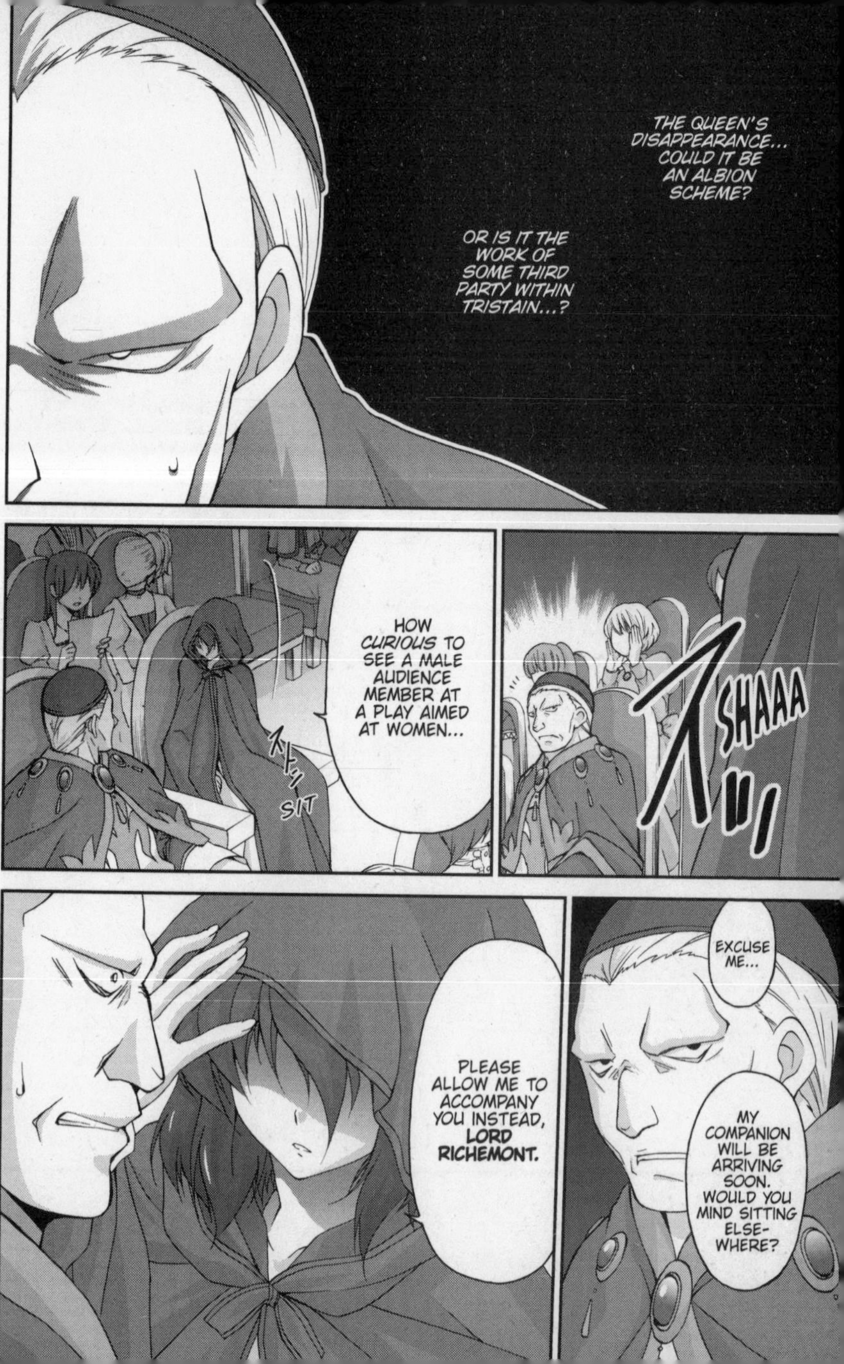
THE QUEEN'S DISAPPEARANCE... COULD IT BE AN ALBION SCHEME?
OR IS IT THE WORK OF SOME THIRD PARTY WITHIN TRISTAIN...?
SHAAA
HOW CURIOUS TO SEE A MALE AUDIENCE MEMBER AT A PLAY AIMED AT WOMEN...
SIT
EXCUSE ME...
MY COMPANION WILL BE ARRIVING SOON. WOULD YOU MIND SITTING ELSE-WHERE?
PLEASE ALLOW ME TO ACCOMPANY YOU INSTEAD, **LORD RICHEMONT.**

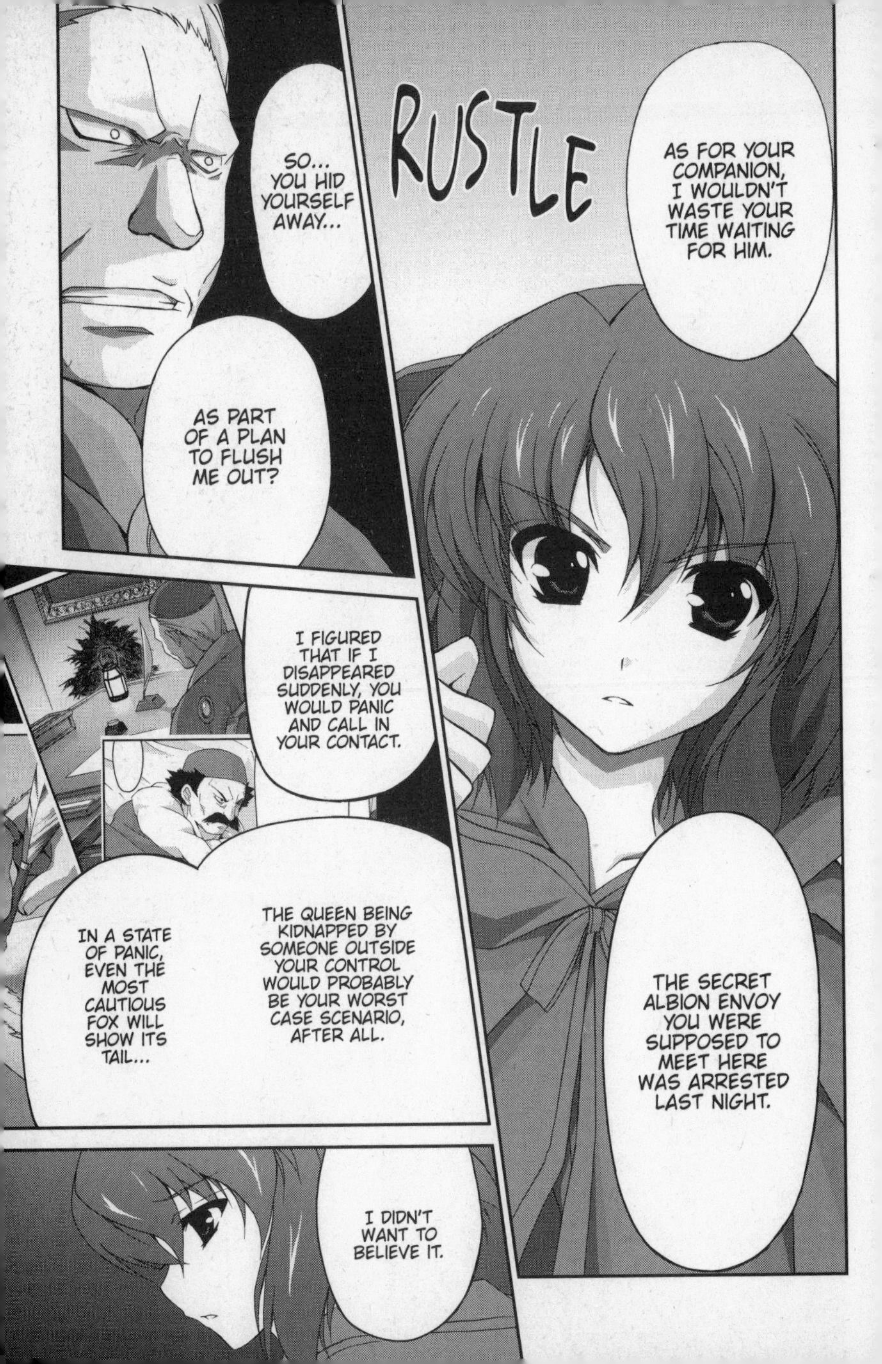
RUSTLE
AS FOR YOUR COMPANION, I WOULDN'T WASTE YOUR TIME WAITING FOR HIM.
THE SECRET ALBION ENVOY YOU WERE SUPPOSED TO MEET HERE WAS ARRESTED LAST NIGHT.
SO... YOU HID YOURSELF AWAY...
AS PART OF A PLAN TO FLUSH ME OUT?
I FIGURED THAT IF I DISAPPEARED SUDDENLY, YOU WOULD PANIC AND CALL IN YOUR CONTACT.
THE QUEEN BEING KIDNAPPED BY SOMEONE OUTSIDE YOUR CONTROL WOULD PROBABLY BE YOUR WORST CASE SCENARIO, AFTER ALL.
IN A STATE OF PANIC, EVEN THE MOST CAUTIOUS FOX WILL SHOW ITS TAIL...
I DIDN'T WANT TO BELIEVE IT.

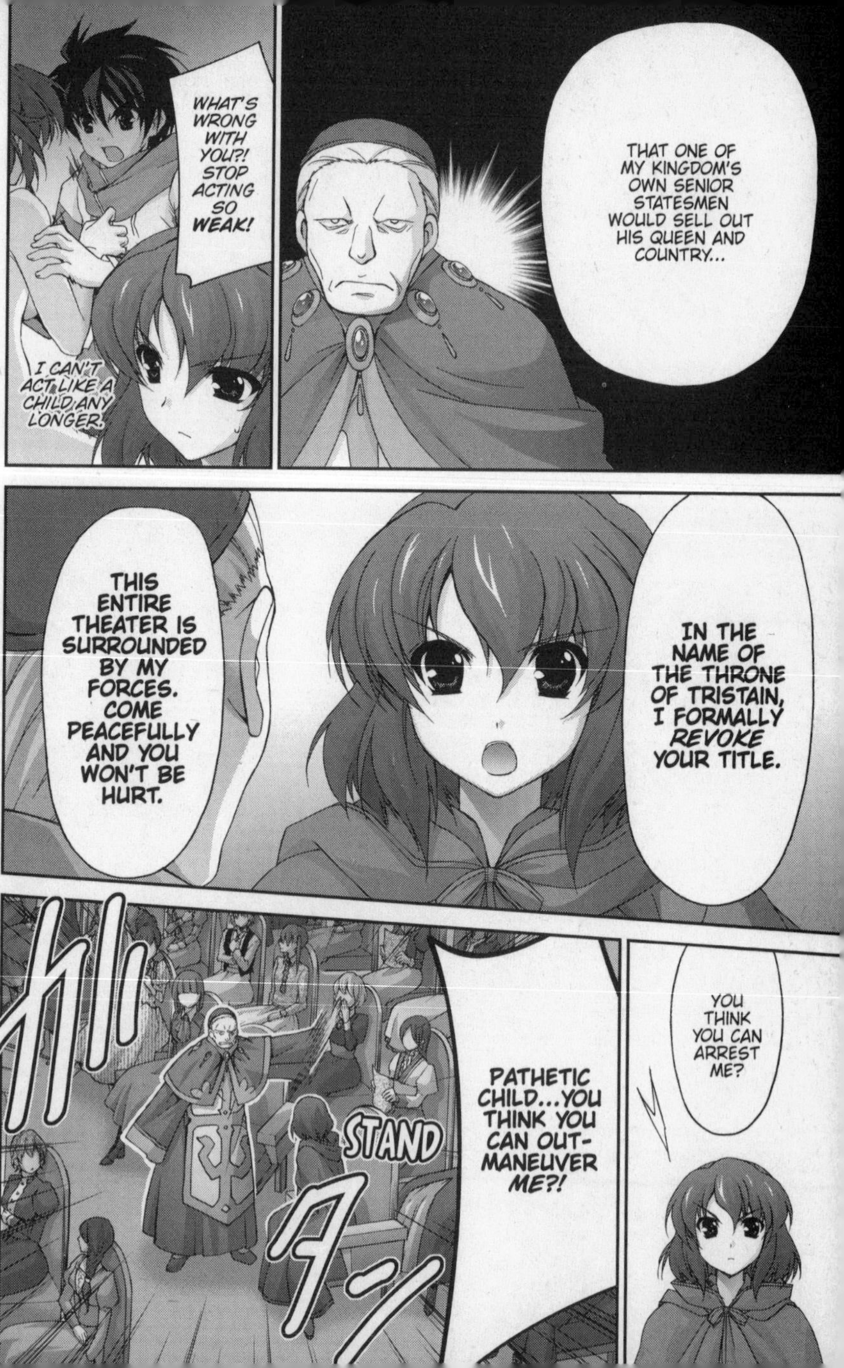
THAT ONE OF MY KINGDOM'S OWN SENIOR STATESMEN WOULD SELL OUT HIS QUEEN AND COUNTRY...
WHAT'S WRONG WITH YOU?! STOP ACTING SO WEAK!
I CAN'T ACT LIKE A CHILD ANY LONGER.
IN THE NAME OF THE THRONE OF TRISTAIN, I FORMALLY REVOKE YOUR TITLE.
THIS ENTIRE THEATER IS SURROUNDED BY MY FORCES. COME PEACEFULLY AND YOU WON'T BE HURT.
YOU THINK YOU CAN ARREST ME?
PATHETIC CHILD...YOU THINK YOU CAN OUT-MANEUVER ME?!
STAND

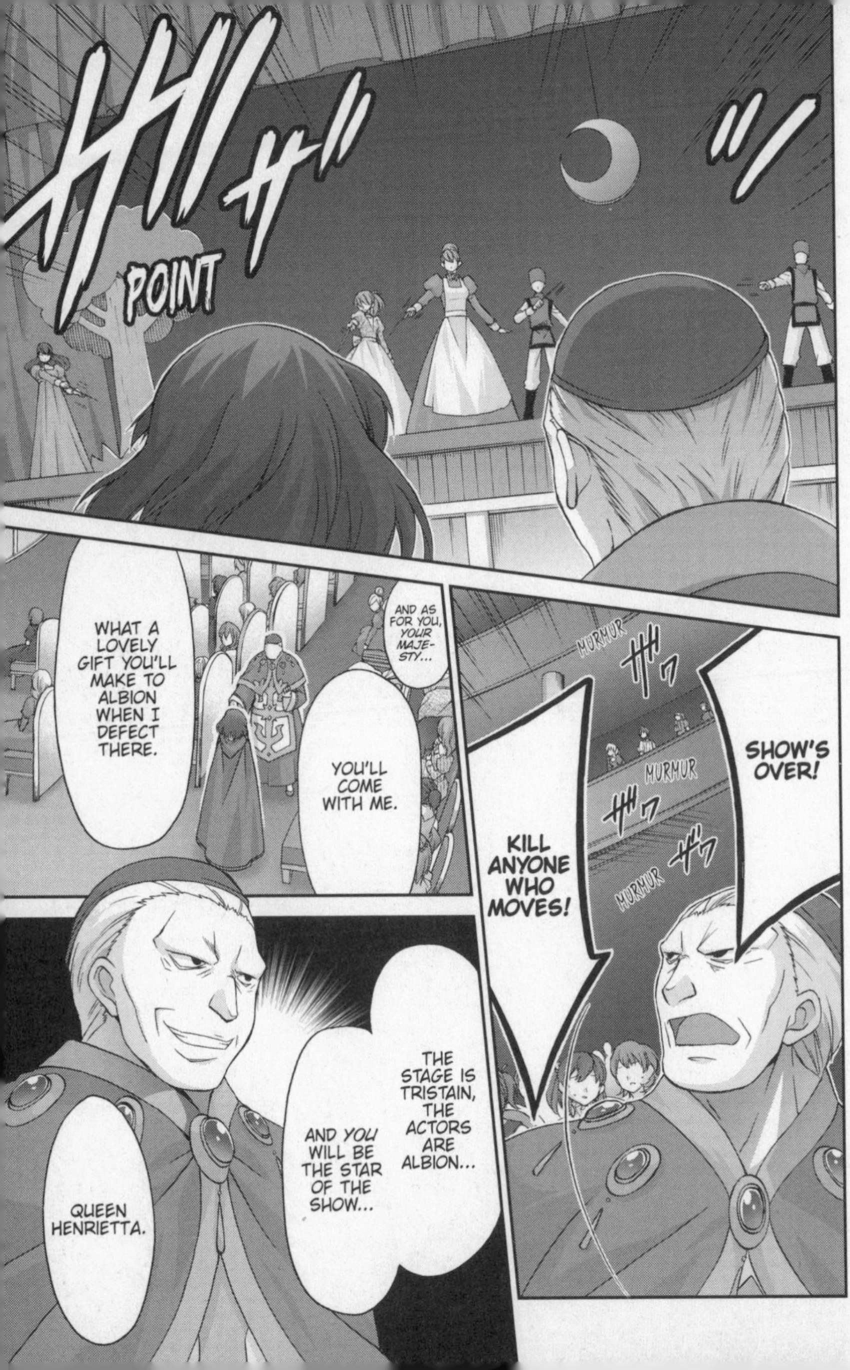
POINT
SHOW'S OVER!
MURMUR
MURMUR
MURMUR
KILL ANYONE WHO MOVES!
AND AS FOR YOU, YOUR MAJESTY...
YOU'LL COME WITH ME.
WHAT A LOVELY GIFT YOU'LL MAKE TO ALBION WHEN I DEFECT THERE.
THE STAGE IS TRISTAIN, THE ACTORS ARE ALBION...
AND YOU WILL BE THE STAR OF THE SHOW...
QUEEN HENRIETTA.

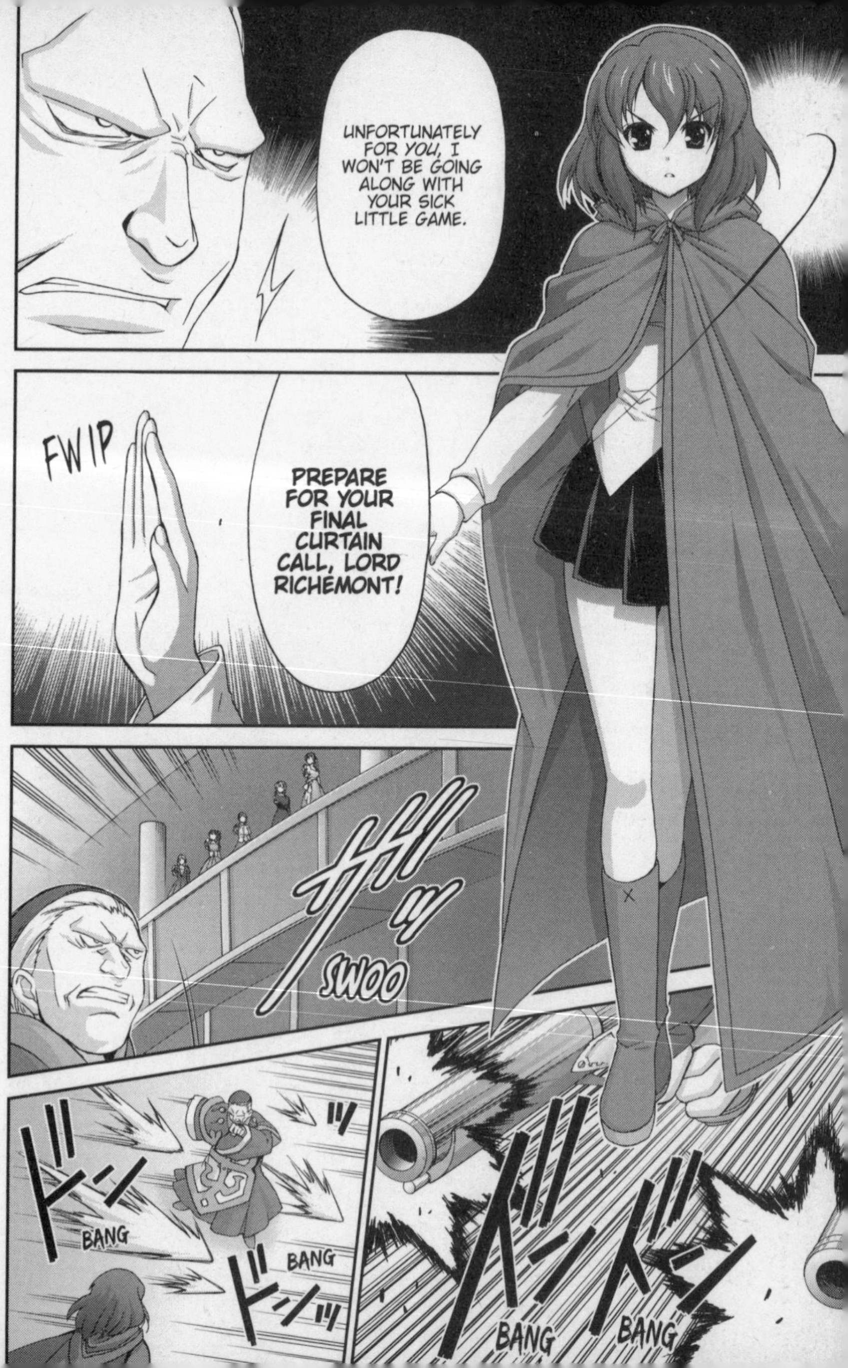
UNFORTUNATELY FOR YOU, I WON'T BE GOING ALONG WITH YOUR SICK LITTLE GAME.
PREPARE FOR YOUR FINAL CURTAIN CALL, LORD RICHEMONT!
FWIP
SWOO
BANG
BANG
BANG
BANG

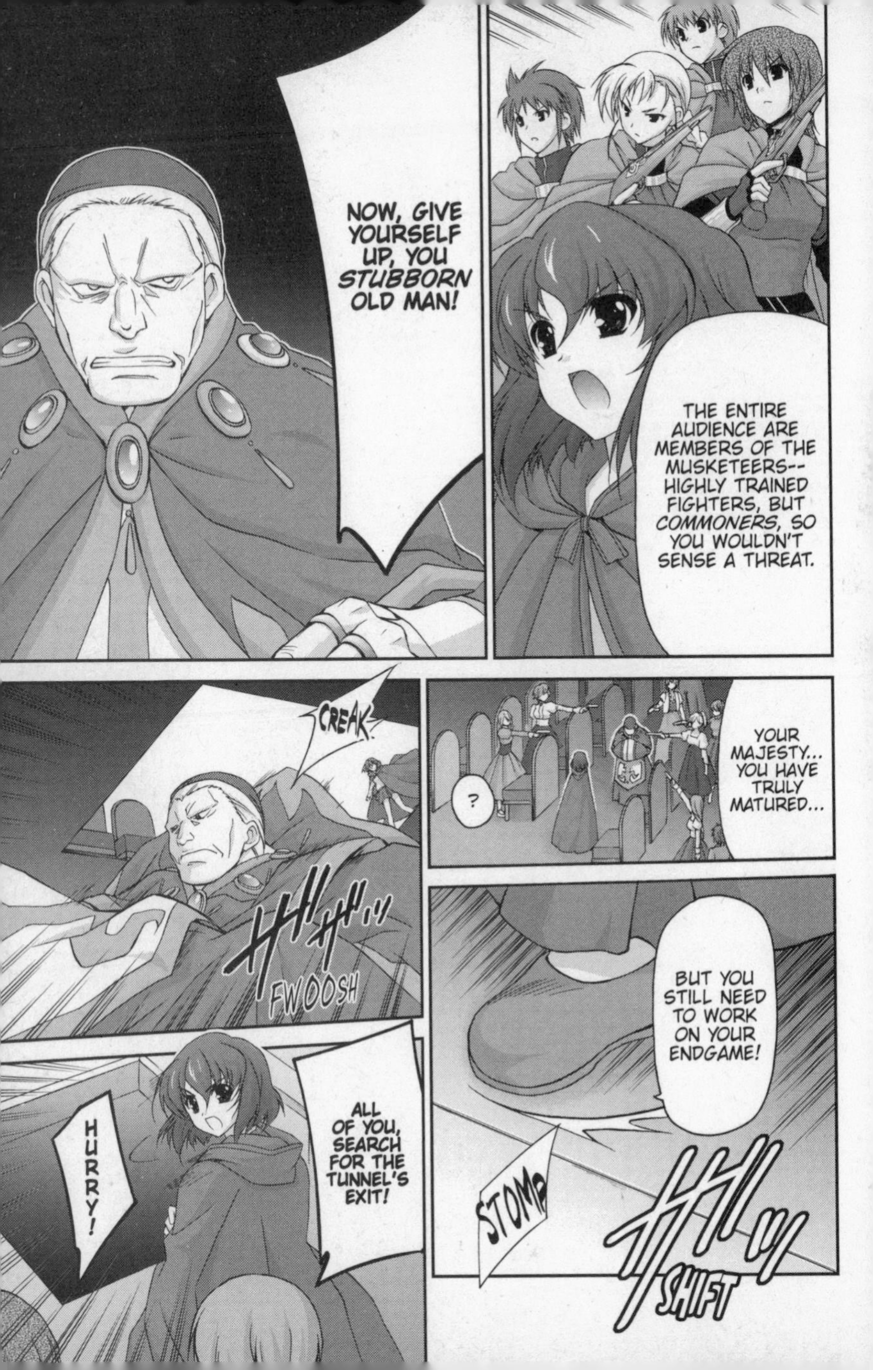
THE ENTIRE AUDIENCE ARE MEMBERS OF THE MUSKETEERS-- HIGHLY TRAINED FIGHTERS, BUT COMMONERS, SO YOU WOULDN'T SENSE A THREAT.
NOW, GIVE YOURSELF UP, YOU STUBBORN OLD MAN!
YOUR MAJESTY... YOU HAVE TRULY MATURED...
?
BUT YOU STILL NEED TO WORK ON YOUR ENDGAME!
STOMP
SHIFT
CREAK
FWOOSH
ALL OF YOU, SEARCH FOR THE TUNNEL'S EXIT!
HURRY!

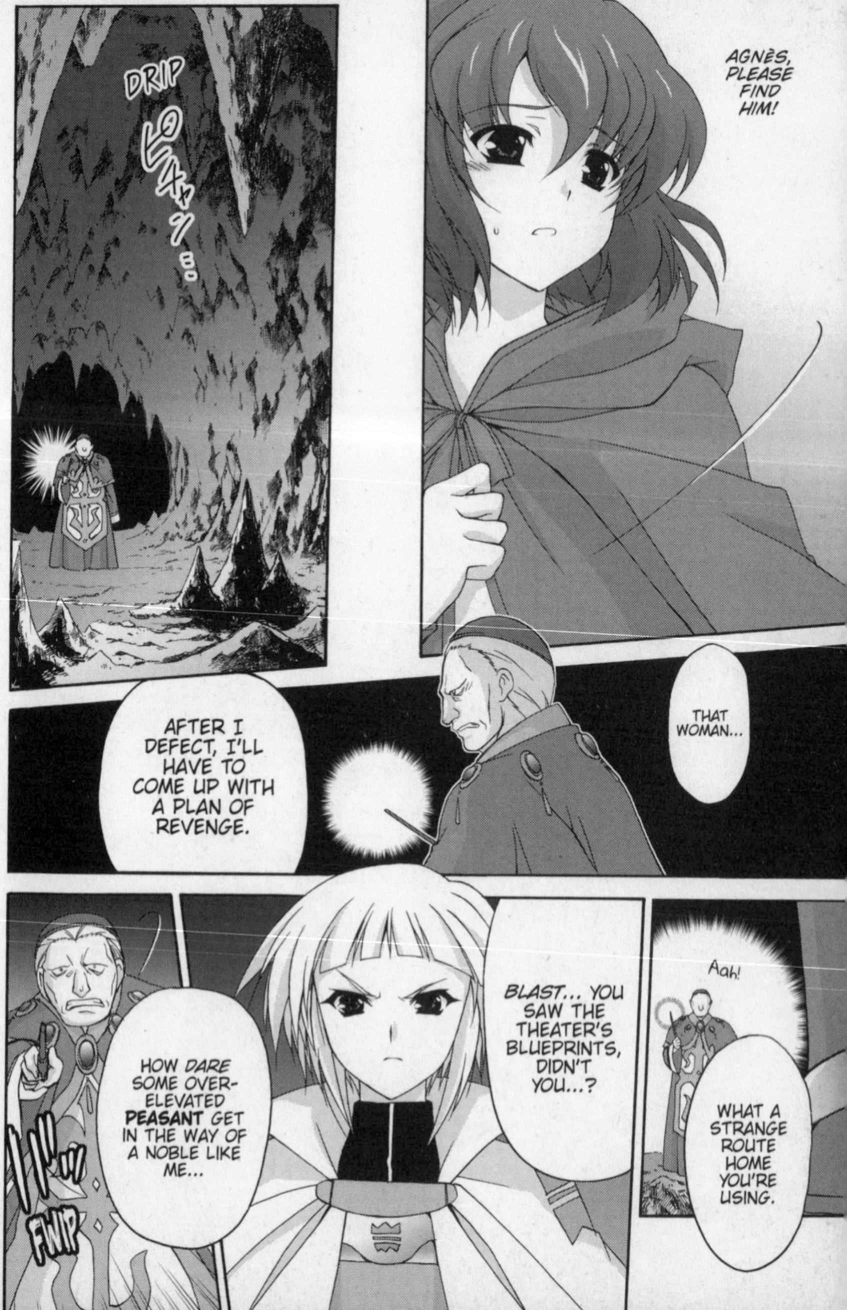
AGNÈS, PLEASE FIND HIM!
DRIP
THAT WOMAN...
AFTER I DEFECT, I'LL HAVE TO COME UP WITH A PLAN OF REVENGE.
Aah!
WHAT A STRANGE ROUTE HOME YOU'RE USING.
BLAST... YOU SAW THE THEATER'S BLUEPRINTS, DIDN'T YOU...?
HOW *DARE* SOME OVER-ELEVATED **PEASANT** GET IN THE WAY OF A NOBLE LIKE ME...
FWIP

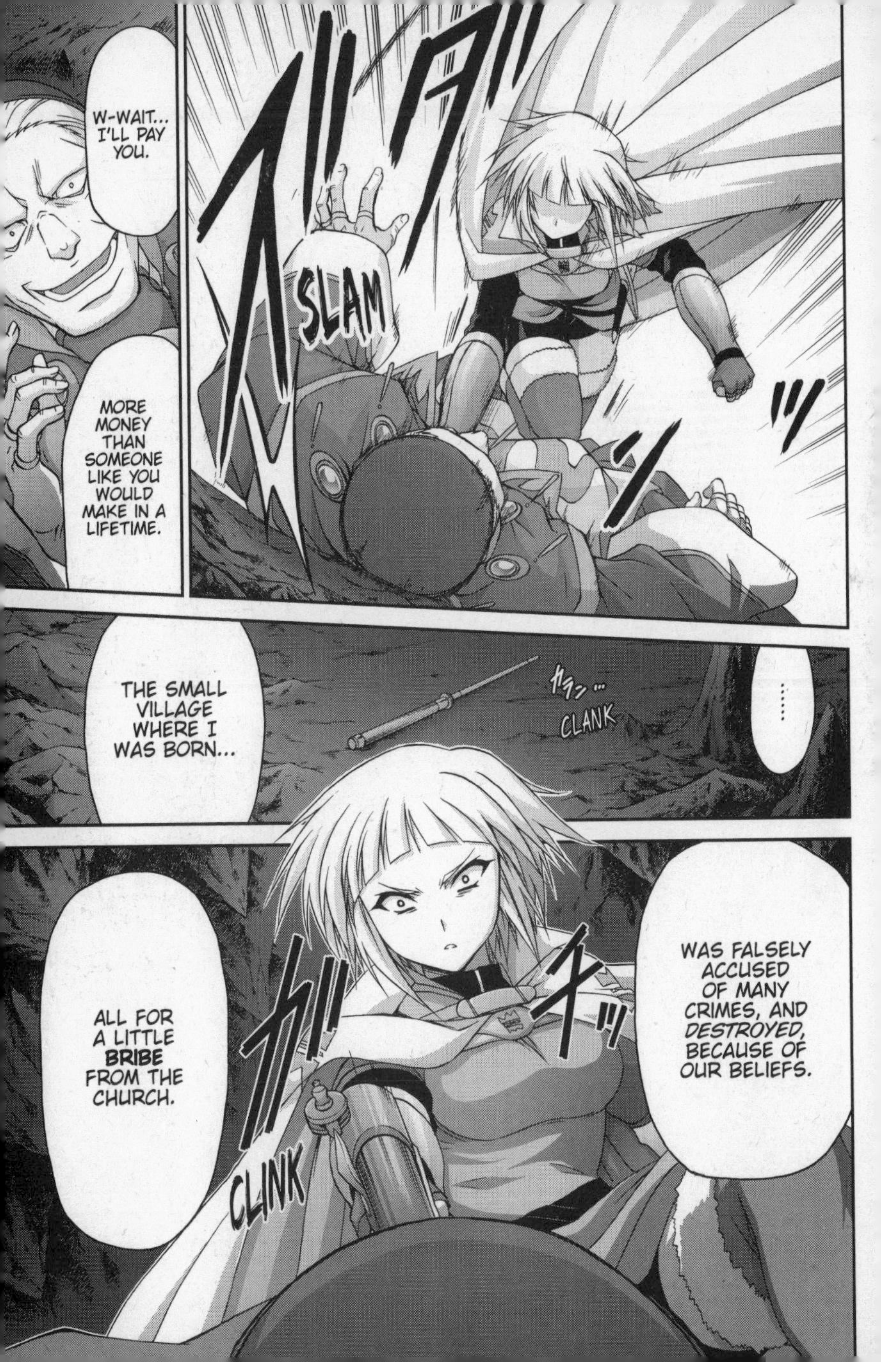
SLAM
W-WAIT... I'LL PAY YOU.
MORE MONEY THAN SOMEONE LIKE YOU WOULD MAKE IN A LIFETIME.
......
CLANK
THE SMALL VILLAGE WHERE I WAS BORN...
WAS FALSELY ACCUSED OF MANY CRIMES, AND *DESTROYED*, BECAUSE OF OUR BELIEFS.
CLINK
ALL FOR A LITTLE **BRIBE** FROM THE CHURCH.

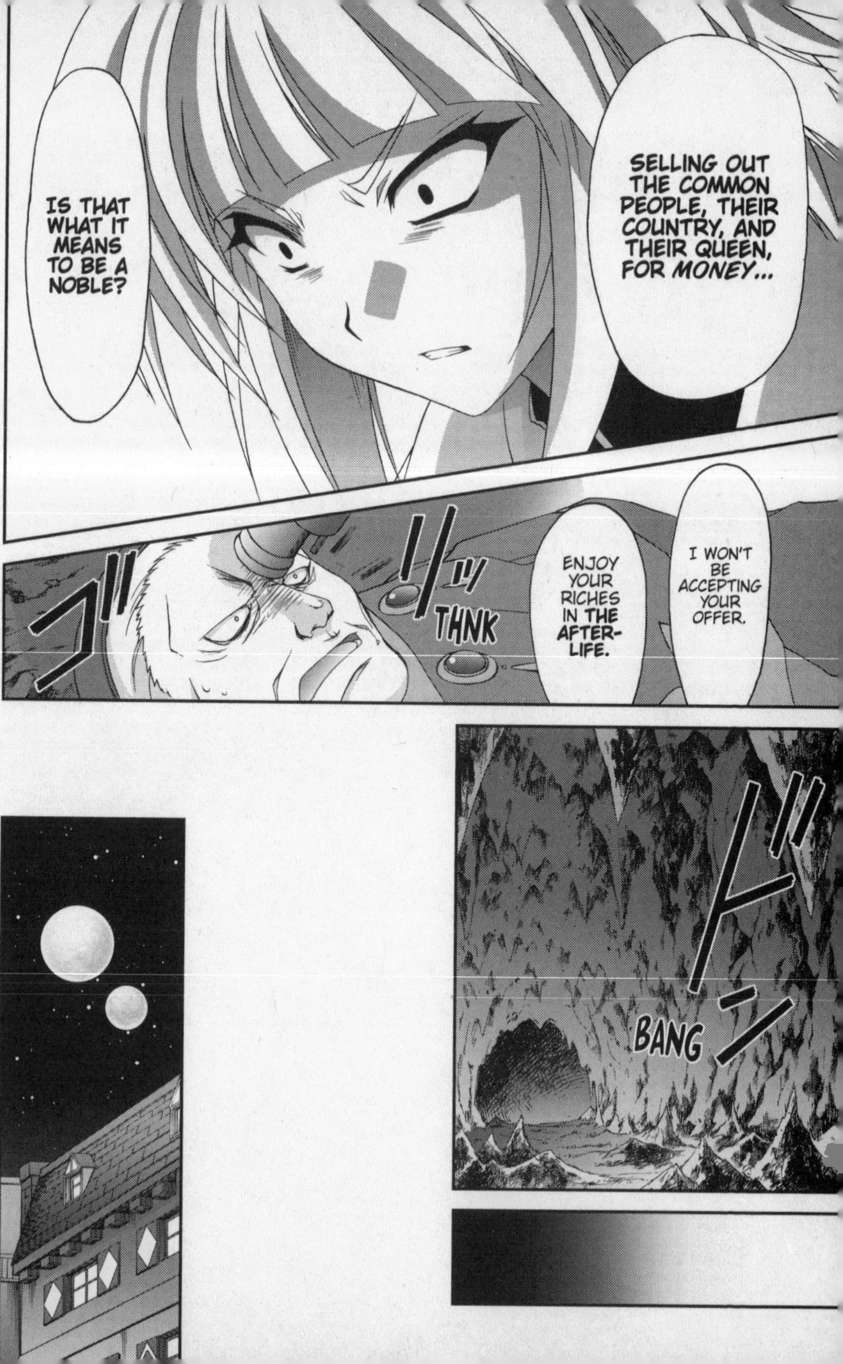
SELLING OUT THE COMMON PEOPLE, THEIR COUNTRY, AND THEIR QUEEN, FOR *MONEY*...
IS THAT WHAT IT MEANS TO BE A NOBLE?
I WON'T BE ACCEPTING YOUR OFFER.
ENJOY YOUR RICHES IN THE AFTER-LIFE.
THNK
BANG

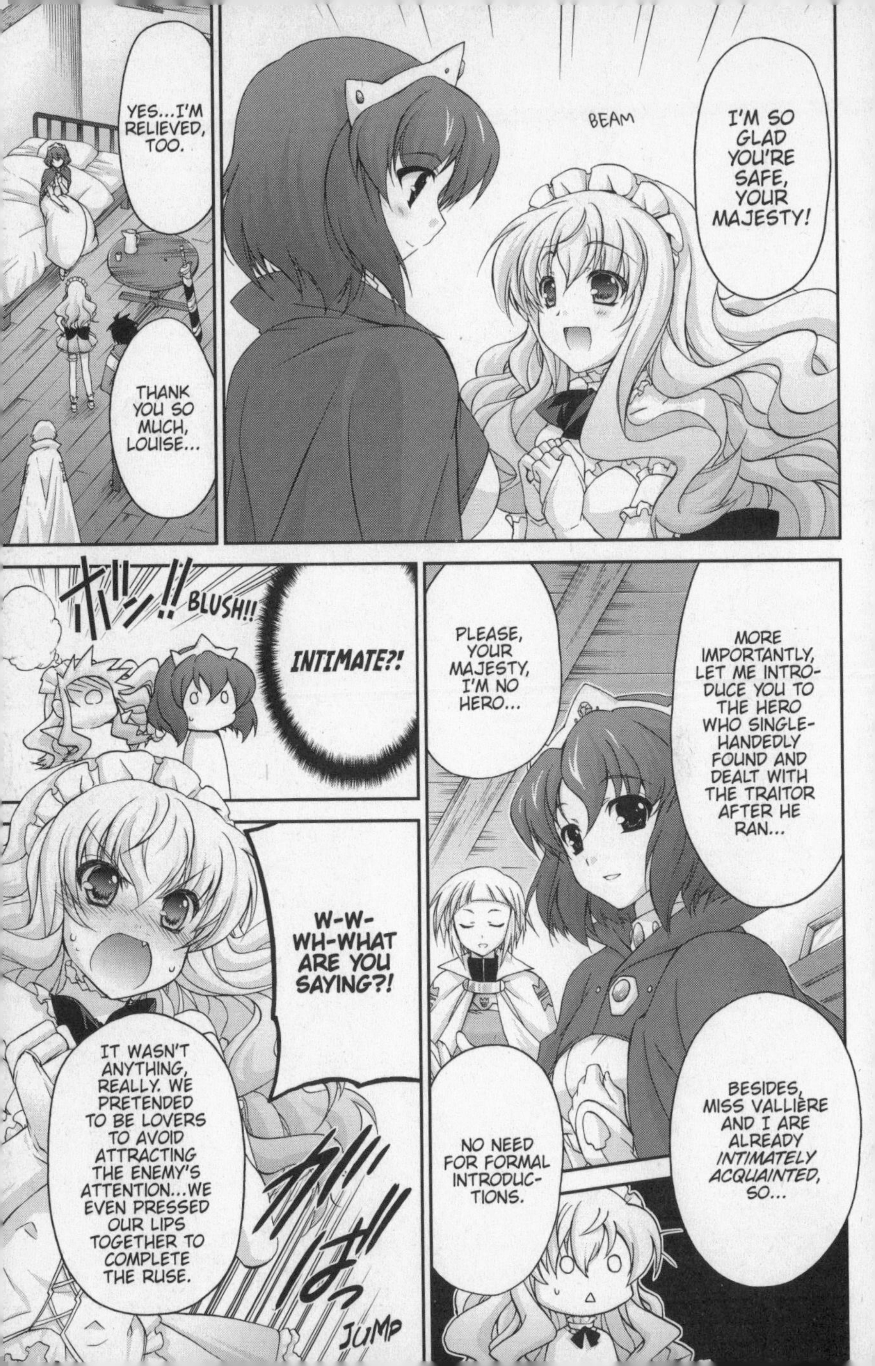
BEAM
I'M SO GLAD YOU'RE SAFE, YOUR MAJESTY!
YES...I'M RELIEVED, TOO.
THANK YOU SO MUCH, LOUISE...
MORE IMPORTANTLY, LET ME INTRODUCE YOU TO THE HERO WHO SINGLE-HANDEDLY FOUND AND DEALT WITH THE TRAITOR AFTER HE RAN...
PLEASE, YOUR MAJESTY, I'M NO HERO...
BESIDES, MISS VALLIÈRE AND I ARE ALREADY *INTIMATELY* ACQUAINTED, SO...
NO NEED FOR FORMAL INTRODUCTIONS.
BLUSH!!
INTIMATE?!
W-W-WH-WHAT ARE YOU SAYING?!
IT WASN'T ANYTHING, REALLY. WE PRETENDED TO BE LOVERS TO AVOID ATTRACTING THE ENEMY'S ATTENTION...WE EVEN PRESSED OUR LIPS TOGETHER TO COMPLETE THE RUSE.
JUMP

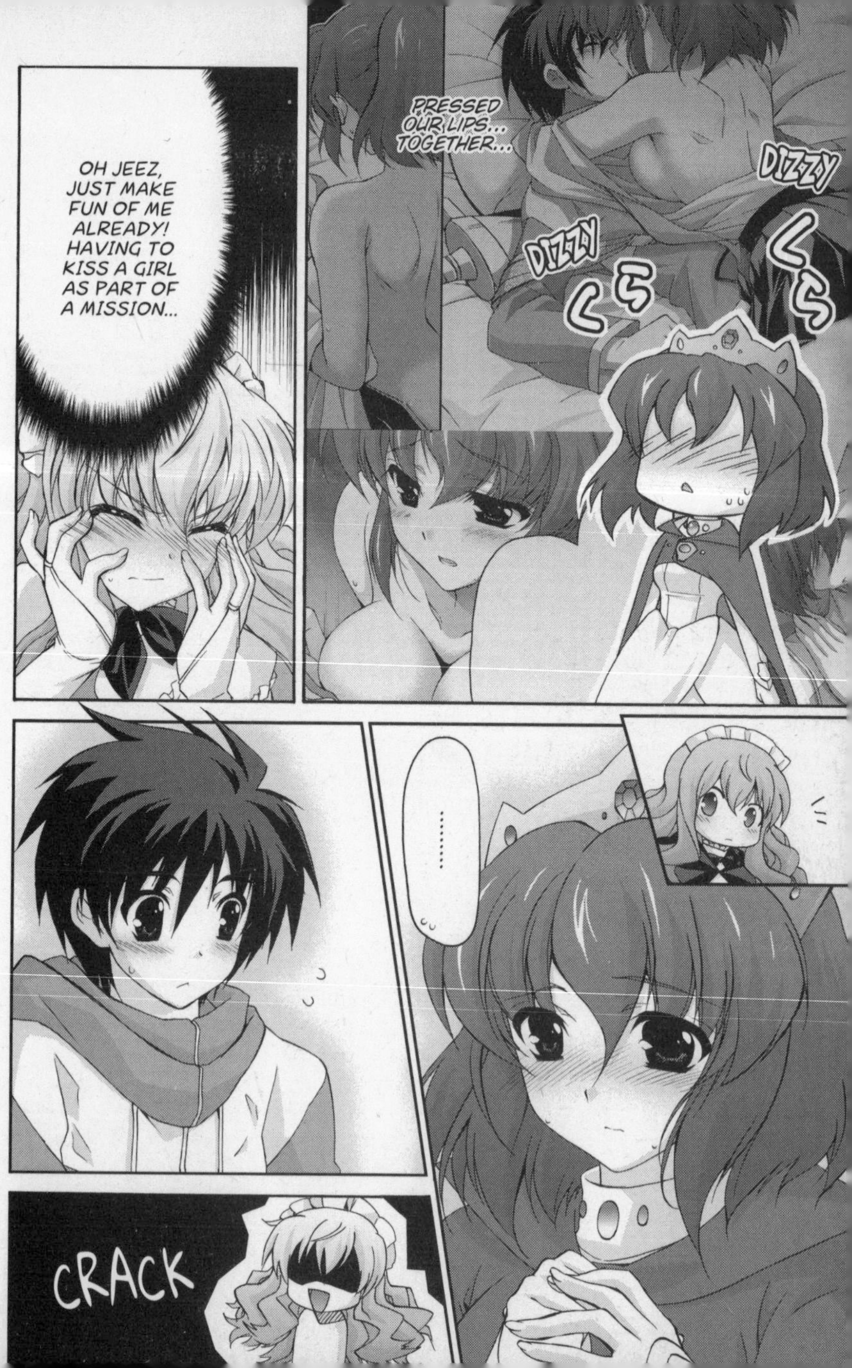
PRESSED OUR LIPS... TOGETHER...
DIZZY
くら
DIZZY
くら
OH JEEZ, JUST MAKE FUN OF ME ALREADY! HAVING TO KISS A GIRL AS PART OF A MISSION...
......
CRACK

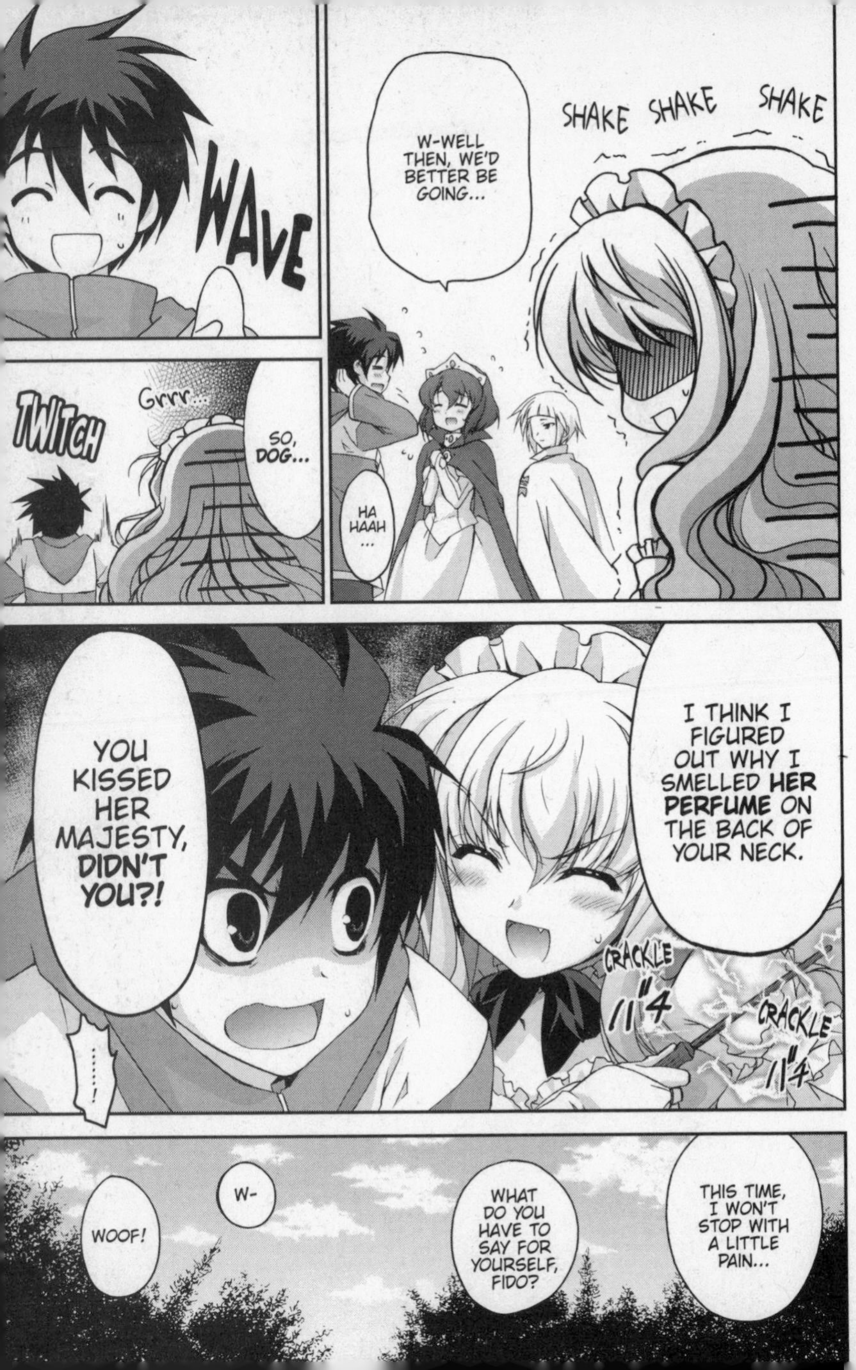
SHAKE SHAKE SHAKE
W-WELL THEN, WE'D BETTER BE GOING...
HA HAAH ...
WAVE
SO, DOG...
Grrr...
TWITCH
I THINK I FIGURED OUT WHY I SMELLED **HER PERFUME** ON THE BACK OF YOUR NECK.
CRACKLE
CRACKLE
YOU KISSED HER MAJESTY, **DIDN'T YOU?!**
......!
THIS TIME, I WON'T STOP WITH A LITTLE PAIN...
WHAT DO YOU HAVE TO SAY FOR YOURSELF, FIDO?
W-
WOOF!

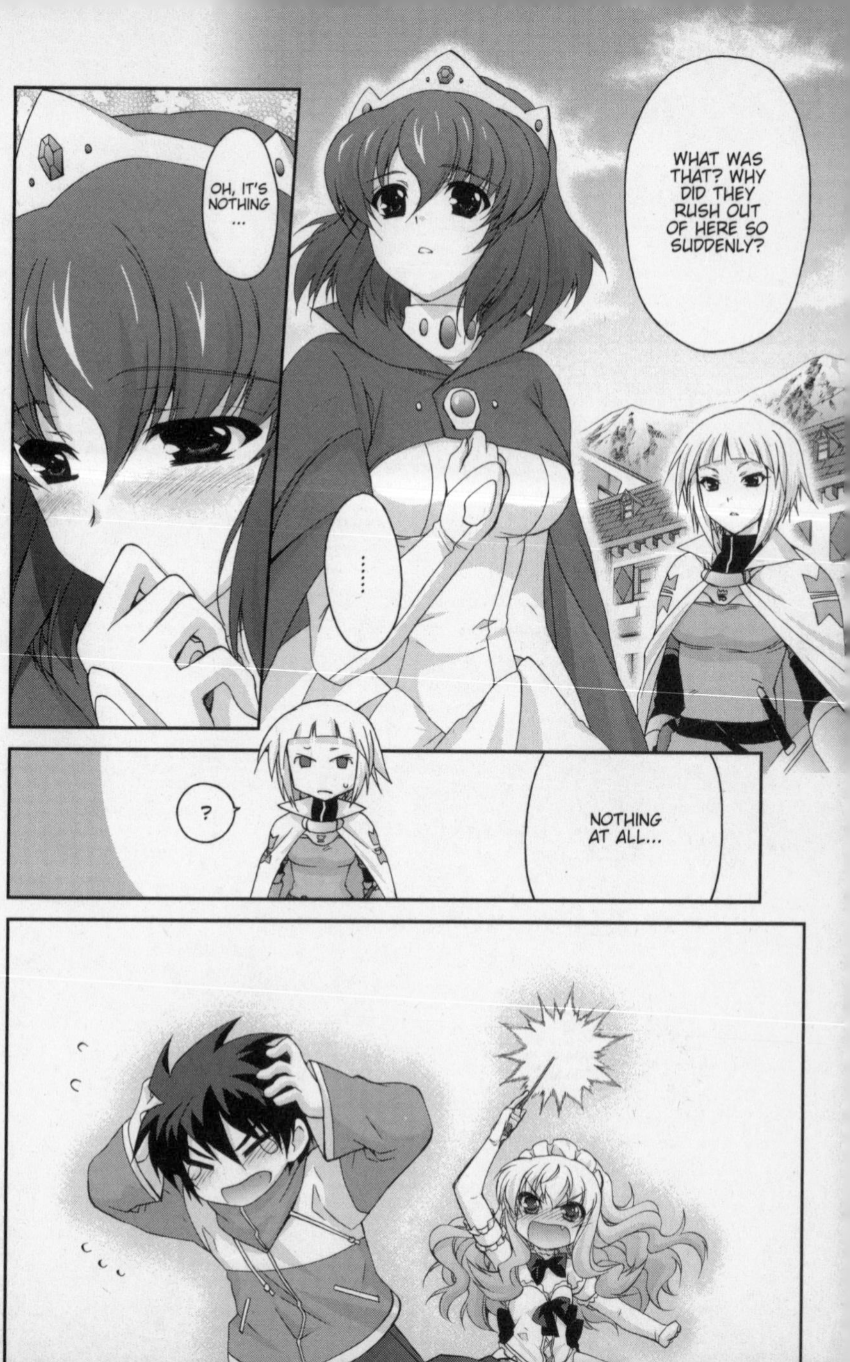
WHAT WAS THAT? WHY DID THEY RUSH OUT OF HERE SO SUDDENLY?
......
OH, IT'S NOTHING ...
NOTHING AT ALL...
?

Le Familier de Zero Chevalier

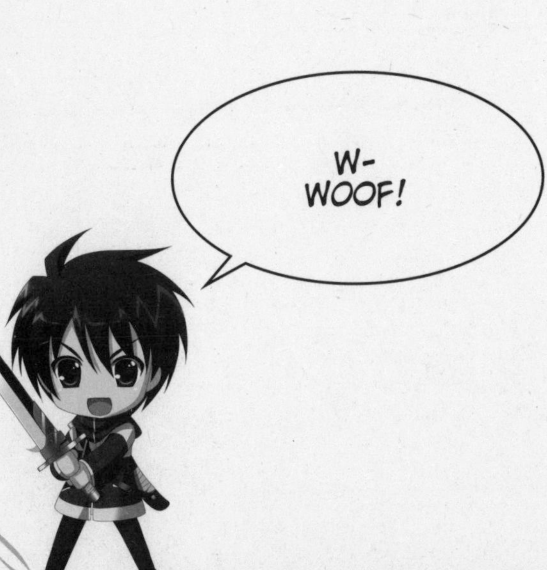

Le Familier de Zero Chevalier

ZERO'S
FAMILIAR
Chevalier

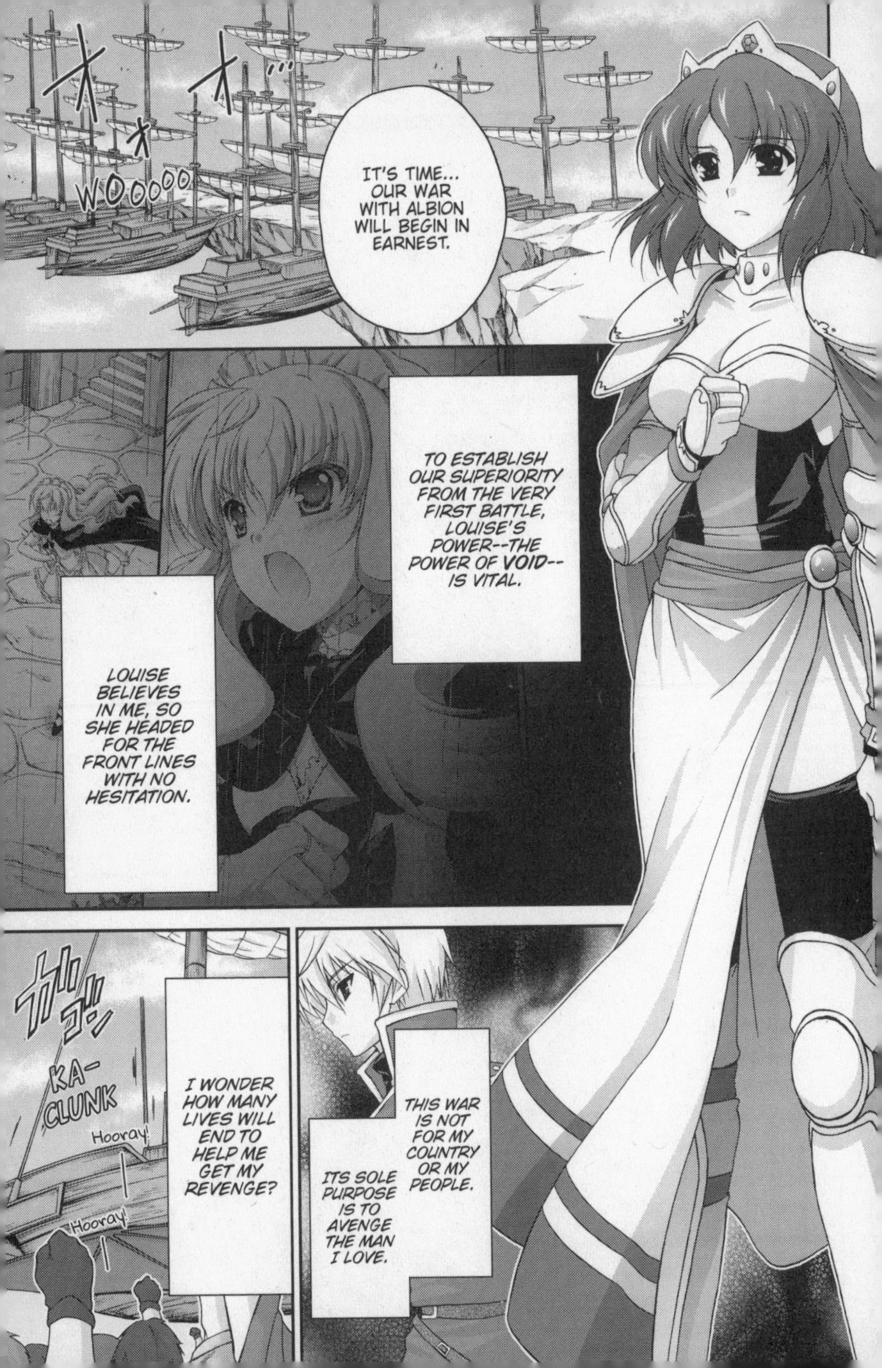

IT'S TIME... OUR WAR WITH ALBION WILL BEGIN IN EARNEST.
WOOOOO
TO ESTABLISH OUR SUPERIORITY FROM THE VERY FIRST BATTLE, LOUISE'S POWER--THE POWER OF VOID--IS VITAL.
LOUISE BELIEVES IN ME, SO SHE HEADED FOR THE FRONT LINES WITH NO HESITATION.
THIS WAR IS NOT FOR MY COUNTRY OR MY PEOPLE.
ITS SOLE PURPOSE IS TO AVENGE THE MAN I LOVE.
I WONDER HOW MANY LIVES WILL END TO HELP ME GET MY REVENGE?
KA-CLUNK
Hooray!
Hooray!

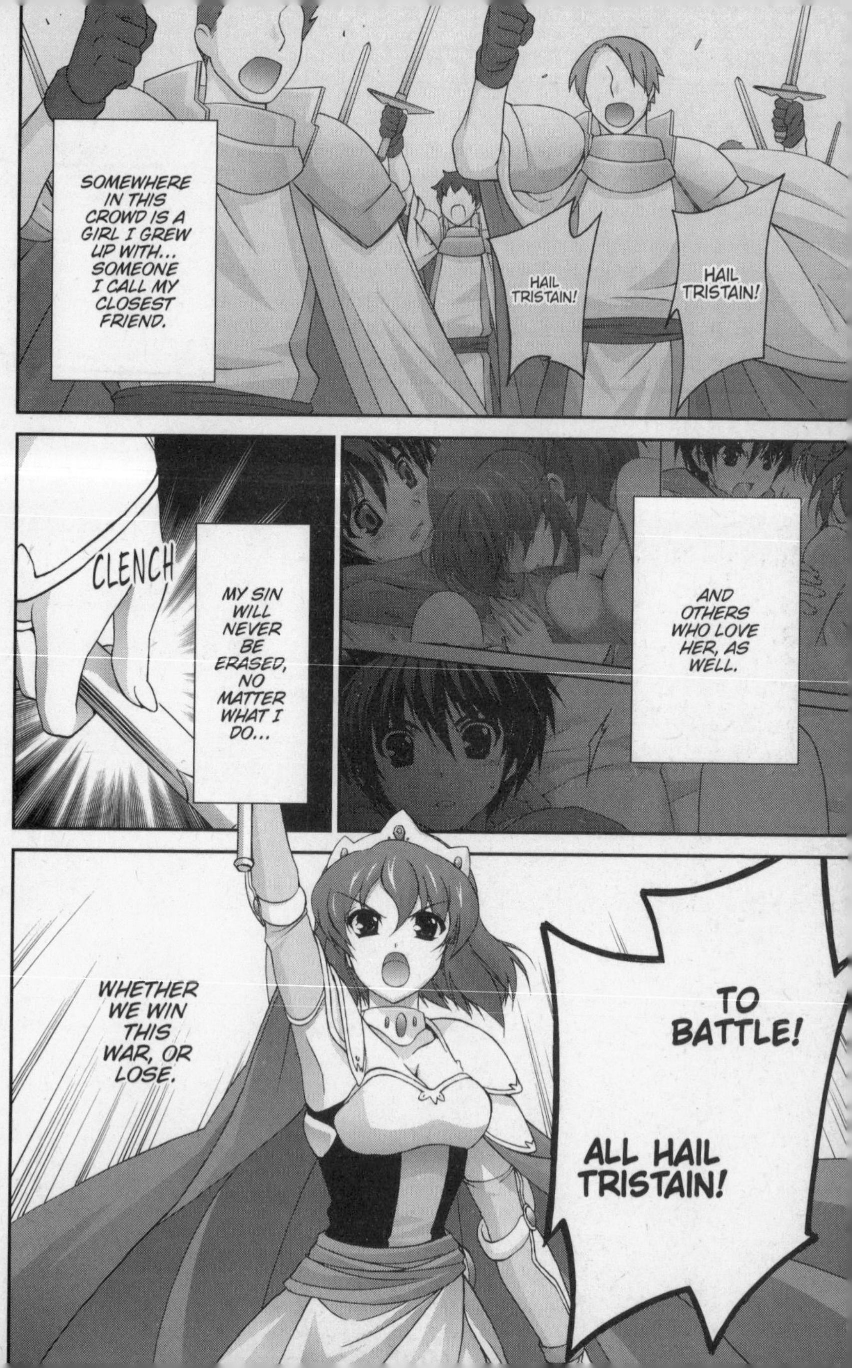
HAIL TRISTAIN!
HAIL TRISTAIN!
SOMEWHERE IN THIS CROWD IS A GIRL I GREW UP WITH... SOMEONE I CALL MY CLOSEST FRIEND.
AND OTHERS WHO LOVE HER, AS WELL.
MY SIN WILL NEVER BE ERASED, NO MATTER WHAT I DO...
CLENCH
TO BATTLE!
ALL HAIL TRISTAIN!
WHETHER WE WIN THIS WAR, OR LOSE.

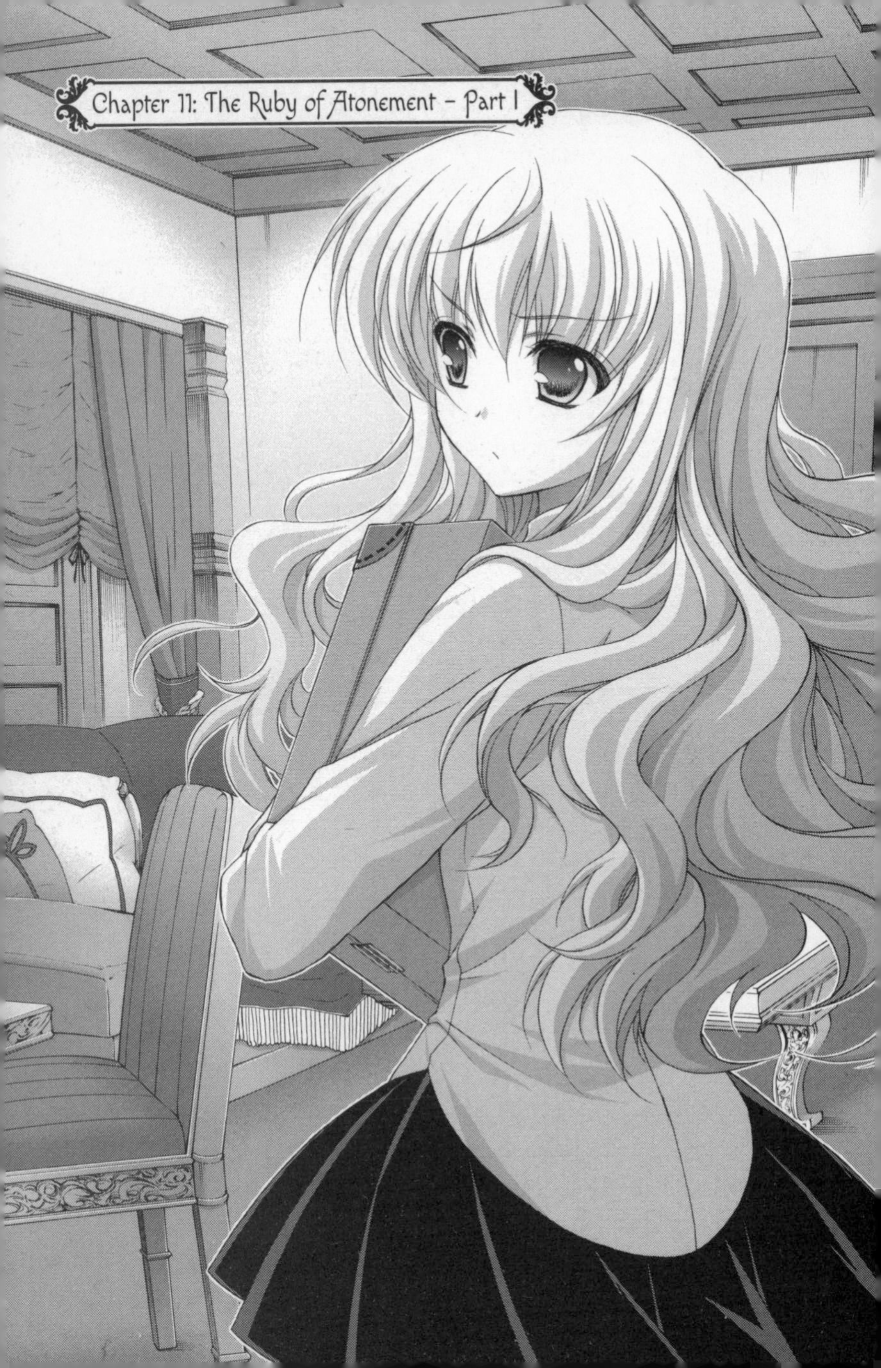
Chapter 11: The Ruby of Atonement - Part 1

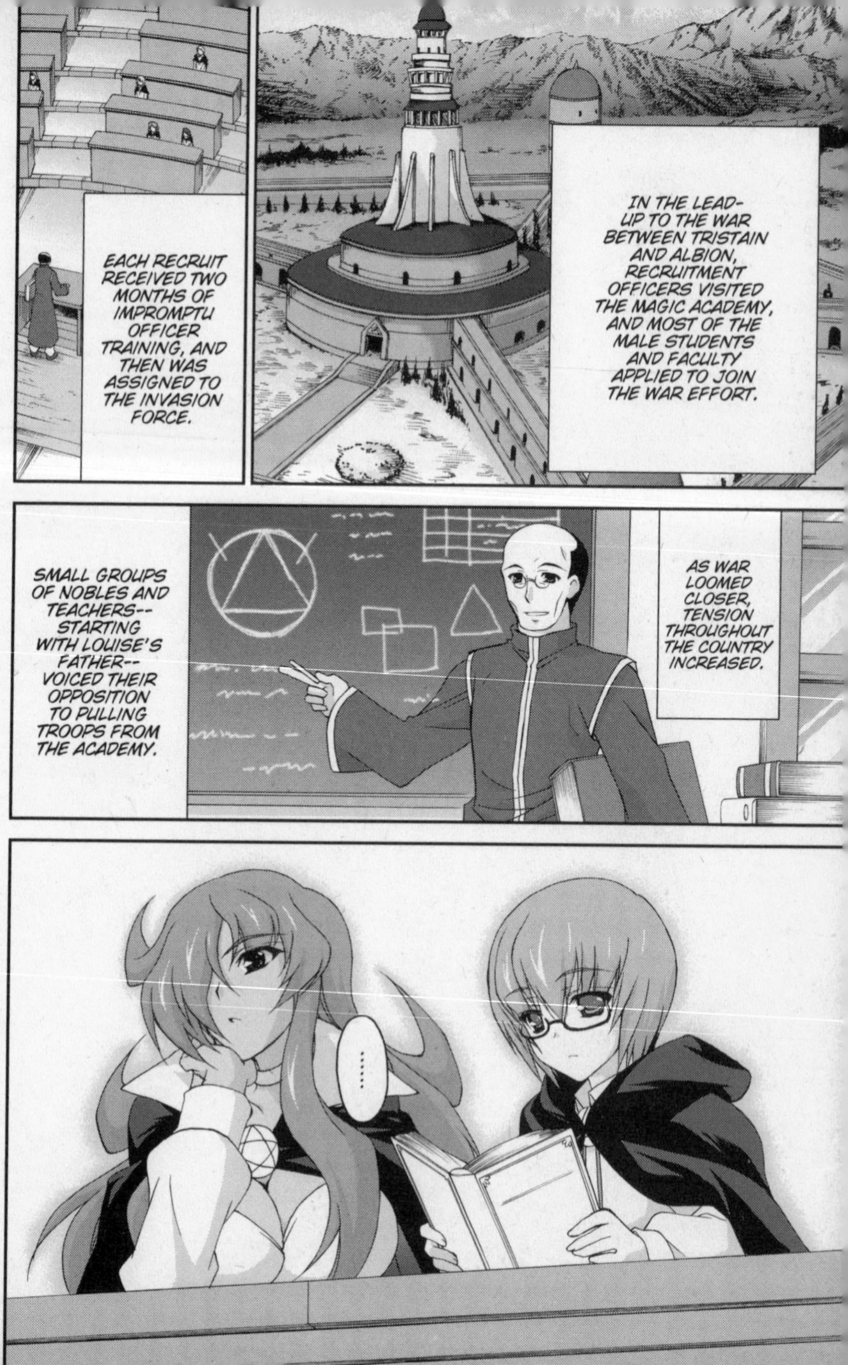
IN THE LEAD-UP TO THE WAR BETWEEN TRISTAIN AND ALBION, RECRUITMENT OFFICERS VISITED THE MAGIC ACADEMY, AND MOST OF THE MALE STUDENTS AND FACULTY APPLIED TO JOIN THE WAR EFFORT.
EACH RECRUIT RECEIVED TWO MONTHS OF IMPROMPTU OFFICER TRAINING, AND THEN WAS ASSIGNED TO THE INVASION FORCE.
AS WAR LOOMED CLOSER, TENSION THROUGHOUT THE COUNTRY INCREASED.
SMALL GROUPS OF NOBLES AND TEACHERS-- STARTING WITH LOUISE'S FATHER-- VOICED THEIR OPPOSITION TO PULLING TROOPS FROM THE ACADEMY.
......

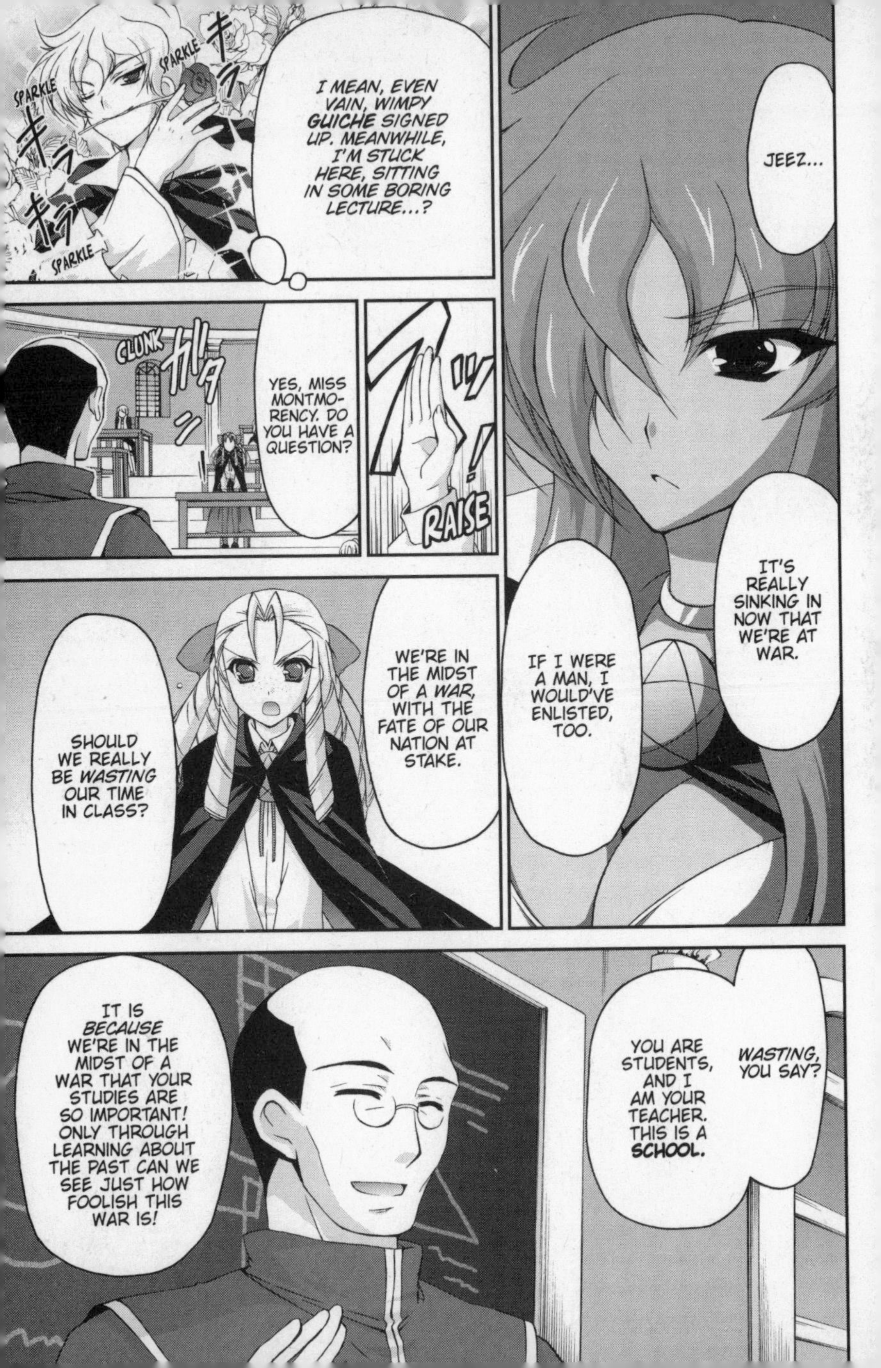
JEEZ...
IT'S REALLY SINKING IN NOW THAT WE'RE AT WAR.
IF I WERE A MAN, I WOULD'VE ENLISTED, TOO.
SPARKLE
SPARKLE
I MEAN, EVEN VAIN, WIMPY GUICHE SIGNED UP. MEANWHILE, I'M STUCK HERE, SITTING IN SOME BORING LECTURE...?
SPARKLE
RAISE
CLUNK
YES, MISS MONTMORENCY. DO YOU HAVE A QUESTION?
WE'RE IN THE MIDST OF A WAR, WITH THE FATE OF OUR NATION AT STAKE.
SHOULD WE REALLY BE WASTING OUR TIME IN CLASS?
WASTING, YOU SAY?
YOU ARE STUDENTS, AND I AM YOUR TEACHER. THIS IS A SCHOOL.
IT IS BECAUSE WE'RE IN THE MIDST OF A WAR THAT YOUR STUDIES ARE SO IMPORTANT! ONLY THROUGH LEARNING ABOUT THE PAST CAN WE SEE JUST HOW FOOLISH THIS WAR IS!

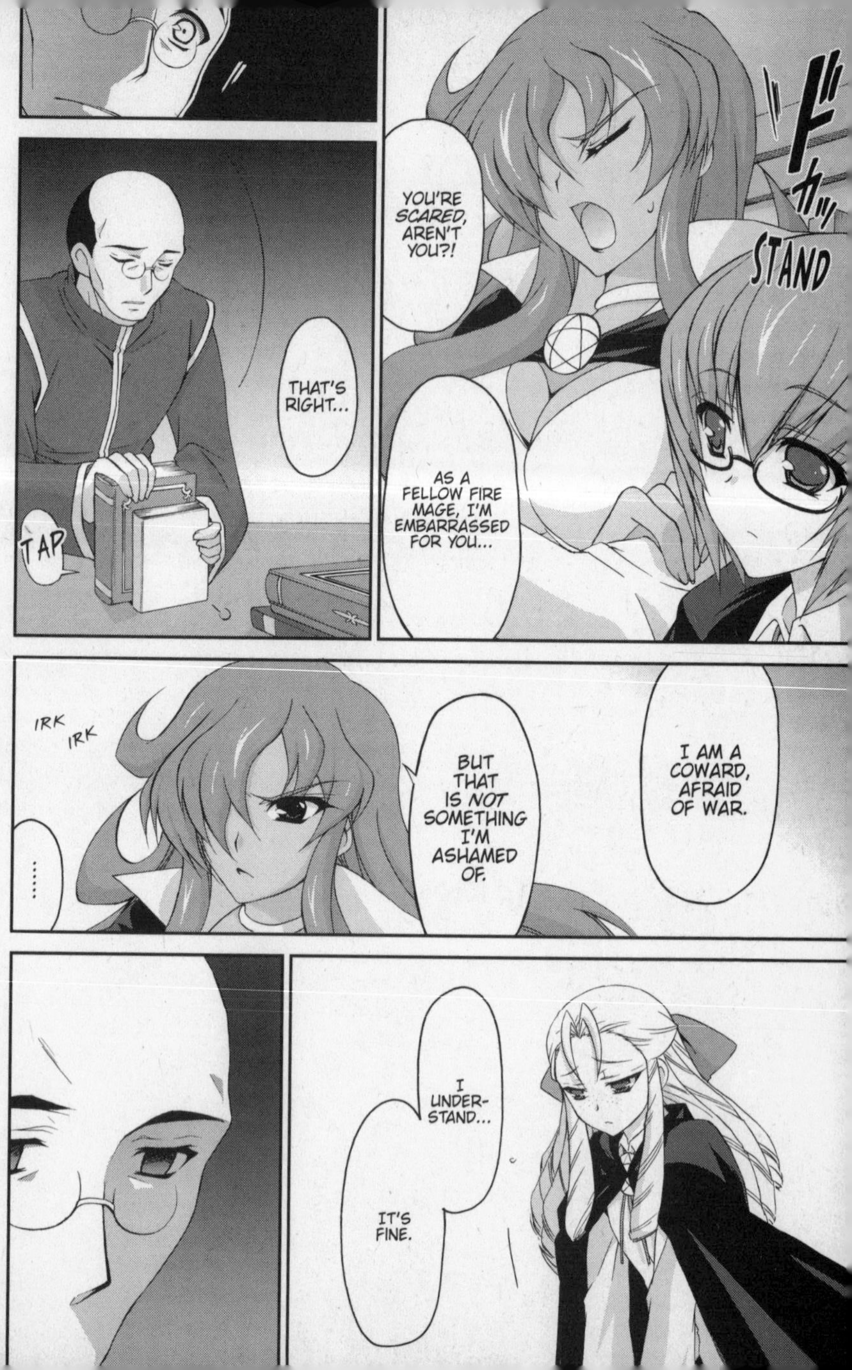
ドカッ
STAND
YOU'RE SCARED, AREN'T YOU?!
AS A FELLOW FIRE MAGE, I'M EMBARRASSED FOR YOU...
THAT'S RIGHT...
TAP
I AM A COWARD, AFRAID OF WAR.
BUT THAT IS *NOT* SOMETHING I'M ASHAMED OF.
IRK IRK
......
I UNDER-STAND...
IT'S FINE.

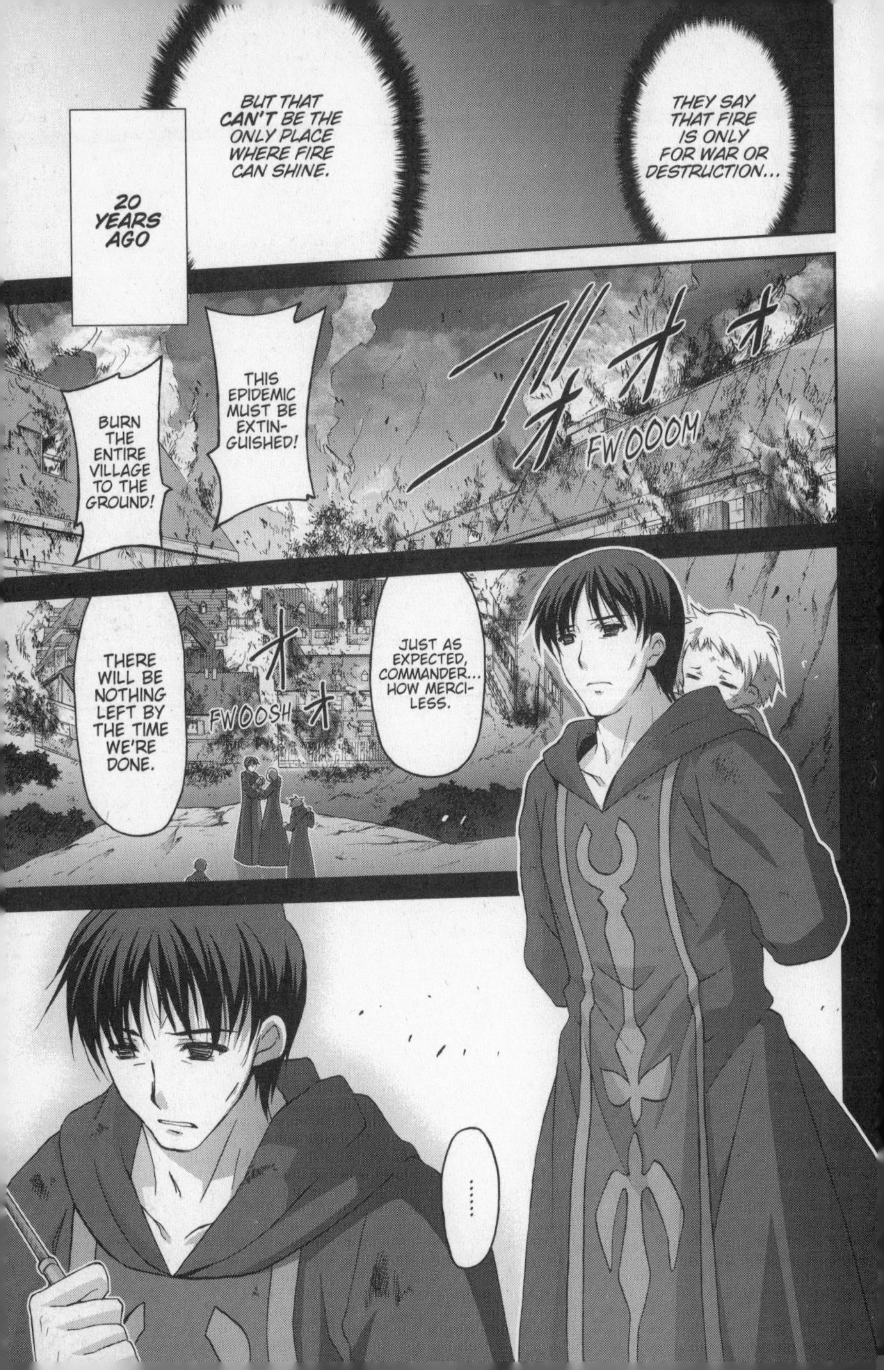
THEY SAY THAT FIRE IS ONLY FOR WAR OR DESTRUCTION...
BUT THAT CAN'T BE THE ONLY PLACE WHERE FIRE CAN SHINE.
20 YEARS AGO
FWOOOM
THIS EPIDEMIC MUST BE EXTIN-GUISHED!
BURN THE ENTIRE VILLAGE TO THE GROUND!
JUST AS EXPECTED, COMMANDER... HOW MERCI-LESS.
FWOOSH
THERE WILL BE NOTHING LEFT BY THE TIME WE'RE DONE.
......

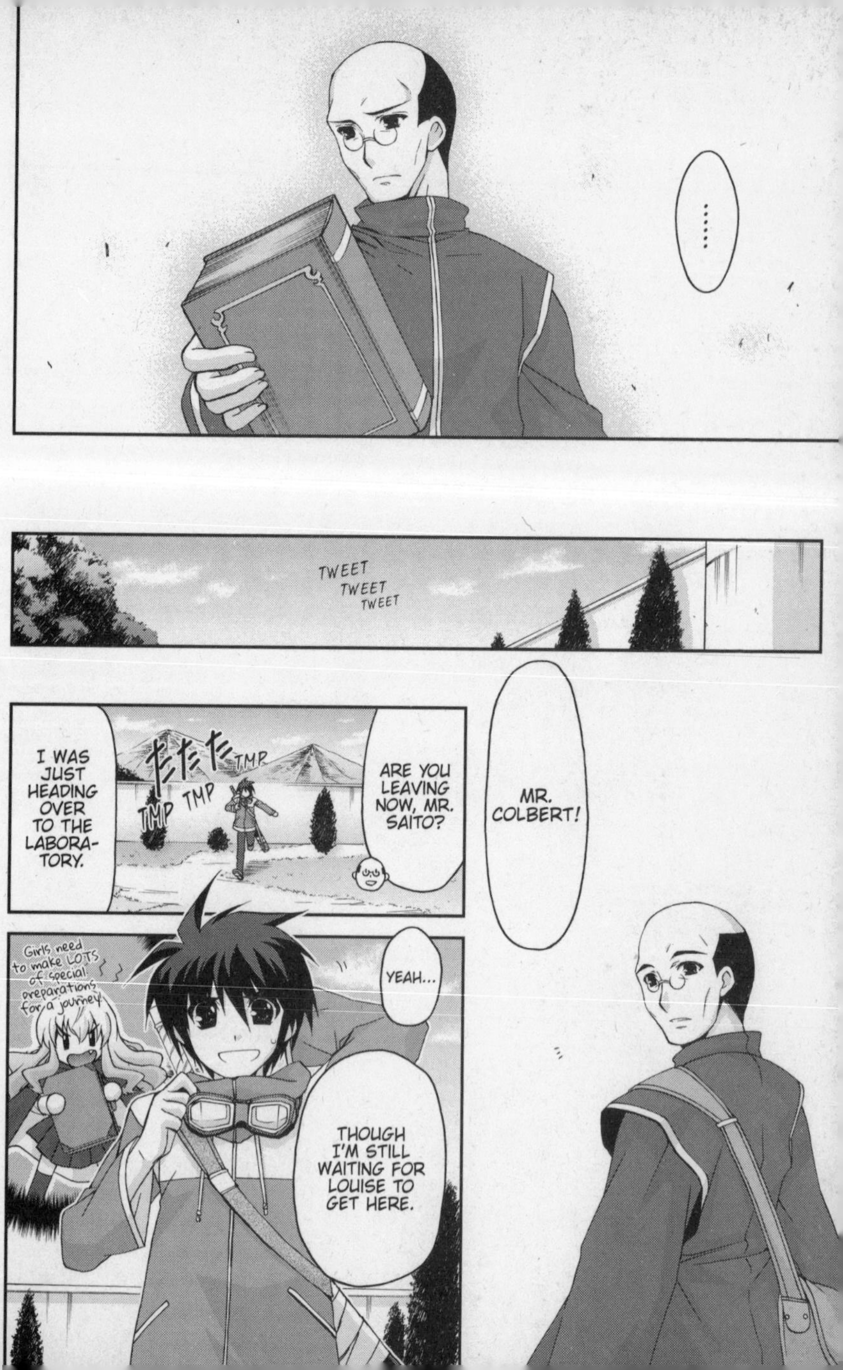
……
TWEET
TWEET
TWEET
MR. COLBERT!
ARE YOU LEAVING NOW, MR. SAITO?
TMP
TMP TMP
I WAS JUST HEADING OVER TO THE LABORA-TORY.
YEAH...
THOUGH I'M STILL WAITING FOR LOUISE TO GET HERE.
Girls need to make LOTS of special preparations for a journey!

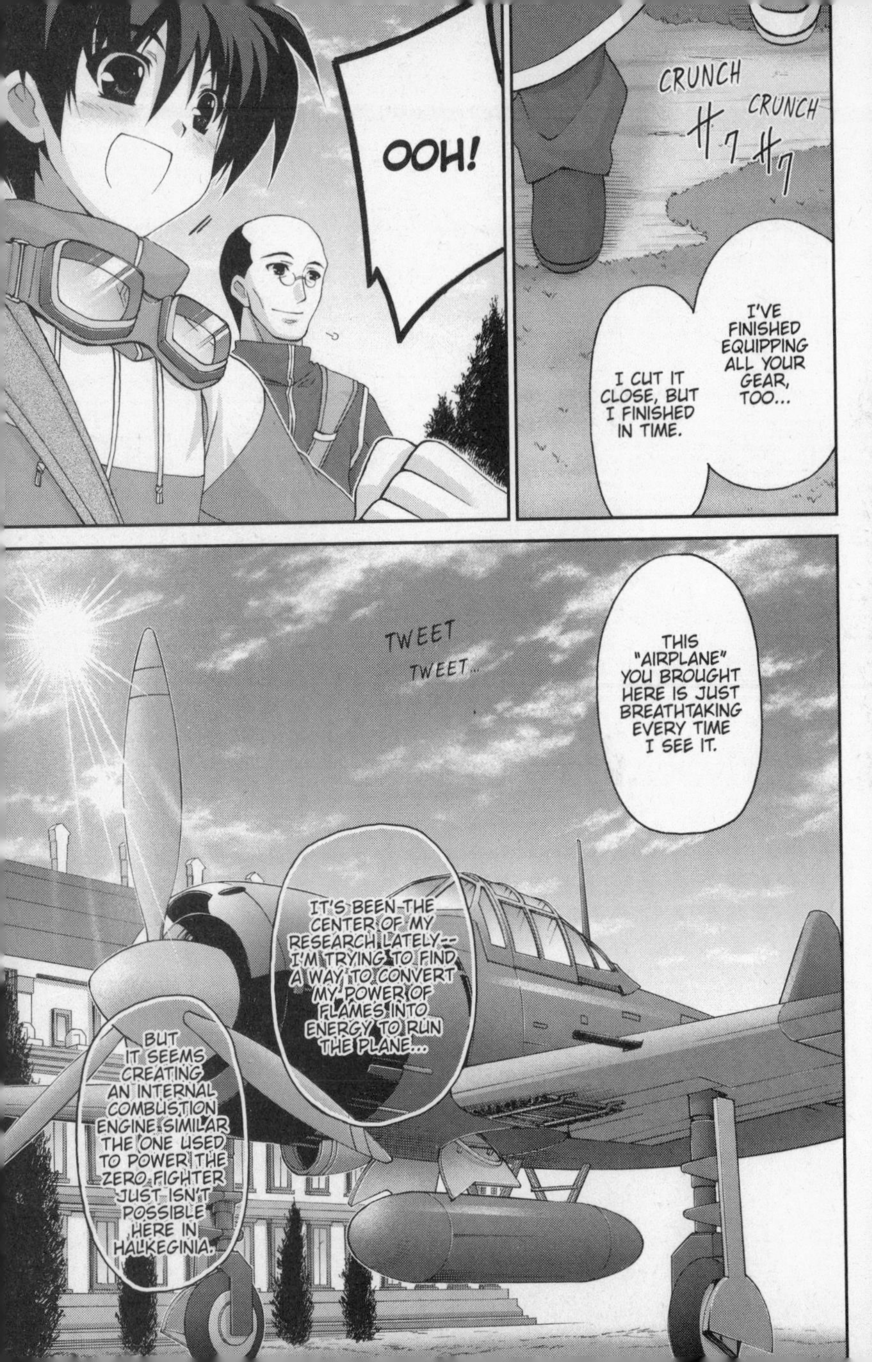
CRUNCH
CRUNCH
サク サク
I'VE FINISHED EQUIPPING ALL YOUR GEAR, TOO...
I CUT IT CLOSE, BUT I FINISHED IN TIME.
OOH!
TWEET
TWEET...
THIS "AIRPLANE" YOU BROUGHT HERE IS JUST BREATHTAKING EVERY TIME I SEE IT.
IT'S BEEN THE CENTER OF MY RESEARCH LATELY-- I'M TRYING TO FIND A WAY TO CONVERT MY POWER OF FLAMES INTO ENERGY TO RUN THE PLANE...
BUT IT SEEMS CREATING AN INTERNAL COMBUSTION ENGINE SIMILAR THE ONE USED TO POWER THE ZERO FIGHTER JUST ISN'T POSSIBLE HERE IN HALKEGINIA.

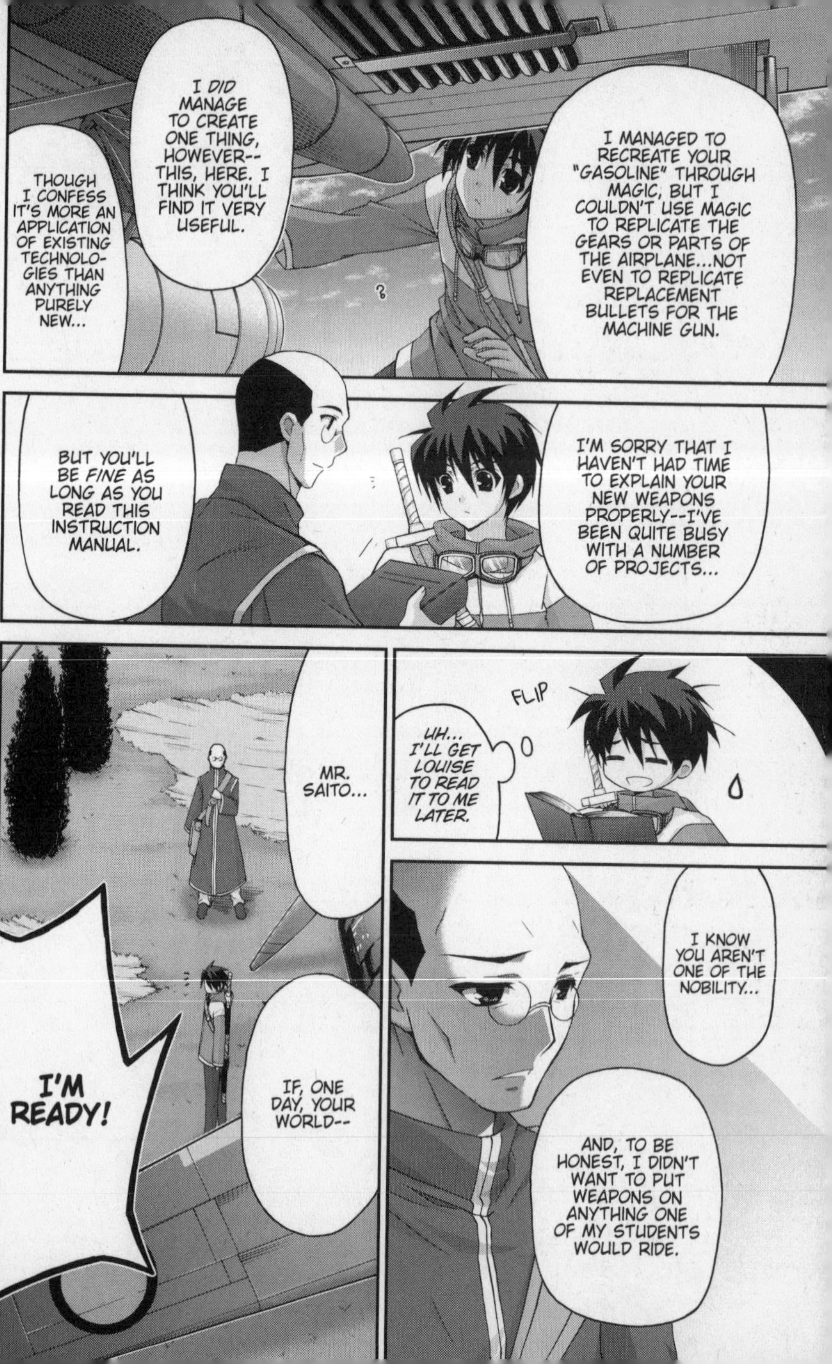
I MANAGED TO RECREATE YOUR "GASOLINE" THROUGH MAGIC, BUT I COULDN'T USE MAGIC TO REPLICATE THE GEARS OR PARTS OF THE AIRPLANE...NOT EVEN TO REPLICATE REPLACEMENT BULLETS FOR THE MACHINE GUN.
I *DID* MANAGE TO CREATE ONE THING, HOWEVER-- THIS, HERE. I THINK YOU'LL FIND IT VERY USEFUL.
THOUGH I CONFESS IT'S MORE AN APPLICATION OF EXISTING TECHNOLOGIES THAN ANYTHING PURELY NEW...
I'M SORRY THAT I HAVEN'T HAD TIME TO EXPLAIN YOUR NEW WEAPONS PROPERLY--I'VE BEEN QUITE BUSY WITH A NUMBER OF PROJECTS...
BUT YOU'LL BE *FINE* AS LONG AS YOU READ THIS INSTRUCTION MANUAL.
FLIP
UH... I'LL GET LOUISE TO READ IT TO ME LATER.
I KNOW YOU AREN'T ONE OF THE NOBILITY...
AND, TO BE HONEST, I DIDN'T WANT TO PUT WEAPONS ON ANYTHING ONE OF MY STUDENTS WOULD RIDE.
MR. SAITO...
IF, ONE DAY, YOUR WORLD--
I'M READY!

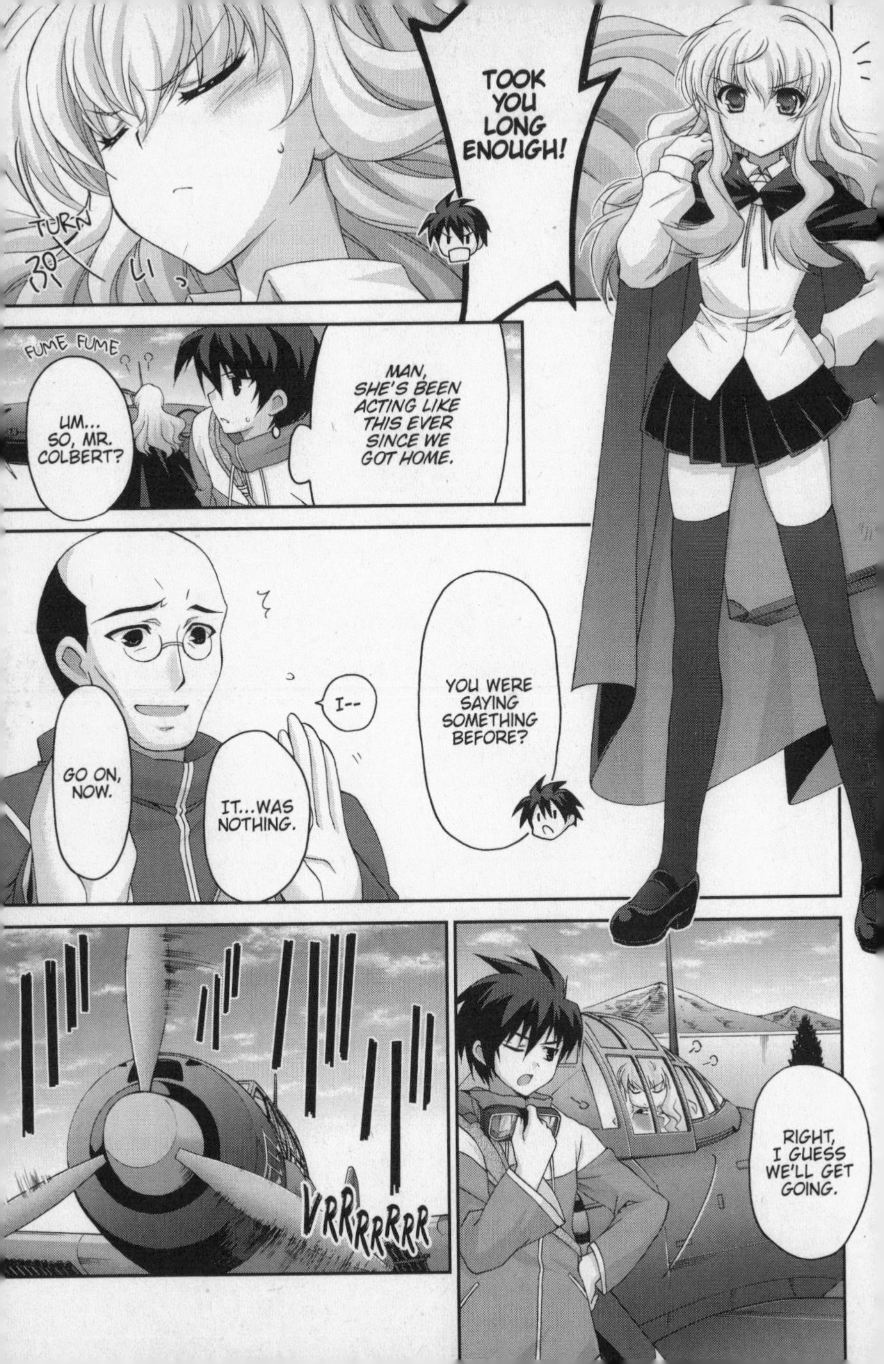
TOOK YOU LONG ENOUGH!
TURN
MAN, SHE'S BEEN ACTING LIKE THIS EVER SINCE WE GOT HOME.
UM... SO, MR. COLBERT?
FUME FUME
YOU WERE SAYING SOMETHING BEFORE?
I--
IT...WAS NOTHING.
GO ON, NOW.
RIGHT, I GUESS WE'LL GET GOING.
VRRRRRRR

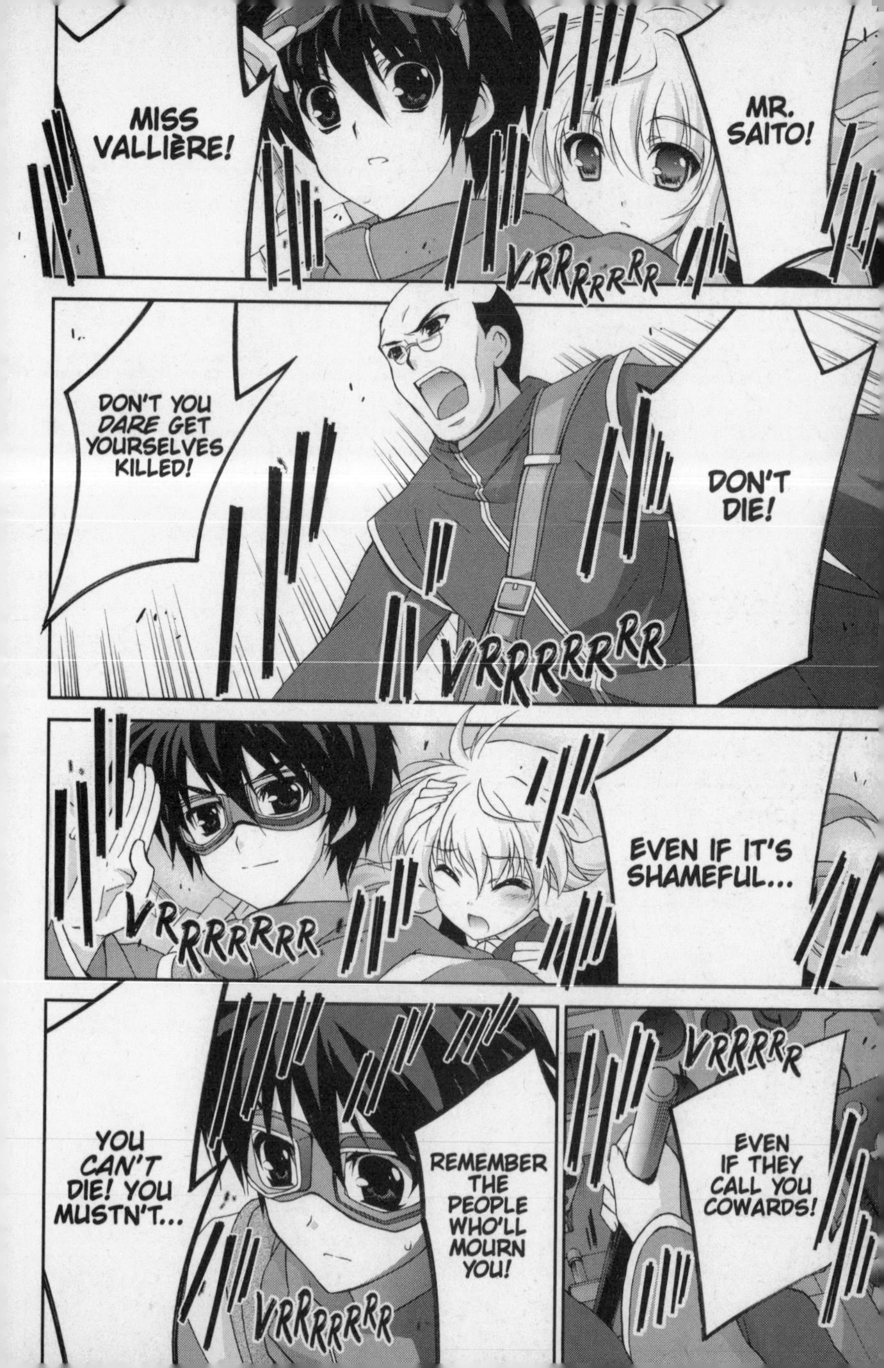
MR. SAITO!
MISS VALLIÈRE!
VRRRRRRR
DON'T DIE!
DON'T YOU DARE GET YOURSELVES KILLED!
VRRRRRRR
EVEN IF IT'S SHAMEFUL...
VRRRRRRR
VRRRRR
EVEN IF THEY CALL YOU COWARDS!
REMEMBER THE PEOPLE WHO'LL MOURN YOU!
YOU CAN'T DIE! YOU MUSTN'T...
VRRRRRRR

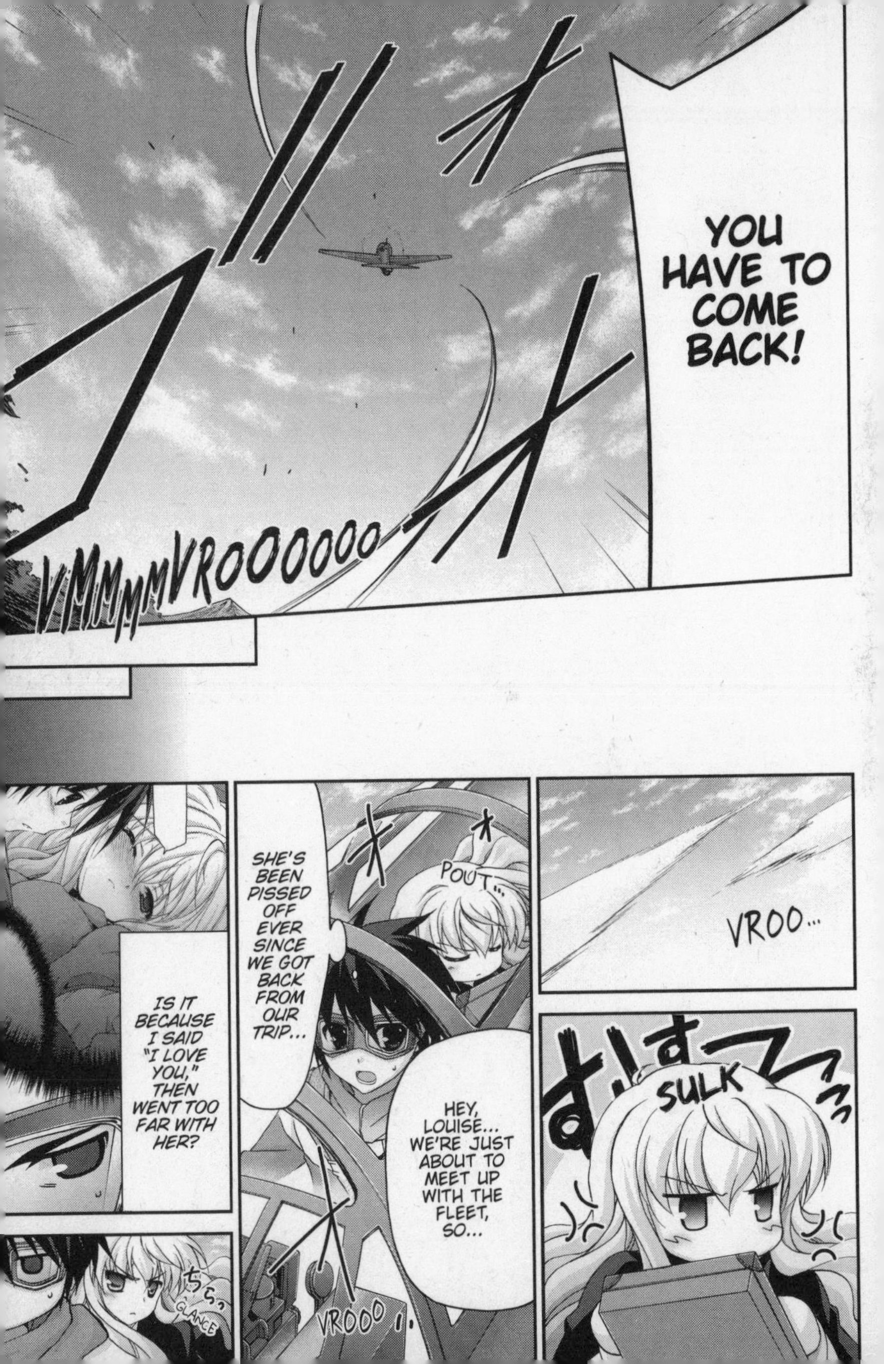

YOU HAVE TO COME BACK!
VMMMMMVROOOOOOO
VROO...
SULK
POUT...
SHE'S BEEN PISSED OFF EVER SINCE WE GOT BACK FROM OUR TRIP...
HEY, LOUISE... WE'RE JUST ABOUT TO MEET UP WITH THE FLEET, SO...
VROOO
IS IT BECAUSE I SAID "I LOVE YOU," THEN WENT TOO FAR WITH HER?
GLANCE

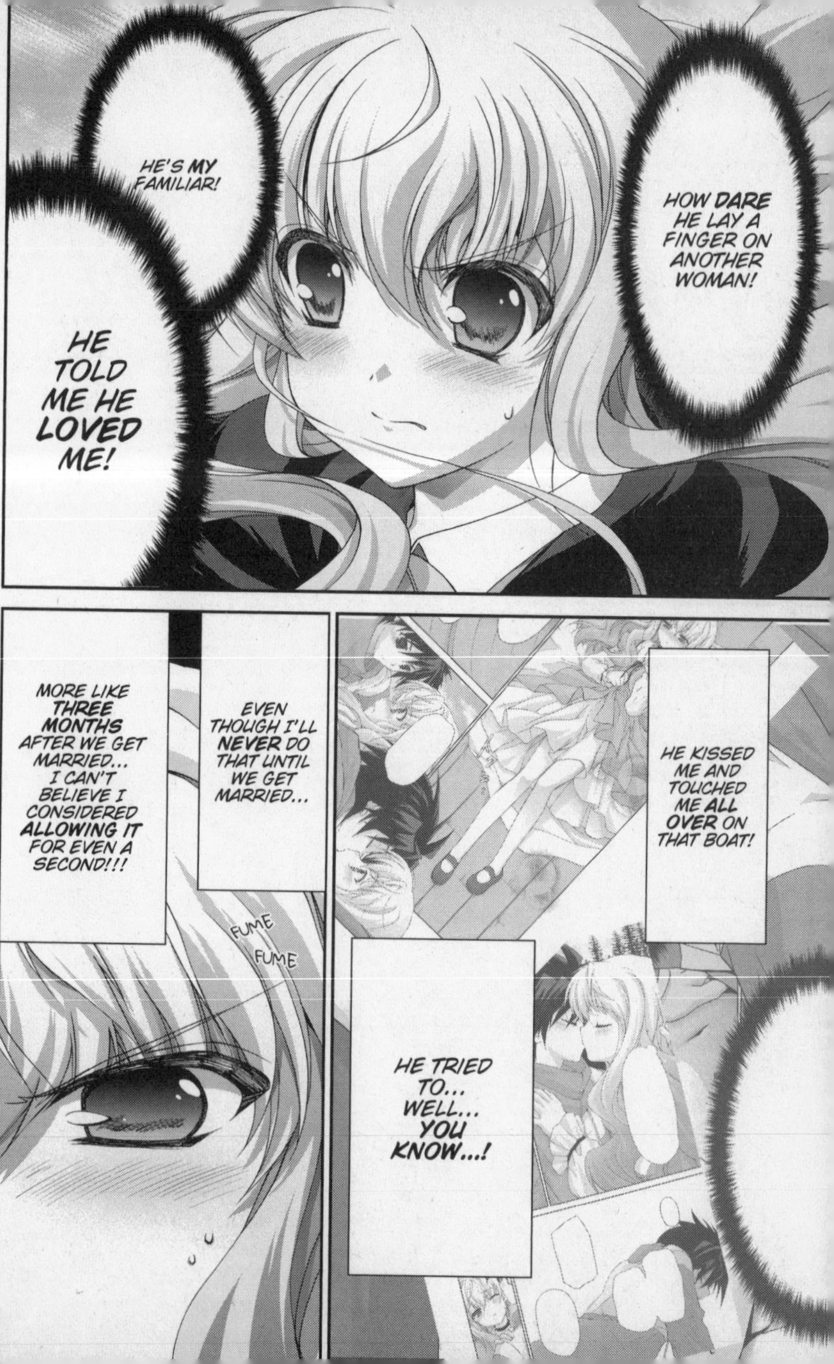
HOW DARE HE LAY A FINGER ON ANOTHER WOMAN!
HE'S MY FAMILIAR!
HE TOLD ME HE LOVED ME!
HE KISSED ME AND TOUCHED ME ALL OVER ON THAT BOAT!
HE TRIED TO... WELL... YOU KNOW...!
EVEN THOUGH I'LL NEVER DO THAT UNTIL WE GET MARRIED...
MORE LIKE THREE MONTHS AFTER WE GET MARRIED... I CAN'T BELIEVE I CONSIDERED ALLOWING IT FOR EVEN A SECOND!!!
FUME
FUME

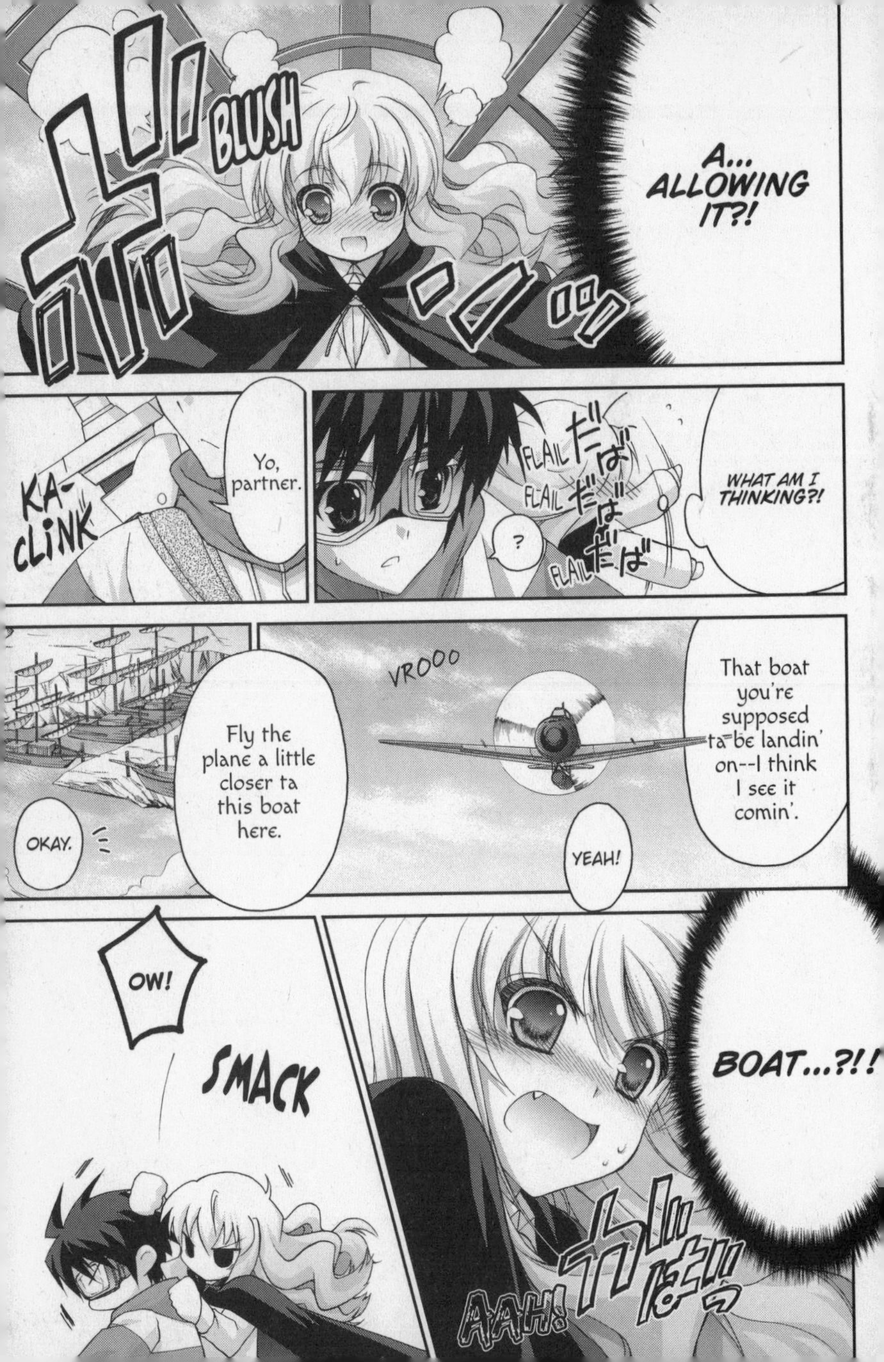
A... ALLOWING IT?!
BLUSH
WHAT AM I THINKING?!
FLAIL だば
FLAIL だば
FLAIL だば
?
Yo, partner.
KA-CLINK
That boat you're supposed ta be landin' on--I think I see it comin'.
YEAH!
VROOO
Fly the plane a little closer ta this boat here.
OKAY.
BOAT...?!!
AAH!
OW!
SMACK

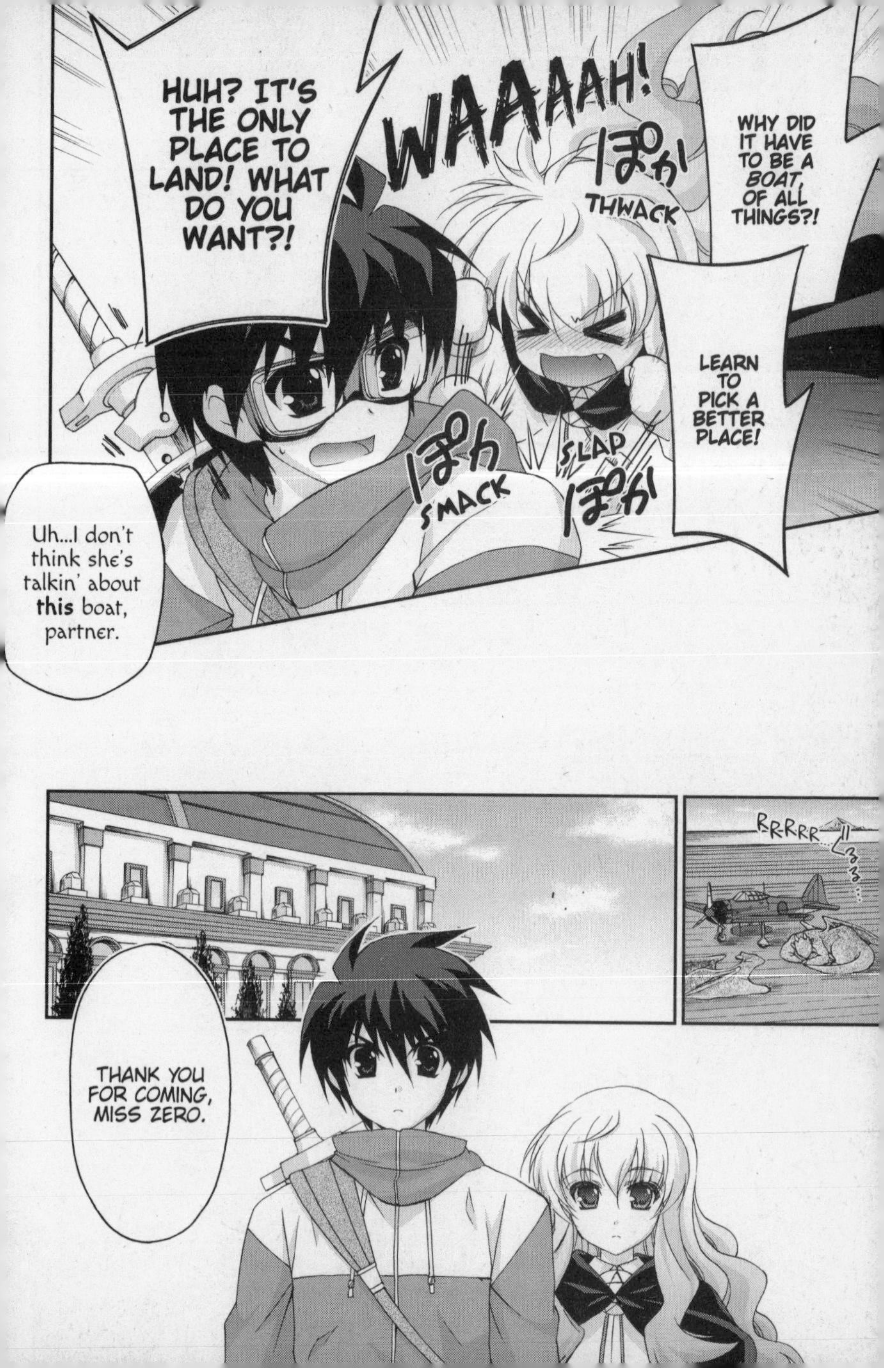
WHY DID IT HAVE TO BE A BOAT, OF ALL THINGS?!
LEARN TO PICK A BETTER PLACE!
WAAAAH!
ぽか THWACK
SLAP ぽか
ぽか SMACK
HUH? IT'S THE ONLY PLACE TO LAND! WHAT DO YOU WANT?!
Uh...I don't think she's talkin' about **this** boat, partner.
RRRRR くるる...
THANK YOU FOR COMING, MISS ZERO.

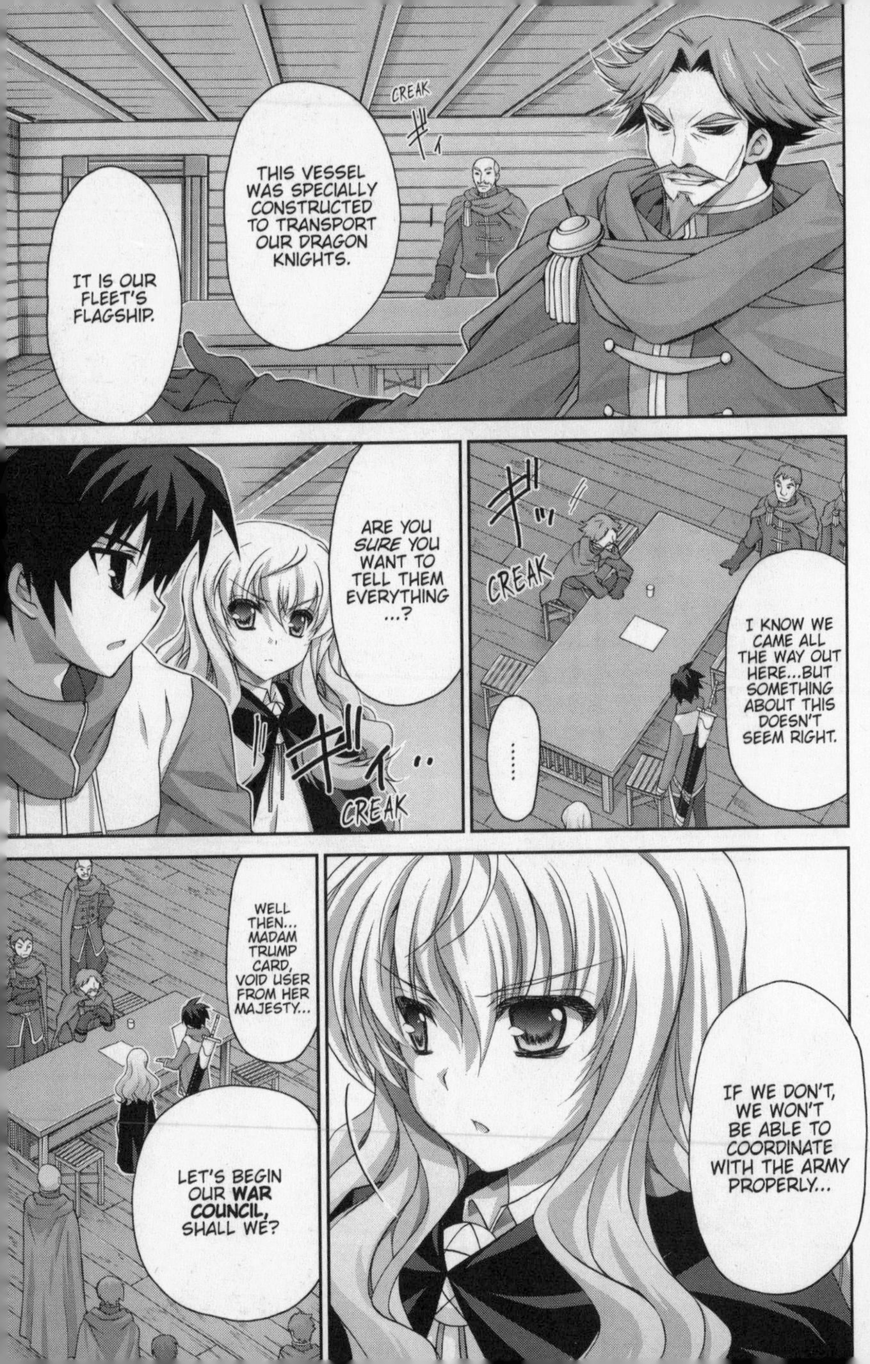
CREAK
THIS VESSEL WAS SPECIALLY CONSTRUCTED TO TRANSPORT OUR DRAGON KNIGHTS.
IT IS OUR FLEET'S FLAGSHIP.
CREAK
I KNOW WE CAME ALL THE WAY OUT HERE...BUT SOMETHING ABOUT THIS DOESN'T SEEM RIGHT.
......
ARE YOU *SURE* YOU WANT TO TELL THEM EVERYTHING ...?
CREAK
IF WE DON'T, WE WON'T BE ABLE TO COORDINATE WITH THE ARMY PROPERLY...
WELL THEN... MADAM TRUMP CARD, VOID USER FROM HER MAJESTY...
LET'S BEGIN OUR **WAR COUNCIL,** SHALL WE?

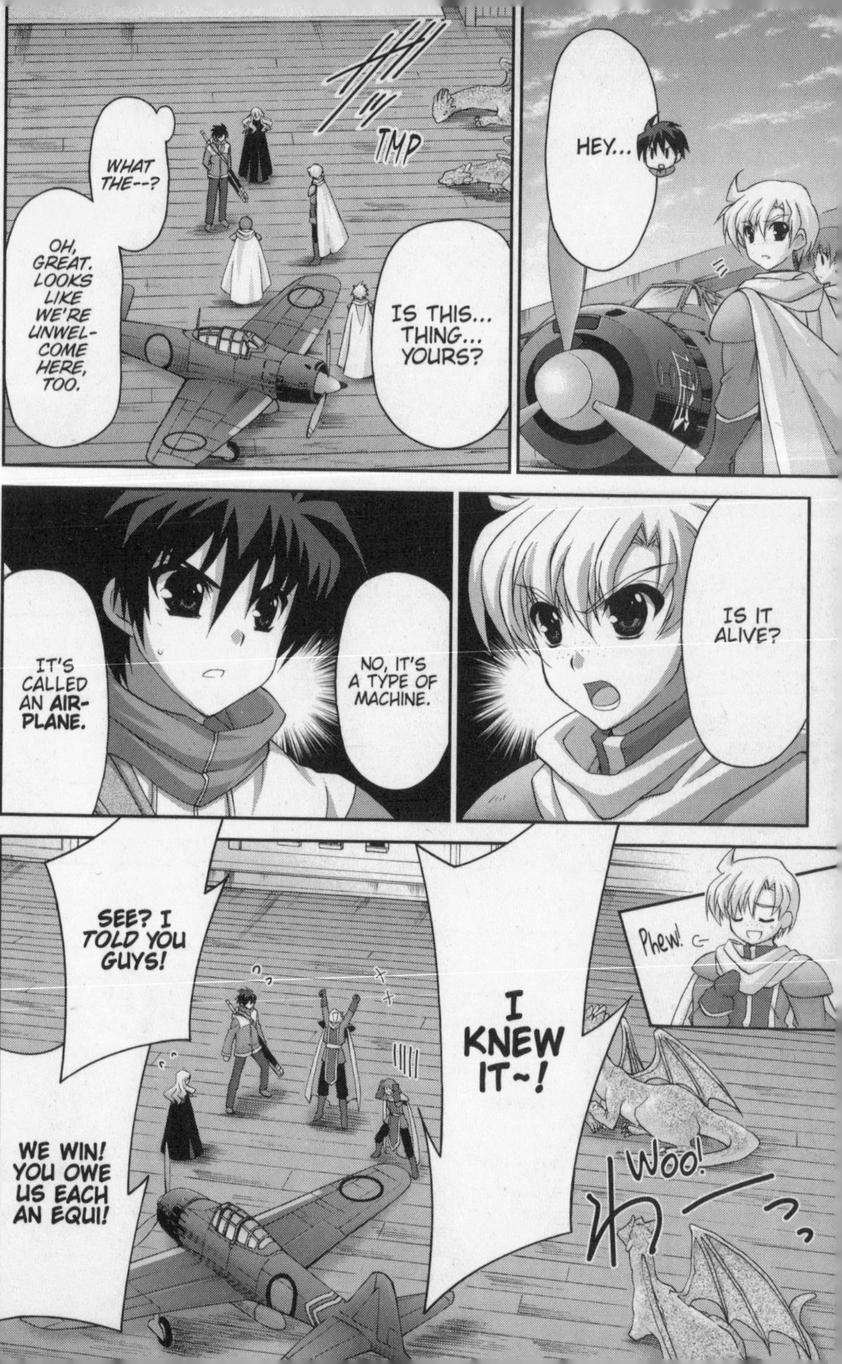
HEY...
IS THIS... THING... YOURS?
TMP
WHAT THE--?
OH, GREAT. LOOKS LIKE WE'RE UNWELCOME HERE, TOO.
IS IT ALIVE?
NO, IT'S A TYPE OF MACHINE.
IT'S CALLED AN AIRPLANE.
Phew!
I KNEW IT~!
Woo!
SEE? I TOLD YOU GUYS!
WE WIN! YOU OWE US EACH AN EQUI!

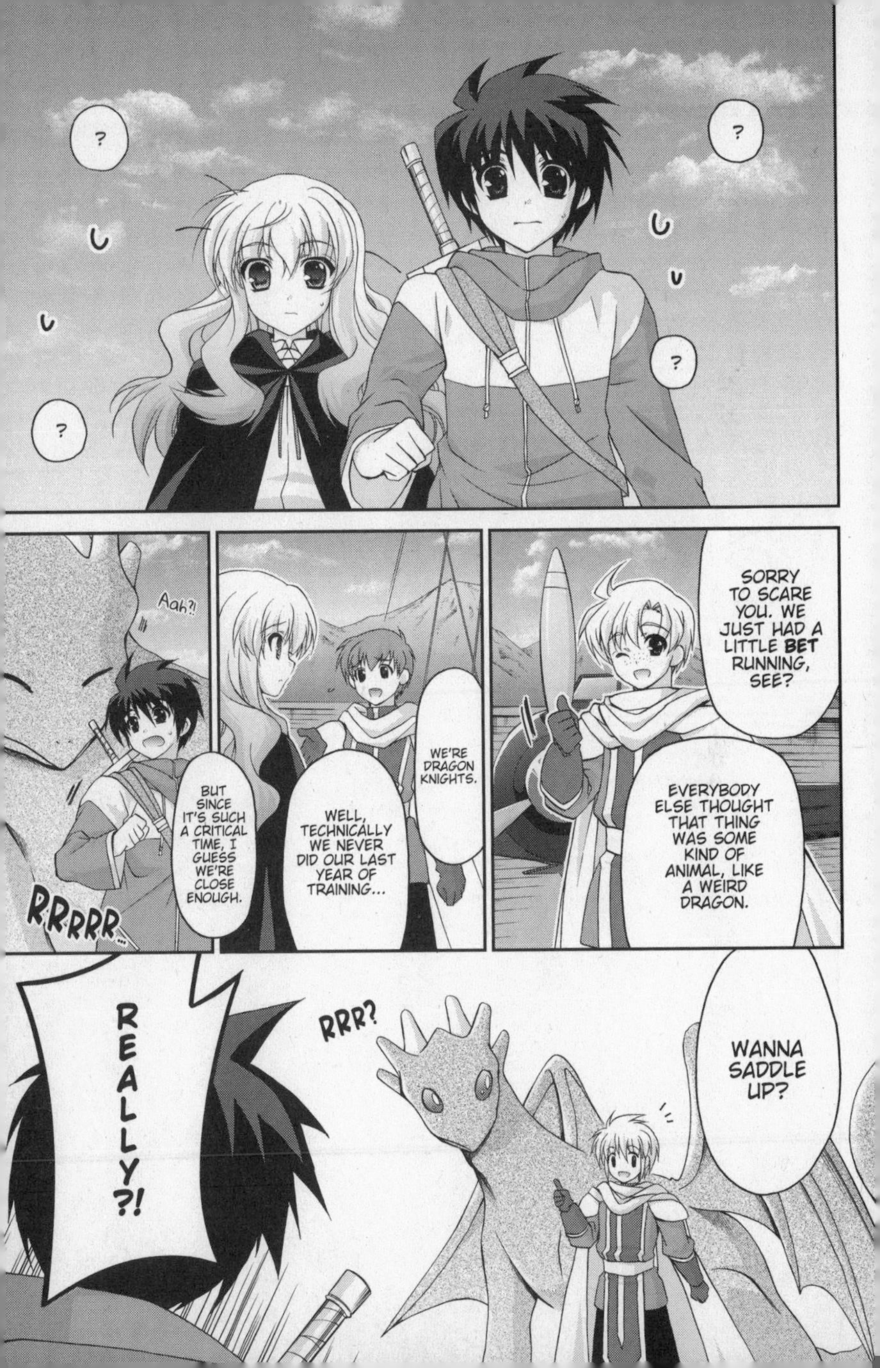
?
?
?
?
SORRY TO SCARE YOU. WE JUST HAD A LITTLE **BET** RUNNING, SEE?
EVERYBODY ELSE THOUGHT THAT THING WAS SOME KIND OF ANIMAL, LIKE A WEIRD DRAGON.
WE'RE DRAGON KNIGHTS.
WELL, TECHNICALLY WE NEVER DID OUR LAST YEAR OF TRAINING...
BUT SINCE IT'S SUCH A CRITICAL TIME, I GUESS WE'RE CLOSE ENOUGH.
Aah?!
RRRRR...
WANNA SADDLE UP?
RRR?
REALLY?!

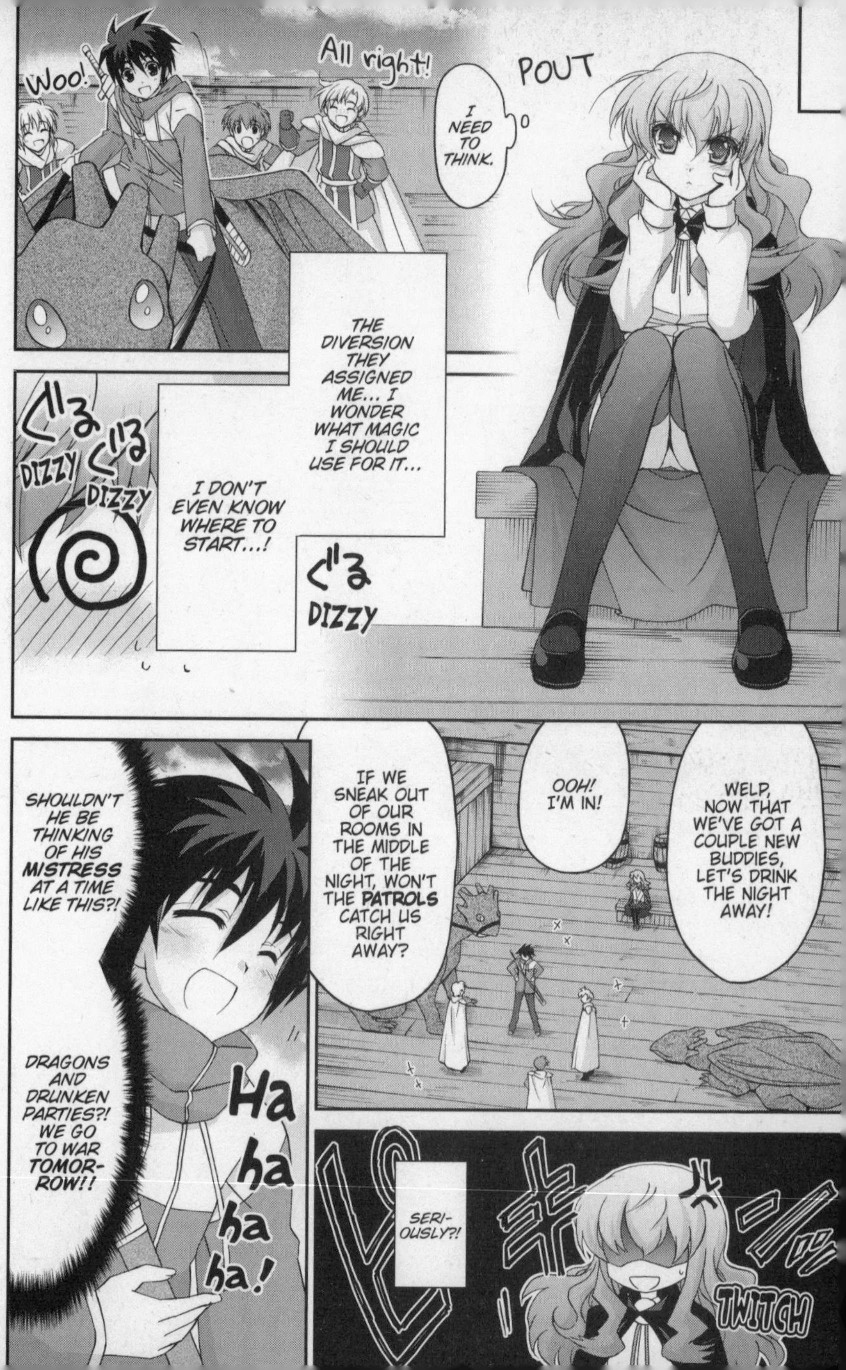
POUT
I NEED TO THINK.
THE DIVERSION THEY ASSIGNED ME... I WONDER WHAT MAGIC I SHOULD USE FOR IT...
I DON'T EVEN KNOW WHERE TO START...!
ぐる DIZZY
All right!
Woo!
ぐる DIZZY
ぐる DIZZY
WELP, NOW THAT WE'VE GOT A COUPLE NEW BUDDIES, LET'S DRINK THE NIGHT AWAY!
OOH! I'M IN!
IF WE SNEAK OUT OF OUR ROOMS IN THE MIDDLE OF THE NIGHT, WON'T THE **PATROLS** CATCH US RIGHT AWAY?
SERI-OUSLY?!
TWITCH
SHOULDN'T HE BE THINKING OF HIS **MISTRESS** AT A TIME LIKE THIS?!
DRAGONS AND DRUNKEN PARTIES?! WE GO TO WAR **TOMOR-ROW!!**
Ha ha ha ha!

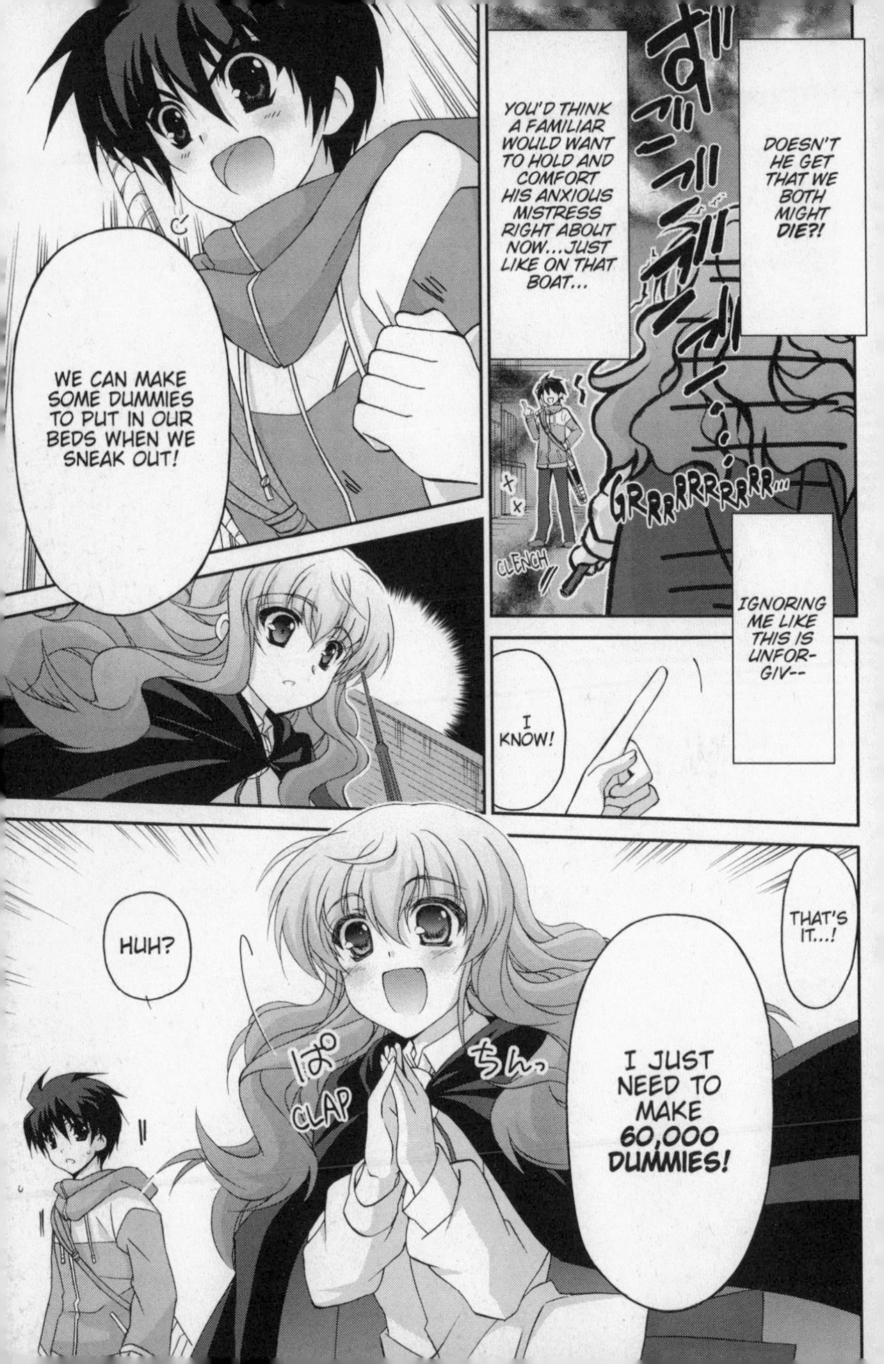

DOESN'T HE GET THAT WE BOTH MIGHT DIE?!
YOU'D THINK A FAMILIAR WOULD WANT TO HOLD AND COMFORT HIS ANXIOUS MISTRESS RIGHT ABOUT NOW... JUST LIKE ON THAT BOAT...
GRRRRRRRRRR...
CLENCH
IGNORING ME LIKE THIS IS UNFORGIV--
WE CAN MAKE SOME DUMMIES TO PUT IN OUR BEDS WHEN WE SNEAK OUT!
I KNOW!
THAT'S IT...!
I JUST NEED TO MAKE 60,000 DUMMIES!
ぱ
ちんっ
CLAP
HUH?

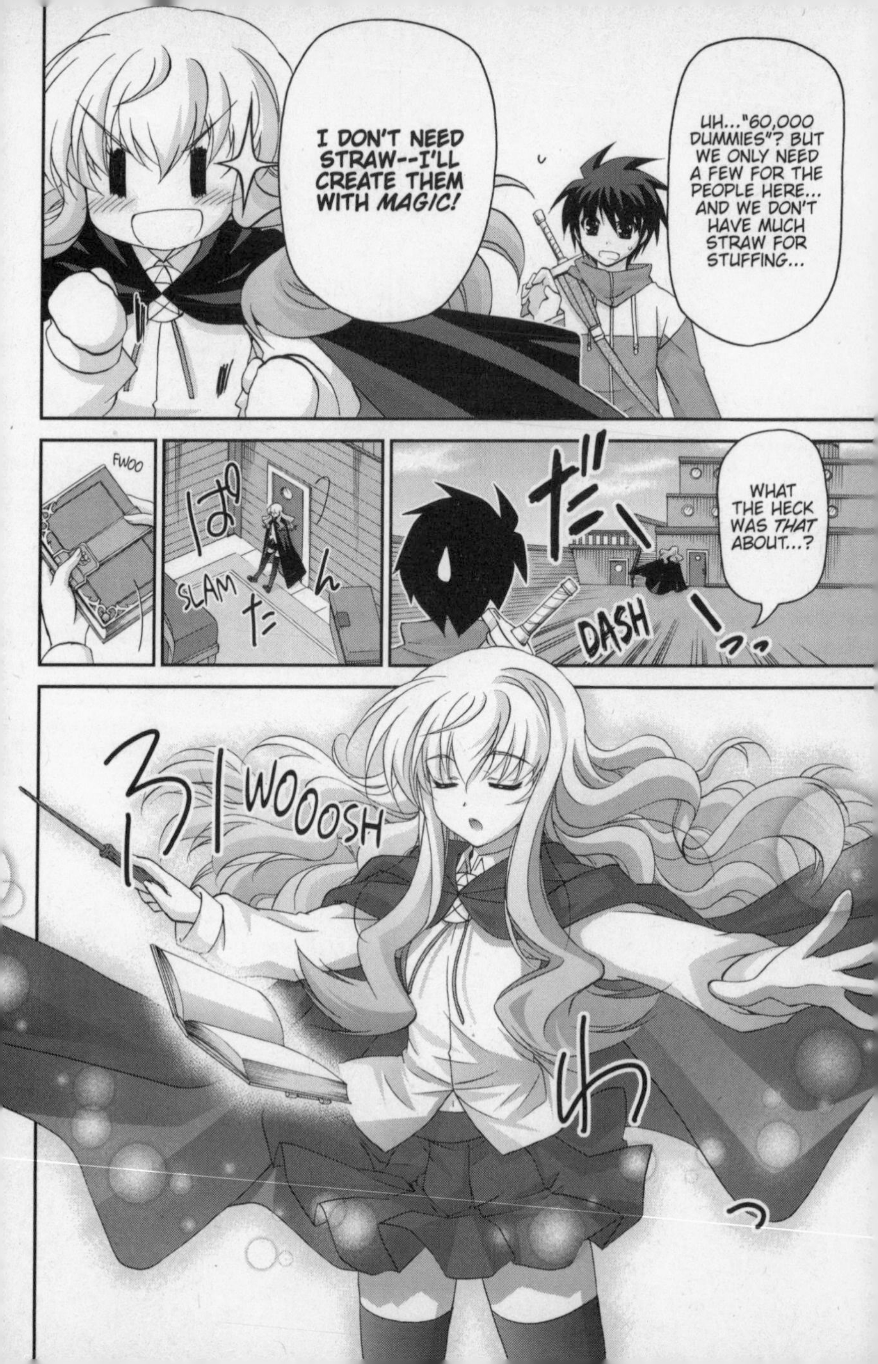
UH..."60,000 DUMMIES"? BUT WE ONLY NEED A FEW FOR THE PEOPLE HERE... AND WE DON'T HAVE MUCH STRAW FOR STUFFING...
I DON'T NEED STRAW--I'LL CREATE THEM WITH *MAGIC!*
WHAT THE HECK WAS *THAT* ABOUT...?
DASH
SLAM
FWOO
WOOOSH

Le Familier de Zero Chevalier

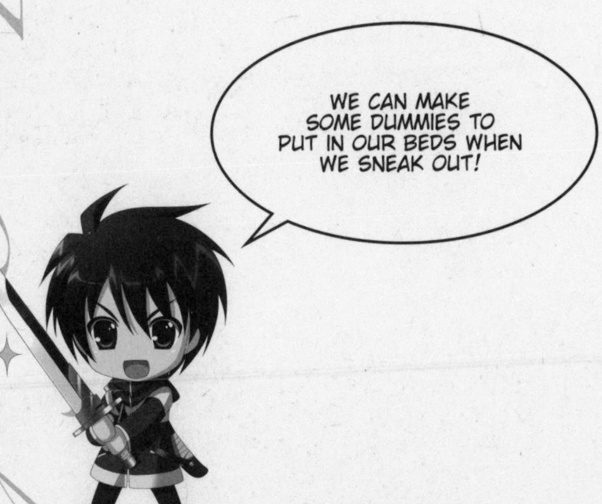
WE CAN MAKE SOME DUMMIES TO PUT IN OUR BEDS WHEN WE SNEAK OUT!

Le Familier de Zero Chevalier

ZERO'S
FAMILIAR
Chevalier

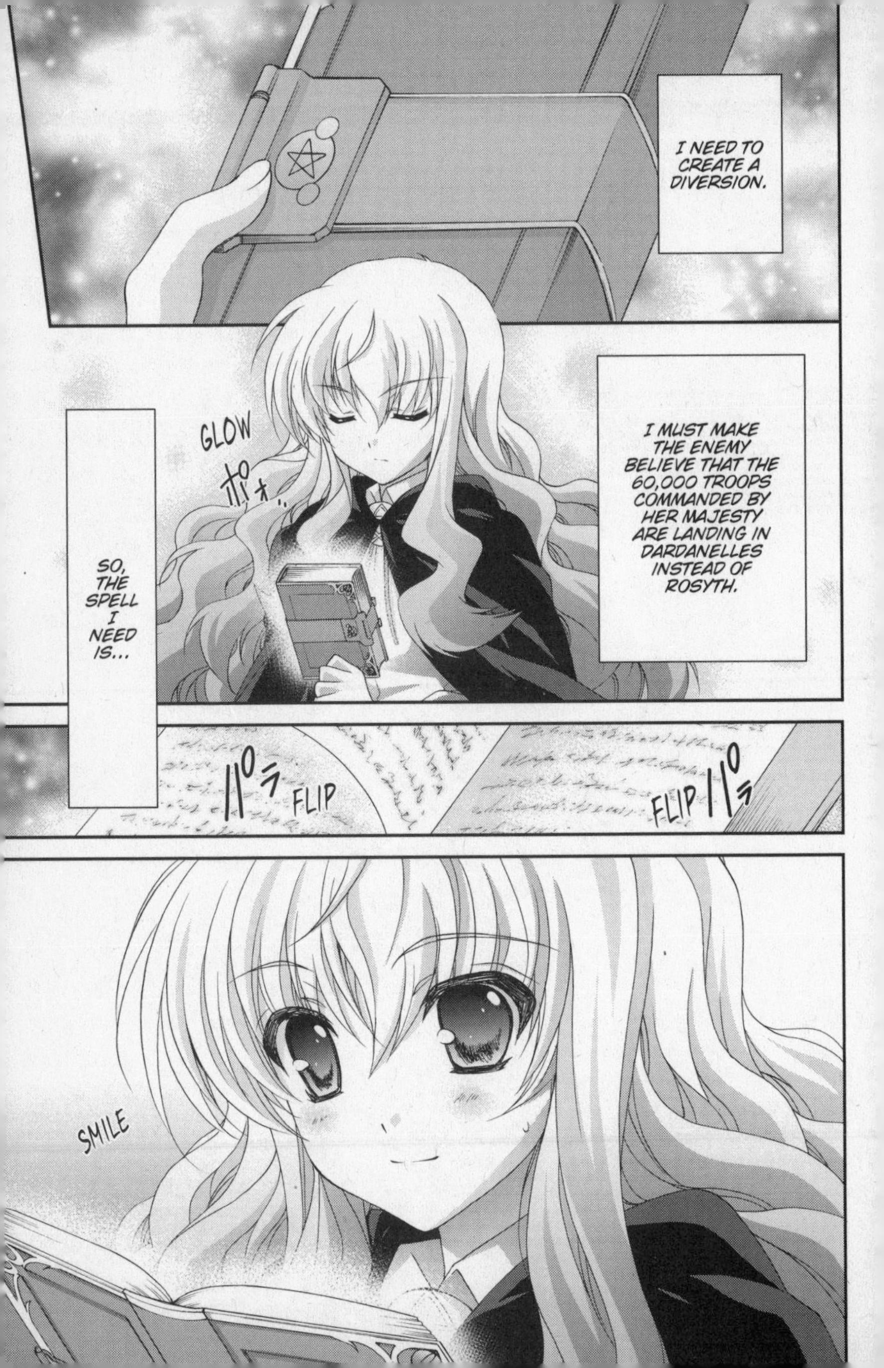
I NEED TO CREATE A DIVERSION.
I MUST MAKE THE ENEMY BELIEVE THAT THE 60,000 TROOPS COMMANDED BY HER MAJESTY ARE LANDING IN DARDANELLES INSTEAD OF ROSYTH.
GLOW
ポォ…
SO, THE SPELL I NEED IS...
パラ
FLIP
FLIP
パラ
SMILE

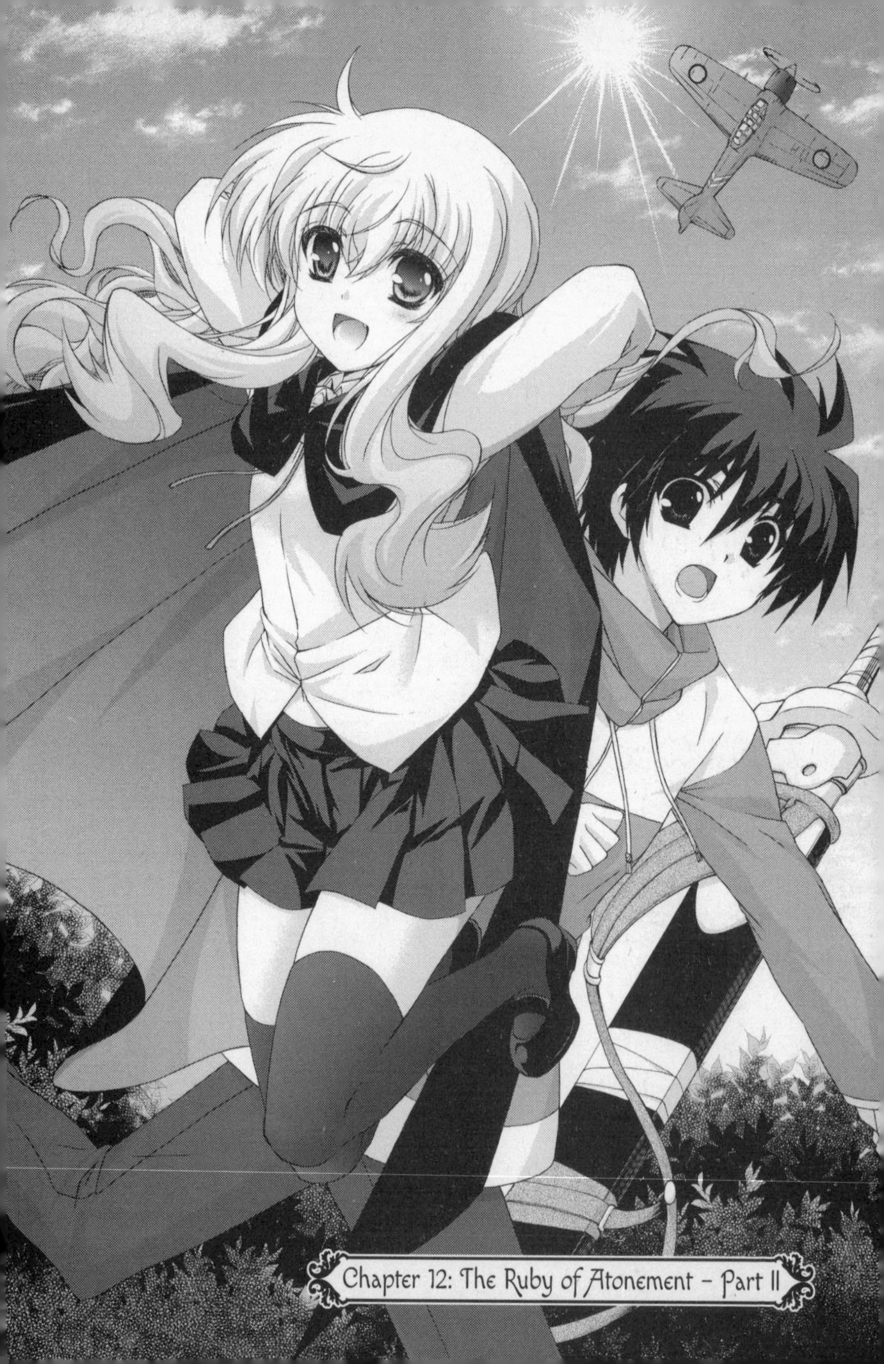
Chapter 12: The Ruby of Atonement - Part II

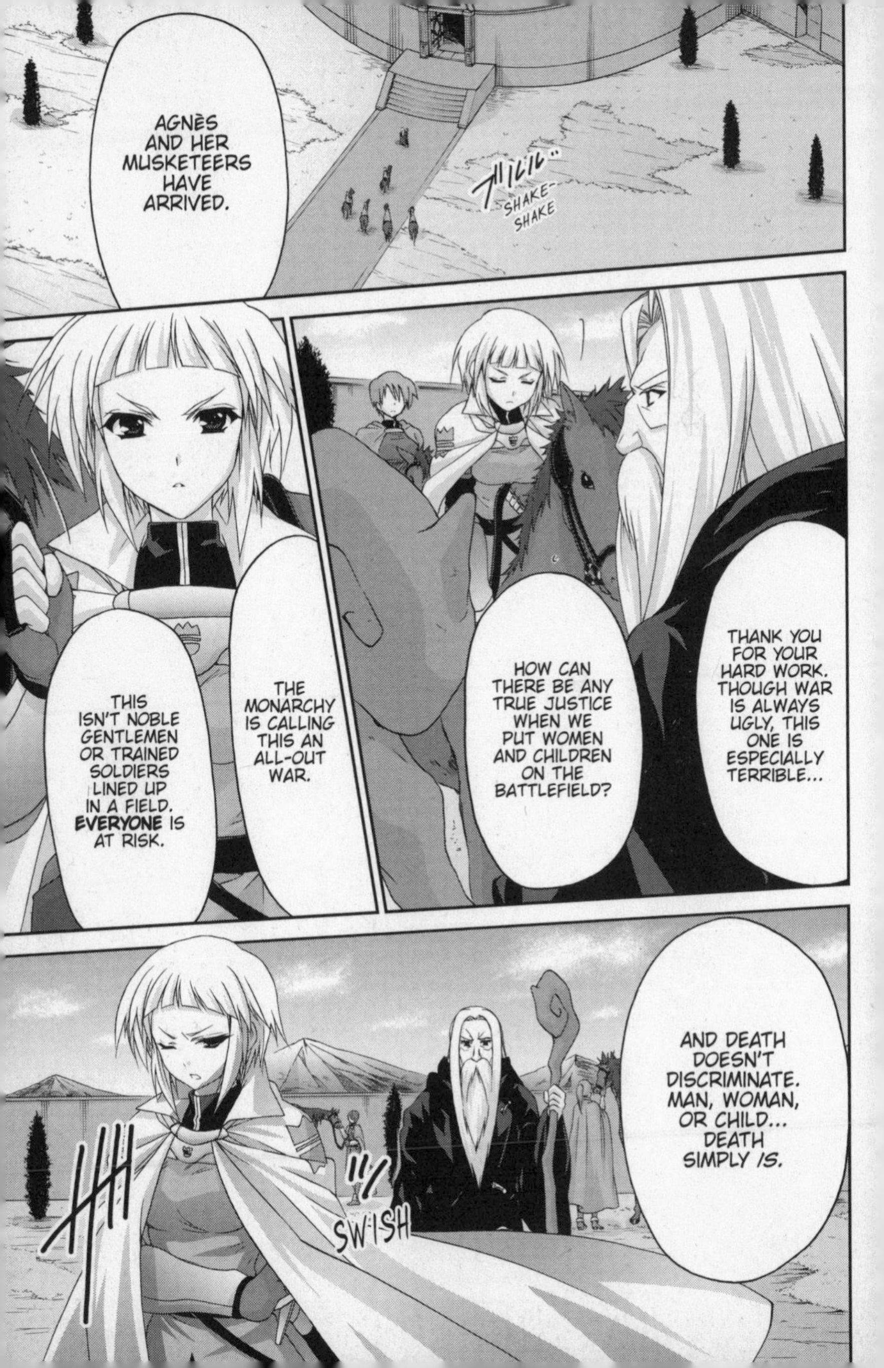
AGNÈS AND HER MUSKETEERS HAVE ARRIVED.
ブルルル‥
SHAKE-SHAKE
THANK YOU FOR YOUR HARD WORK. THOUGH WAR IS ALWAYS UGLY, THIS ONE IS ESPECIALLY TERRIBLE...
HOW CAN THERE BE ANY TRUE JUSTICE WHEN WE PUT WOMEN AND CHILDREN ON THE BATTLEFIELD?
THE MONARCHY IS CALLING THIS AN ALL-OUT WAR.
THIS ISN'T NOBLE GENTLEMEN OR TRAINED SOLDIERS LINED UP IN A FIELD. **EVERYONE** IS AT RISK.
AND DEATH DOESN'T DISCRIMINATE. MAN, WOMAN, OR CHILD... DEATH SIMPLY *IS*.
SWISH

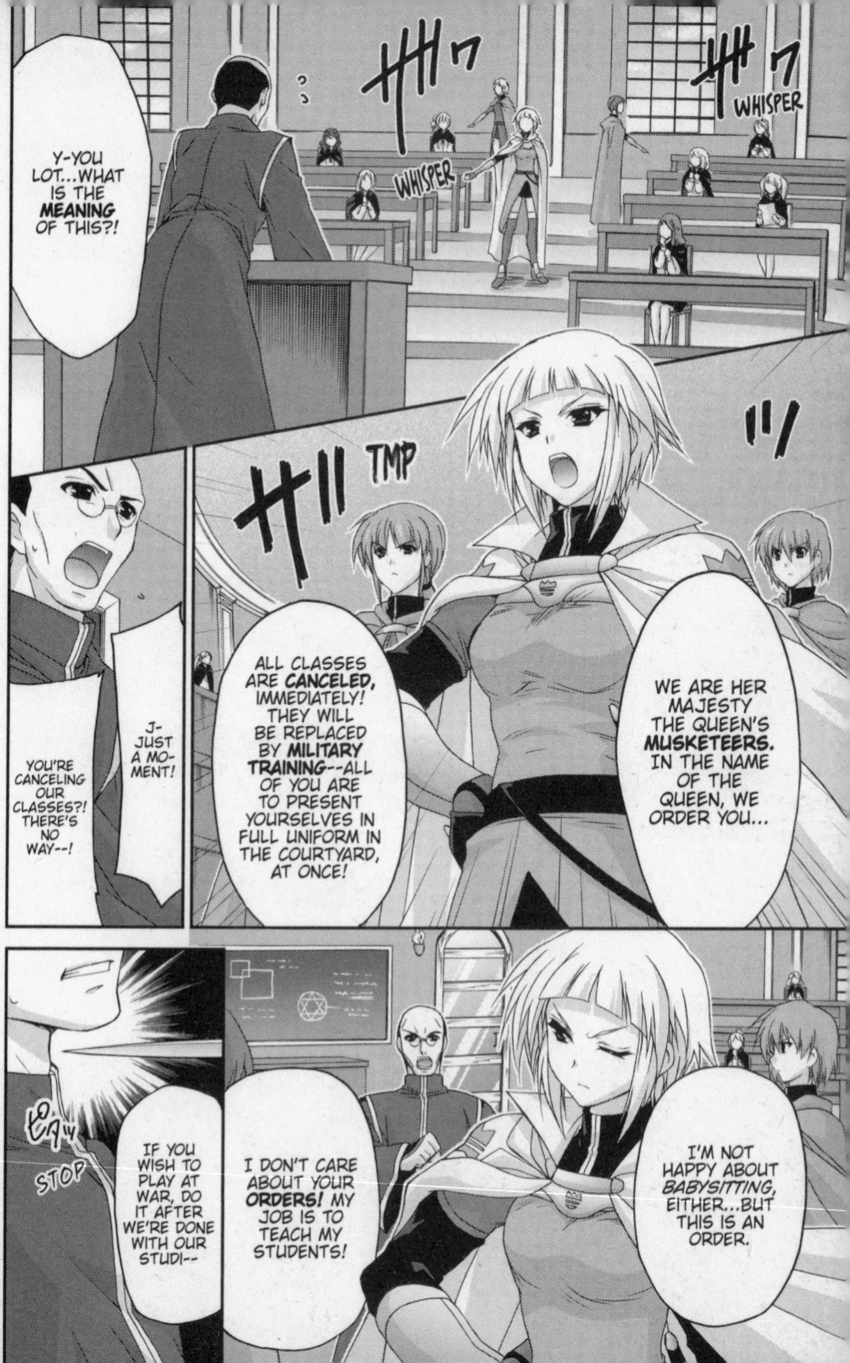
WHISPER
WHISPER
Y-YOU LOT...WHAT IS THE **MEANING** OF THIS?!
WE ARE HER MAJESTY THE QUEEN'S **MUSKETEERS.** IN THE NAME OF THE QUEEN, WE ORDER YOU...
ALL CLASSES ARE **CANCELED,** IMMEDIATELY! THEY WILL BE REPLACED BY **MILITARY TRAINING**--ALL OF YOU ARE TO PRESENT YOURSELVES IN FULL UNIFORM IN THE COURTYARD, AT ONCE!
TMP
J-JUST A MO-MENT!
YOU'RE CANCELING OUR CLASSES?! THERE'S NO WAY--!
I'M NOT HAPPY ABOUT *BABYSITTING,* EITHER...BUT THIS IS AN ORDER.
I DON'T CARE ABOUT YOUR **ORDERS!** MY JOB IS TO TEACH MY STUDENTS!
IF YOU WISH TO PLAY AT WAR, DO IT AFTER WE'RE DONE WITH OUR STUDI--
STOP

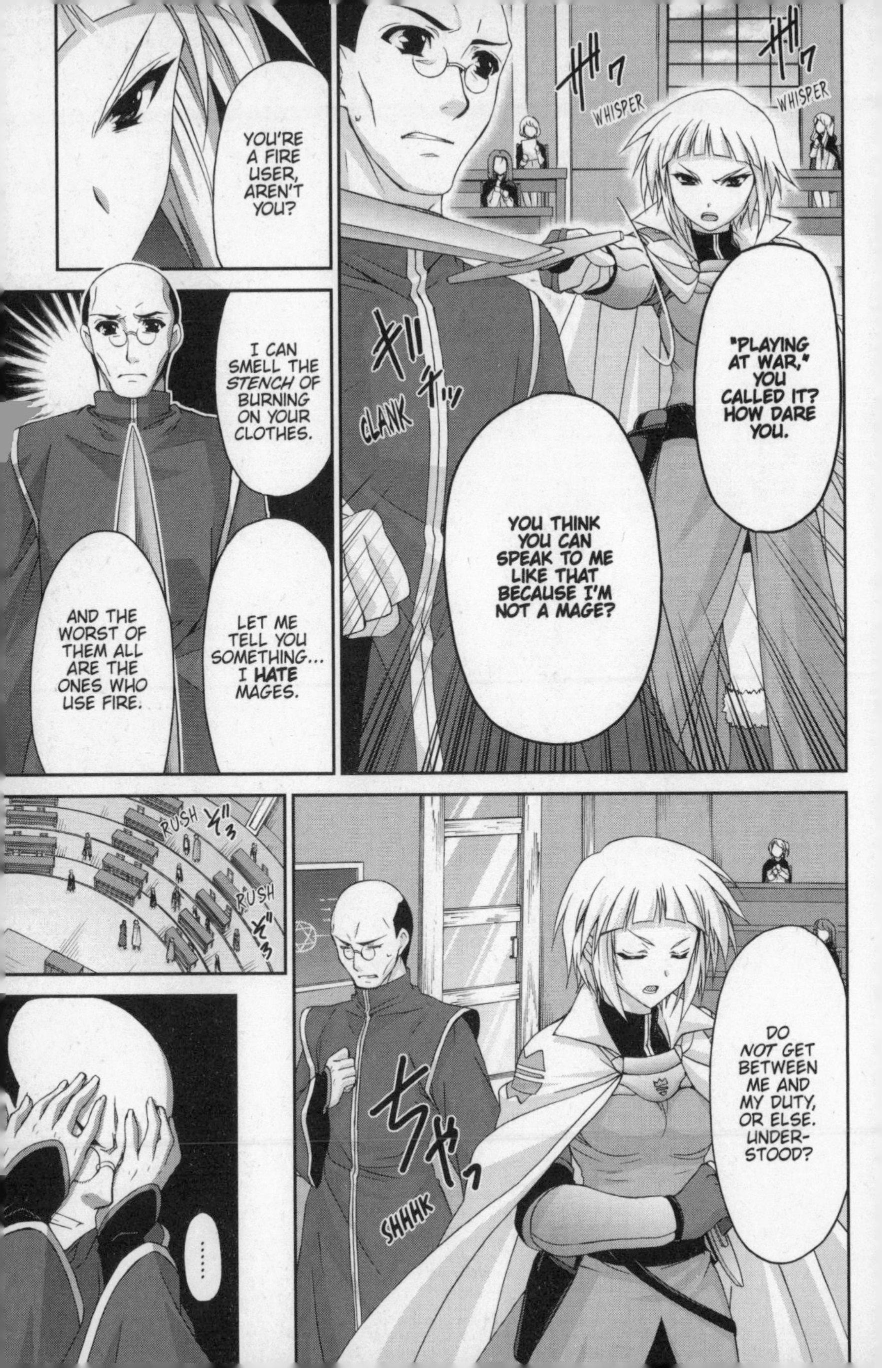
WHISPER
WHISPER
"PLAYING AT WAR," YOU CALLED IT? HOW DARE YOU.
CLANK
YOU THINK YOU CAN SPEAK TO ME LIKE THAT BECAUSE I'M NOT A MAGE?
YOU'RE A FIRE USER, AREN'T YOU?
I CAN SMELL THE *STENCH* OF BURNING ON YOUR CLOTHES.
LET ME TELL YOU SOMETHING... I **HATE** MAGES.
AND THE WORST OF THEM ALL ARE THE ONES WHO USE FIRE.
DO *NOT* GET BETWEEN ME AND MY DUTY, OR ELSE. UNDER-STOOD?
SHHHK
RUSH
RUSH
......

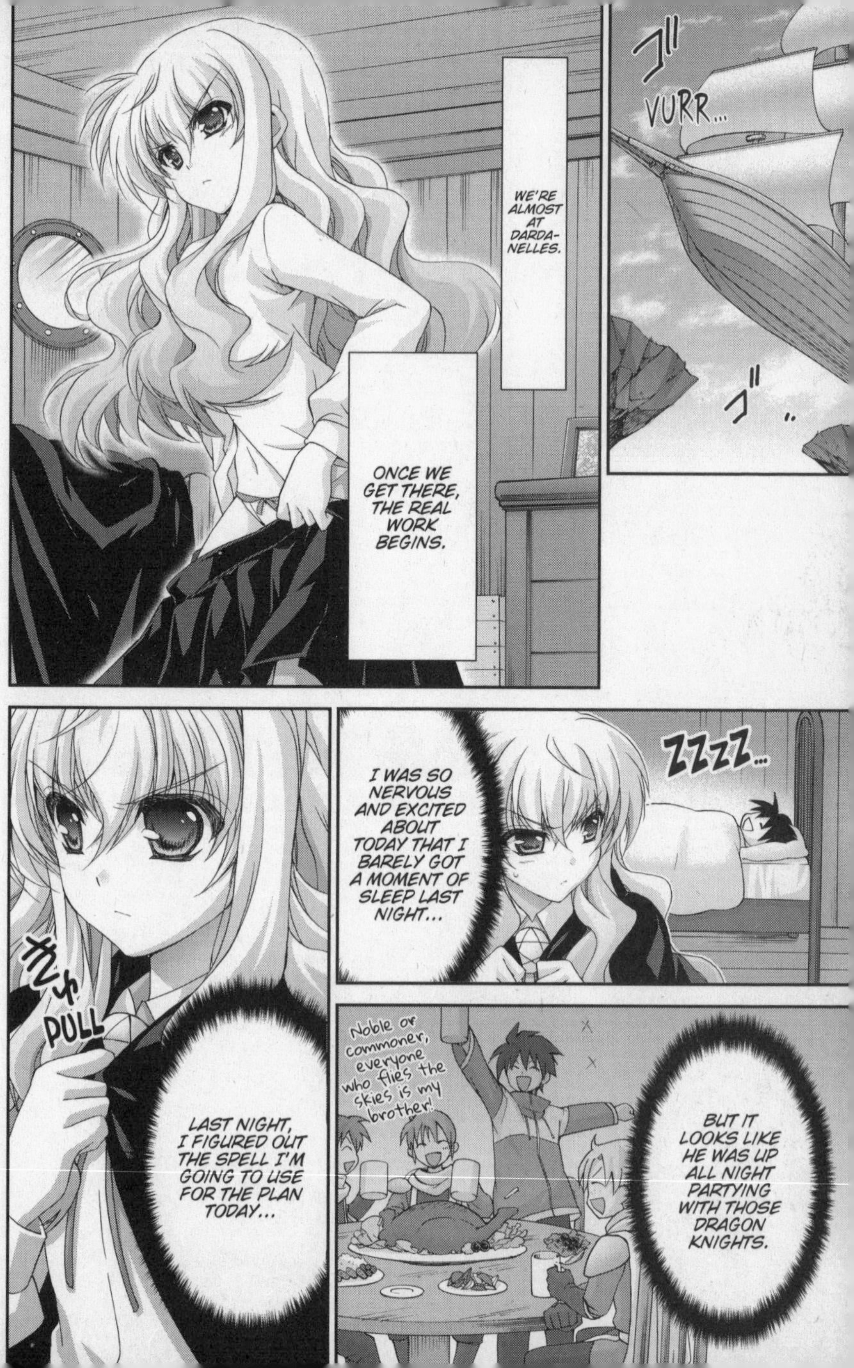

VURR...
WE'RE ALMOST AT DARDANELLES.
ONCE WE GET THERE, THE REAL WORK BEGINS.
ZZZZ...
I WAS SO NERVOUS AND EXCITED ABOUT TODAY THAT I BARELY GOT A MOMENT OF SLEEP LAST NIGHT...
BUT IT LOOKS LIKE HE WAS UP ALL NIGHT PARTYING WITH THOSE DRAGON KNIGHTS.
Noble or commoner, everyone who flies the skies is my brother!
PULL
LAST NIGHT, I FIGURED OUT THE SPELL I'M GOING TO USE FOR THE PLAN TODAY...

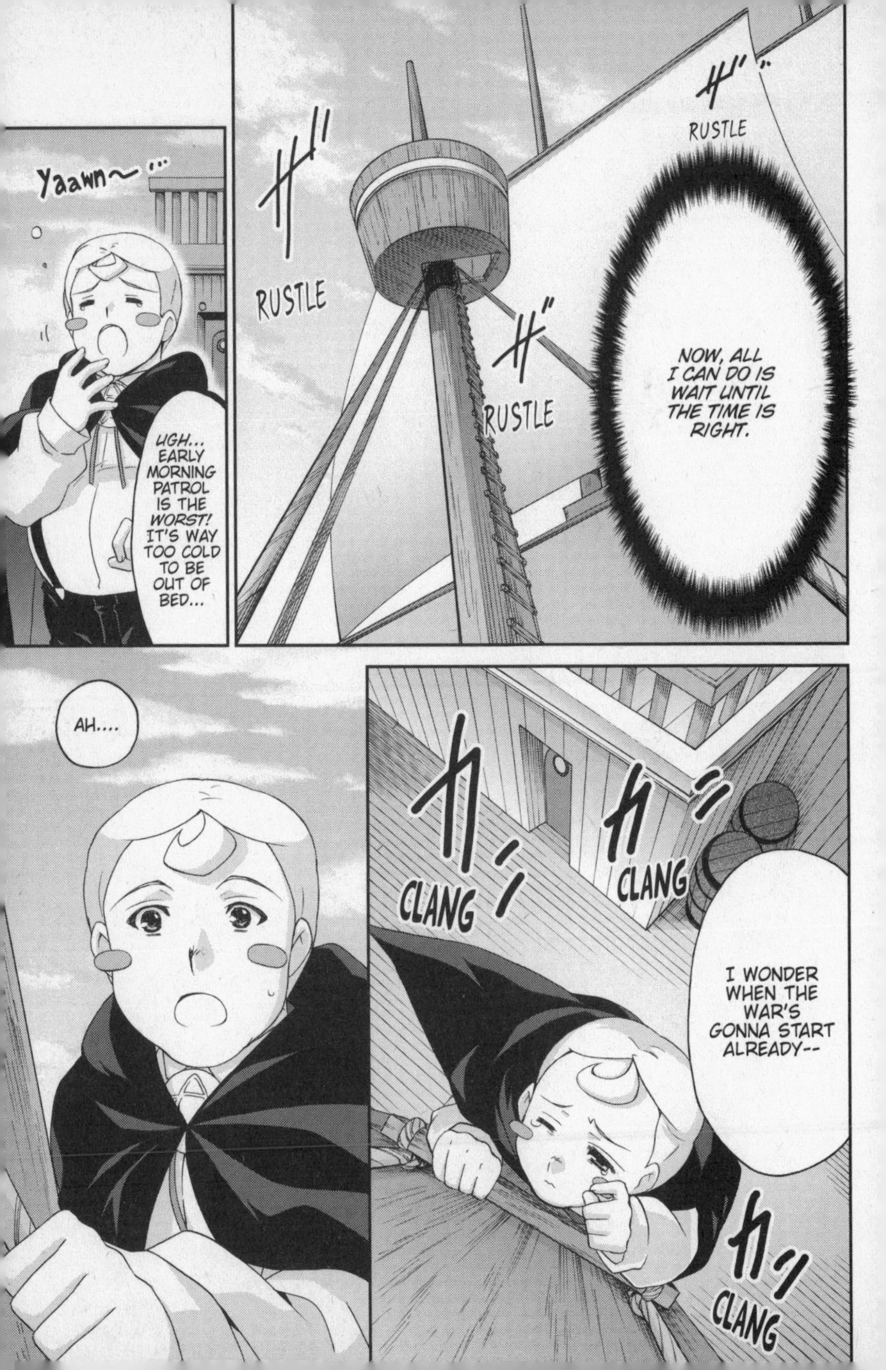
RUSTLE
RUSTLE
RUSTLE
NOW, ALL I CAN DO IS WAIT UNTIL THE TIME IS RIGHT.
Yaawn~...
UGH... EARLY MORNING PATROL IS THE WORST! IT'S WAY TOO COLD TO BE OUT OF BED...
CLANG
CLANG
I WONDER WHEN THE WAR'S GONNA START ALREADY--
CLANG
AH....

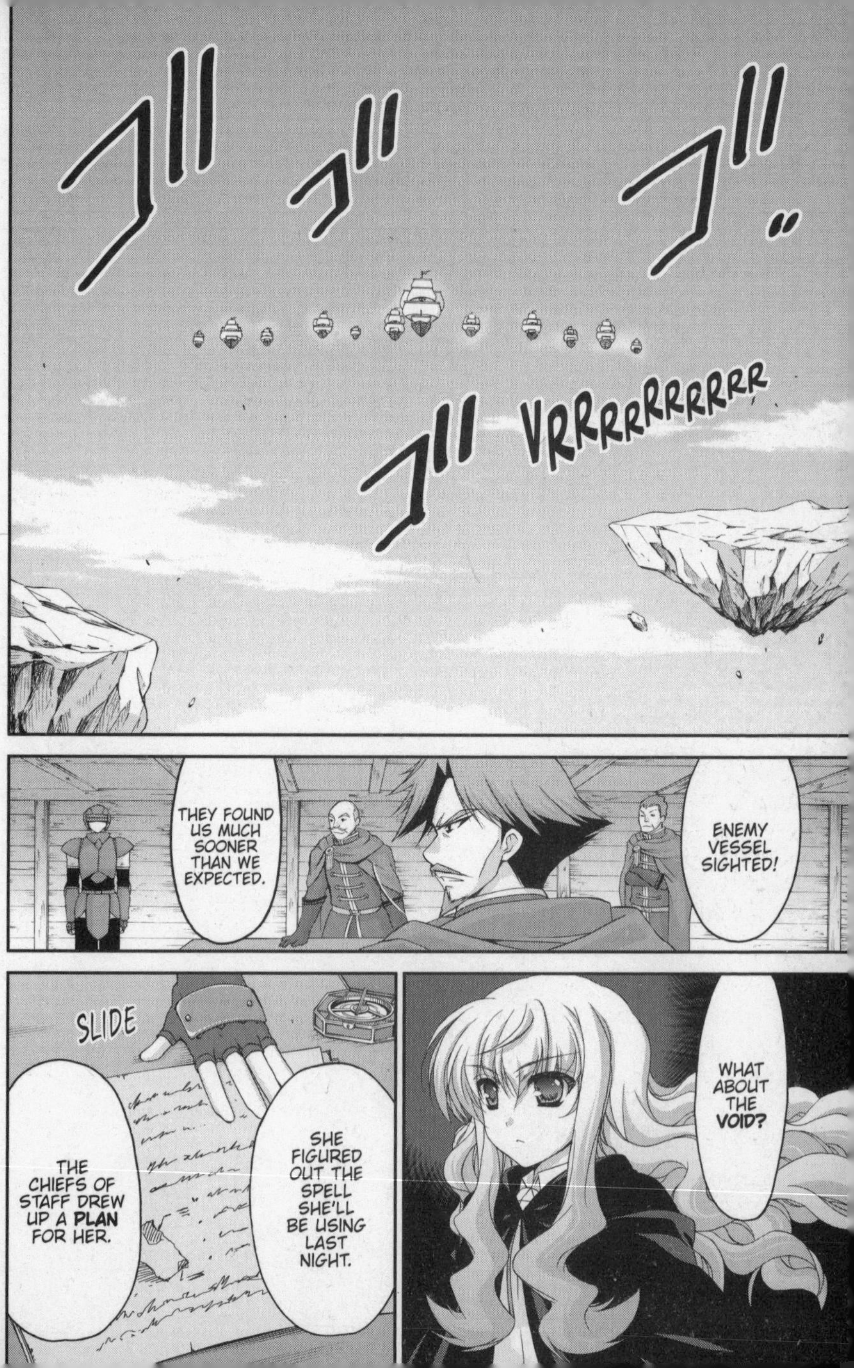
VRRRRRRRRR
ENEMY VESSEL SIGHTED!
THEY FOUND US MUCH SOONER THAN WE EXPECTED.
WHAT ABOUT THE **VOID?**
SLIDE
SHE FIGURED OUT THE SPELL SHE'LL BE USING LAST NIGHT.
THE CHIEFS OF STAFF DREW UP A **PLAN** FOR HER.

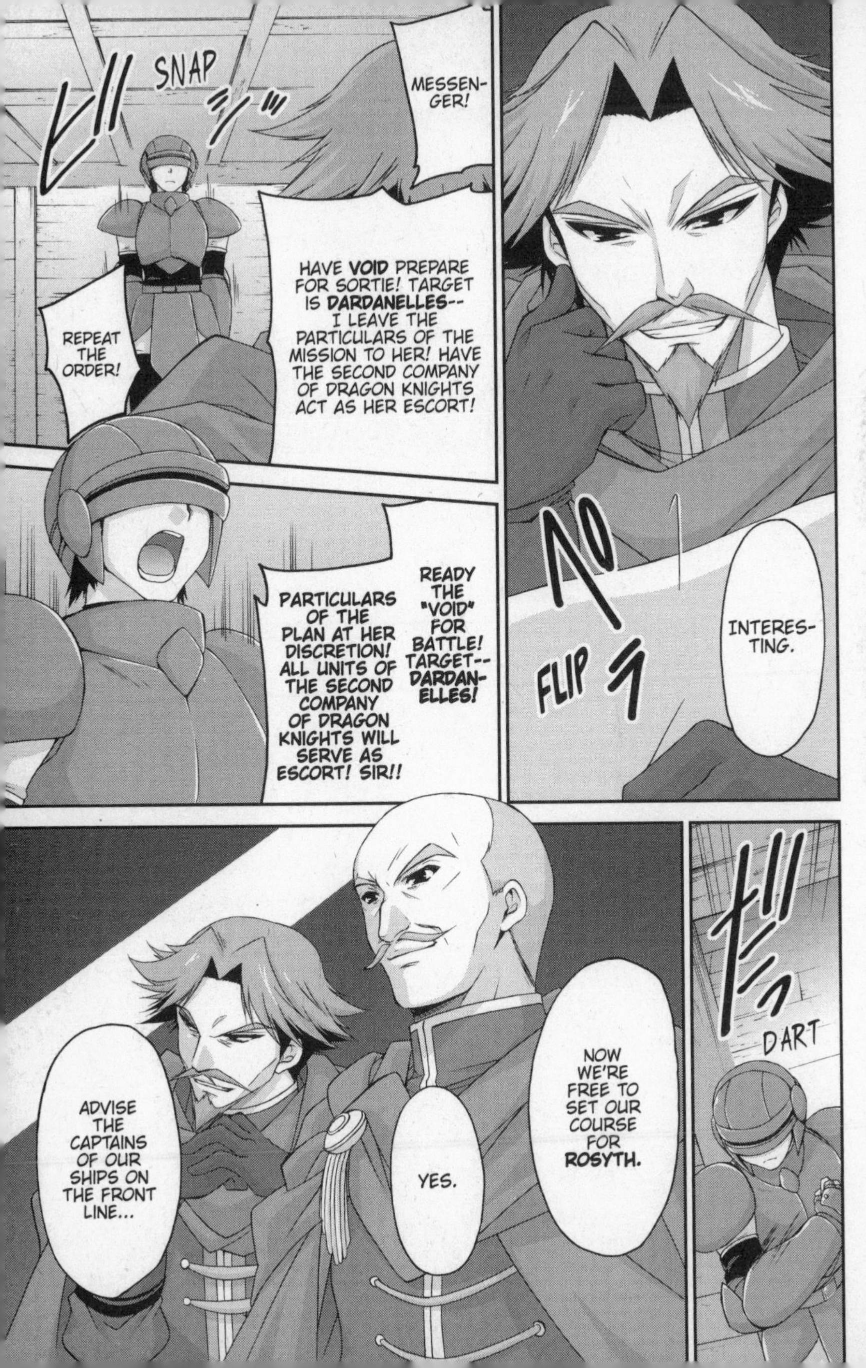

FLIP
INTERESTING.
SNAP
MESSENGER!
HAVE **VOID** PREPARE FOR SORTIE! TARGET IS **DARDANELLES**-- I LEAVE THE PARTICULARS OF THE MISSION TO HER! HAVE THE SECOND COMPANY OF DRAGON KNIGHTS ACT AS HER ESCORT!
REPEAT THE ORDER!
READY THE "VOID" FOR BATTLE! TARGET-- DARDANELLES!
PARTICULARS OF THE PLAN AT HER DISCRETION! ALL UNITS OF THE SECOND COMPANY OF DRAGON KNIGHTS WILL SERVE AS ESCORT! SIR!!
DART
NOW WE'RE FREE TO SET OUR COURSE FOR **ROSYTH.**
YES.
ADVISE THE CAPTAINS OF OUR SHIPS ON THE FRONT LINE...

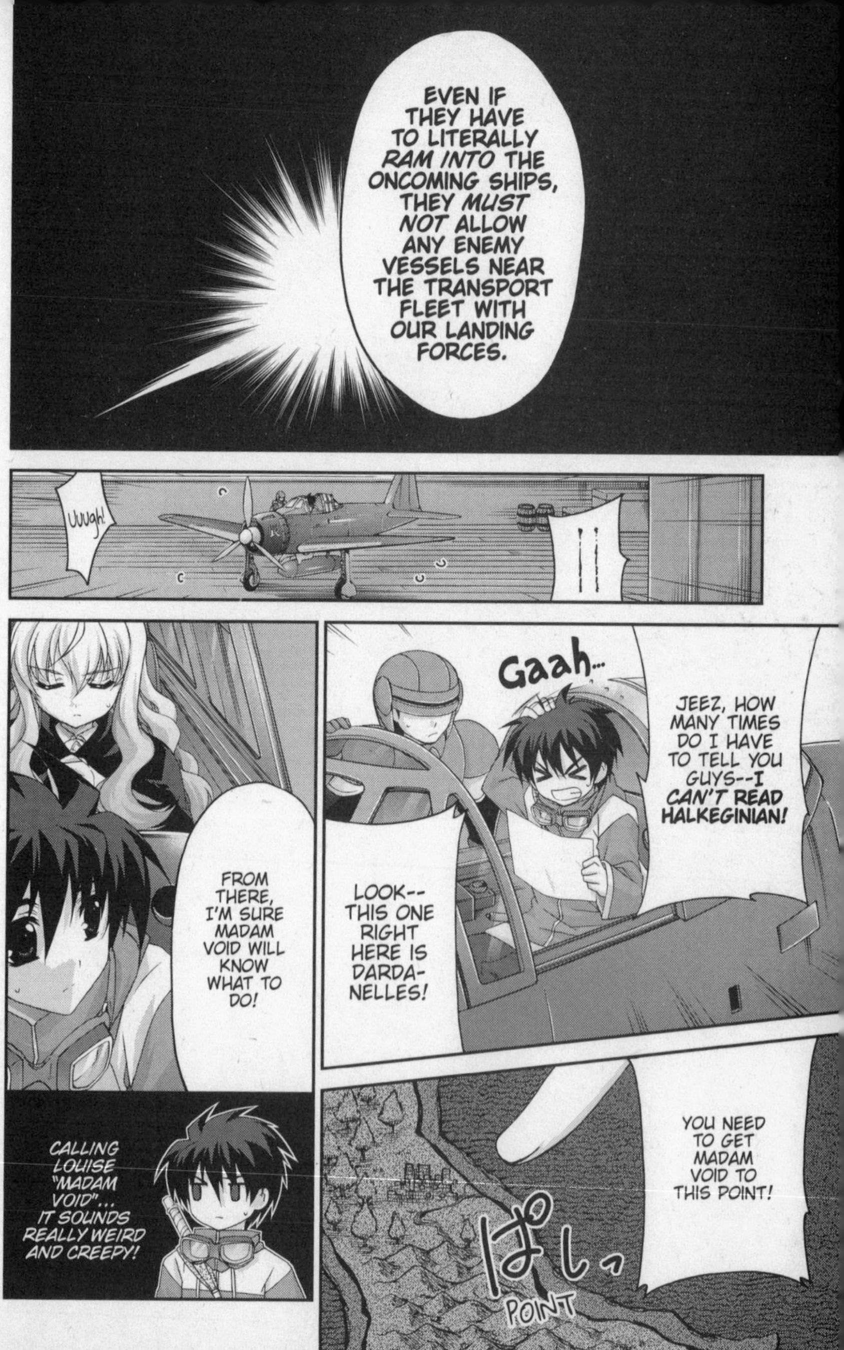

EVEN IF THEY HAVE TO LITERALLY *RAM INTO* THE ONCOMING SHIPS, THEY *MUST NOT* ALLOW ANY ENEMY VESSELS NEAR THE TRANSPORT FLEET WITH OUR LANDING FORCES.
Uuugh!
JEEZ, HOW MANY TIMES DO I HAVE TO TELL YOU GUYS--**I *CAN'T* READ HALKEGINIAN!**
Gaah...
LOOK-- THIS ONE RIGHT HERE IS DARDA-NELLES!
FROM THERE, I'M SURE MADAM VOID WILL KNOW WHAT TO DO!
YOU NEED TO GET MADAM VOID TO THIS POINT!
ぱしっ
POINT
CALLING LOUISE "MADAM VOID"... IT SOUNDS REALLY WEIRD AND CREEPY!

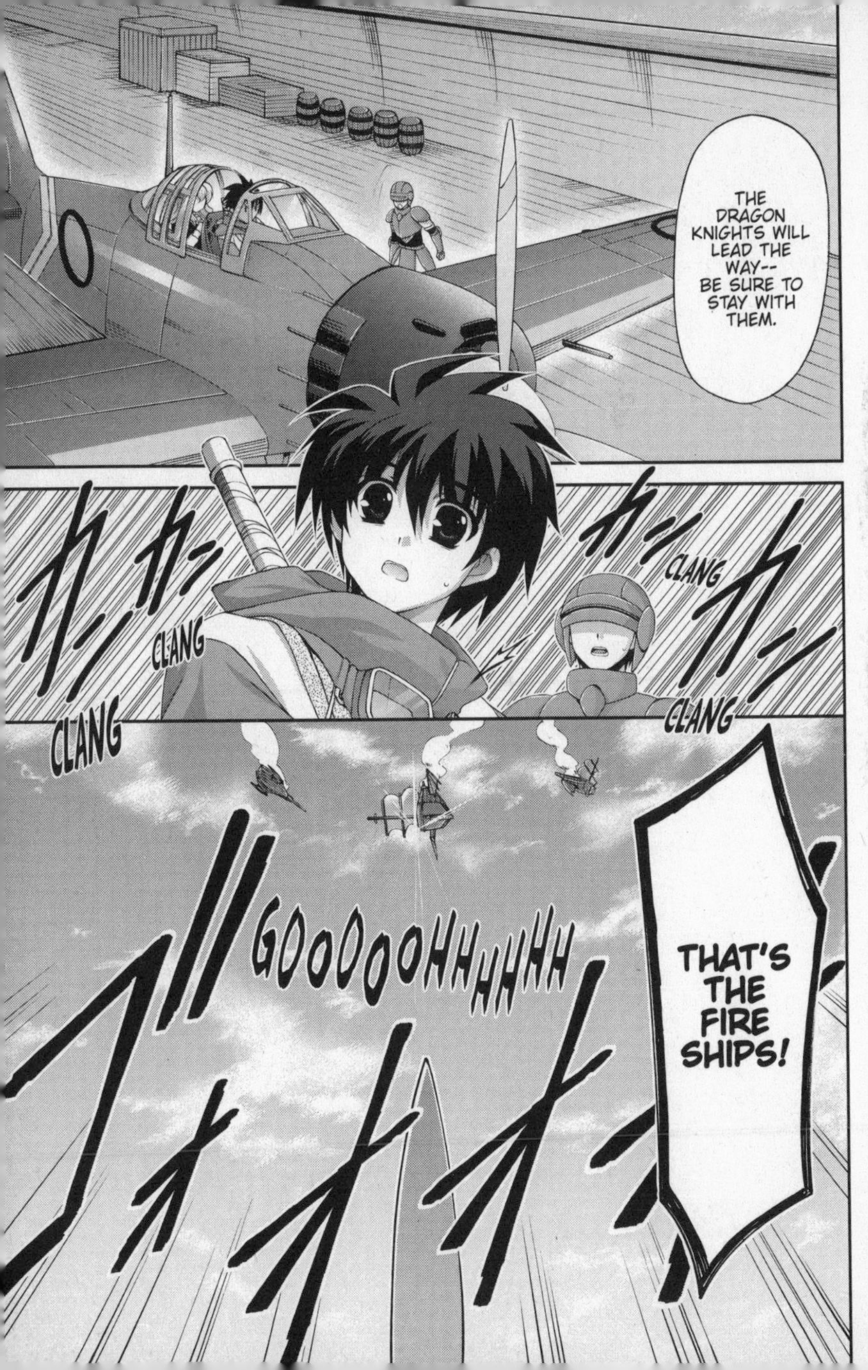
THE DRAGON KNIGHTS WILL LEAD THE WAY-- BE SURE TO STAY WITH THEM.
CLANG
CLANG
CLANG
CLANG
THAT'S THE FIRE SHIPS!
GOOOOOHHHHHH

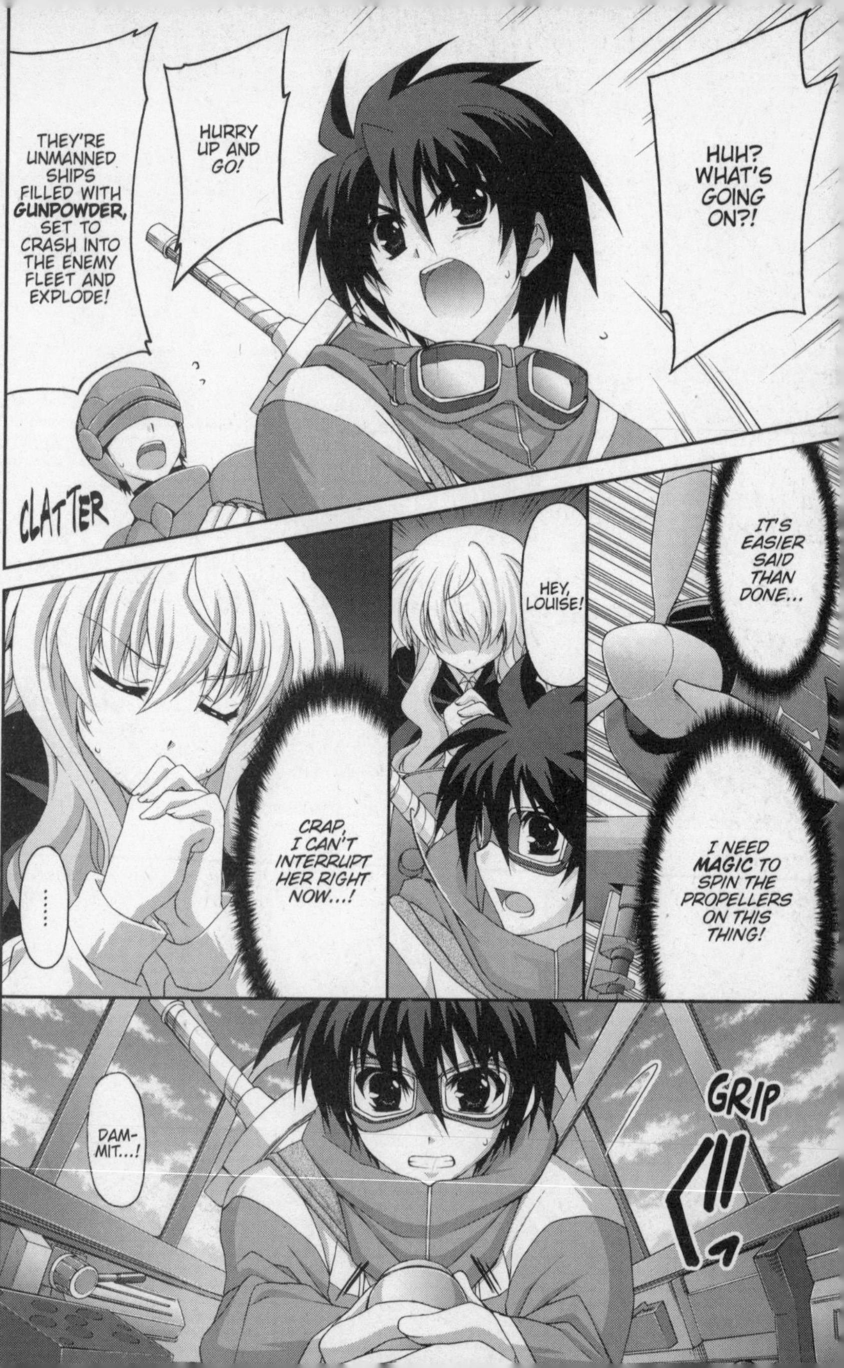
HUH? WHAT'S GOING ON?!
HURRY UP AND GO!
THEY'RE UNMANNED SHIPS FILLED WITH **GUNPOWDER,** SET TO CRASH INTO THE ENEMY FLEET AND EXPLODE!
CLATTER
IT'S EASIER SAID THAN DONE...
I NEED **MAGIC** TO SPIN THE PROPELLERS ON THIS THING!
HEY, LOUISE!
CRAP, I CAN'T INTERRUPT HER RIGHT NOW...!
......
GRIP
DAM-MIT...!

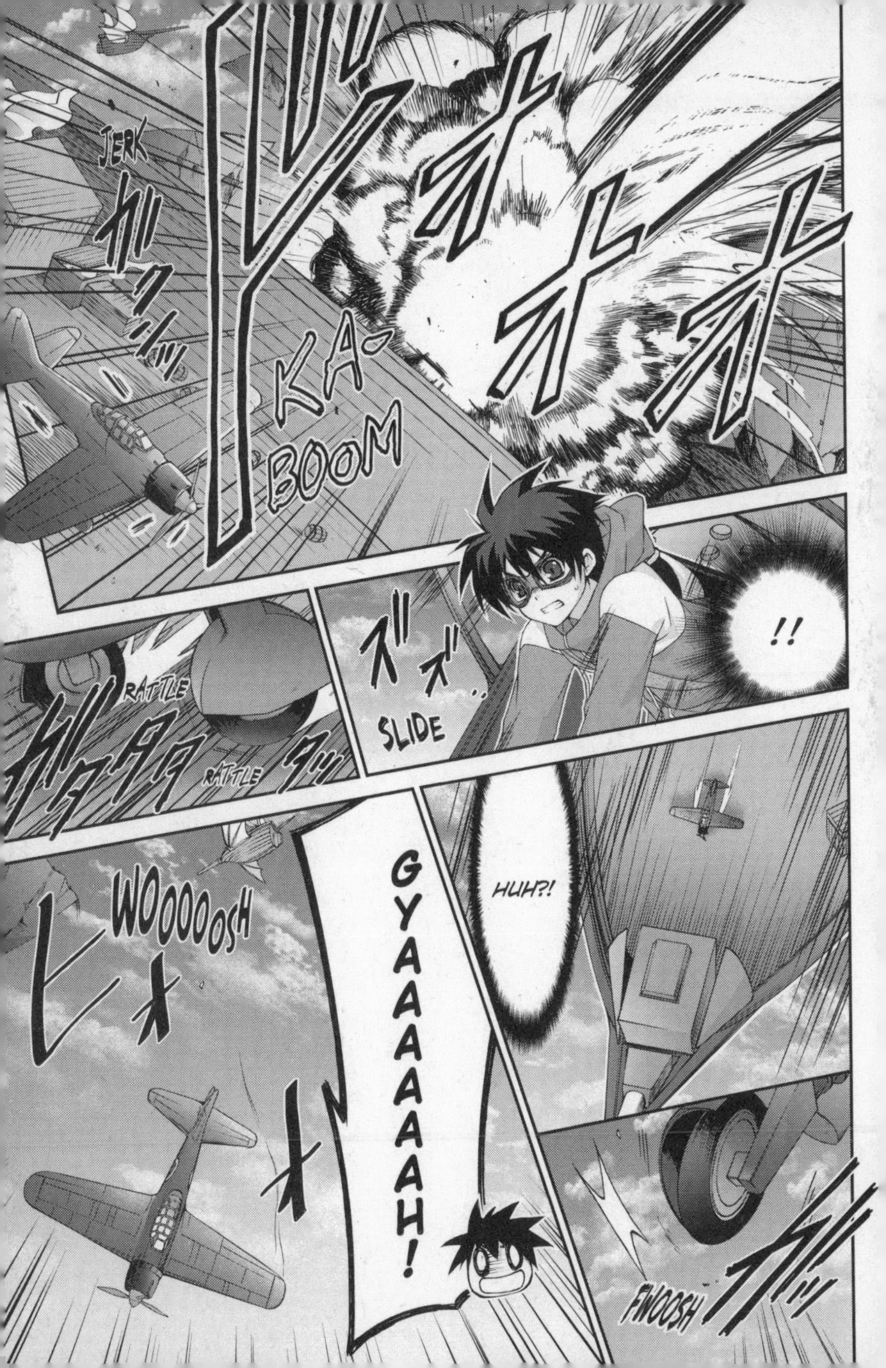
KA-BOOM
JERK
!!
SLIDE
RATTLE
RATTLE
HUH?!
FWOOSH
GYAAAAAAAH!
WOOOOOSH

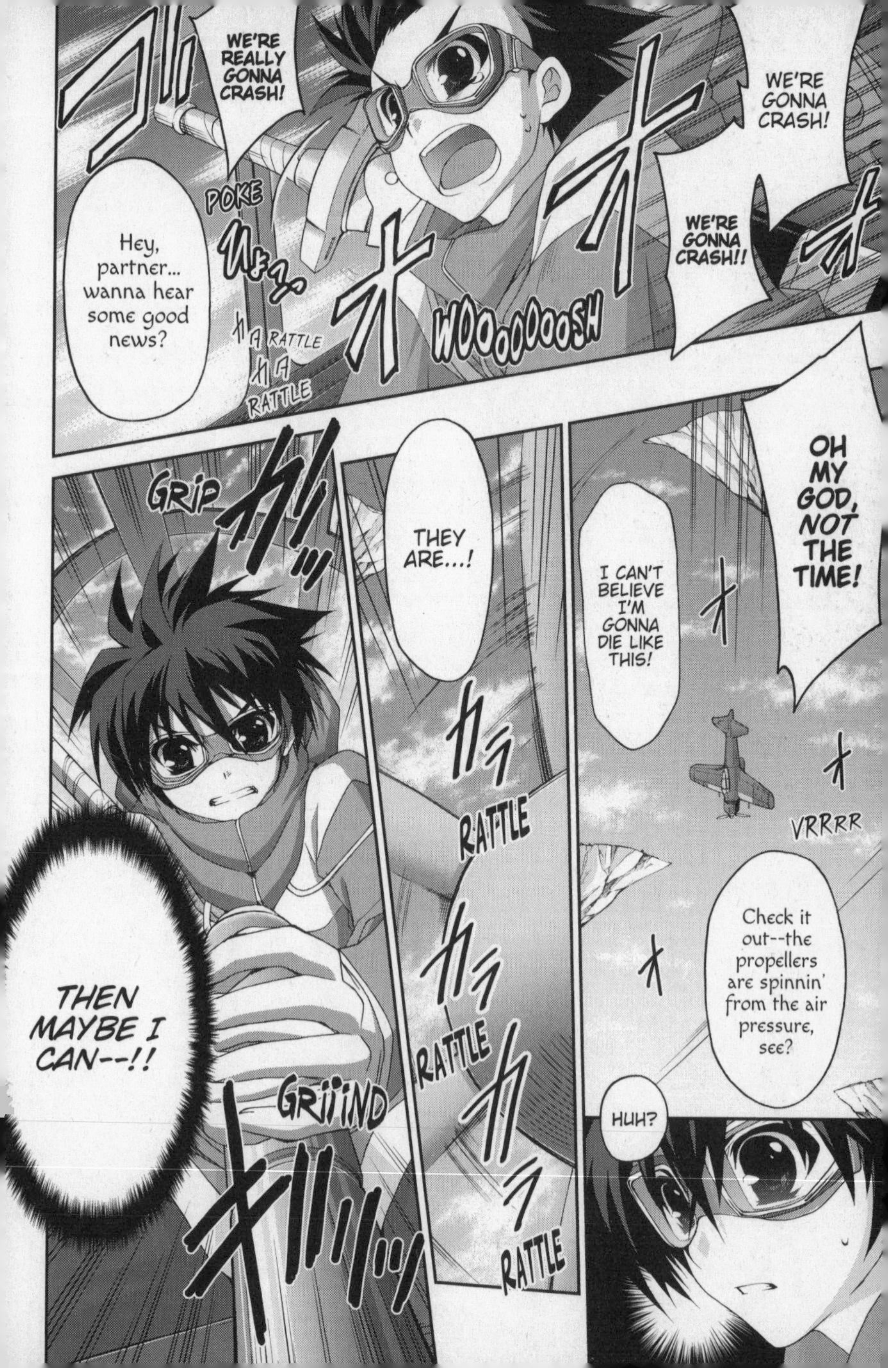
WE'RE GONNA CRASH!
WE'RE GONNA CRASH!!
WE'RE REALLY GONNA CRASH!
WOOOOOOOSH
POKE
RATTLE
RATTLE
Hey, partner... wanna hear some good news?
OH MY GOD, NOT THE TIME!
I CAN'T BELIEVE I'M GONNA DIE LIKE THIS!
VRRRR
Check it out--the propellers are spinnin' from the air pressure, see?
HUH?
THEY ARE...!
RATTLE
RATTLE
RATTLE
GRIP
GRIIIND
THEN MAYBE I CAN--!!

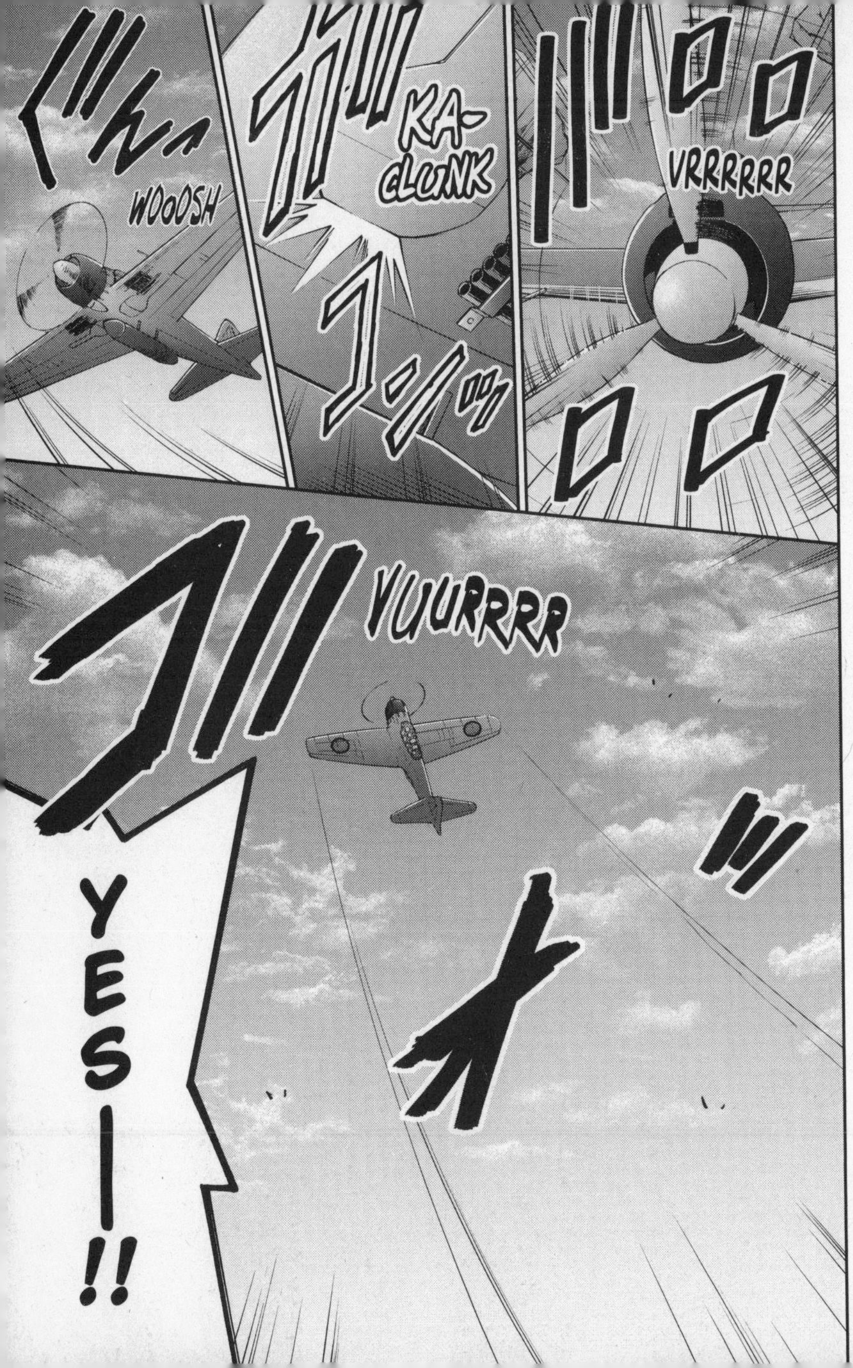
VRRRRRR
KA-CLUNK
WOOOSH
YUURRRR
YES—!!

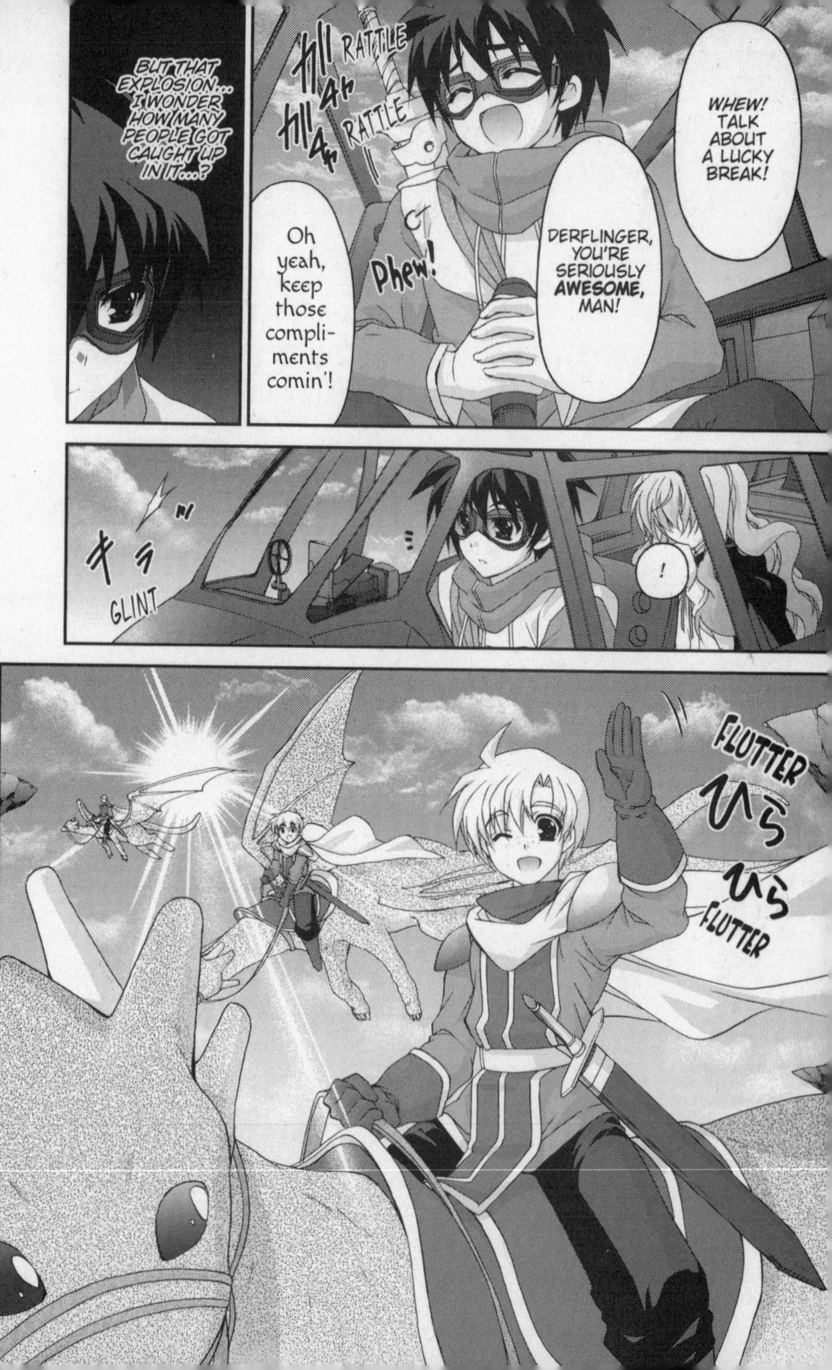
WHEW! TALK ABOUT A LUCKY BREAK!
DERFLINGER, YOU'RE SERIOUSLY **AWESOME,** MAN!
RATTLE
RATTLE
Phew!
Oh yeah, keep those compliments comin'!
BUT THAT EXPLOSION... I WONDER HOW MANY PEOPLE GOT CAUGHT UP IN IT...?
!
キラ
GLINT
FLUTTER
ひら
ひら
FLUTTER

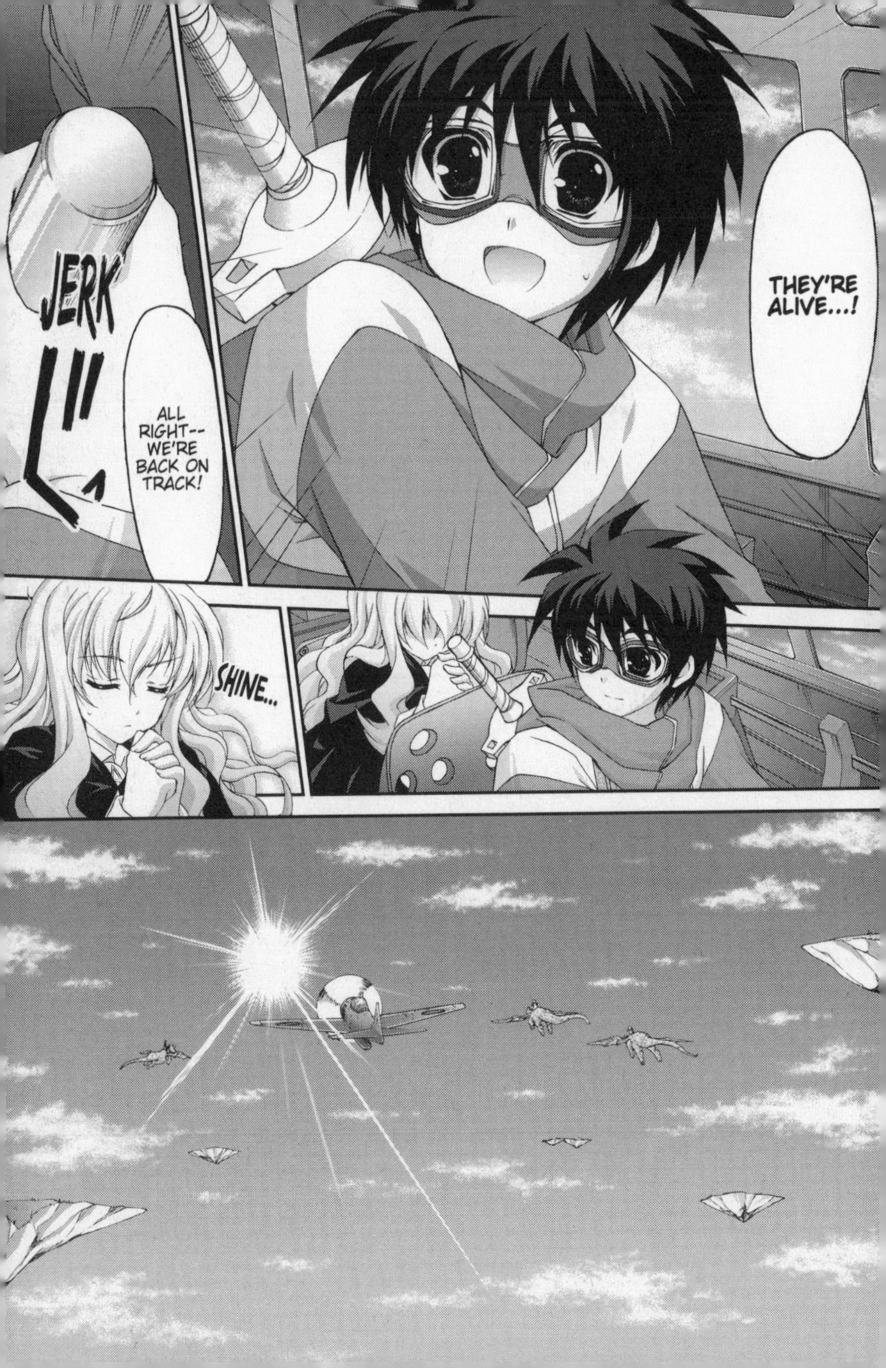
THEY'RE ALIVE...!
ALL RIGHT-- WE'RE BACK ON TRACK!
JERK
SHINE...

Le Familier de Zero Chevalier

ZERO'S
FAMILIAR
Chevalier

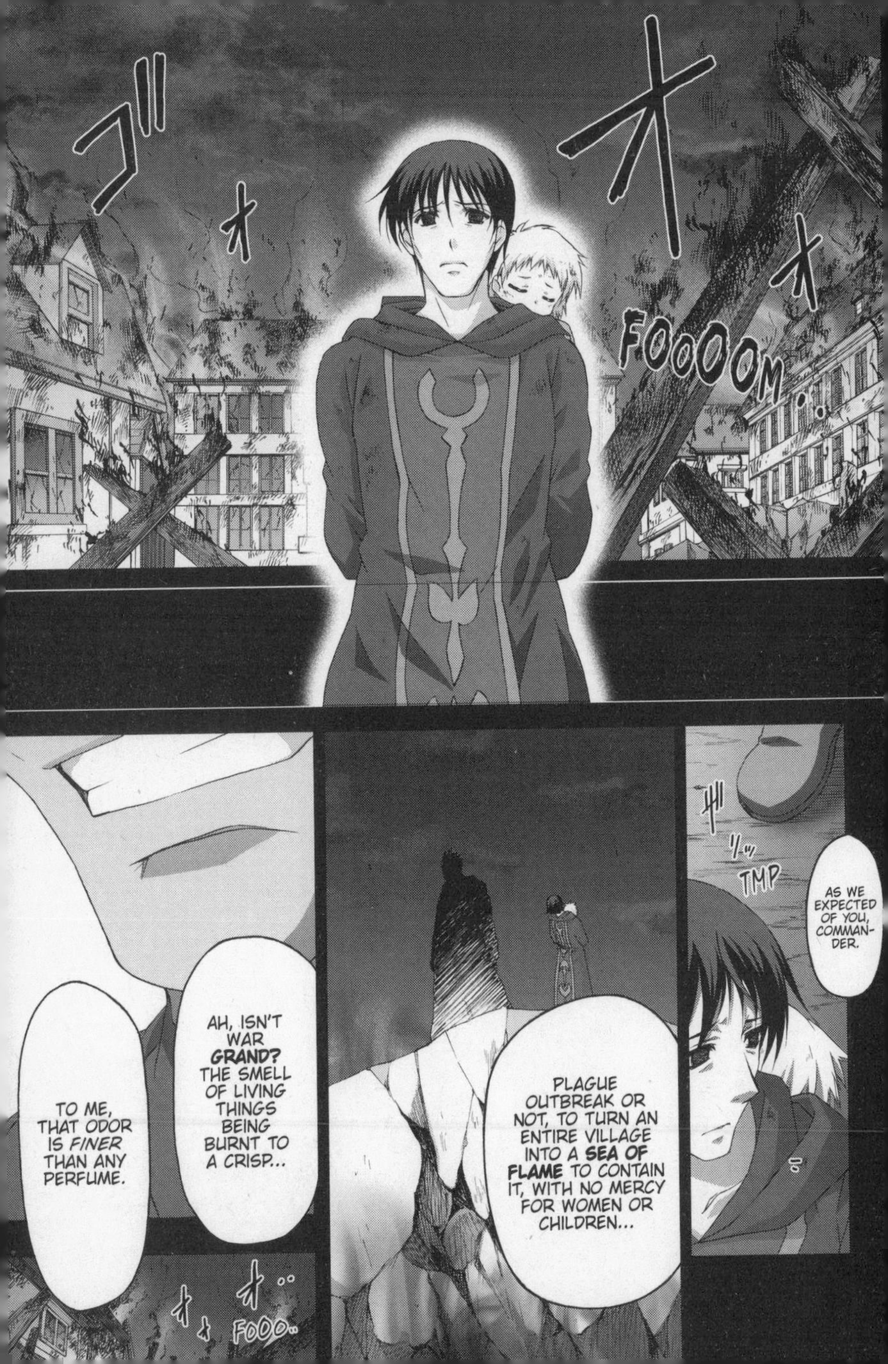
FOOOOM..
TMP
AS WE EXPECTED OF YOU, COMMANDER.
PLAGUE OUTBREAK OR NOT, TO TURN AN ENTIRE VILLAGE INTO A **SEA OF FLAME** TO CONTAIN IT, WITH NO MERCY FOR WOMEN OR CHILDREN...
AH, ISN'T WAR **GRAND?** THE SMELL OF LIVING THINGS BEING BURNT TO A CRISP...
TO ME, THAT ODOR IS *FINER* THAN ANY PERFUME.
FOOO..

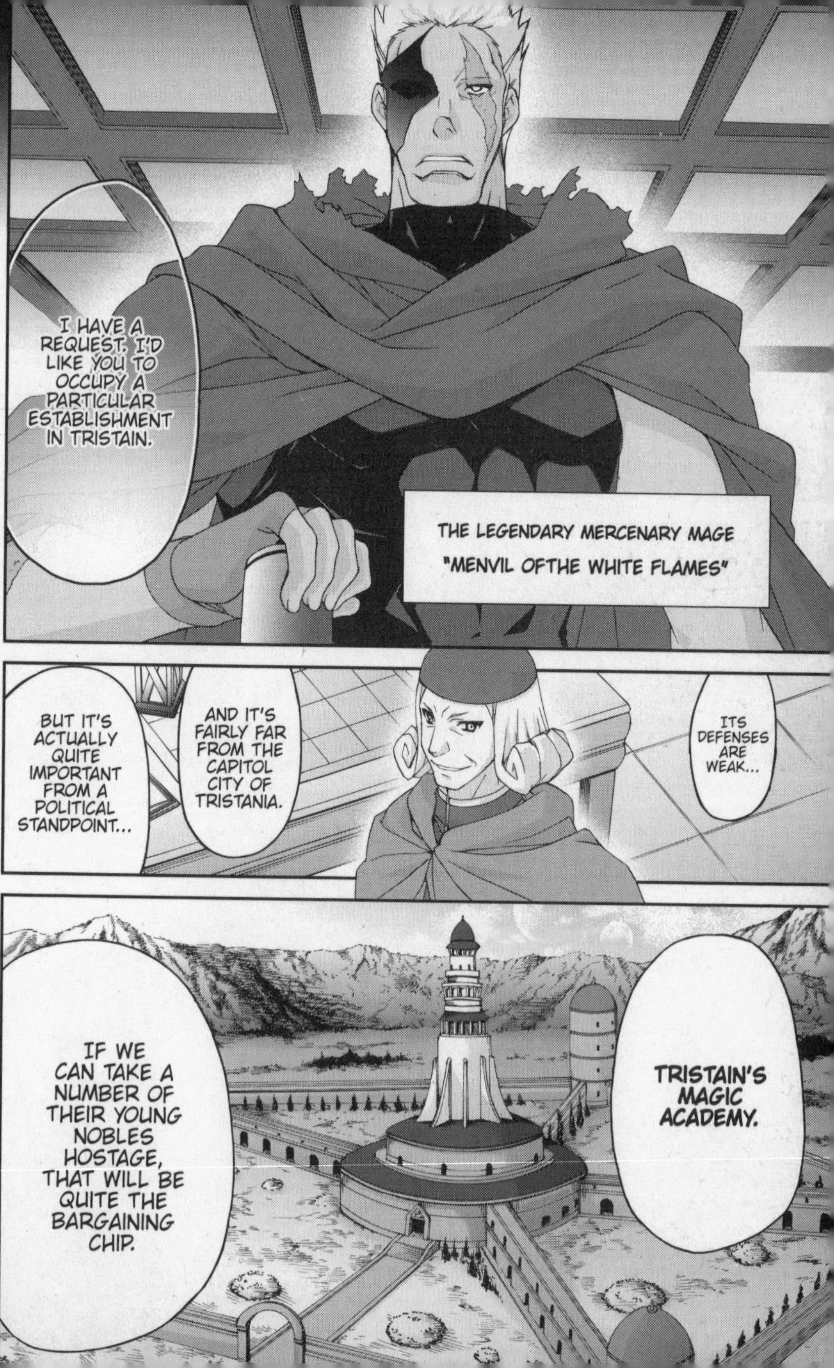
THE LEGENDARY MERCENARY MAGE "MENVIL OFTHE WHITE FLAMES"
I HAVE A REQUEST. I'D LIKE YOU TO OCCUPY A PARTICULAR ESTABLISHMENT IN TRISTAIN.
ITS DEFENSES ARE WEAK...
AND IT'S FAIRLY FAR FROM THE CAPITOL CITY OF TRISTANIA.
BUT IT'S ACTUALLY QUITE IMPORTANT FROM A POLITICAL STANDPOINT...
TRISTAIN'S MAGIC ACADEMY.
IF WE CAN TAKE A NUMBER OF THEIR YOUNG NOBLES HOSTAGE, THAT WILL BE QUITE THE BARGAINING CHIP.

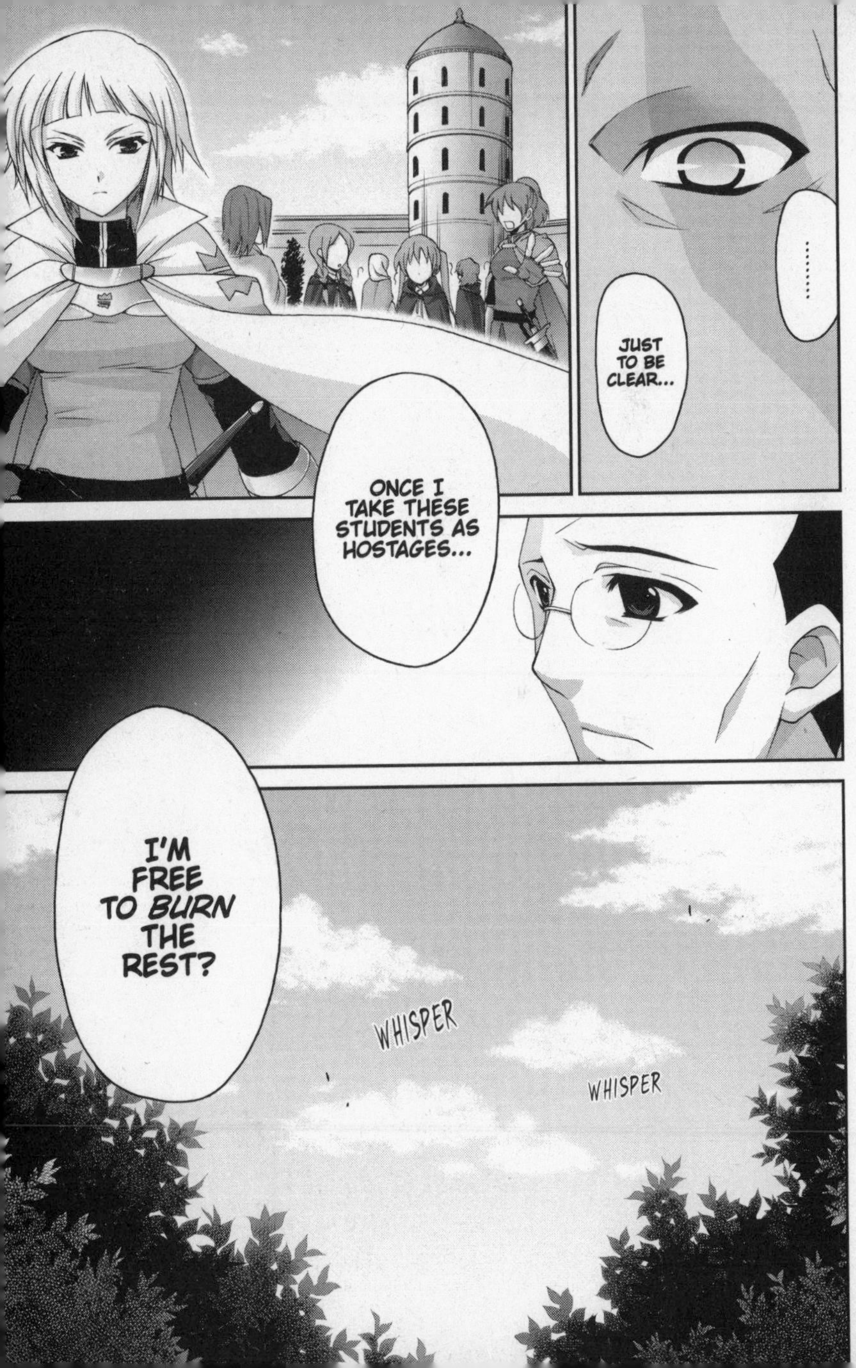
......
JUST TO BE CLEAR...
ONCE I TAKE THESE STUDENTS AS HOSTAGES...
I'M FREE TO *BURN* THE REST?
WHISPER
WHISPER

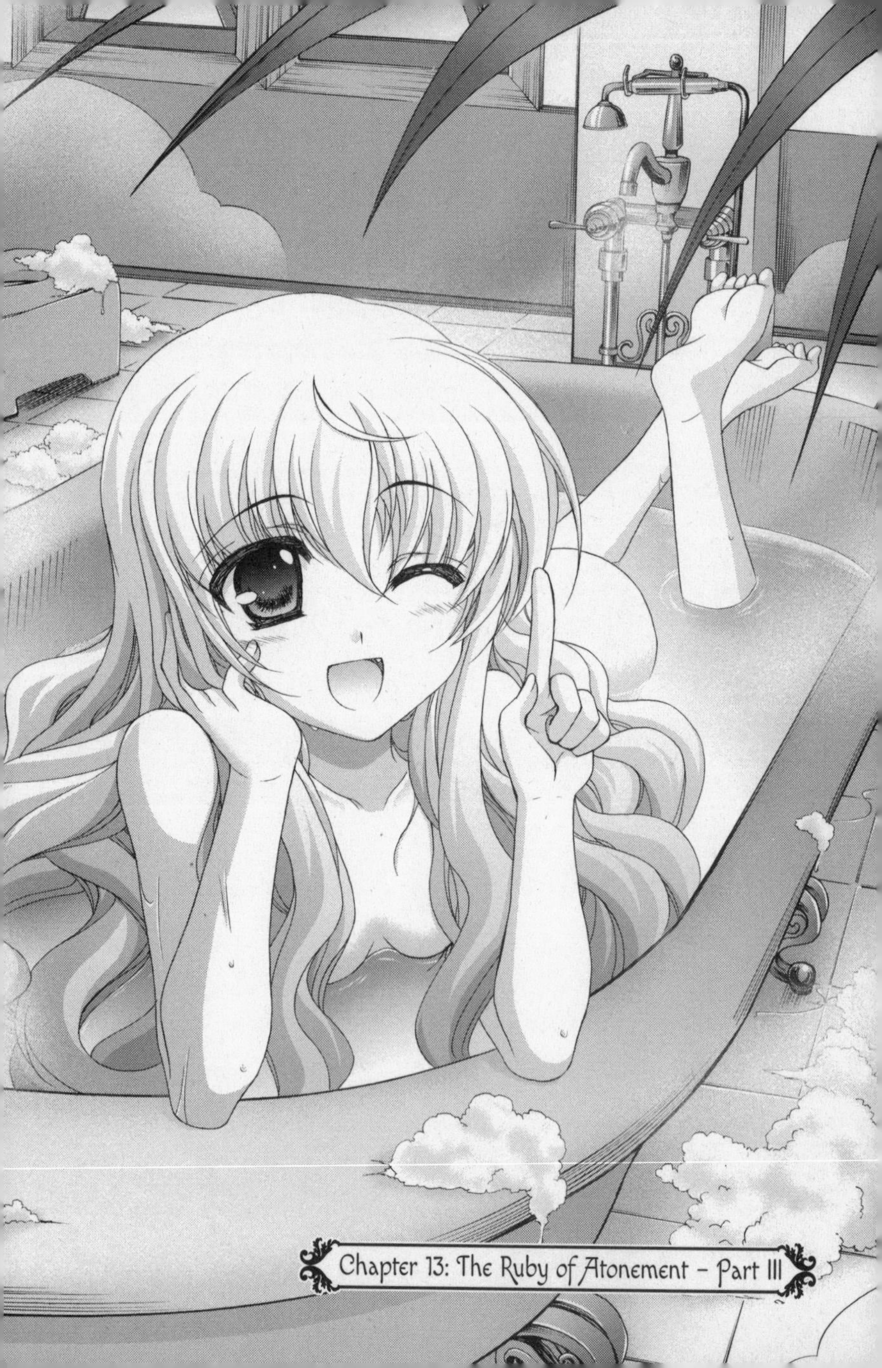
Chapter 13: The Ruby of Atonement – Part III

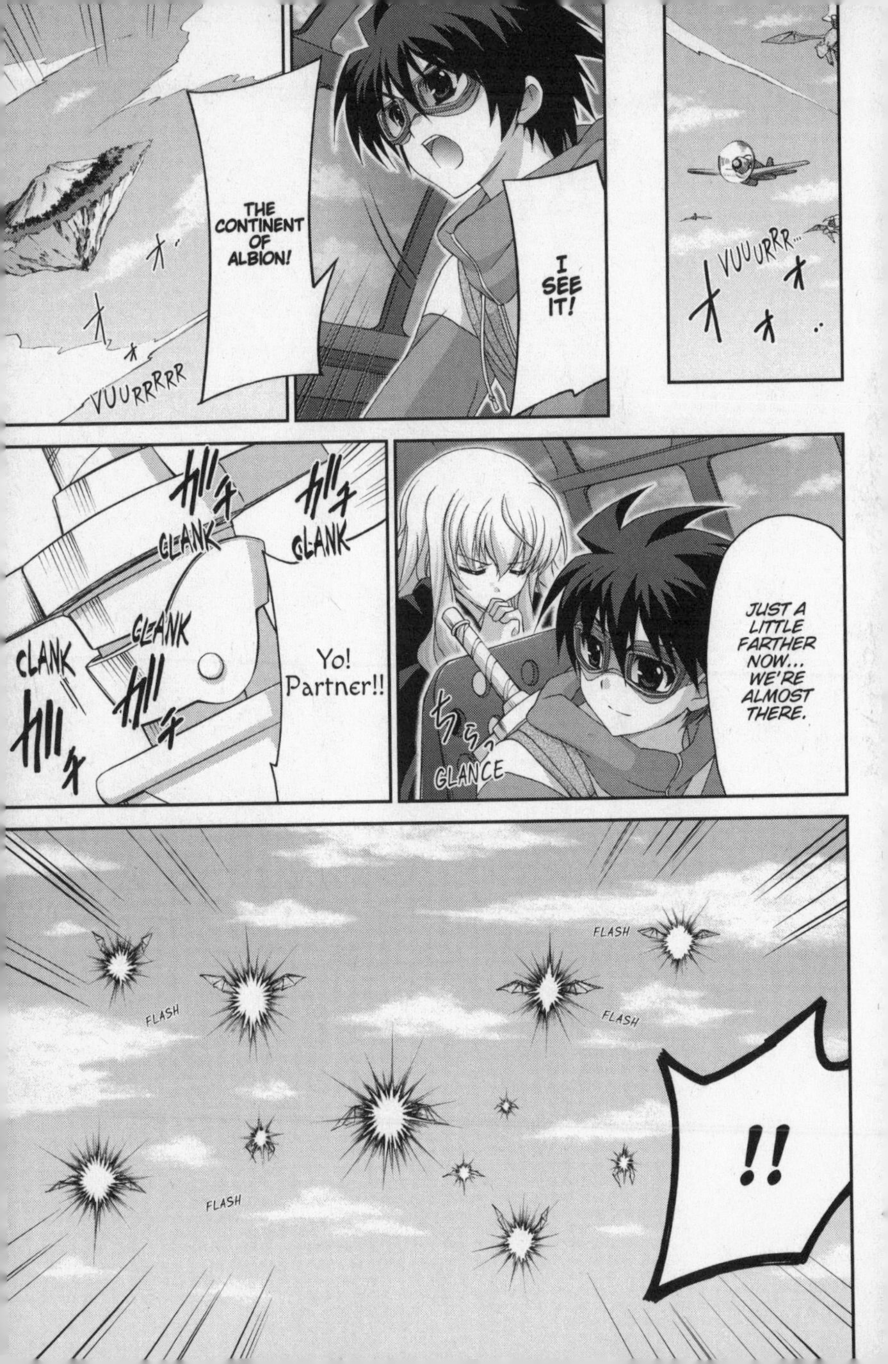
VUUURRR...
I SEE IT!
THE CONTINENT OF ALBION!
VUURRRR
JUST A LITTLE FARTHER NOW... WE'RE ALMOST THERE.
GLANCE
Yo! Partner!!
CLANK
CLANK
CLANK
CLANK
!!
FLASH
FLASH
FLASH
FLASH

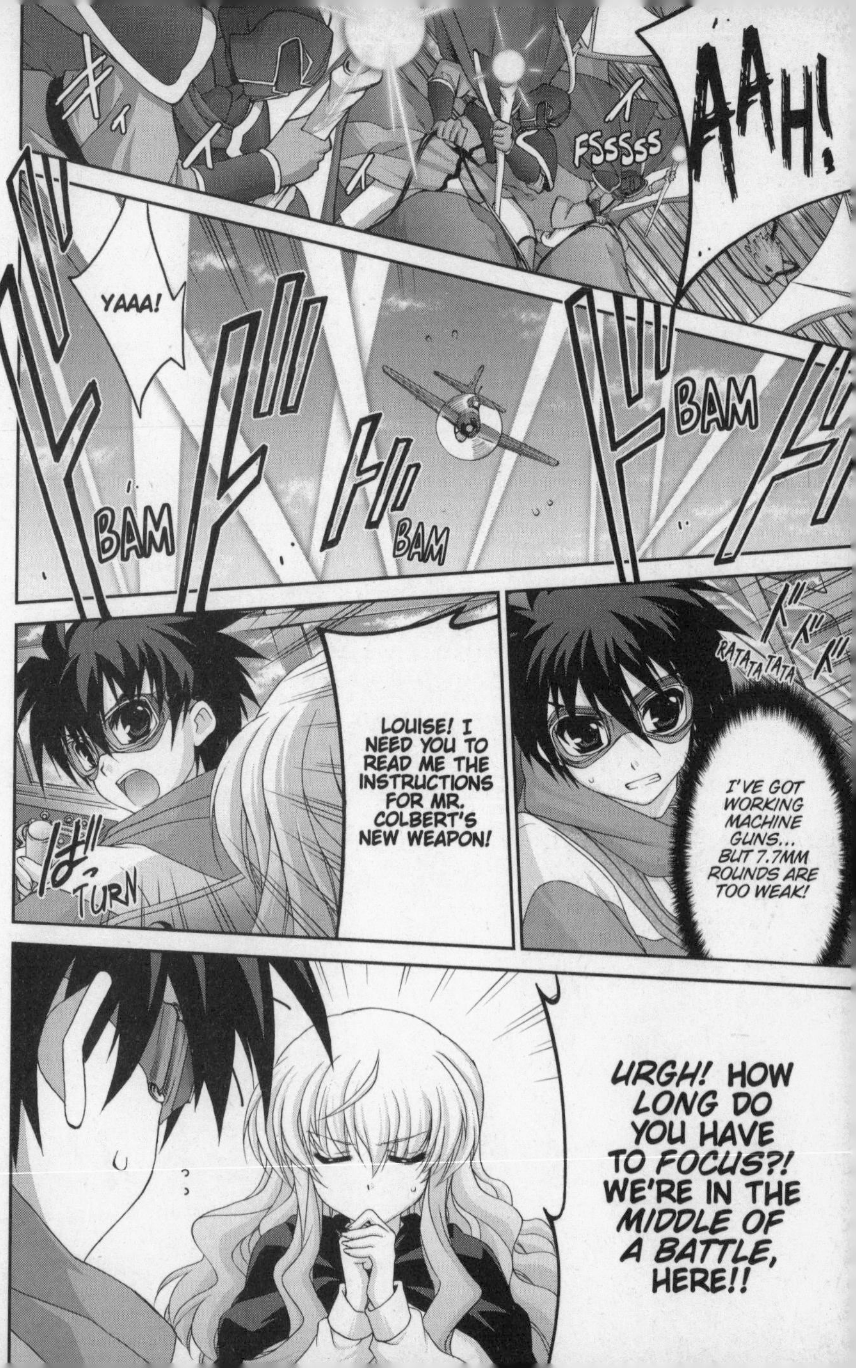
AAH!
FSSSSS
BAM
YAAA!
BAM
BAM
RATATATATA
I'VE GOT WORKING MACHINE GUNS... BUT 7.7MM ROUNDS ARE TOO WEAK!
LOUISE! I NEED YOU TO READ ME THE INSTRUCTIONS FOR MR. COLBERT'S NEW WEAPON!
TURN
URGH! HOW LONG DO YOU HAVE TO FOCUS?! WE'RE IN THE MIDDLE OF A BATTLE, HERE!!

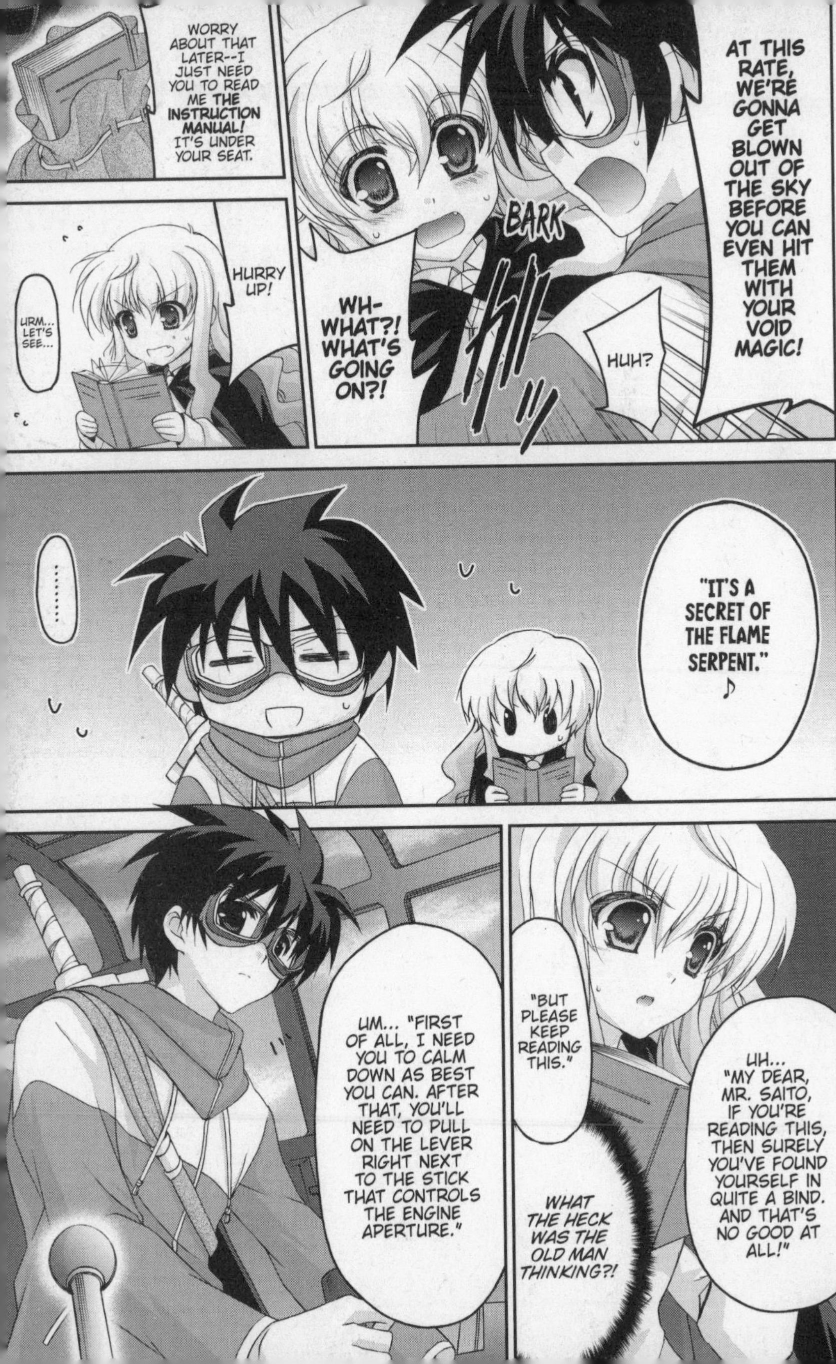
AT THIS RATE, WE'RE GONNA GET BLOWN OUT OF THE SKY BEFORE YOU CAN EVEN HIT THEM WITH YOUR VOID MAGIC!
BARK
HUH?
WH- WHAT?! WHAT'S GOING ON?!
WORRY ABOUT THAT LATER--I JUST NEED YOU TO READ ME THE INSTRUCTION MANUAL! IT'S UNDER YOUR SEAT.
HURRY UP!
URM... LET'S SEE...
"IT'S A SECRET OF THE FLAME SERPENT." ♪
......
UH... "MY DEAR, MR. SAITO, IF YOU'RE READING THIS, THEN SURELY YOU'VE FOUND YOURSELF IN QUITE A BIND. AND THAT'S NO GOOD AT ALL!"
"BUT PLEASE KEEP READING THIS."
WHAT THE HECK WAS THE OLD MAN THINKING?!
UM... "FIRST OF ALL, I NEED YOU TO CALM DOWN AS BEST YOU CAN. AFTER THAT, YOU'LL NEED TO PULL ON THE LEVER RIGHT NEXT TO THE STICK THAT CONTROLS THE ENGINE APERTURE."

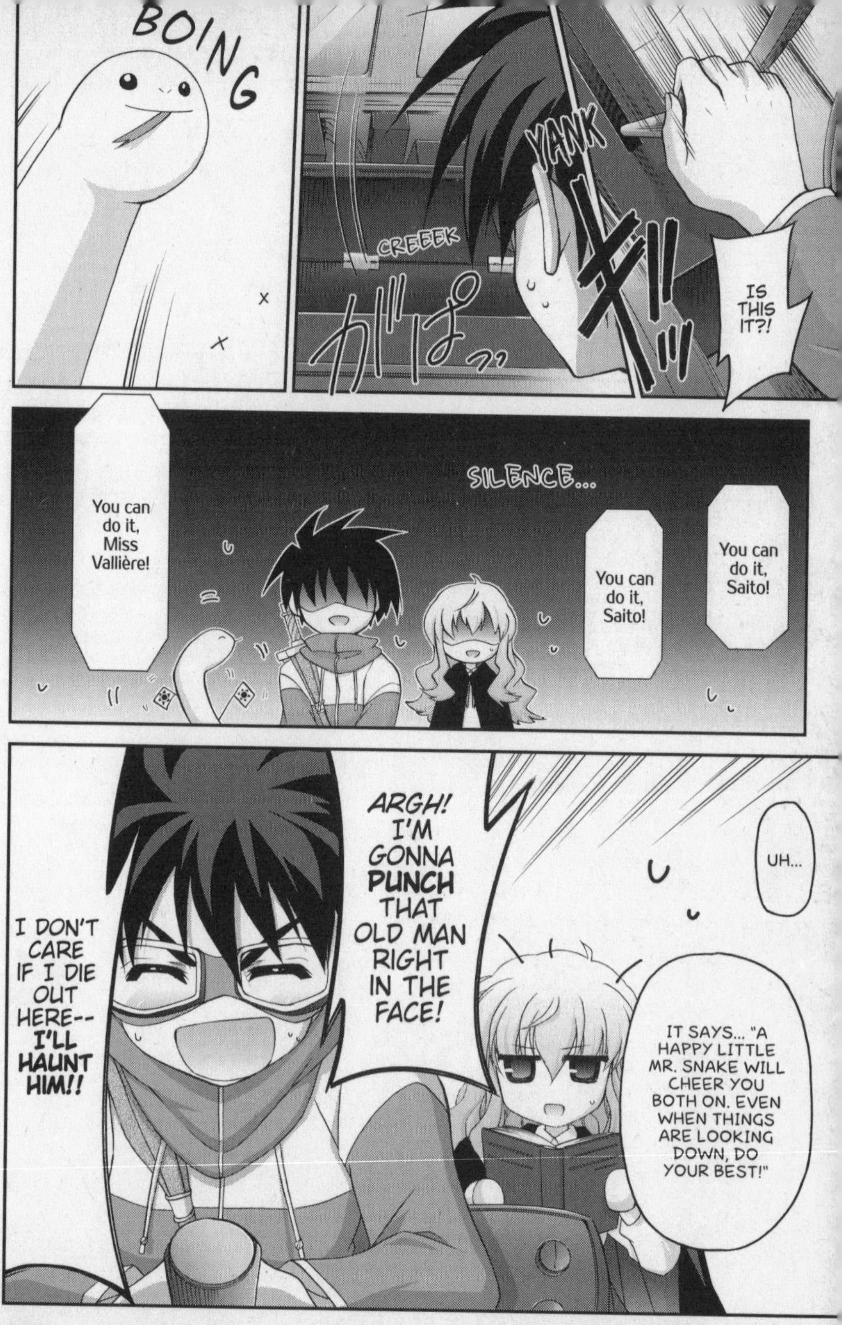
YANK
CREEEK
がぱっ
IS THIS IT?!
BOING
You can do it, Saito!
You can do it, Saito!
SILENCE...
You can do it, Miss Vallière!
UH...
IT SAYS... "A HAPPY LITTLE MR. SNAKE WILL CHEER YOU BOTH ON. EVEN WHEN THINGS ARE LOOKING DOWN, DO YOUR BEST!"
ARGH! I'M GONNA PUNCH THAT OLD MAN RIGHT IN THE FACE!
I DON'T CARE IF I DIE OUT HERE-- I'LL HAUNT HIM!!

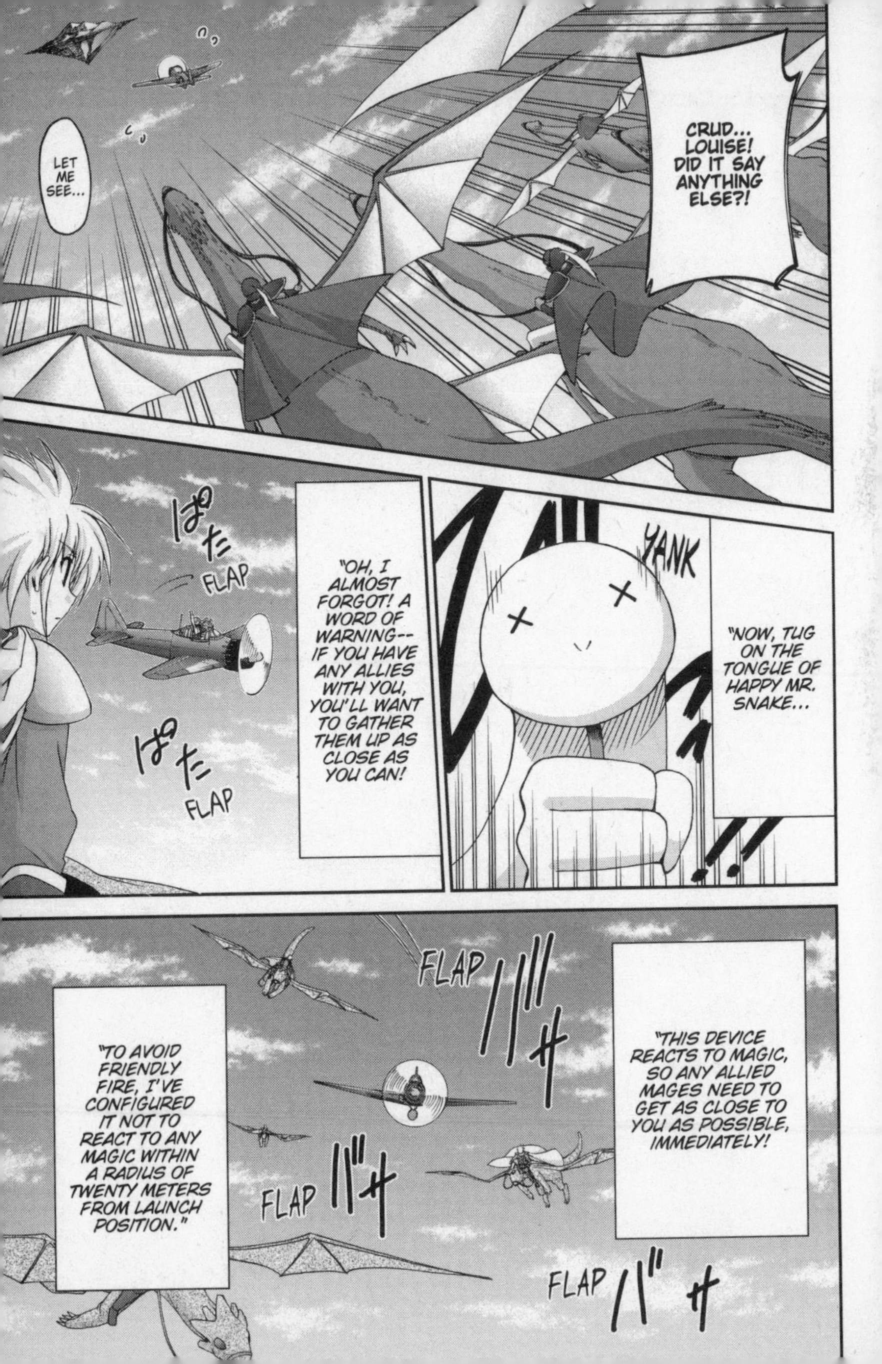
CRUD... LOUISE! DID IT SAY ANYTHING ELSE?!
LET ME SEE...
"NOW, TUG ON THE TONGUE OF HAPPY MR. SNAKE...
YANK
"OH, I ALMOST FORGOT! A WORD OF WARNING-- IF YOU HAVE ANY ALLIES WITH YOU, YOU'LL WANT TO GATHER THEM UP AS CLOSE AS YOU CAN!
ぱた
FLAP
ぱた
FLAP
"THIS DEVICE REACTS TO MAGIC, SO ANY ALLIED MAGES NEED TO GET AS CLOSE TO YOU AS POSSIBLE, IMMEDIATELY!
FLAP
バッ
FLAP
バッ
"TO AVOID FRIENDLY FIRE, I'VE CONFIGURED IT NOT TO REACT TO ANY MAGIC WITHIN A RADIUS OF TWENTY METERS FROM LAUNCH POSITION."
FLAP
バッ

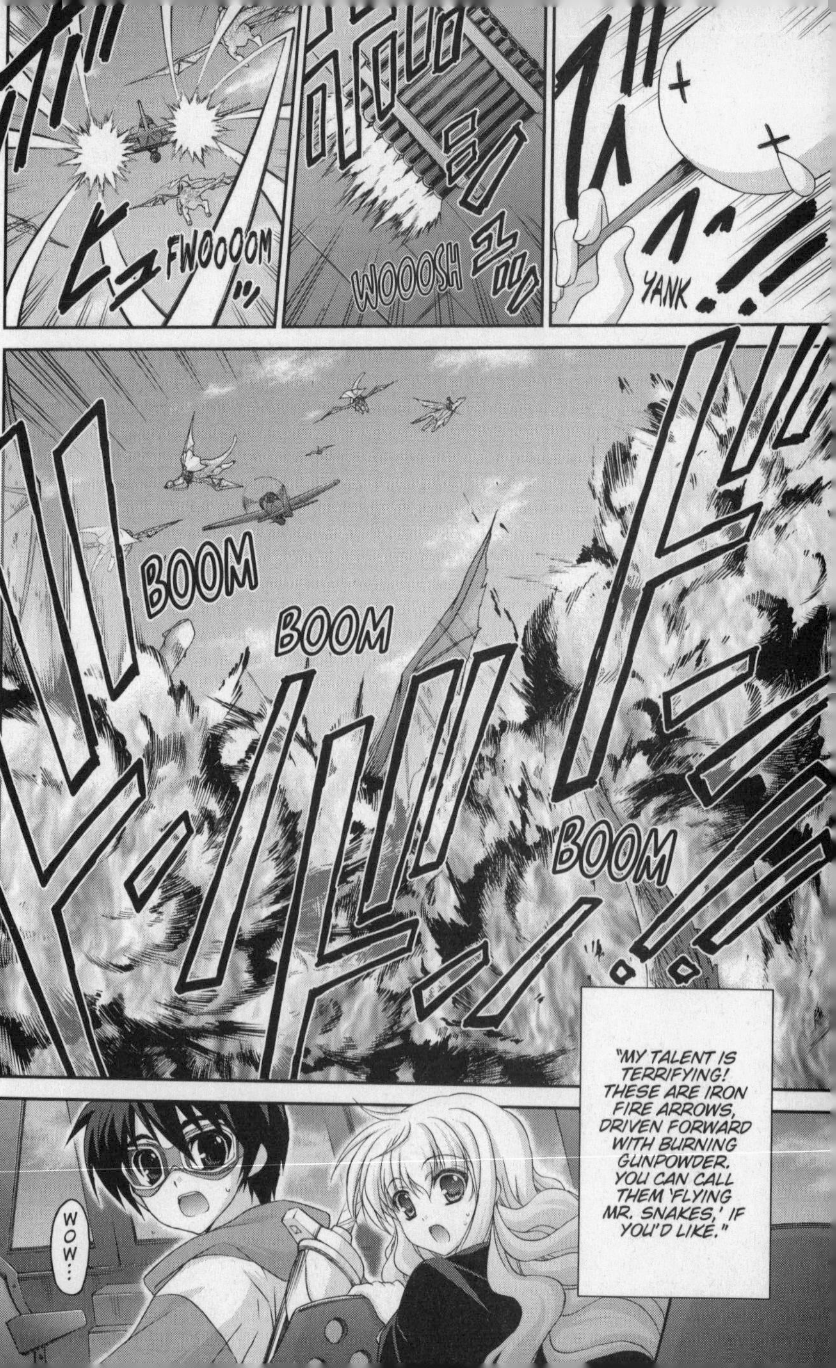
YANK
WOOOSH
FWOOOOM
BOOM
BOOM
BOOM
"MY TALENT IS TERRIFYING! THESE ARE IRON FIRE ARROWS, DRIVEN FORWARD WITH BURNING GUNPOWDER. YOU CAN CALL THEM 'FLYING MR. SNAKES,' IF YOU'D LIKE."
WOW...

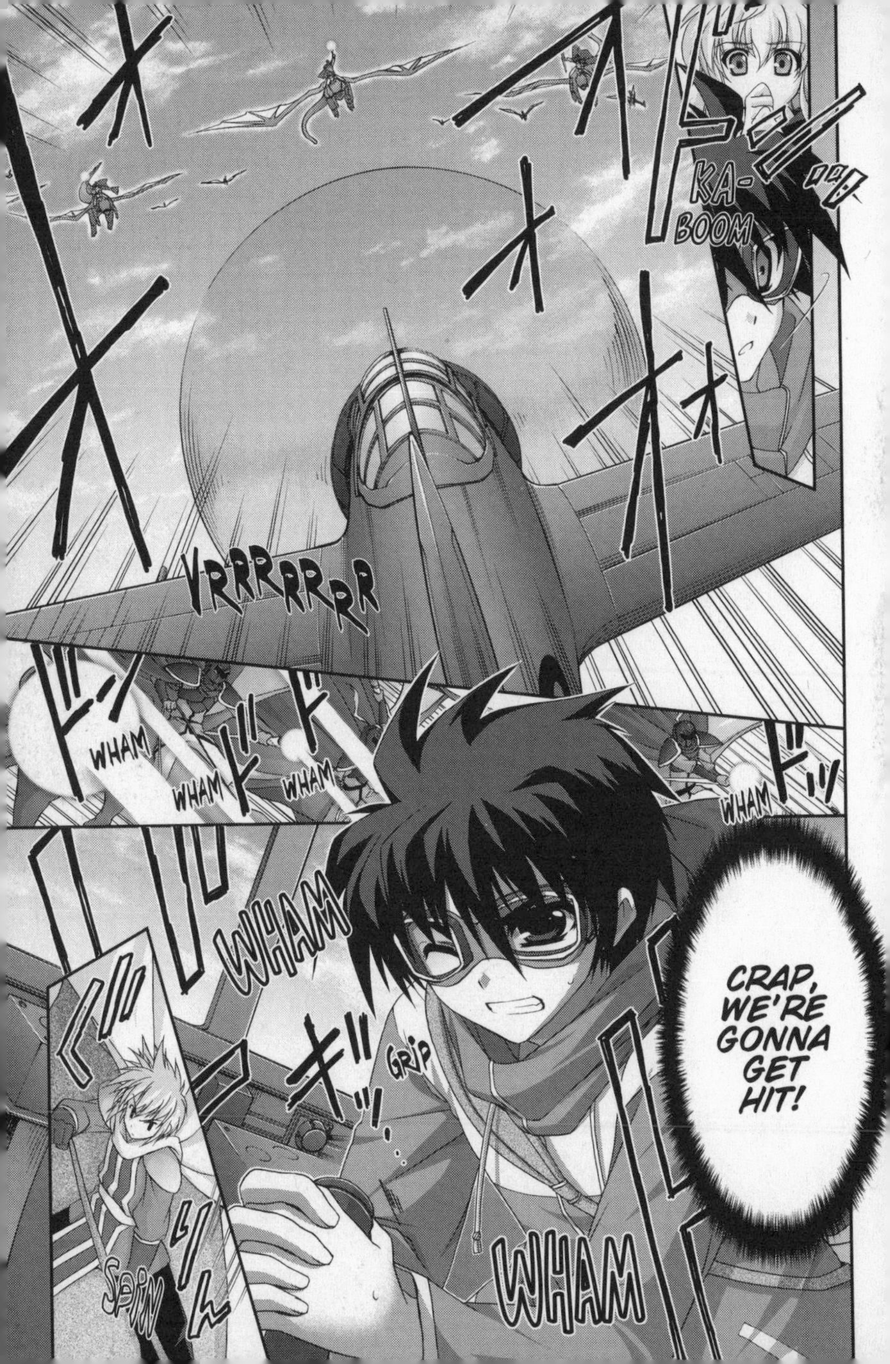
KA-BOOM
VRRRRRRR
WHAM
WHAM
WHAM
WHAM
CRAP, WE'RE GONNA GET HIT!
WHAM
GRIP
WHAM
SPIN

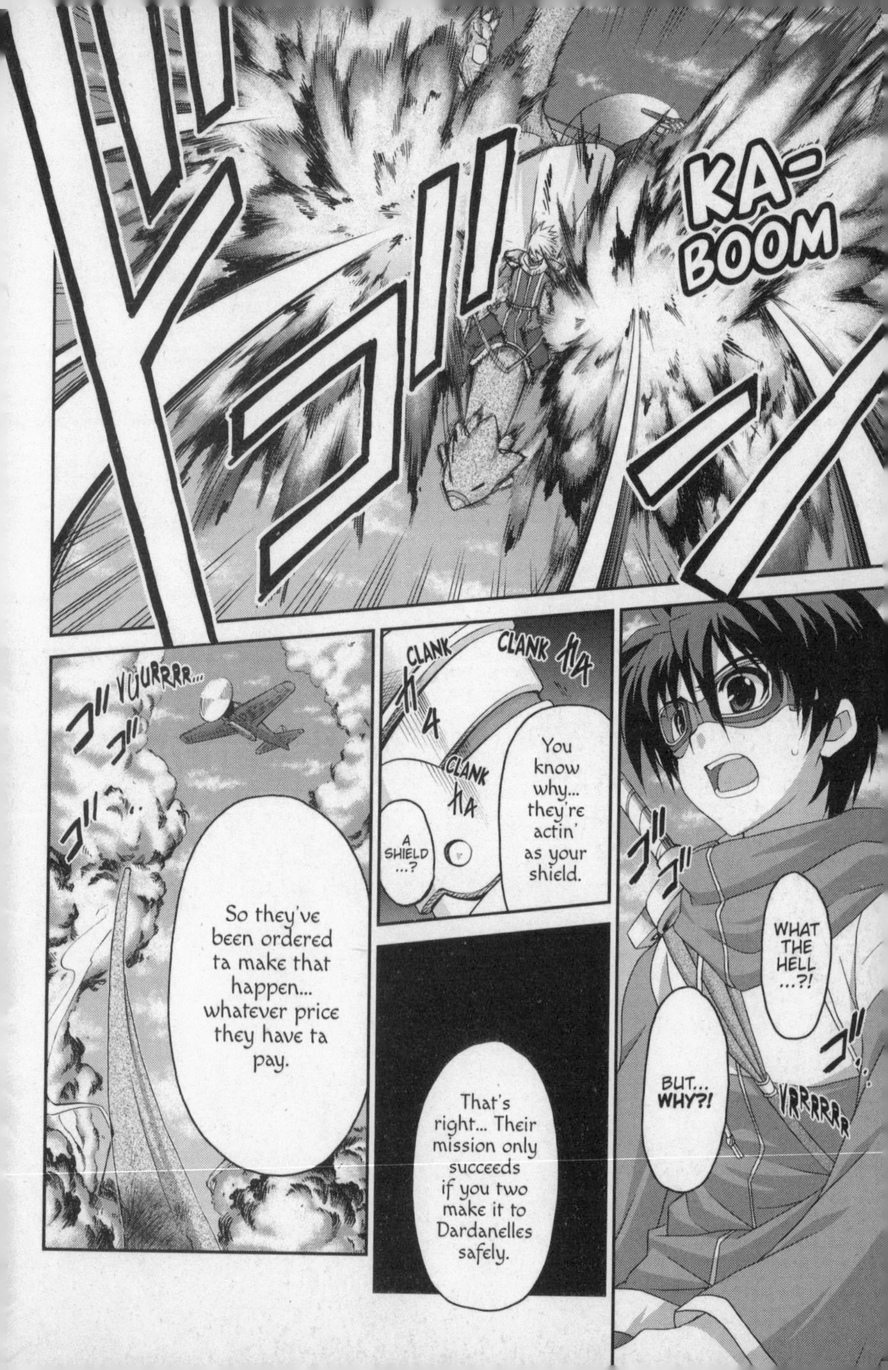
KA-
BOOM
WHAT THE HELL ...?!
BUT... WHY?!
VRRRRRR
CLANK
CLANK
CLANK
You know why... they're actin' as your shield.
A SHIELD ...?
That's right... Their mission only succeeds if you two make it to Dardanelles safely.
VUURRRR...
So they've been ordered ta make that happen... whatever price they have ta pay.

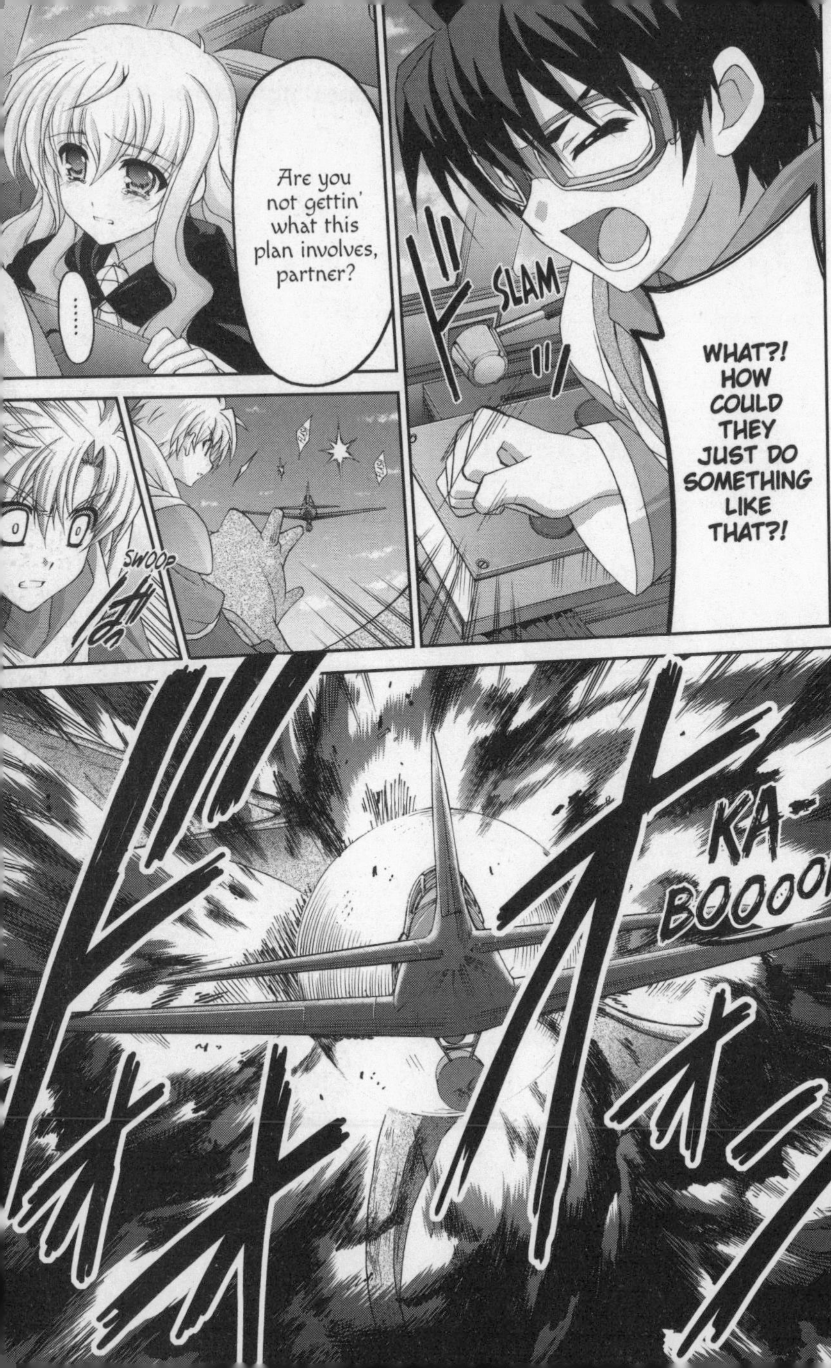
WHAT?! HOW COULD THEY JUST DO SOMETHING LIKE THAT?!
SLAM
Are you not gettin' what this plan involves, partner?
......
SWOOP
KA-BOOOOOM

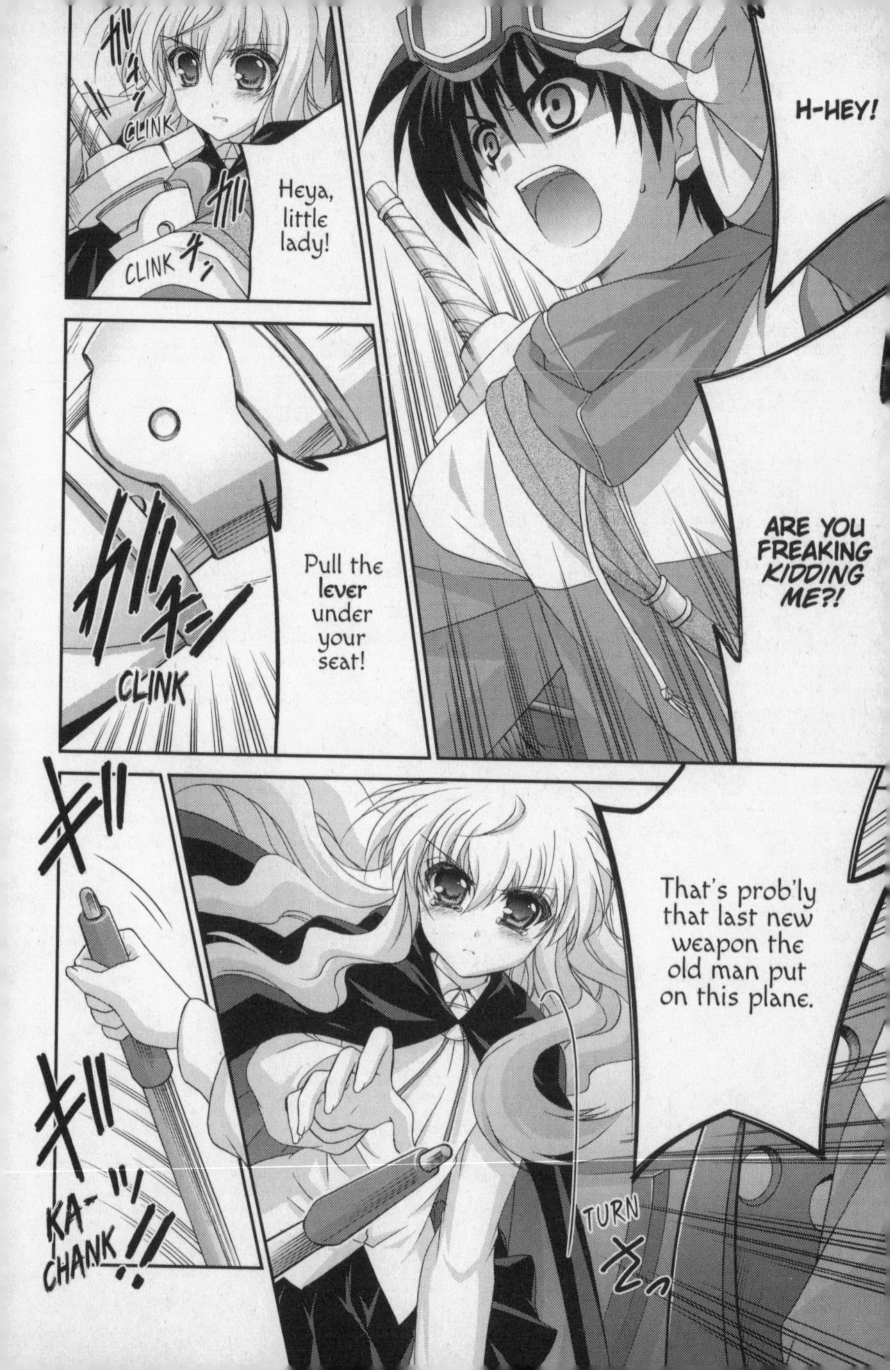
H-HEY!
ARE YOU FREAKING KIDDING ME?!
CLINK
Heya, little lady!
CLINK
Pull the lever under your seat!
CLINK
That's prob'ly that last new weapon the old man put on this plane.
TURN
KA-CHANK!!

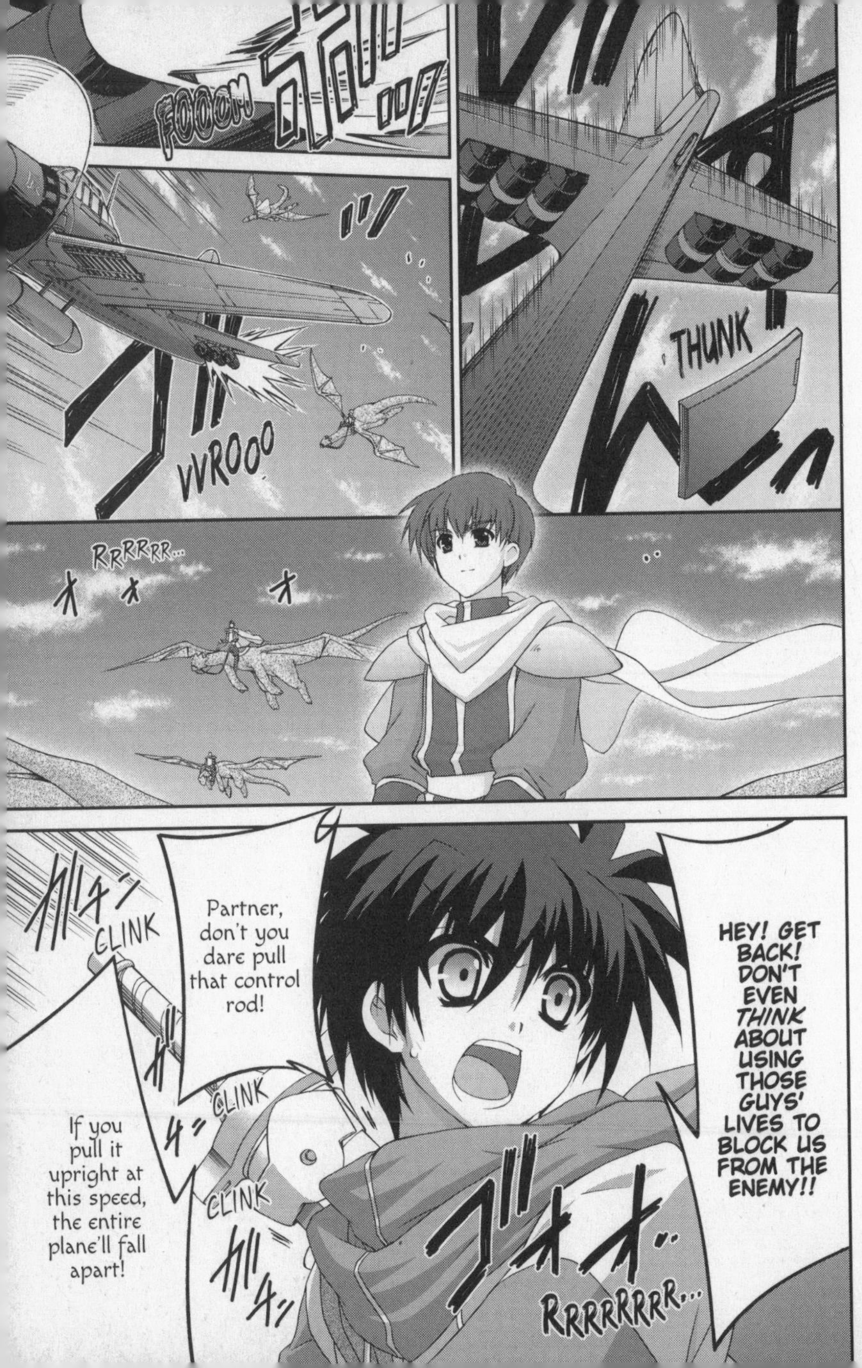
THUNK
FOOOM
VVROOO
RRRRRR...
HEY! GET BACK! DON'T EVEN *THINK* ABOUT USING THOSE GUYS' LIVES TO BLOCK US FROM THE ENEMY!!
Partner, don't you dare pull that control rod!
CLINK
CLINK
CLINK
If you pull it upright at this speed, the entire plane'll fall apart!
RRRRRRRR...

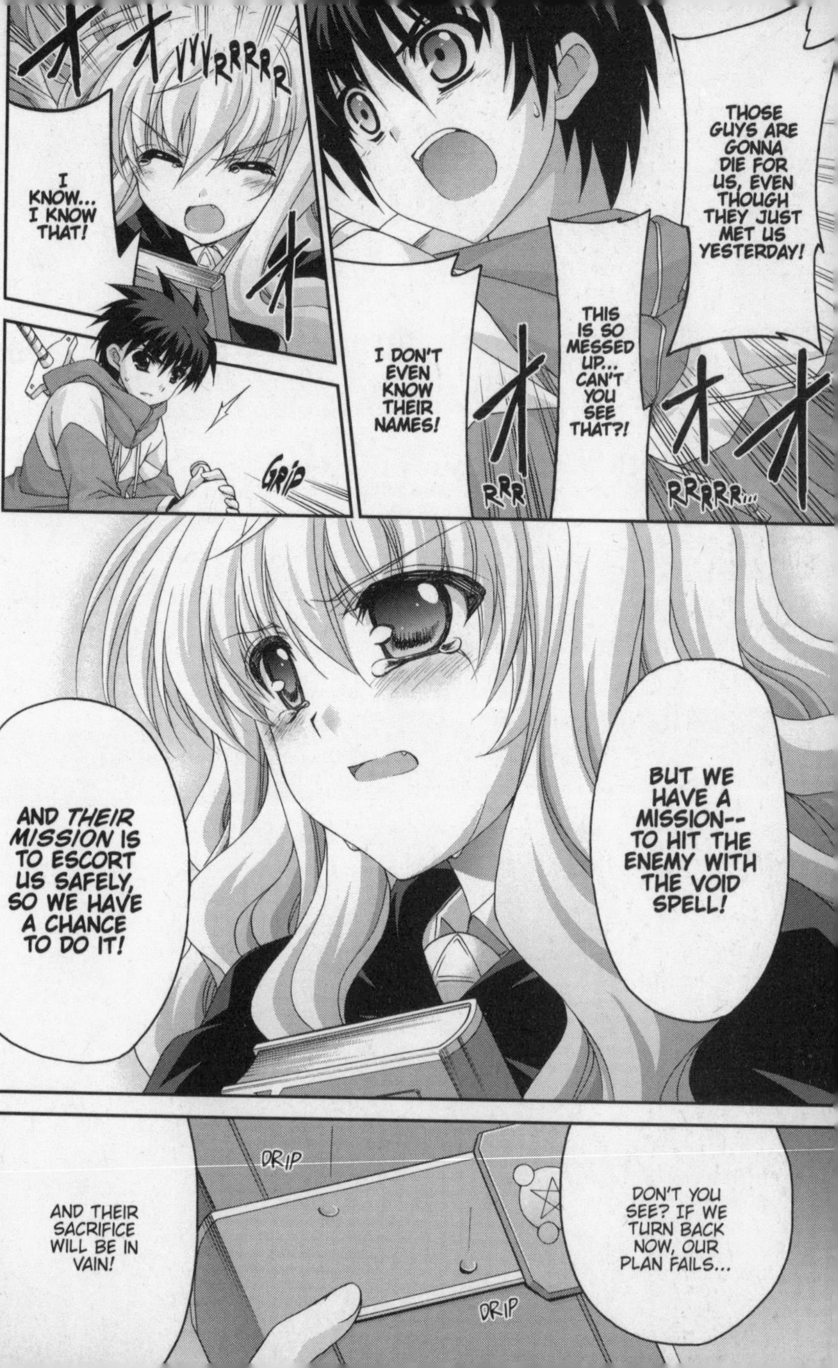
THOSE GUYS ARE GONNA DIE FOR US, EVEN THOUGH THEY JUST MET US YESTERDAY!
THIS IS SO MESSED UP... CAN'T YOU SEE THAT?!
I DON'T EVEN KNOW THEIR NAMES!
RRRRR...
RRR
VVVRRRRRR
I KNOW... I KNOW THAT!
GRIP
BUT WE HAVE A MISSION-- TO HIT THE ENEMY WITH THE VOID SPELL!
AND *THEIR MISSION* IS TO ESCORT US SAFELY, SO WE HAVE A CHANCE TO DO IT!
DRIP
DON'T YOU SEE? IF WE TURN BACK NOW, OUR PLAN FAILS...
AND THEIR SACRIFICE WILL BE IN VAIN!
DRIP

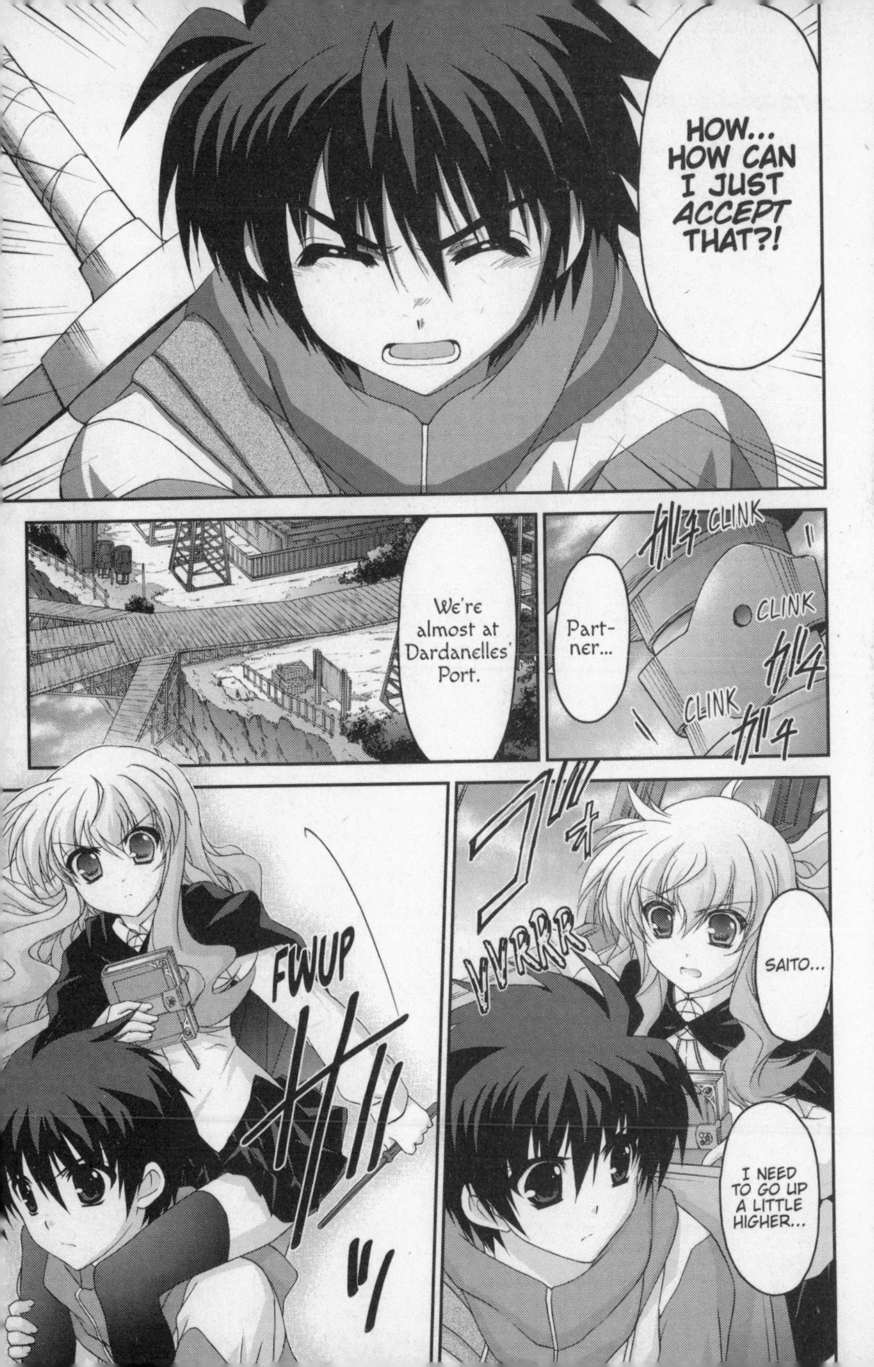
HOW... HOW CAN I JUST ACCEPT THAT?!
CLINK
Part-ner...
CLINK
CLINK
We're almost at Dardanelles' Port.
VVRRR
SAITO...
I NEED TO GO UP A LITTLE HIGHER...
FWUP

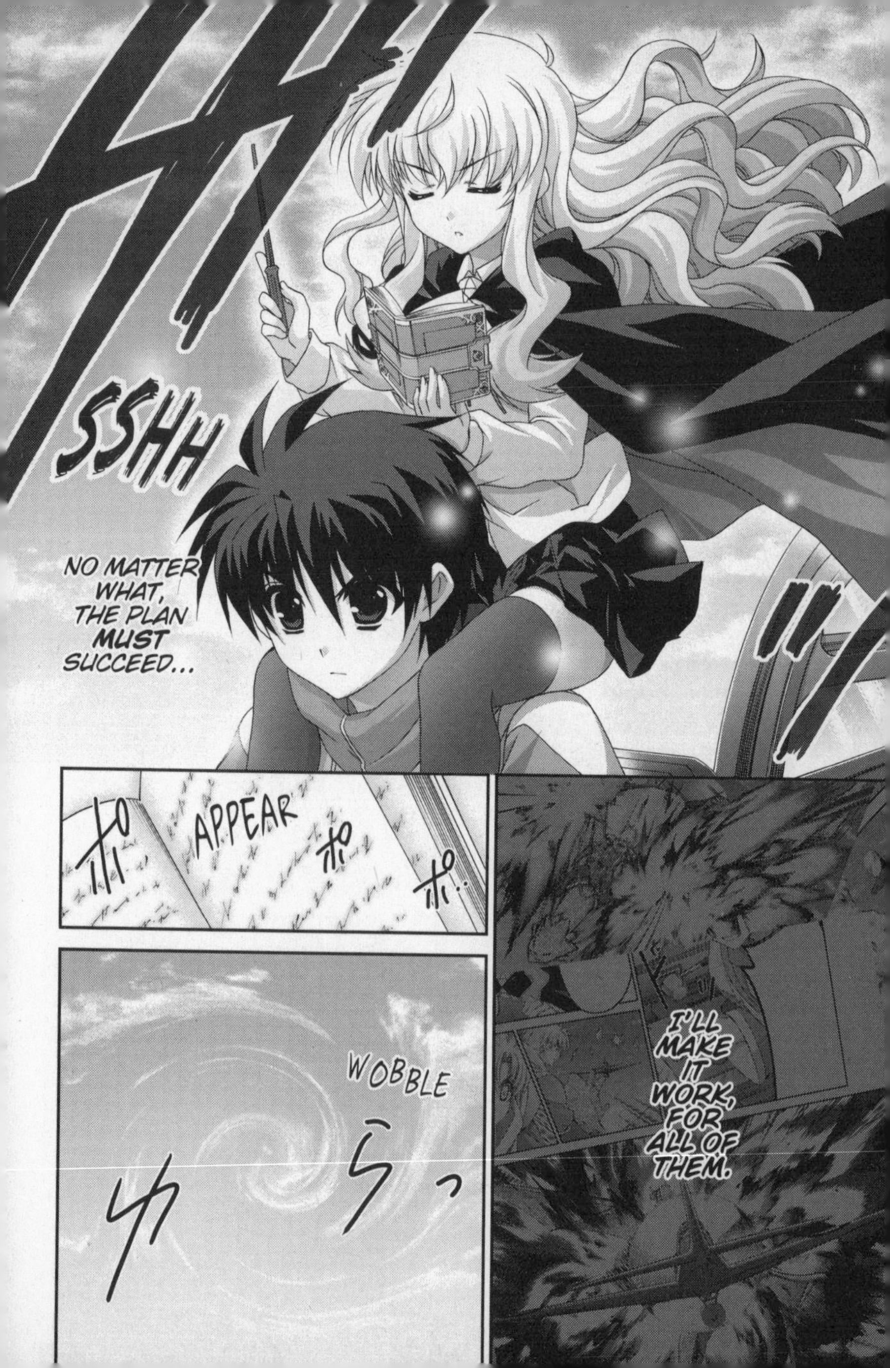
SSHH
NO MATTER WHAT, THE PLAN MUST SUCCEED...
I'LL MAKE IT WORK, FOR ALL OF THEM.
APPEAR
WOBBLE
ゆらっ

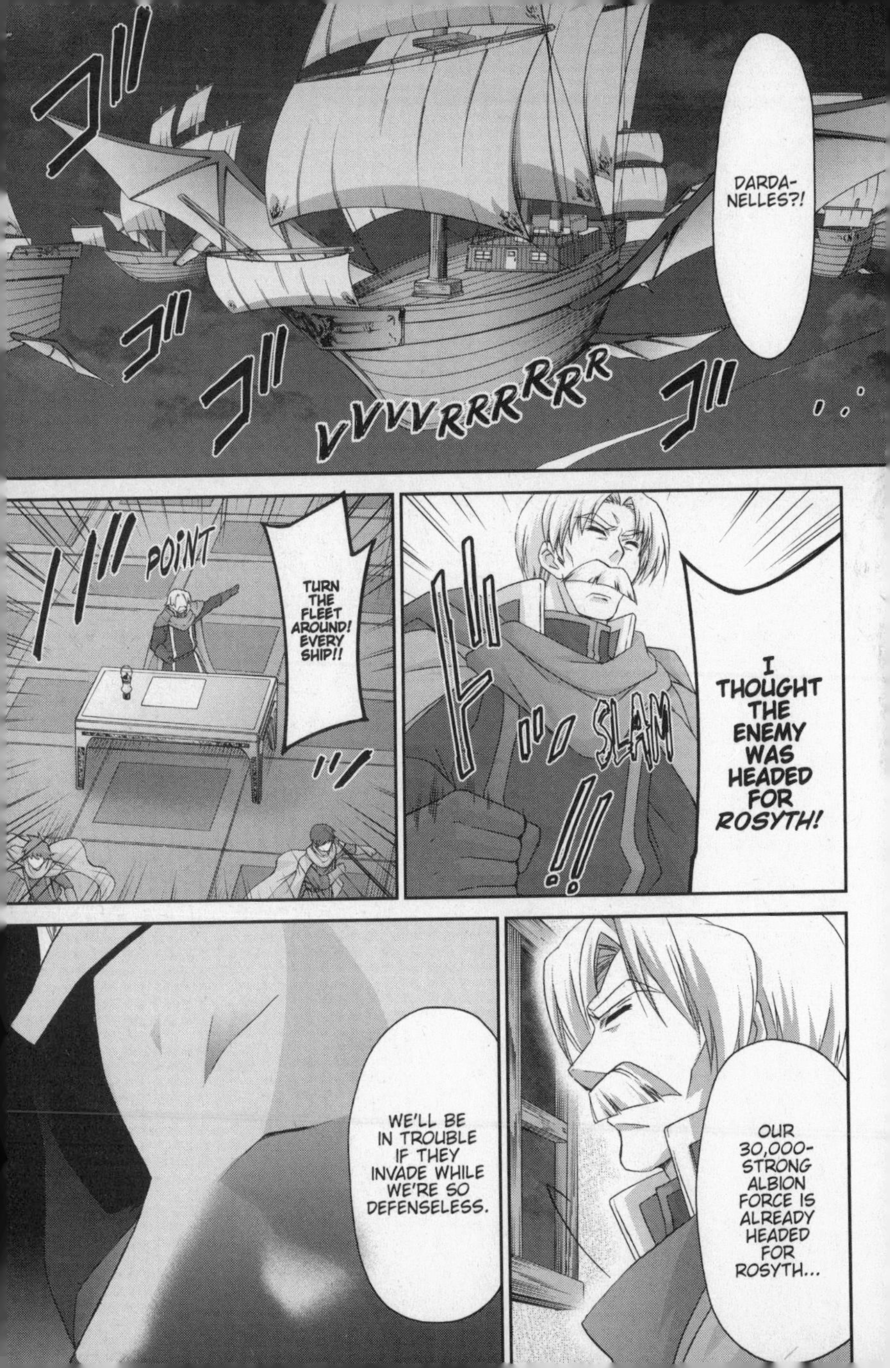
DARDA-NELLES?!
VVVVRRRRRR
I THOUGHT THE ENEMY WAS HEADED FOR ROSYTH!
SLAM
TURN THE FLEET AROUND! EVERY SHIP!!
POINT
OUR 30,000-STRONG ALBION FORCE IS ALREADY HEADED FOR ROSYTH...
WE'LL BE IN TROUBLE IF THEY INVADE WHILE WE'RE SO DEFENSELESS.

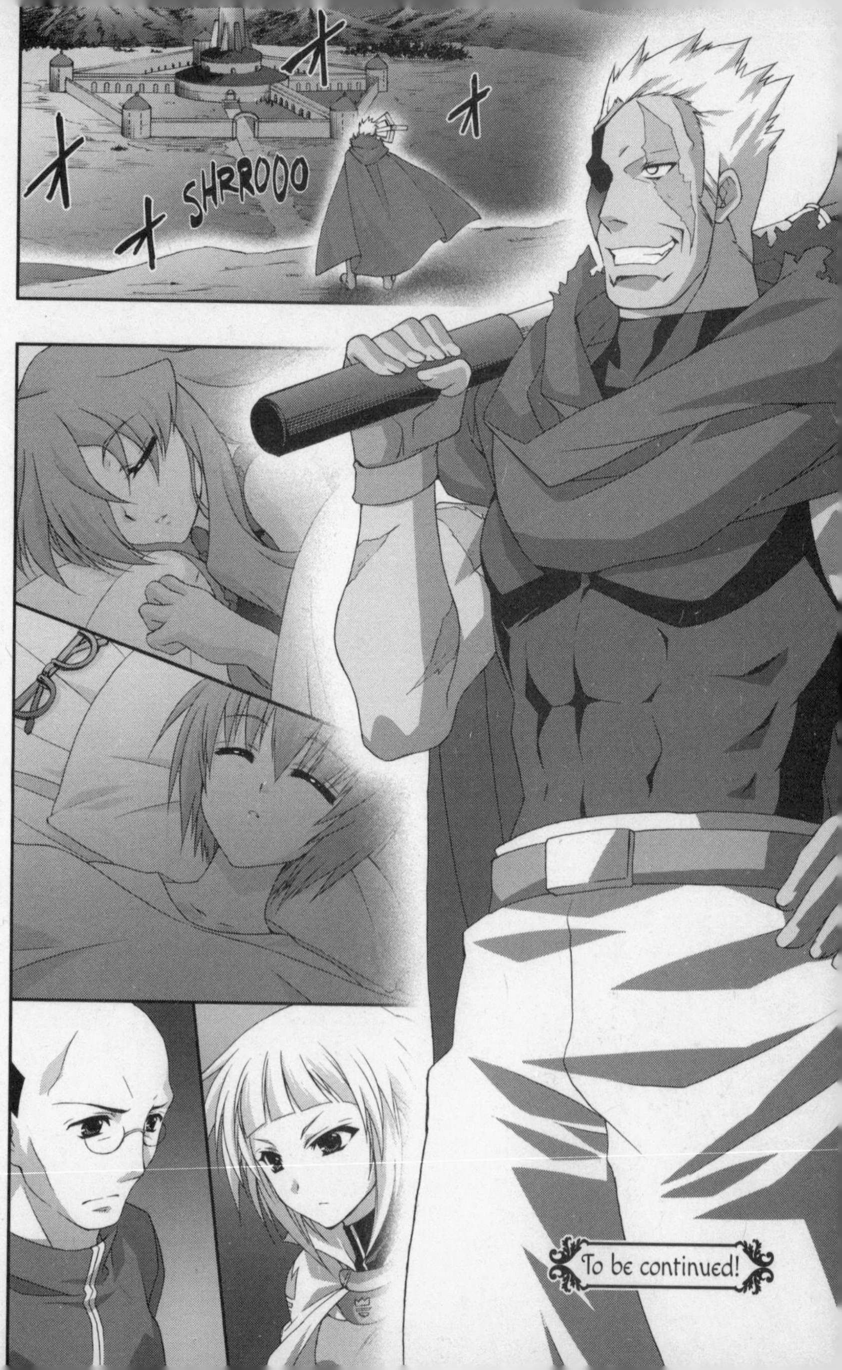
SHRROOO
To be continued!

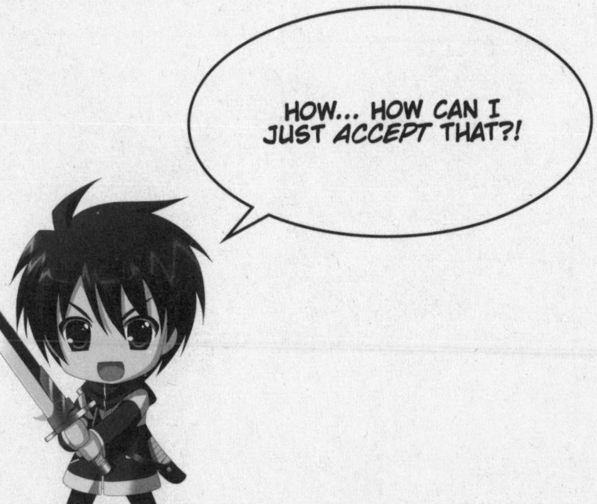
HOW... HOW CAN I JUST ACCEPT THAT?!

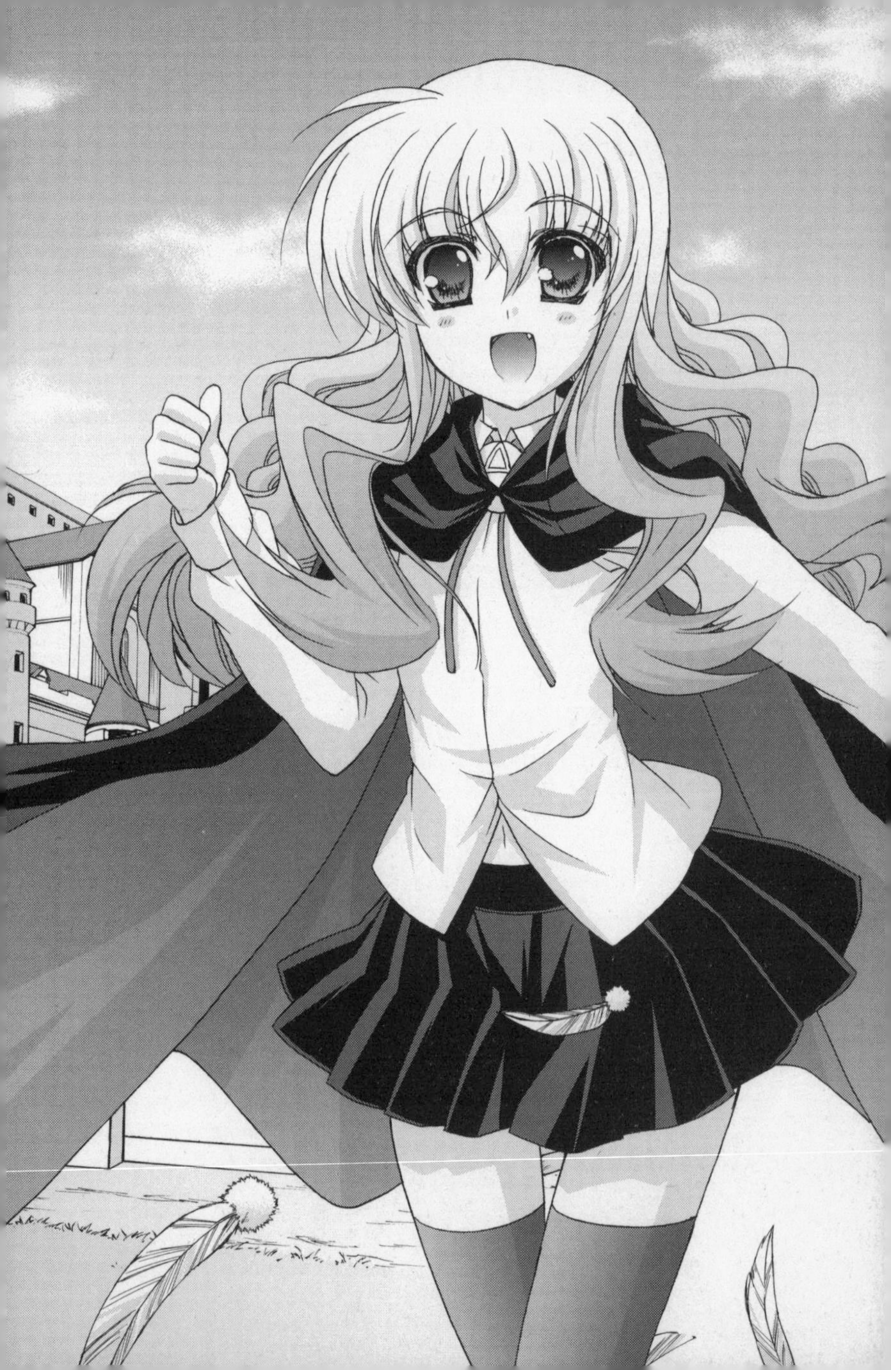

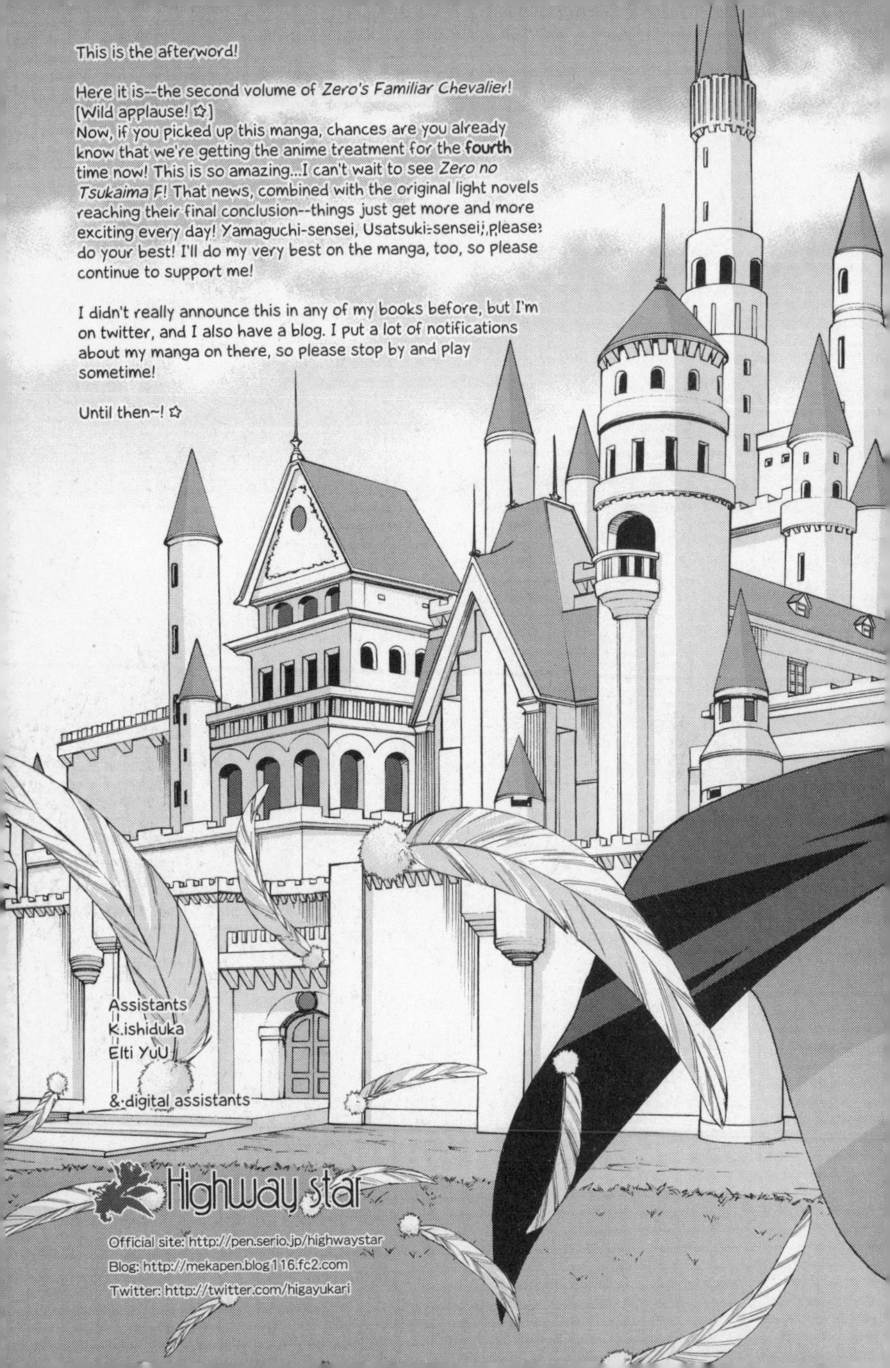

This is the afterword!

Here it is--the second volume of *Zero's Familiar Chevalier*! [Wild applause! ✩]
Now, if you picked up this manga, chances are you already know that we're getting the anime treatment for the **fourth** time now! This is so amazing...I can't wait to see *Zero no Tsukaima F*! That news, combined with the original light novels reaching their final conclusion--things just get more and more exciting every day! Yamaguchi-sensei, Usatsuki-sensei, please do your best! I'll do my very best on the manga, too, so please continue to support me!

I didn't really announce this in any of my books before, but I'm on twitter, and I also have a blog. I put a lot of notifications about my manga on there, so please stop by and play sometime!

Until then~! ✩

Assistants
K.ishiduka
Elti YuU

& digital assistants

Highway star

Official site: http://pen.serio.jp/highwaystar
Blog: http://mekapen.blog116.fc2.com
Twitter: http://twitter.com/higayukari

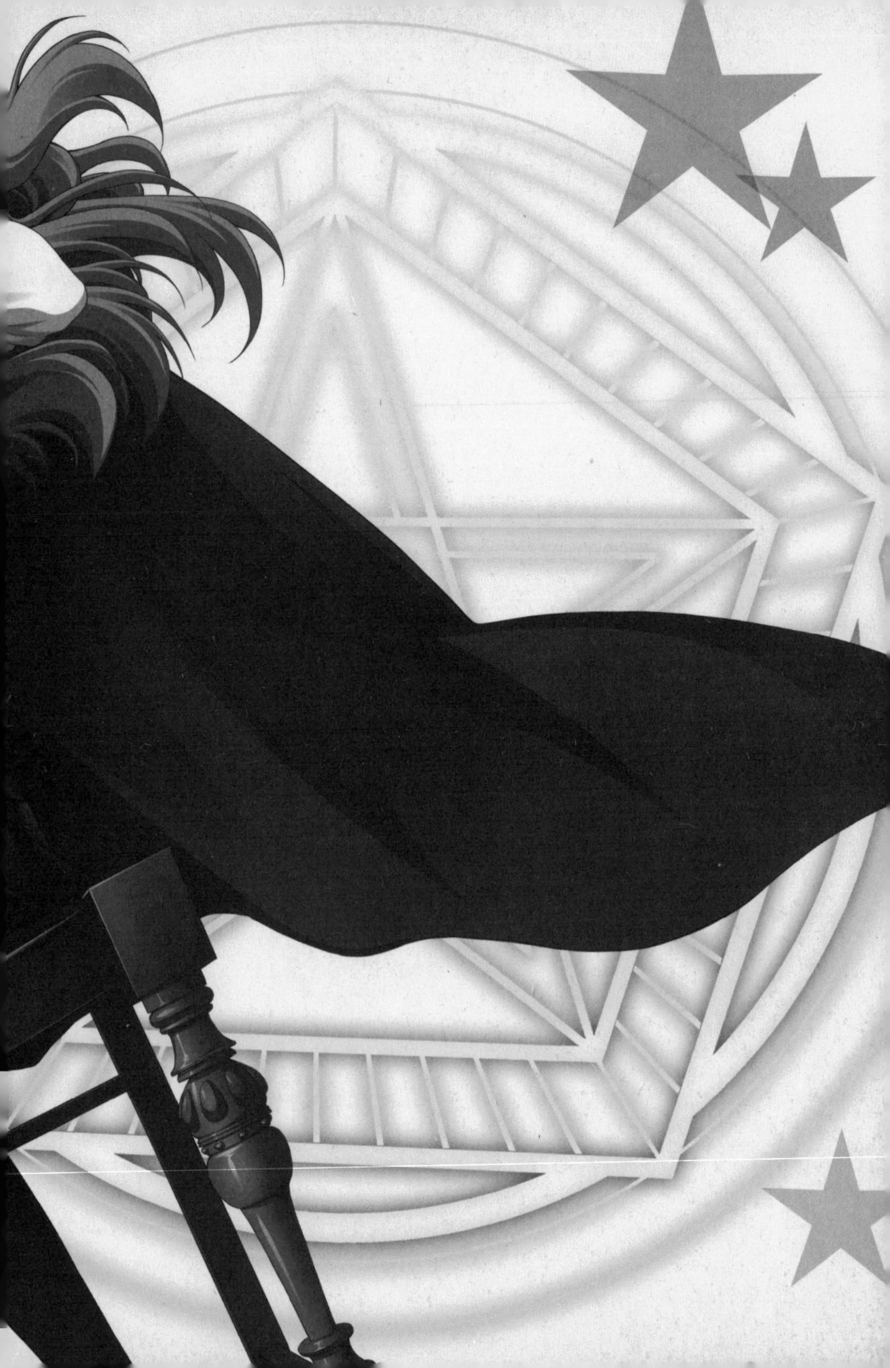

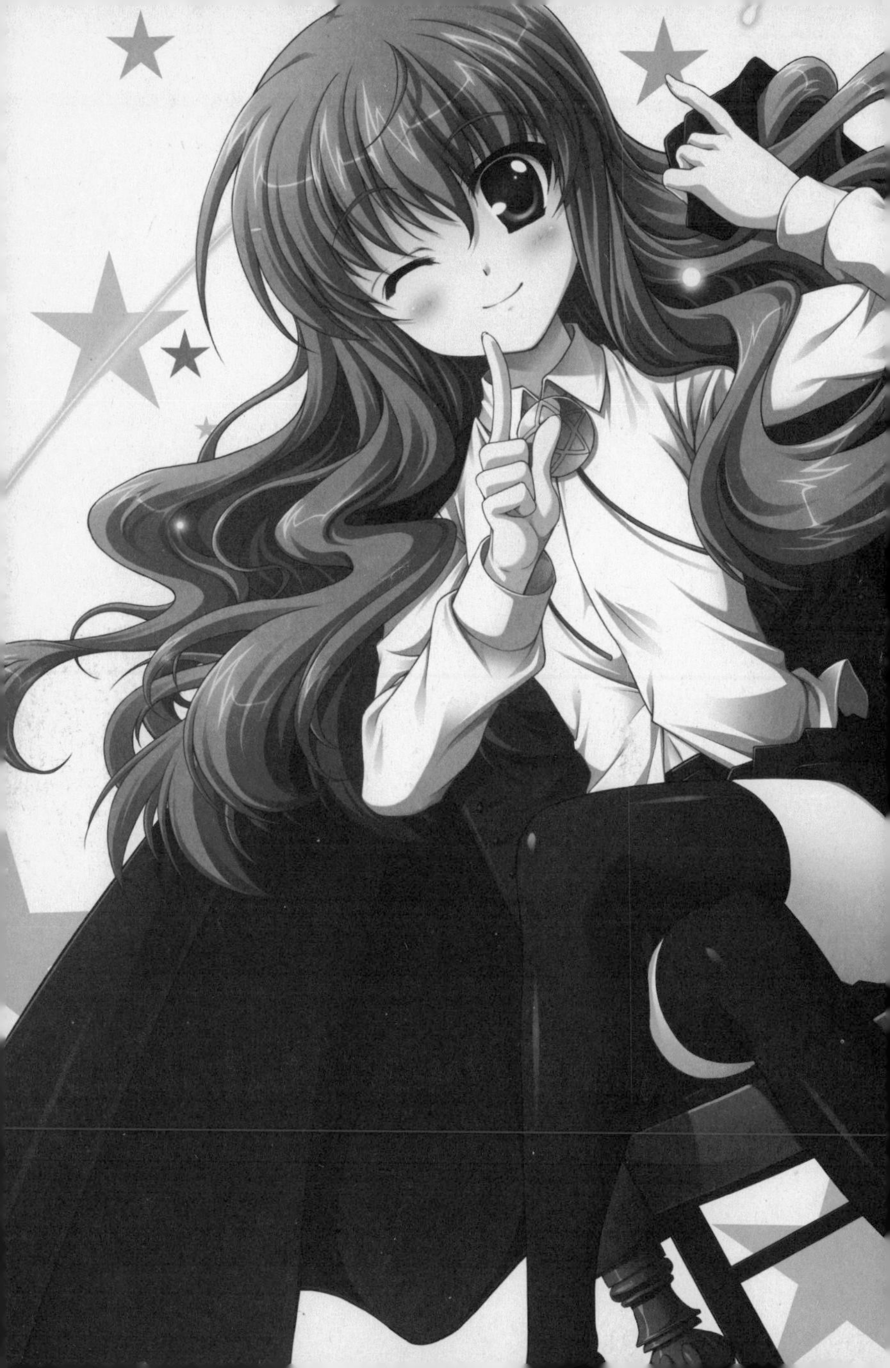

Le Familier de Zero Chevalier

ZERO'S
FAMILIAR
Chevalier

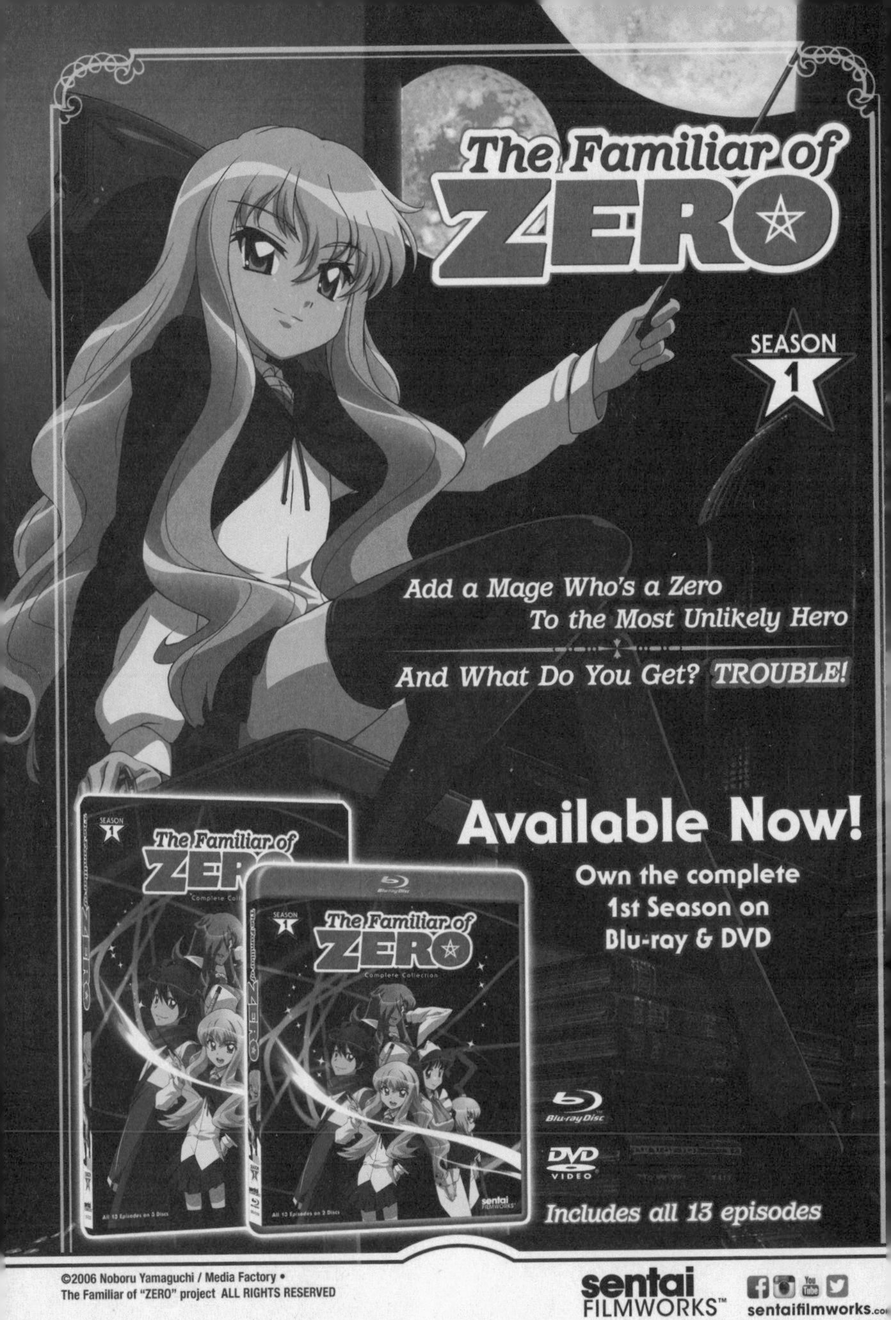

The Familiar of ZERO
SEASON 1
Add a Mage Who's a Zero
To the Most Unlikely Hero
And What Do You Get? TROUBLE!
Available Now!
Own the complete
1st Season on
Blu-ray & DVD
Includes all 13 episodes

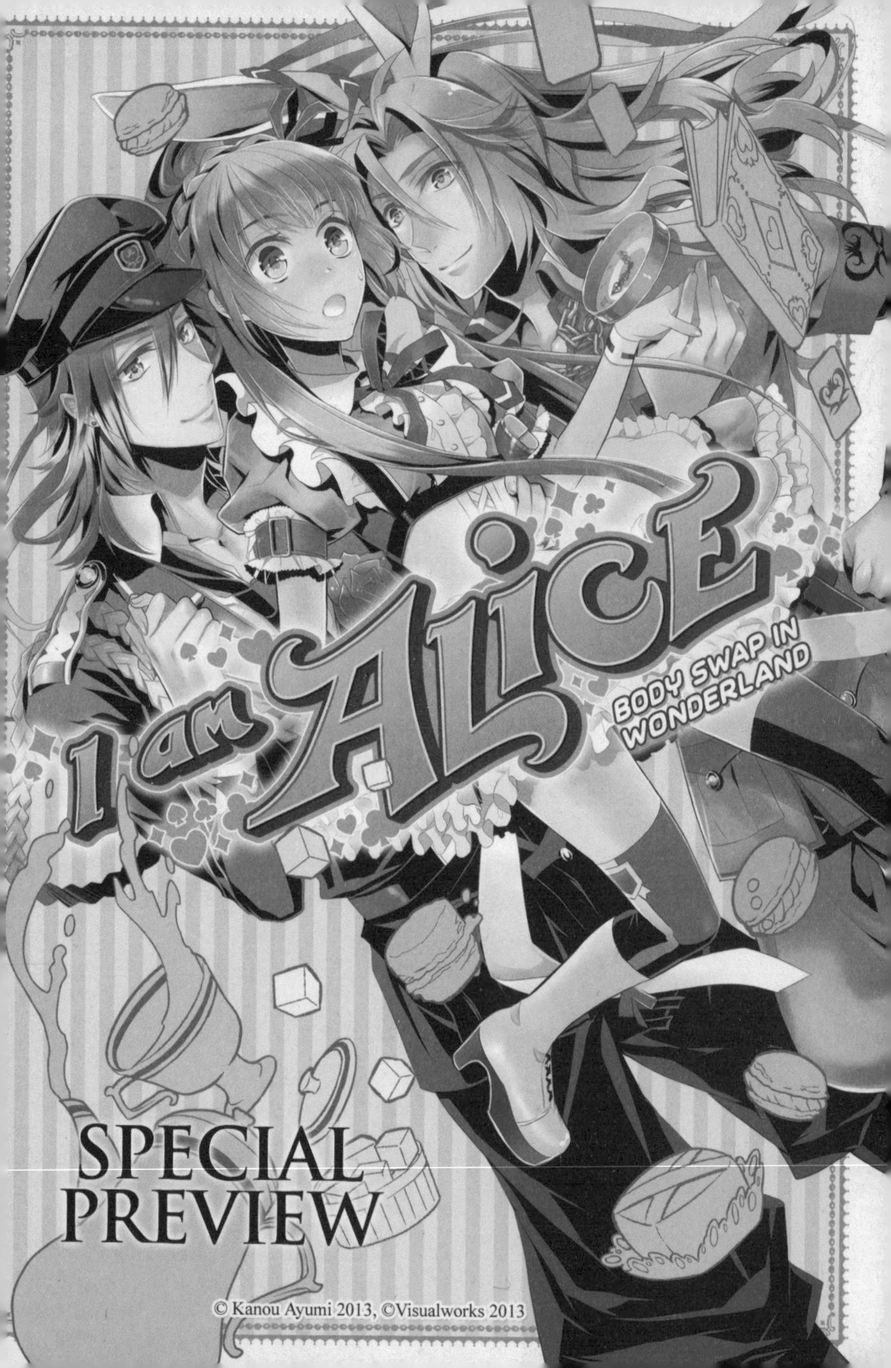
I am ALICE
BODY SWAP IN WONDERLAND
SPECIAL PREVIEW

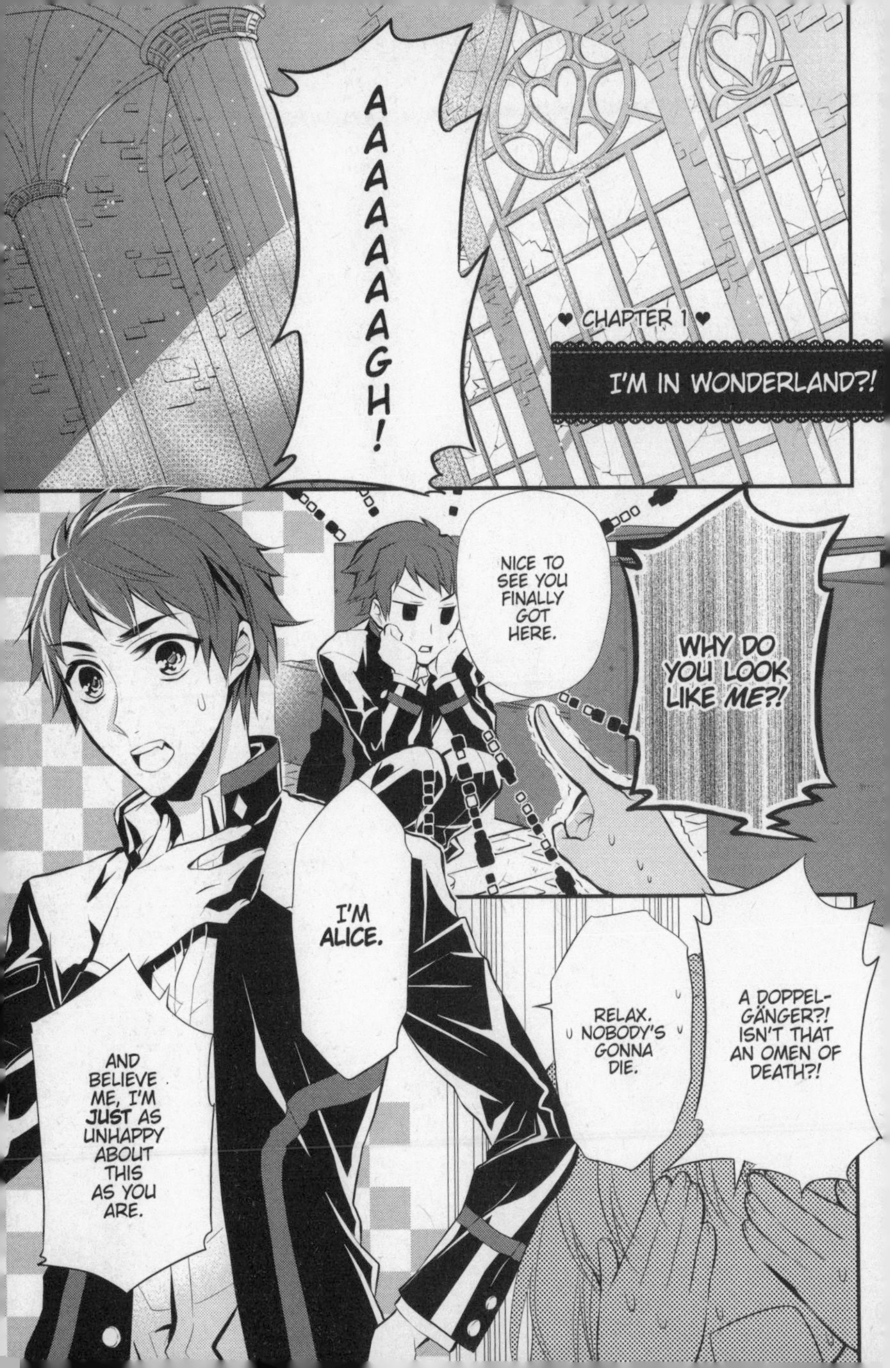
♥ CHAPTER 1 ♥
I'M IN WONDERLAND?!
AAAAAAAGH!
WHY DO YOU LOOK LIKE ME?!
NICE TO SEE YOU FINALLY GOT HERE.
A DOPPEL-GÄNGER?! ISN'T THAT AN OMEN OF DEATH?!
RELAX. NOBODY'S GONNA DIE.
I'M ALICE.
AND BELIEVE ME, I'M JUST AS UNHAPPY ABOUT THIS AS YOU ARE.

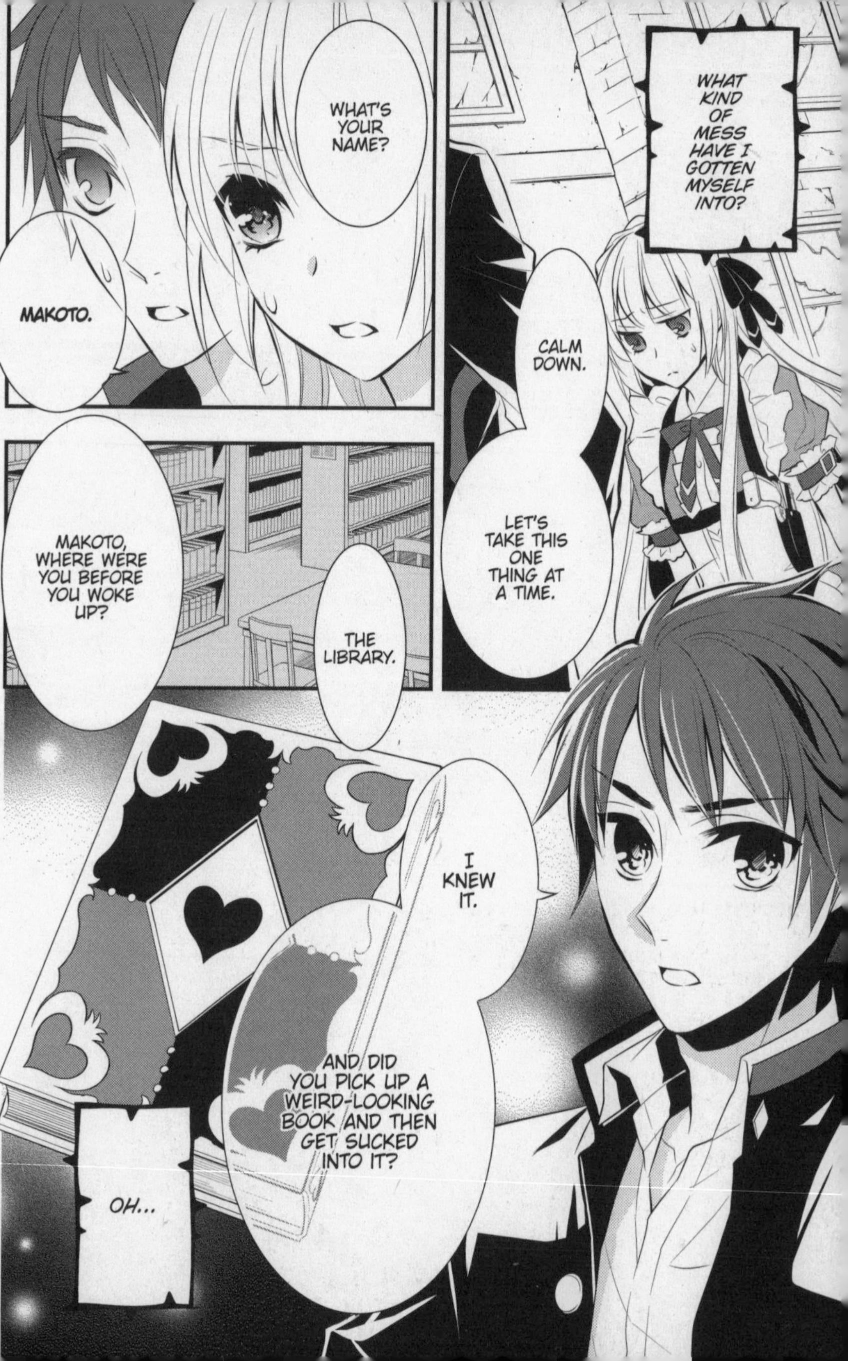
WHAT KIND OF MESS HAVE I GOTTEN MYSELF INTO?
CALM DOWN.
LET'S TAKE THIS ONE THING AT A TIME.
WHAT'S YOUR NAME?
MAKOTO.
MAKOTO, WHERE WERE YOU BEFORE YOU WOKE UP?
THE LIBRARY.
I KNEW IT.
AND DID YOU PICK UP A WEIRD-LOOKING BOOK AND THEN GET SUCKED INTO IT?
OH...

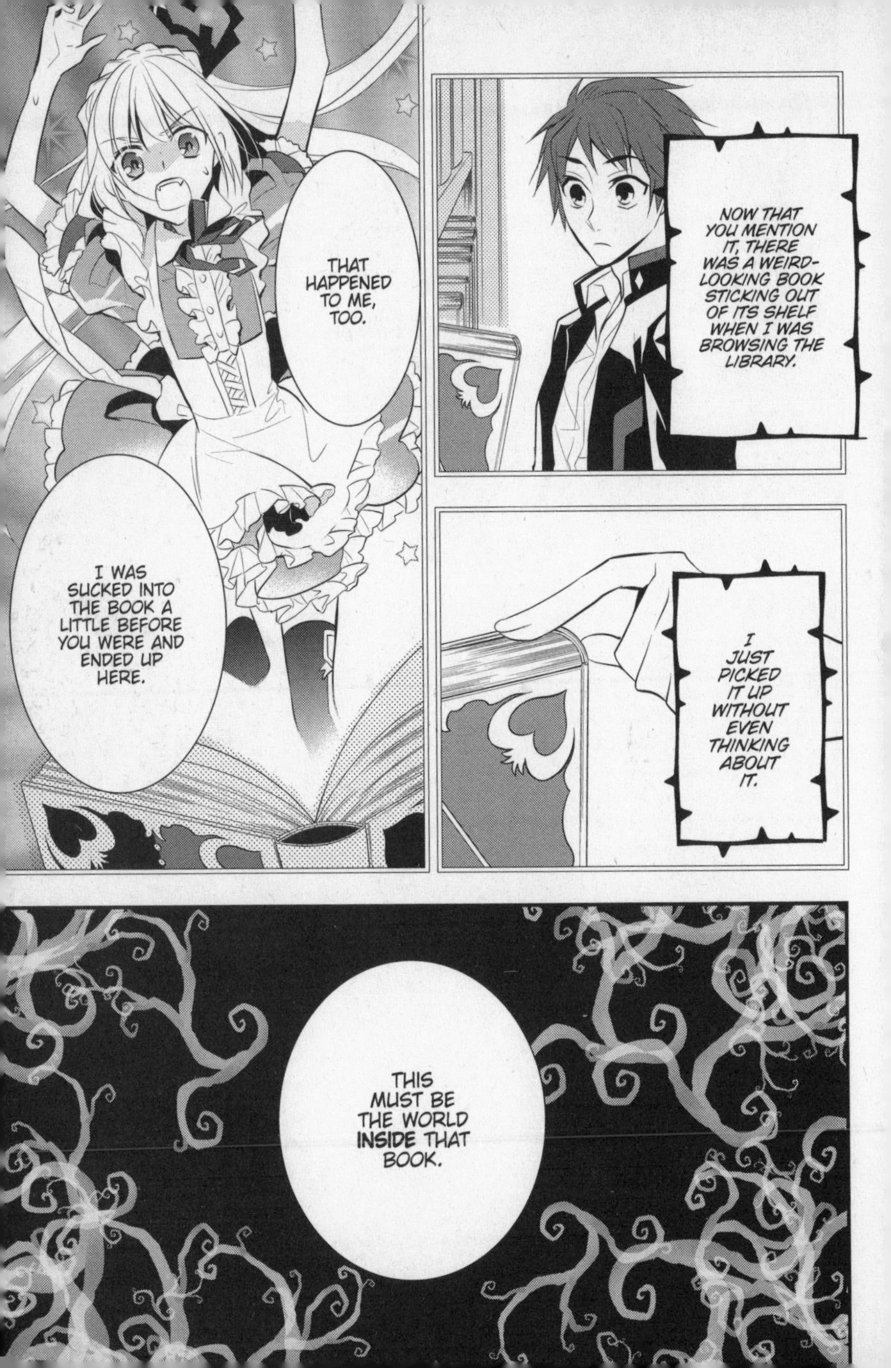
NOW THAT YOU MENTION IT, THERE WAS A WEIRD-LOOKING BOOK STICKING OUT OF ITS SHELF WHEN I WAS BROWSING THE LIBRARY.
I JUST PICKED IT UP WITHOUT EVEN THINKING ABOUT IT.
THAT HAPPENED TO ME, TOO.
I WAS SUCKED INTO THE BOOK A LITTLE BEFORE YOU WERE AND ENDED UP HERE.
THIS MUST BE THE WORLD **INSIDE** THAT BOOK.

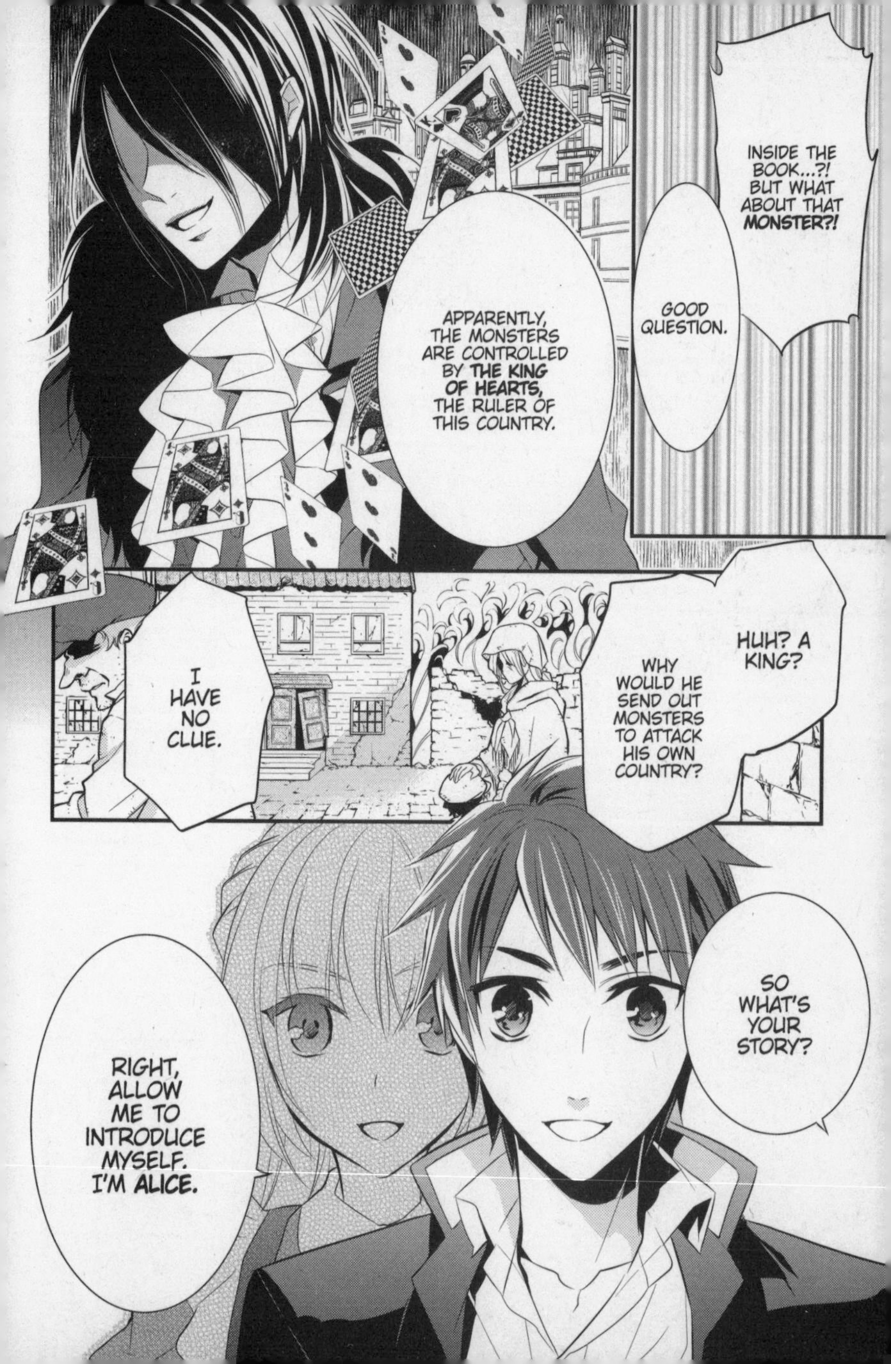
INSIDE THE BOOK...?! BUT WHAT ABOUT THAT MONSTER?!
GOOD QUESTION.
APPARENTLY, THE MONSTERS ARE CONTROLLED BY THE KING OF HEARTS, THE RULER OF THIS COUNTRY.
HUH? A KING?
WHY WOULD HE SEND OUT MONSTERS TO ATTACK HIS OWN COUNTRY?
I HAVE NO CLUE.
SO WHAT'S YOUR STORY?
RIGHT, ALLOW ME TO INTRODUCE MYSELF. I'M ALICE.

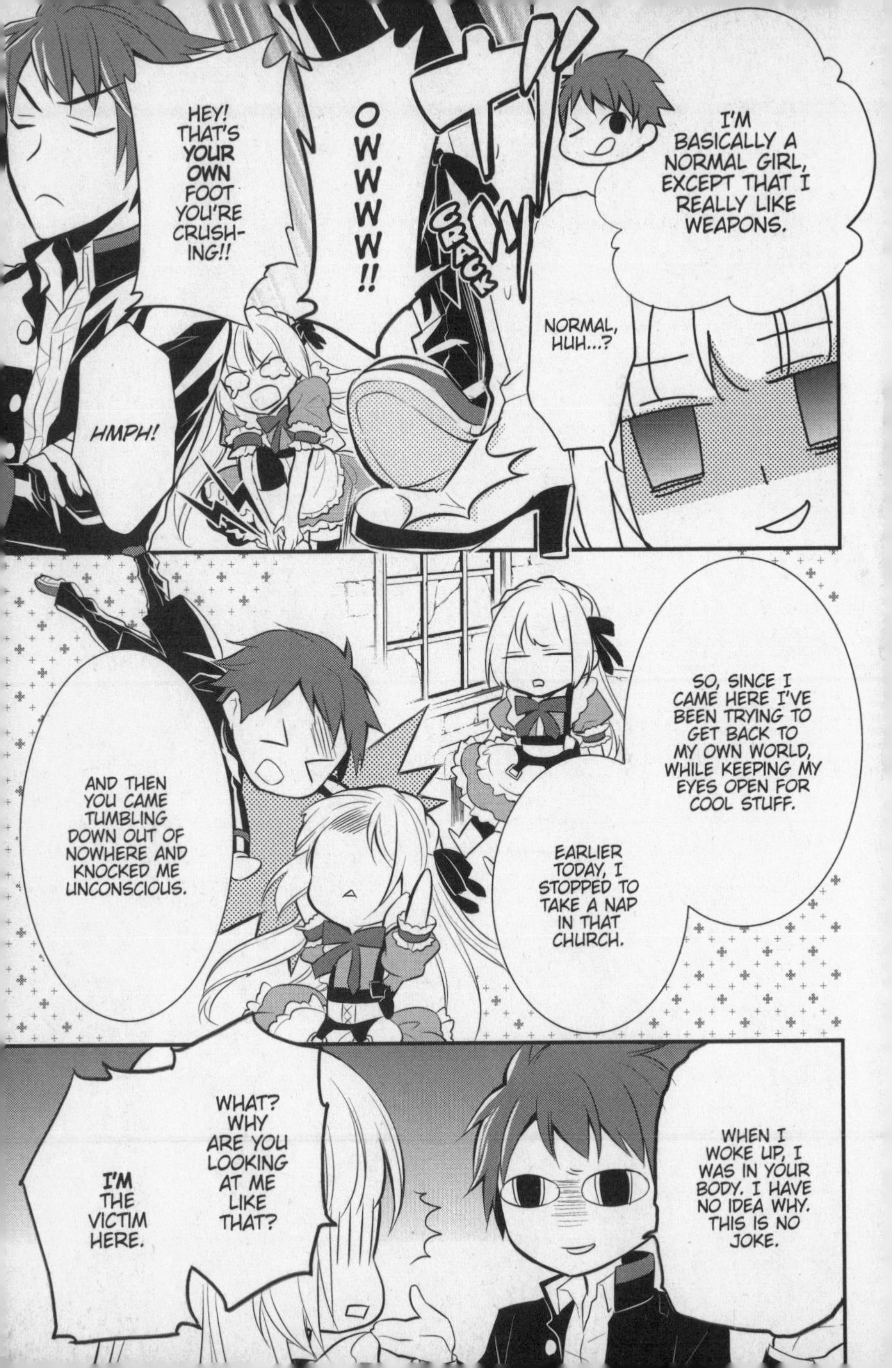
I'M BASICALLY A NORMAL GIRL, EXCEPT THAT I REALLY LIKE WEAPONS.
NORMAL, HUH...?
CRACK
OWWWWW!!
HEY! THAT'S YOUR OWN FOOT YOU'RE CRUSHING!!
HMPH!
SO, SINCE I CAME HERE I'VE BEEN TRYING TO GET BACK TO MY OWN WORLD, WHILE KEEPING MY EYES OPEN FOR COOL STUFF.
EARLIER TODAY, I STOPPED TO TAKE A NAP IN THAT CHURCH.
AND THEN YOU CAME TUMBLING DOWN OUT OF NOWHERE AND KNOCKED ME UNCONSCIOUS.
WHEN I WOKE UP, I WAS IN YOUR BODY. I HAVE NO IDEA WHY. THIS IS NO JOKE.
WHAT? WHY ARE YOU LOOKING AT ME LIKE THAT?
I'M THE VICTIM HERE.

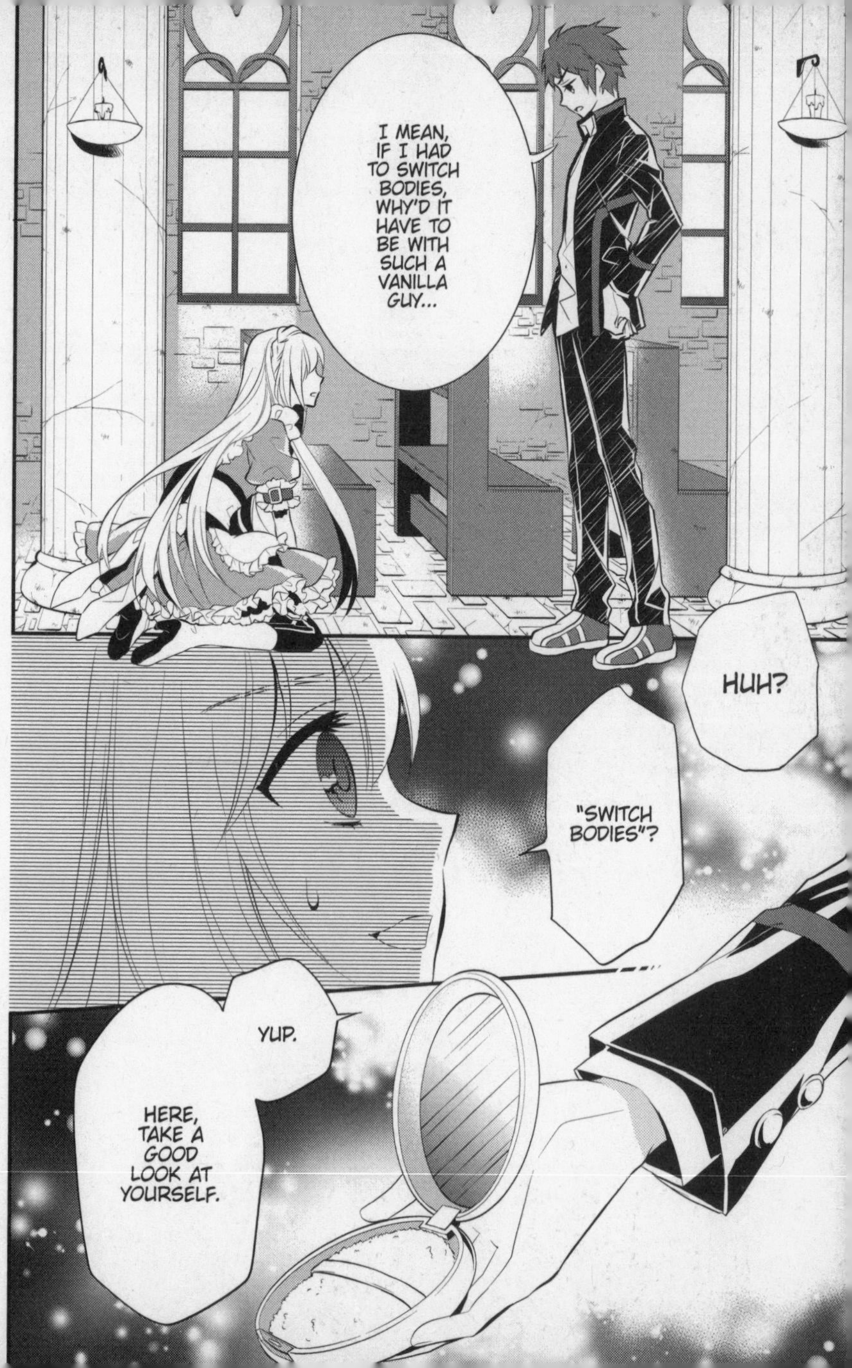
I MEAN, IF I HAD TO SWITCH BODIES, WHY'D IT HAVE TO BE WITH SUCH A VANILLA GUY...
HUH?
"SWITCH BODIES"?
YUP.
HERE, TAKE A GOOD LOOK AT YOURSELF.

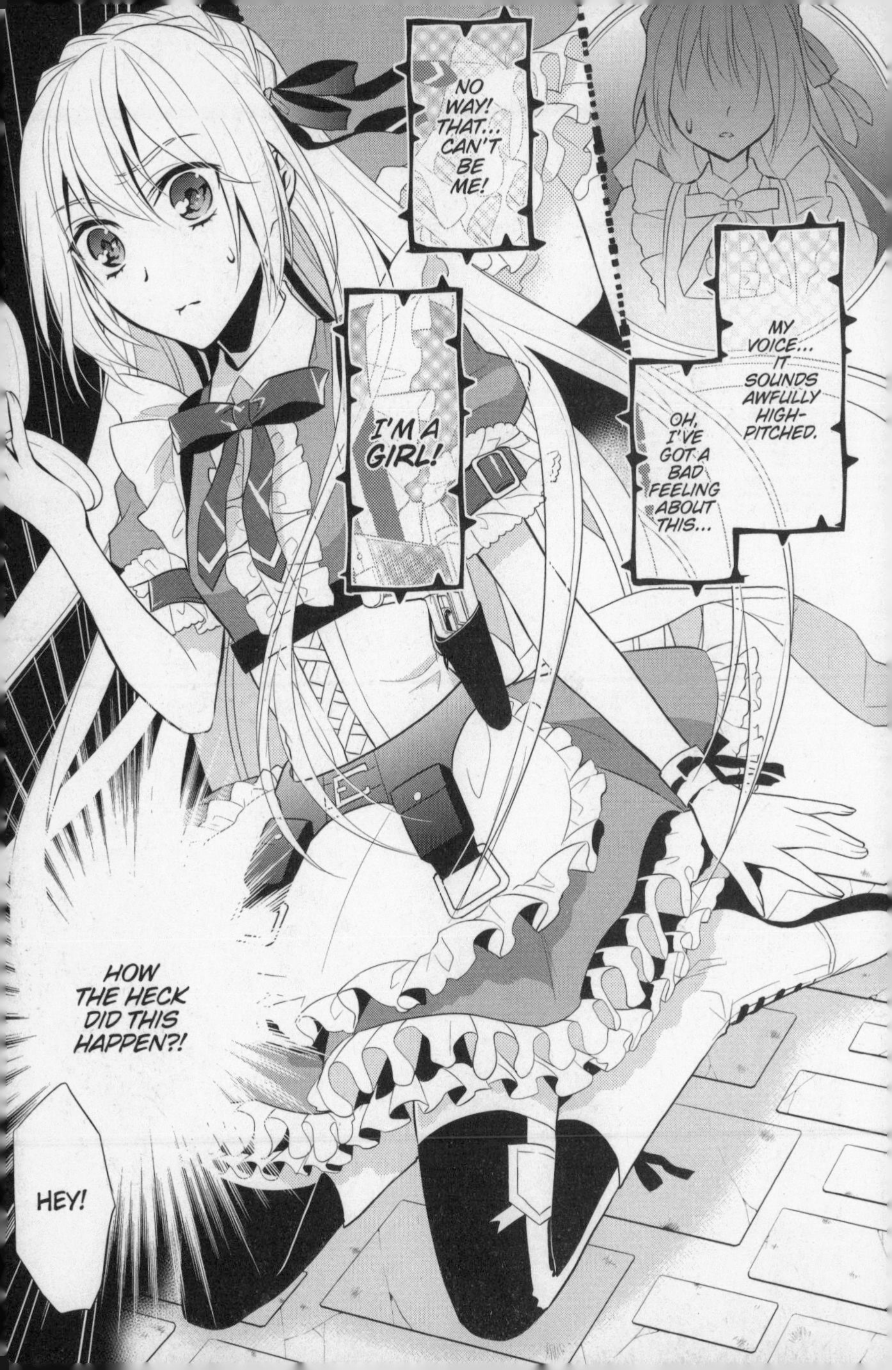
MY VOICE... IT SOUNDS AWFULLY HIGH-PITCHED.
OH, I'VE GOT A BAD FEELING ABOUT THIS...
NO WAY! THAT... CAN'T BE ME!
I'M A GIRL!
HOW THE HECK DID THIS HAPPEN?!
HEY!

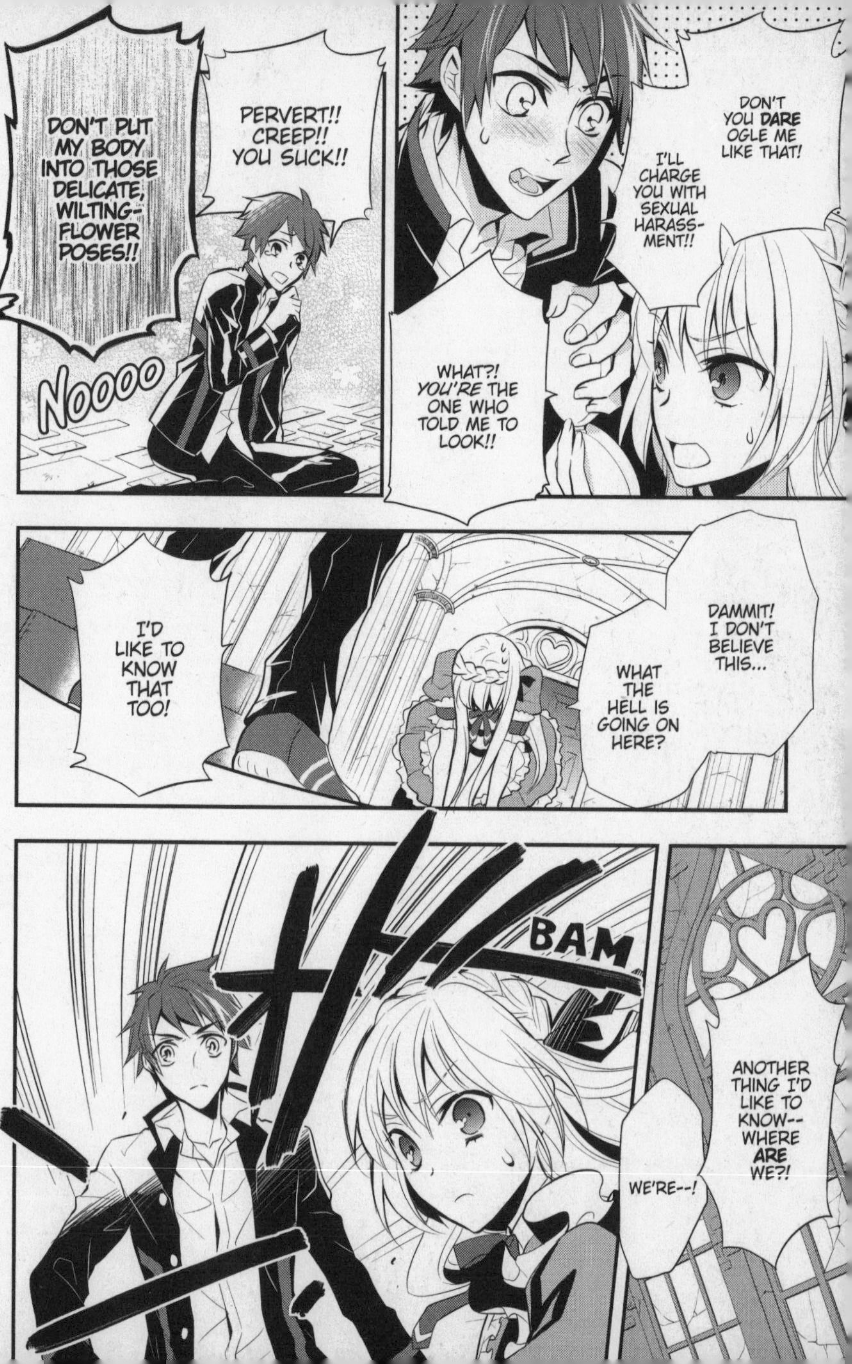
DON'T YOU DARE OGLE ME LIKE THAT!
I'LL CHARGE YOU WITH SEXUAL HARASS-MENT!!
WHAT?! YOU'RE THE ONE WHO TOLD ME TO LOOK!!
PERVERT!! CREEP!! YOU SUCK!!
DON'T PUT MY BODY INTO THOSE DELICATE, WILTING-FLOWER POSES!!
NOOOO
DAMMIT! I DON'T BELIEVE THIS...
WHAT THE HELL IS GOING ON HERE?
I'D LIKE TO KNOW THAT TOO!
ANOTHER THING I'D LIKE TO KNOW-- WHERE ARE WE?!
WE'RE--!
BAM

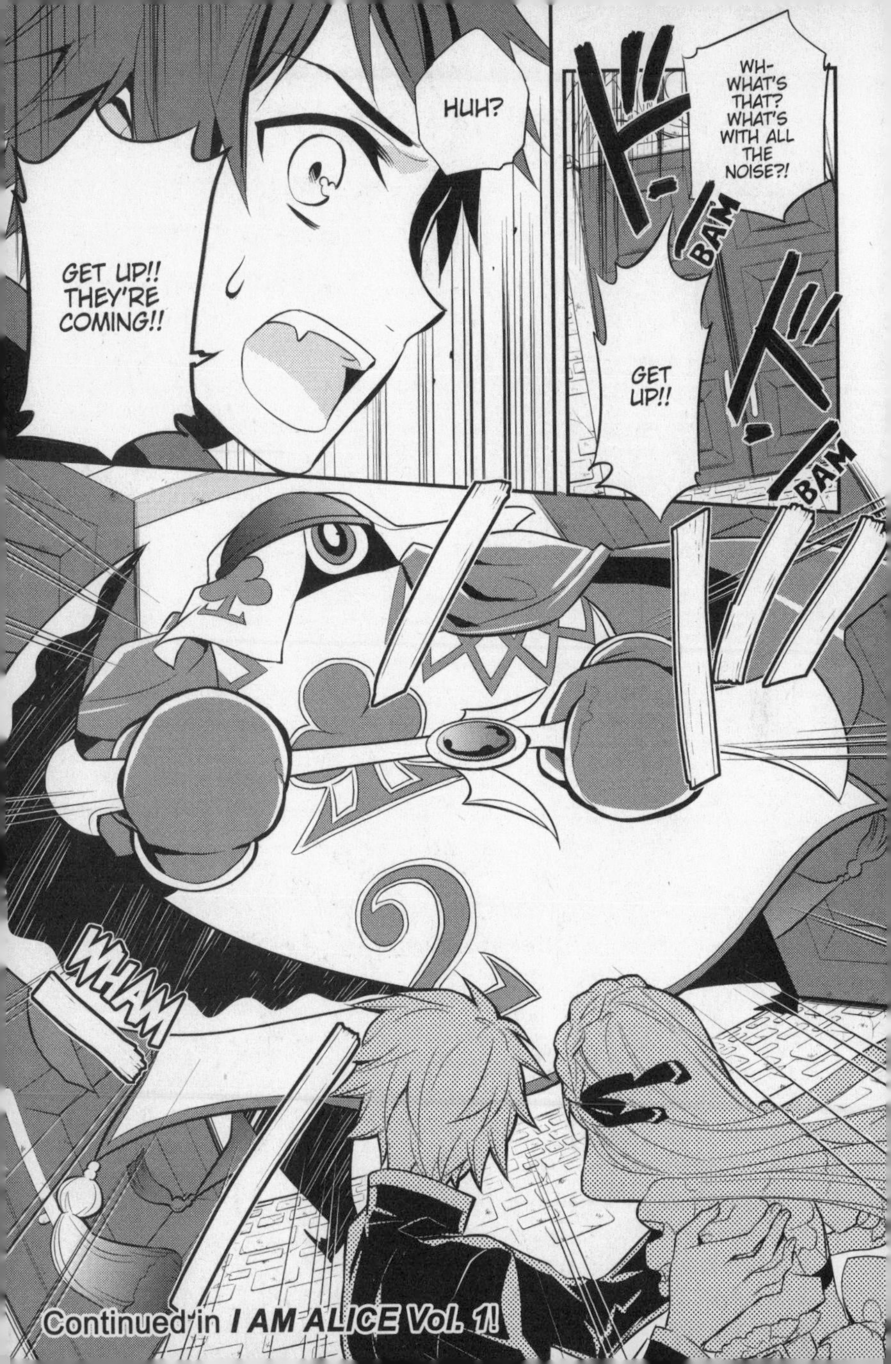
WH-WHAT'S THAT? WHAT'S WITH ALL THE NOISE?!
BAM
GET UP!!
BAM
HUH?
GET UP!! THEY'RE COMING!!
WHAM

Continued in ***I AM ALICE* Vol. 1!**

SEVEN SEAS ENTERTAINMENT PRESENTS

ZERO'S FAMILIAR Chevalier

art by YUKARI HIGA / story by NOBORU YAMAGUCHI   VOLUME 2
Original Character Designs by EIJI USATSUKA

TRANSLATION
Nan Rymer

ADAPTATION
Rebecca Scoble

LETTERING AND LAYOUT
Alice Baker

COVER DESIGN
Nicky Lim

PROOFREADER
Katherine Bell
Conner Crooks

MANAGING EDITOR
Adam Arnold

PUBLISHER
Jason DeAngelis

ZERO'S FAMILIAR CHEVALIER VOL. 2
© Yukari Higa 2011, © Noboru Yamaguchi 2011
Edited by MEDIA FACTORY.
First published in Japan in 2011 by KADOKAWA CORPORATION, Tokyo.
English translation rights reserved by Seven Seas Entertainment, LLC.
under the license from KADOKAWA CORPORATION, Tokyo.

No portion of this book may be reproduced or transmitted in any form without
written permission from the copyright holders. This is a work of fiction. Names,
characters, places, and incidents are the products of the author's imagination
or are used fictitiously. Any resemblance to actual events, locals, or persons,
living or dead, is entirely coincidental.

Seven Seas books may be purchased in bulk for educational, business, or
promotional use. For information on bulk purchases, please contact Macmillan
Corporate & Premium Sales Department at 1-800-221-7945 (ext 5442)
or write specialmarkets@macmillan.com.

Seven Seas and the Seven Seas logo are trademarks of
Seven Seas Entertainment, LLC. All rights reserved.

ISBN: 978-1-626920-67-5

Printed in Canada

First Printing: September 2014

10 9 8 7 6 5 4 3 2 1

FOLLOW US ONLINE: *www.gomanga.com*

READING DIRECTIONS

This book reads from *right to left*, Japanese style.
If this is your first time reading manga, you start
reading from the top right panel on each page and
take it from there. If you get lost, just follow the
numbered diagram here. It may seem backwards at
first, but you'll get the hang of it! Have fun!!

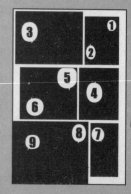